W9-AUM-779

Charles H. Huber
The Samaritan Center
Jacksonville, Florida

Leroy G. Baruth
University of South Carolina

Ethical, Legal, and Professional Issues in the Practice of Marriage and Family Therapy

Merrill Publishing Company
A Bell & Howell Company
Columbus • Toronto • London • Melbourne

Published by Merrill Publishing Company
A Bell & Howell Company
Columbus, Ohio 43216

This book was set in Garamond ITC

Administrative Editor: Vicki Knight
Production Coordinator: Linda Hillis Bayma
Cover Designer: Cathy Watterson

Photo Credits: All photos copyrighted by individuals or companies listed. Merrill
Publishing/photographs by Jan Hall, p. 182; and Bruce Johnson, pp. x, 84, 86, 126, 154,
204. Additional photography by Jo Hall, pp. 2, 36, 236; Tom Hubbard, p. 184;
Christopher B. Reddick, p. 62.

Copyright © 1987 by Merrill Publishing Company. All rights reserved. No part of this
book may be reproduced in any form, electronic or mechanical, including photocopy,
recording, or any information storage and retrieval system, without permission in writing
from the publisher. "Merrill Publishing Company" and "Merrill" are registered trademarks
of Merrill Publishing Company.

Library of Congress Catalog Card Number: 86-61421
International Standard Book Number: 0-675-20703-7
Printed in the United States of America
4 5 6 7 8 9 — 91 90

Contents

Preface   vii

Part One / Ethical Issues in Marriage and Family Therapy

1 Acceptance of and Adherence to a Professional Code of Ethics   2
   Ethical Decision Making   5
   Client Welfare   10
   Confidentiality   16
   Informed Consent   26
   Summary and Conclusions   35

2 Ethical Considerations in the Interactional Context
   of Marriage and Family Therapy   36
   Defining The Problem   38
   Complications in Convening Therapy   41
   The Therapist as Agent for Change   46
   Paradoxical Procedures   52
   Agency Triangulation   54
   Summary and Conclusions   59

3 Ethical Accountability: A Casebook   62
   Principle 1: Responsibility to Clients   64
   Principle 2: Confidentiality   68
   Principle 3: Professional Competence and Integrity   71
   Principle 4: Responsibility to Students, Employees, and Supervisees   75
   Principle 5: Responsibility to the Profession   77
   Principle 6: Fees   80
   Principle 7: Advertising   82

Part Two / Legal Issues in Marriage and Family Therapy

4 The Marriage and Family Therapist:
Roles and Responsibilities Within the Legal System   86
Legal Education   88
The Marriage and Family Therapist as Source of Information   92
The Marriage and Family Therapist as Referral Resource   101
The Marriage and Family Therapist as Expert Witness   108
Professional Liability Under the Law   116
Summary and Conclusions   124
Recommended Resources   125

5 Family Law   126
Marriage and Cohabitation   128
Parent-Child Relationships   133
Parental Rights and Responsibilities   139
Annulment and Divorce   141
Child Custody and Support After Divorce   148
Summary and Conclusions   153
Recommended Resources   153

6 Legal Considerations   154
Divorce Mediation   155
Liability in Crisis Counseling   158
Informed Consent?   160
Criminal Liability   163
The Buckley Amendment   167
The Premarital Agreement   170
Child Custody and Privileged Communications   173
Legal Responsibility of Clinical Supervisors   177

**Part Three / Professional Issues in Marriage
and Family Therapy**

7 Valuing: Basis for Professional Therapeutic Practice   184
Values Clarification   186
An Expanding Epistemology   187
Negotiation: The Nature of Valuing   190
The Practice Implications of Valuing   193
Valuing Components   197
Summary and Conclusions   202

10/17

8 Professional Identity as a Marriage and Family Therapist   204
Profession or Professional Specialization   205
Professional Affiliation   206
Legislative Regulation of Marriage and Family Therapy   212
Interdisciplinary Difficulties Faced by Marriage
and Family Therapists   219
Pragmatic Issues and Professional Identity   225
Summary and Conclusions   235

0/24

9 Professional Questions   236
Question 1: Tandem Counseling   238
Question 2: Extending the Systemic Perspective   241
Question 3: Therapeutic Influence   243
Question 4: Values Analysis   246
Question 5: Gender Equality   251
Question 6: Advertising   254
Question 7: Fee Collection   257
Question 8: Independent Practice   260

Epilogue   263
References   265
Name Index   282
Subject Index   288

Charles H. Huber is Director of Psychological Services at the Samaritan Center in Jacksonville, Florida. A Licensed Psychologist in both the states of Florida and Connecticut, he is also an Approved Supervisor for the AAMFT and the Institute for Rational-Emotive Therapy. Along with being a Fellow for the latter, he has consulted at the West Duval Child Guidance Clinic; the Clay County Mental Health, Drug, and Alcohol Services; and the Children's Crisis Center in Florida. He conducts presentations and workshops on counseling and crisis intervention within the profession and throughout communities all over the United States.

Dr. Huber received his B.A. from Upsala College, his M.Ed. and Ed.S. from Florida Atlantic University, and his Ph.D. from University of South Carolina. The editor of several books and articles, he has also written for numerous professional journals. He has coauthored three textbooks with Leroy Baruth: *Coping with Marital Conflict: An Adlerian Approach to Succeeding in Marriage* (1981), *An Introduction to Marital Theory and Therapy* (1984), and *Counseling and Psychotherapy: Theoretical Analyses and Skills Applications* (1985). Active in several professional organizations including the American Association for Marriage and Family Therapy, the American Psychological Association, and the American School Counselors Association, he received the American Mental Health Counselors Professional Service Award for 1982–84.

Leroy G. Baruth is Professor of Educational Psychology at the University of South Carolina. He also serves on numerous university, college, and departmental committees. An Approved Clinical Supervisor for the AAMFT, he is also a licensed Counseling Psychologist in the state of South Carolina. Active in the American Association of Counseling and Development, the American Association of Marriage and Family Therapy, the American Psychological Association, and the American School Counselor Association, Dr. Baruth has received a number of awards from these and other organizations. He has served as an advisor to public school systems, social service departments, and college and university personnel. In addition, he has done numerous presentations at state, regional, and national association conventions.

Dr. Baruth obtained his B.S. and M.S. from Mankato State University and his Ed.D. from the University of Arizona. His numerous articles on various aspects of counseling have appeared in professional journals. He has authored and coauthored ten books, including *A Single Parent's Survival Guide: How to Raise the Children* (1979), *The ABC's of Classroom Discipline* with Dan G. Eckstein (1982), and *Child Psychology* with Alaine Lane (1980).

Preface

Increasing numbers of psychotherapists are practicing marriage and family therapy. This is most evident in the "army of professionals doing research, developing theory, counseling, conducting workshops, and writing articles and books for both professionals and lay audiences in the area of marriage and the family" (Becvar, Becvar, & Bender, 1982, p. 385).

As the practice of marriage and family therapy has evolved, training procedures have become more explicit, replicable, and accessible. Specific theories and techniques have been identified, broad curricular components for training compiled, and specific content, goals, and teaching methods for university coursework and professional workshops delineated. Noticeably lacking, however, are sources addressing "nontherapy" issues necessary to supplement the therapeutic training of marriage and family therapists (Piercy & Sprenkle, 1983).

One such source would logically consider ethical, legal, and professional issues in marriage and family therapy (Margolin, 1982). The importance of this is exemplified in an article entitled "Family Therapy May Be Dangerous for Your Health" (Hare-Mustin, 1980). In it, the author states:

> In sum, family therapy may not be in the best interests of individual family members. Family therapists and their clients need to be aware of possible risks to the rights of the individual member. By being required to participate, individuals may have to subordinate their own goals and give up limited confidentiality and privacy. In addition, therapists who idealize the traditional family may foster stereotyped roles and expectations in the family that disadvantage individuals and limit their well-being and mental health. (p. 938)

The simple fact that marriage and family therapy contrasts with individual therapy on both conceptual and pragmatic levels requires that therapists be adequately prepared to encounter controversial issues that arise when a marriage and family perspective is pursued. For example, ethical standards for psychologists have been established by the American Psychological Association (APA). The *Ethical Standards of Psychologists* (APA, 1981a) and the accompanying *Specialty Guidelines for the Delivery of Services by Clinical Psychologists* (APA, 1981b) are both primarily formulated in terms of a therapeutic relationship that consists of one therapist and one client. Yet difficult ethical questions that may need to be confronted in individual therapy can become significantly more complicated when a couple or a whole family presents itself for services (Margolin, 1982).

The *Guidelines for Psychologists Conducting Growth Groups* (APA, 1973) offer a supplement to the APA ethical standards in addressing situations with multiple clients. These guidelines still do not directly pertain to the concerns of psychologists practicing marriage and family therapy. Levels of intimacy and intensity in relationships among marital partners and significant family members compared to relationships among group members call for further clarification of appropriate professional conduct (Margolin, 1982). With the exception of the *AAMFT Code of Ethical Principles for Marriage and Family Therapists* (AAMFT,1985), expressly formulated for marriage and family therapy, similar exigencies are evident in the ethical codes of other professional organizations whose members may engage in the practice of marriage and family therapy. Likewise, legal and various professional issues arising in marriage and family therapy can collide with traditional individual and group training.

The American Association for Marriage and Family Therapy, the primary professional affiliation for marriage and family therapists, has specified graduate-level coursework in "Professional Studies" (AAMFT, 1983) as a requirement within its educational requirements for clinical membership. In response, "Ethical, Legal, and Professional Issues" courses have been developed and are a core component of marriage and family therapy training programs (Piercy & Sprenkle, 1983). There is, however, a dearth of available sources in the literature for both beginning students as well as practicing professionals seeking to expand their knowledge of ethical, legal, and professional issues in marriage and family therapy.

This book is structured to encourage an expanded understanding of ethical, legal, and professional issues in the practice of marriage and family therapy. It is divided into three parts. Part One addresses ethical issues in marriage and family therapy. Chapter 1 examines major ethical issues confronting all therapists with an emphasis on both the beginning marriage and family therapist and the experienced individually oriented practitioner initially assuming a marriage and family therapy approach. Chapter 2 critiques ethical issues endemic to the interactional context of marriage and family therapy. Chapter 3 offers a "casebook" of case illustrations with critiques from the *AAMFT Code of Ethical Principles for Marriage and Family Therapists.* Part Two considers legal issues in marriage and family therapy. Chapter 4 investigates roles and relationships marriage and family therapists take within the legal system. Chapter 5 examines relevant family law. Chapter 6, like Chapter 3, is a casebook of examples with critiques discussing the impact of legal issues on marriage and family therapy. Finally, Part Three contains three chapters addressing, respectively, the implications of "valuing" for professional therapeutic practice, professional identity as a marriage and family therapist, and another casebook addressing professional questions.

Special attention needs to be given to the three casebook chapters: 3, 6, and 9. The authors recall their concerns as clinicians-in-training seeking to fully comprehend notions garnered from readings. Classroom instructors and clinical supervisors, knowledgeable and skilled from years of experience, provided case examples to illustrate concepts more clearly. These illustrations made learning a more pragmatic endeavor from which we emerged well-prepared.

We would like to thank a number of reviewers for their constructive suggestions during manuscript development. They include David Drum, University of Texas at Austin; Leonard Haas and Robert Stahmann, both at Brigham Young University; Charlotte Kahn, Syracuse University; Tom Lovett, Southeast Missouri State University; John Pietrofesa, Wayne State University; Holly Stadler, University of Missouri—Kansas City; and David Rosenthal, University of Iowa.

We are each especially grateful to certain people for their support and encouragement during the writing of this book: colleagues at the Samaritan Center who offer a model of professional excellence (C.H.H.) and at the University of South Carolina (L.G.B.). We are particularly indebted to Vicki Knight and Linda Bayma of Merrill Publishing; Sandie Gurvis, copy editor; and Benie Preacher, graduate assistant.

PART ONE

Ethical Issues in Marriage and Family Therapy

The training of the family therapist requires attention to ethical issues as well as to techniques. Self-awareness and social responsibility are an important part of the professional ethics of therapists. By being demanding of ourselves in our professional role, we may be able to be more reasonable toward our patients.

(Fieldsteel, 1982, p. 267)

1

Acceptance of and Adherence to a Professional Code of Ethics

Ethics is concerned with the conduct of human beings as they make moral decisions. These decisions reflect judgments leading to action and involve the use of words known as *moral predicates:* "ought," "should," "right," "good," and their opposites (Brandt, 1959). Unlike a discipline such as mathematics, ethics is normative as opposed to factual. It addresses principles that *ought* to govern human conduct rather than *do* govern it (Daubner & Daubner, (1970).

Although morality is frequently considered to be synonymous with ethics, the distinction between the two terms is critical. Barry (1982) defined *ethics* as "the study of what constitutes good and bad human conduct, including related actions and values" (p. 4). While recognizing the difficulty of maintaining a separation between ethics and morality, he proposed that the terms *moral* and *morality* be restricted to the *conduct* itself and ethics and ethical be employed for the *study* of moral conduct or a code a person follows. Mowrer (1967) likewise reported finding the two terms being used interchangeably, but cautioned that morals definitively referred to the goodness or badness of behavior while ethics represented an objective inquiry.

Ethics addresses questions that have no ultimate answers yet are important in planning, justifying, and carrying out decisions. Consider the following situation:

> A woman initially presented for individual therapy sought to resolve a number of personal conflicts, only one of which was the state of her marriage resulting from her extramarital affair. Later, her husband accompanied her to therapy for conjoint efforts. The woman was still engaged in the affair and it was obvious to the therapist that this impeded progress with her husband. She demanded, however, that the therapist maintain the confidentiality of what was discussed during the individual sessions.

"Should" the therapist respect the individual confidences of one marital partner when doing so clearly impedes those goals overtly agreed to by both? A code of ethics offers guidance in answering such a question. Ethics, however, is primarily concerned with helping the therapist decide what is right, not with getting the persons involved to do what is believed to be right (Jones, Sontag, Beckner, & Fogelin, 1977).

Webster's New World Dictionary of the American Language defines *ethics* as "standards of conduct and moral judgment . . . of a particular philosophy, religion, or group." As such, ethical codes are standards of moral conduct for a society or subgroup. A code of ethics for a profession contains standards of conduct subscribed to by the members of the profession. Van Hoose and Kottler (1985) identified the universality of ethical codes among the professions. These codes reflect concerns and define basic principles that "ought" to guide professional activities. They provide a position on standards of practice to aid members in deciding how to act when areas of conflict arise. They assist in clarifying professionals' responsibility to clients and society. They give society some guarantee that professionals will demonstrate a sensible regard for the

3

mores and expectations of the society. Finally, they give professionals themselves grounds for safeguarding their freedom and integrity.

With regard to this last point, Van Hoose and Kottler (1985) posited that codes of ethics aid professionals in dealing with potential dangers from three groups: government, themselves, and the public:

> First, codes of ethics are designed to protect the profession from the government. All professions desire autonomy and seek to avoid undue interference and regulations by lawmakers. Professional codes assert a self-regulatory stance.
>
> Second, codes of ethics offer protection to a profession from potential self-destruction occasioned by internal discord in the absence of such areas of common agreement. For example, it is unethical to entice colleagues' clients to leave them. Such a standard enables professionals to live in harmony.
>
> Third, codes of ethics protect professionals from the public. Professionals who act according to accepted professional codes have some protection if sued for malpractice.

With respect to the field of psychotherapy, the first two require little explanation; the latter can be clarified in light of recent litigation.

Ethical codes are adopted by professional associations by virtue of their representation of the profession. Self-regulation through established ethical codes involves informal and formal discipline. *Informal discipline* is seen in subtle and overt pressure colleagues exert upon one another in the form of consultations regarding practices and referrals of clients. *Formal discipline* is seen in the power exercised by professional associations in publicly criticizing or censuring members and in extreme cases, barring violators from membership. Although this threat of formal discipline does have some influence on professionals who are not members of their representative professional associations, the association's code of ethics is binding only on actual members. Consequently, sanctions can be imposed only on those violators who are members of the association.

If sued for malpractice, a therapist will be judged in terms of actions appropriate to other therapists with similar qualifications and duties. Ethical standards of the profession will be a probable basis for comparison (Corey, Corey, & Callanan, 1984). If therapists act in good faith, they are not likely to be found responsible for a client's lack of progress or mistake in judgment if the mistake were the type a "careful and skillful" therapist could make (Burgum & Anderson, 1975).

Precedent for the application of ethical standards as acceptable careful and skillful factors emanate from medical ethics, representative portions of which have been made into law. Physicians are expected to display behavior suitable to their profession:

> The law imposes on a physician who undertakes the care of a patient the obligation of due care, the exercise of an amount of skill common to his profession, without which he should not have taken the case, and a degree of care commensurate with this position. (61 Am. Jur. 2d 99)

Standards from the codes of ethics of relevant professional associations mirror this assertion. Corresponding standards from these ethical codes are illustrated in Table 1–1.

Table 1–1   Ethical Considerations Relating to Due Care/Therapist Competence

American Association for Counseling and Development (1981)

   "With regard to the delivery of professional services, members should accept only those positions for which they are professionally qualified."

American Association for Marriage and Family Therapy (1985)

   "Marriage and family therapists do not attempt to diagnose, treat, or advise on problems outside the recognized boundaries of their competence."

American Psychological Association (1981a)

   "Psychologists recognize the boundaries of their competence and the limitations of their techniques. They only provide services and only use techniques for which they are qualified by training and experience."

National Association of Social Workers (1979)

   "The social worker should accept responsibility or employment only on the basis of existing competence or the intention to acquire the necessary competence."

Physicians also have a duty to act in good faith and advise patients regarding the best possible treatment:

> A physician occupies a position of trust and confidence as regards his patient, and it is his duty to act with the utmost good faith; if he knows that the treatment adopted by him will probably be of little or no benefit, and that there is another method of treatment that is more likely to be successful, which he has not the training or facilities to give . . . he must advise his patient. (61 Am. Jur. 2d 99)

Standards from the codes of ethics of relevant professional associations are clearly in alignment with this position as well. Applicable standards are offered in Table 1–2.

ETHICAL DECISION MAKING

Van Hoose (1980) proposed that therapists have a clear process in understanding ethical decision making. Such an understanding should allow therapists to critically evaluate and interpret their code of ethics. Furthermore, it should provide direction in analyzing feelings as appropriate or inappropriate bases for ethical behavior. Kitchener (1986) synthesized the work of Rest (1983) in identifying four major psychological processes underlying applied ethics in psychotherapy. Ethical decision making involves becoming proficient in all four processes.

Table 1–2   Ethical Considerations Relating to Good Faith/Client Referrals

American Association for Counseling and Development (1981)

> "If a member determines an inability to be of professional assistance to the client, the member must either avoid initiating the counseling relationship or immediately terminate that relationship. In either event, the member must suggest appropriate alternatives."

American Association for Marriage and Family Therapy (1985)

> "Marriage and family therapists continue therapeutic relationships only so long as it is reasonably clear that clients are benefiting from the relationship."

American Psychological Association (1981a)

> "Psychologists terminate a clinical or consulting relationship when it is reasonably clear that the consumer is not benefiting from it. They offer to help the consumer locate alternative sources of assistance."

National Association of Social Workers (1979)

> "The social worker should terminate service to clients, and professional relationships with them, when such service and relationships are no longer required or no longer serve the clients' needs or interests."

> "The social worker who anticipates the termination or interruption of service to clients should notify clients promptly and seek the transfer, referral, or continuation of services in relation to the clients' needs and preferences."

Process 1: Interpreting a Situation as Requiring an Ethical Decision

This process involves the ability to perceive the effect of one's actions on the welfare of others. Several relevant psychological research findings have important implications here. First, many persons have difficulty interpreting the meaning of even simple situations. Sometimes failure to intervene in an ethical situation may be attributable to a misunderstanding about what is actually occurring. Second, individuals differ in their ability to be sensitive to the needs and welfare of others (Schwartz, 1977). Welfel and Lipsitz (1984), for example, estimated from a number of research studies that between 5–10% of mental health practitioners are substantially insensitive to the ethical dimensions of their work. Third, the ability to infer the effect of one's actions on others as well as to infer others' needs develops with age and experience. Fourth, a social situation may arouse a strong emotional response before there is time to reflect on it (Zajonc, 1980); thus, to interpret a situation, persons must understand their feelings about it.

Process 1 points to the importance of therapists' development of ethical sensitivity and empathy. Therapists must be continually aware that their actions have real ethical consequences that can potentially harm as well as help others. Codes of ethics function to establish a central framework for professional behavior and responsibility. They serve to provide guidance in identifying situations where an ethical decision is needed (e.g., confidentiality in therapy).

Process 1 furthermore supports the fact that feelings may not always be good guides for ethical action. For example. the therapist who breaks confidentiality to prevent serious harm to the client or another will feel badly. On the other hand, the therapist would feel worse if the client or another suffered unduly at the expense of maintaining confidentiality. The ethical dilemma balances a lesser harm against a greater harm. As Nozick (1968) asserted, such situations ought to leave therapists with feelings of dissatisfaction and regret that, to make the most ethical decision, they had to violate other ethical responsibilities. Ethical action does not always feel good, nor does it always lead to choices that are "good" in an absolute sense.

Process 2: Formulating an Ethical Course of Action

It is not enough to be aware that an ethical situation exists. One must also be able to integrate various considerations into an ethically justifiable course of action. Process 2 underscores the importance of fundamental ethical guidelines.

Kitchener (1984, 1985) distinguished between levels of justification in proposing a model for ethical reasoning. The model includes the intuitive and critical-evaluative levels of ethical justification. The *intuitive level* addresses immediate feeling responses to situations. It affords a basis for immediate action that is necessary in some situations (e.g., dealing with a suicidal client). Many situations, however, are not amenable to intuitive responses alone (e.g., when intuition leads to sexual relations with clients).

The *critical-evaluative level* of justification is composed of three tiers. At the first tier, an ethical course of action can be judged by formal ethical rules (e.g., one's professional code of ethics). Therapists can receive ready guidance regarding sexual contact with clients from their code of ethics. If the ethical standards of such a code are insufficient, movement to a second tier is in order. This tier consists of more general and fundamental ethical principles. Such principles serve as a foundation for formal codes of ethics. For example, if therapists were asked why a particular standard in their ethical code is important, principles provide the justification (e.g., the right to make one's own decisions; the need to respect the rights of others to make free choices). The third tier of critical evaluation is that of ethical theory. For example, many 20th century ethicists (Abelson & Nielson, 1967; Baier, 1958; Toulmin, 1950) have posited that when principles are in conflict, ethical actions should emanate from what one would want for oneself or significant others in the same circumstances, or what produces the least amount of avoidable harm.

Process 3: Integrating Competing Personal/Professional Values

It is possible for persons to know what they "should" do ethically (Process 2) but decide against taking ethical action because of competing values and motives. Process 3 recognizes that how individuals decide to act is heavily influenced by factors such as ambition, money, and self-interest. Research and ordinary observation has consistently shown that persons do not always do what they think they "should" do. For example, a therapist may know a colleague is acting unethically, but because of friendship or loyalty, decides not to intervene.

Therapists must clearly comprehend that they have a stake in acting according to the code of ethics of their profession. Public trust is easily eroded if professionals are perceived to be overly self-serving at the cost of their clients.

Process 4: Implementing an Action Plan

Perseverance, resoluteness, and character are elements involved in acting on any decision (Rest, 1982). Process 4 addresses the need to develop and maintain a sense of ethical responsibility. It is not enough to be aware of and concerned about ethical issues, nor even to think wisely about them. Professional practice requires that therapists take responsibility for their actions and the subsequent consequences.

An important aspect of assuming responsibility is the ability to tolerate the ambiguity that accompanies ethical decision making. Therapists must understand that few absolute answers exist; certainty is frequently impossible. At the same time, ethical reasoning can be precise and can in many cases resolve dilemmas. In more difficult situations, it can at least identify the precise nature of the dilemma.

Van Hoose (1980) offered a summarizing rule of thumb for therapists faced with ethical decisions:

> The counselor or psychotherapist is *probably* acting in an ethically responsible way concerning a client if (a) he or she has maintained personal and professional honesty, coupled with (b) the best interests of the client, (c) without malice or personal gain, and (d) can justify his or her actions as the best judgment of what should be done based upon the current state of the profession. When these four components are present, ethically responsible behavior is likely to be demonstrated. (p. 11)

Codes of ethics provide the bases from which responsibilities of professionals are articulated. A code of ethics represents the consensus of a large number of reputable members of a profession. As such, it demands primary attention from those seeking to practice in an ethical manner. Consider the following case circumstances:

> A male therapist has been working for several months with a couple seeking a divorce. He finds the wife attractive and exciting. He is aware that she has intimate feelings toward him and would like to become involved with him socially and sexually. His own feelings favor doing so to the extent that he often finds it difficult to concentrate during sessions because of his desire to become intimate with her.

Standards set by the codes of ethics of a number of major professional associations can offer relatively explicit guidance in this regard. Applicable standards are illustrated in Table 1–3.

These standards imply that the therapist's considerable influence must be properly used: the creation of a dual relationship (therapeutic and intimately personal/sexual) with a client is clearly unethical. Codes of ethics, however, more frequently offer only general philosophical guidance in conceptualizing and responding to conflicts. It is not their purpose to recommend specific behaviors in limited situations. Were this the case, codes would become voluminous, lack broad-based support, and infringe upon the role of the individual professional in ethical decision making (Huston, 1984). Stude and McKelvey (1979) reflected this in stating:

> They (code of ethics) are statements of principle, which must be interpreted and applied by the individual or group to a particular context. They present a rationale for ethical behavior. Their exact interpretation, however, will depend on the situation to which they are being applied. (p. 453)

In order to conceptualize solidly grounded ethical solutions, it is important to first reference one's professed code of ethics. One must also, however, identify basic ethical concepts that can serve to both supple-

---

Table 1–3   Ethical Considerations Relating to Sexual Relationships With Clients

American Association for Counseling and Development (1981)

"Dual relationships with clients that might impair the member's objectivity and professional judgement (e.g., as with close friends or relatives, sexual intimacies with any client) must be avoided and/or the counseling relationship terminated through referral to another competent professional."

American Association for Marriage and Family Therapy (1985)

"Marriage and family therapists are cognizant of their potentially influential position with respect to clients, and they avoid exploiting the trust and dependency of such persons. Marriage and family therapists therefore make every effort to avoid dual relationships with clients that could impair their professional judgement or increase the risk of exploitation. Examples of such dual relationships include, but are not limited to, business or close personal relationships with clients. Sexual intimacy with clients is prohibited."

American Psychiatric Association (1981)

"The necessary intensity of the therapeutic relationship may tend to activate sexual and other needs and fantasies on the part of both patient and therapist, while weakening the objectivity necessary for control. Sexual activity with a patient is unethical."

American Psychological Association (1981a)

"Psychologists make every effort to avoid dual relationships that could impair their professional judgement or increase the risk of exploitation. Examples of such relationships include supervisees, close friends, or relatives. Sexual intimacies with clients are unethical."

National Association of Social Workers (1979)

"The social worker should under no circumstances engage in sexual intimacies with clients."

---

ment the code and as additional sources of guidance in ethical decision making. Tymchuk, Drapkin, Major-Kingsley, Ackerman, Coffman, and Baum (1982) drew a similar conclusion in surveying psychologists. They found there was low ethical consensus on dilemmas about situations that were either not addressed by the *Ethical Standards of Psychologists* (APA, 1981a) or not at the forefront of the professionals' attention. They called for a model of ethical conceptualization as an adjunct to the code.

Margolin (1982) cautioned that insufficiencies in the *Ethical Standards of Psychologists* (APA, 1981a) as they apply to practitioners of marriage and family therapy have not been fully appreciated. With the exception of the American Association for Marriage and Family Therapy's *Code of Ethical Principles for Marriage and Family Therapists* (AAMFT, 1985), similar insufficiencies can be found in the codes of ethics of other professional associations with members engaging in the practice of marriage and family therapy. These codes are established in an atmosphere where traditional individual and group therapy models predominate.

The generality inherent in codes of ethics relating to client welfare, confidentiality, and informed consent can make ethical decision making troublesome with individual clients. Complications are compounded when the primary treatment unit consists of a cohabitating couple or multiple family members. The balance of this chapter addresses ethical decision making around these thorny issues, first from a therapist-individual client perspective and then from a therapist-couple/family perspective.

CLIENT WELFARE

The codes of ethics of all major professional associations affirm a therapist's *primary* responsibility as being to the client. The needs of clients, not therapists, assume primary importance in the therapeutic relationship. Also implied is that therapeutic relationships should be maintained only as long as clients are benefiting. Standards from the codes of ethics of relevant professional organizations are excerpted in Table 1–4.

Recognition of the primacy of the clients' welfare is relatively clear. Corey, Corey, and Callanan (1984), however, raised several cogent questions that tend to cloud this simple assertion:

— What criteria should be used to determine whether a client is benefiting from the therapeutic relationship?
— What should be done if a client reports he or she is benefiting from therapy but the therapist is unable to identify any signs of progress?
— What courses of action are available to the therapist who believes that a client is seeking only to purchase friendship and has no intention of pursuing therapeutic change?

Table 1–4   Ethical Considerations Relating to Client Welfare

---

American Association for Counseling and Development (1981)

"The member's *primary* obligation is to respect the integrity and promote the welfare of the client(s), whether the client(s) is (are) assisted individually or in a group relationship."

American Association for Marriage and Family Therapy (1985)

"Marriage and family therapists are dedicated to advancing the welfare of families and individuals, including respecting the rights of those persons seeking their assistance, and making reasonable efforts to ensure that their services are used appropriately."

American Psychiatric Association (1981)

"A physician shall be dedicated to providing competent medical service with compassion and respect for human dignity."

American Psychological Association (1981a)

"Psychologists respect the dignity and worth of the individual and strive for the preservation and protection of fundamental human rights. They are committed to increasing knowledge of human behavior and of people's understanding of themselves and others and to the utilization of such knowledge for the promotion of human welfare. While pursuing these objectives, they make every effort to protect the welfare of those who seek their services."

National Association of Social Workers (1979)

"The social worker's primary responsibility is to clients."

These and other questions call for a conceptual framework for ethical decision making as an adjunct to the guidance available from formal ethical standards. Kitchener (1984) recommended five principles applied by Beauchamp and Childress (1979) to biomedical ethics as specifically relevant to issues of client welfare in psychotherapy: autonomy, beneficence, nonmaleficence, justice, and fidelity.

Autonomy refers to a stance that all human beings have the right to make decisions and act on them in an independent fashion. *Beneficence* is the expectation that one must actively attempt to benefit another in a positive manner. The principle that one must avoid causing harm to another is *nonmaleficence*. *Justice* summarizes the belief that all individuals should be treated fairly; equals must be treated as equals and unequals must be treated in a way most beneficial to their specific circumstances. *Fidelity* implies a commitment to keep promises; truth and loyalty.

Treatment recommendations pose many of the more perplexing ethical dilemmas relative to client welfare. A notable illustration that has evolved from studies of the "battered woman's syndrome" has been that a battered woman should be encouraged by her therapist to leave her abusive relationship (Huston, 1984). Ethically, this creates a dilemma: Should the therapist encourage her to leave the relationship? One side of the issue is respect for her autonomy and an assumption that she possesses sufficient psychological competence to act in her own best interests. The other side urges that because of experiencing the battered woman's syndrome, the client's right to maintain autonomous functioning must be compromised. Beauchamp and Childress' (1979) five principles can be of guidance in delineating just what would best serve the standard of primacy of the client's welfare.

Beneficence demands that therapists confer benefits and promote clients' well-being. The literature describing the battered women syndrome often notes a woman's separation from the batterer will maximize her psychological growth, facilitate a more objective assessment of the relationship, and reduce the immediate potential of injury or death. "Only after women feel protected from another assault, can they begin to deal with the reality of the battering situation" (L. Walker, 1981, p. 88).

"The symbiotic dependency bonds must be broken and each partner taught independence and new communication skills" (McG Mullin & Carroll, 1983, p. 34).

"Marriage counseling cannot proceed while the wife is living in fear" (Wentzel & Ross, 1983, p. 427). These suggest a therapist should actively encourage a battered woman client to leave the batterer.

Beneficence also demands that benefits and harms be balanced; that is, positive outcomes weighed against the risks (Beauchamp & Childress, 1979). Studies have shown that battered women who leave the batterer and go to a shelter where help is available have far greater success in overcoming the emotional and motivational deficits emanating from the feelings of helplessness they experience (Walker, 1977–78). Less success in overcoming these feelings of helplessness has been reported when women remain with battering partners and try to change the relationship to a nonbattering one (Flax, 1977). Because the benefits outweigh the harms, a therapist should assert the value for a battered woman client in leaving the batterer.

The principle of nonmaleficence is best applied utilizing the adage, "above all, do no harm." Not encouraging a battered woman to leave circumstances that are certainly dangerous violates this principle. Although a therapist may not personally be inflicting the harm, he or she is allowing the client to return to a setting in which she will most probably be abused in the future (Walker, 1979; Wentzel & Ross, 1983). The principle of justice demands that clients with equal needs not be discriminated against by either therapist incompetence or denial of treatment. However, clients with unique needs requiring special interventions are entitled to unique treatment (Huston, 1984). Battered women, because of the psychological reactions concomitant to living in a violent environment, display unique characteristics and needs (Roy, 1977; Straus, 1977–78; Walker, 1977–78, 1979). Justice, therefore, lends support to the use of a distinct treatment approach for a battered woman client.

Fidelity emphasizes the importance of therapists' faithfulness and loyalty to clients. L. Walker (1981) reported battered women generally believe that their batterer's charm will seduce anyone, even professionals:

"a battered woman may misinterpret any attempt at developing a thera-peutic alliance with the batterer" (p. 85). A battered woman client must be assured that the therapist will be loyal to her above any connection with the batterer or to the unconditional maintenance of the marriage. Fidelity also demands therapists to be truthful with clients. Herein sug-gested is the therapist's obligation to inform a battered woman client of research findings indicating it is dangerous and not psychologically help-ful to her to return to the batterer (Huston, 1984).

The ethical dilemma created by potential infringement upon the cli-ent's autonomous functioning is less easily resolved. Autonomy proposes that an individual has a right to make his or her own decisions if those decisions do not violate the rights of others. To assert that a client leave her home can be viewed as an infringement of her autonomy. It can also be argued that respect for the autonomous functioning of battered women is vital because of their vulnerable and dependent nature, partic-ularly given the inherent transference aspects of the therapist-client rela-tionship. Transference issues with battered women tend to include withholding anger from and/or being overly compliant with persons of authority (Heppner, 1978; McG Mullin & Carroll, 1983). Therapists must be cautious lest they misuse their position as object of the transference phenomenon by being overly directive with these clients (Huston, 1984).

Individuals' right to autonomy can be affected by their deemed level of psychological competence. An individual whose psychological com-petence is limited is unable to make consistent rational judgments (Beau-champ & Childress, 1979). Walker (1979) described battered women as experiencing a form of learned helplessness. They experience this be-cause of a consistent and well-reinforced message that nothing they can do will change their situation. Because battered women can conse-quently become immobilized, they may be viewed as having limited psy-chological competence and therefore, in desperate need of someone to assist them to get out of their "hopeless" situation (Huston, 1984).

Battered women can also be immobilized by a state of extreme fear. Symonds (1979) cited research findings indicating how many victims of violent crimes become reduced to an infantile obedience and coopera-tion with their attacker. Symonds suggested a battered woman follows this response pattern and "experiences terror which traumatically in-fantilizes her" (p. 169). Heppner (1978) reported battered women describing how they remain in abusive relationships out of fear of the consequences of leaving. Hilberman and Munson (1977–78) found bat-tered women to be living in constant and debilitating fear that affected their ability to sever the relationship. These findings suggest that bat-tered women are in need of directive assistance.

It would thus seem ethically justifiable to encourage a battered woman to leave her relationship were she judged to have limited psychological competence because of the severity of her circumstances. Whether it is ethically justifiable to force her to leave or deny her treatment should she refuse to leave would be questionable. Forcing her to leave can amount to an overt violation of her right to autonomy. Were an initial effort unsuccessfully exerted, the therapist might better maintain a position of respect for autonomous decision making. As Ball and Wyman (1977–78) asserted, "There is a fine line, in counseling battered wives, between the need to be initially directive and the danger of playing 'rescue' " (p. 448).

Huston (1984) proposed that a therapist should then adopt more of a "maternalistic" treatment stance:

> Maternalism as the recommended treatment approach for battered women can be defined as offering a nurturing, directive stance at early stages of the client's development and an acceptance of more autonomy at later developmental stages. This approach recognizes that battered women as clients move through developmental stages of growth in objectively understanding their battering relationships. The women demonstrate different needs at different stages, and treatment must vary accordingly. . . . This stance is congruent with feminist treatment beliefs, because it acknowledges a deep respect for the autonomous functioning of the individual and yet recognizes the unique needs of specific populations and developmental tasks. (p. 831)

The literature in the women's movement has pointed out that paternalism can be a debilitating mode of interaction with many women, reinforcing predominant societal conditioning of them as passive and dependent. The maternalistic alternative espoused by Huston involves initial assertion, but recognizes the potential need to patiently await developmental movement toward increased independence, positive self-worth, and autonomous action.

Multiple Client Considerations

North American culture is highly individualistic; each person's rights take precedence. Consequently, multiple clients such as in marriage and family therapy can create dilemmas for therapists. In some situations, an intervention that serves one member's best interest may be countertherapeutic to another. Indeed, the very reason couples and families seek out professional assistance is that they have conflicting goals and interests (Margolin, 1982). Consider the following illustration:

> Two parents come to family therapy with their 17-year-old son. They seek to have their son acquiesce more readily to their directives, invoking a rather rigid "honor thy father and mother" dictum. The son's actions as described during the therapy are not destructive, but he has been actively disobedient.

The parents' goal of having their son respond more readily to their commands might ease their tension as well as perhaps provide secondary benefits for their marriage. The son, however, is at a developmental life stage wherein he is attempting to launch himself from the family. The parents' goal would not be necessarily advantageous to the son's overall development.

Marriage and family therapists must strive to see that improvement in the status of one partner or family member does not occur at the expense of the other partner or another family member. This objective is not entirely unique to marriage and family therapy (Margolin, 1982). Persons in individual therapy can also make changes causing discomfort to, or conflicting with, the desires of significant others. Individually oriented therapists are always wise in encouraging clients to explore potential ramifications of their actions upon those around them. What sets marriage and family therapists apart, however, is their commitment to promote the welfare of each family member. Through direct involvement with all members, marriage and family therapists are able to assess how each member's actions affect the others. Thus, marriage and family therapists take on more responsibility for exercising judgment regarding the welfare of more than one individual.

Marriage and family therapists can respond to this dilemma by identifying the marital or family system, rather than a single individual, as the "client." Such a stance should be a natural outgrowth of their theoretical position. The therapist who is an advocate of the system avoids becoming an agent of any one marital partner or family member. Working within a framework that conceptualizes change as affecting and being affected by all family members, marriage and family therapists define problems and consider plans for change in the context of the entire family. Consider the following situation:

> A couple presents themselves for therapy stating opposite goals. She wants divorce counseling; he is seeking to save/improve the marriage.

The system advocate works to define the couple's problem as a relationship concern, seeking to help them establish and pursue relationship goals. Whether marriage enhancement or divorce is the ultimate result, reorganizing their relationship interactions so that they can problem-solve more effectively can only be in the best interests of both.

Functioning as a system advocate occasionally has the paradoxical effect of actually creating greater variance between the aims of the therapist and those of marital partners or family members. Functioning as a system advocate suggests a knowledge that often goes beyond the specific and sometimes self-centered goals of the individual members (Margolin, 1982). Most couples and family members enter treatment wanting to change their partner or a specific family member's behavior or attitude. "If only he/she/they would change" is likely the most frequent complaint communicated to marriage and family therapists. The system advocate's problem definition and goal orientation is at odds with those of some couples and families and must be reconciled when unacceptable. Marriage and family therapists should clearly communicate the nature of their commitment as system advocate. Informed of the therapist's stance as advocate of the system, most marital partners and family members generally understand and accept this position, although during therapy they may at times seek to solicit the therapist as a personal ally (Margolin, 1982).

While the stance of system advocate works well in the majority of instances, it does not eliminate the problems of conflicting interests. The recommended emphasis in certain circumstances such as treatment of the battered women's syndrome client call for the primacy of individual needs as an immediate course of action. The system is not set aside, but rather given an apparent secondary focus as when the welfare of an individual member is in jeopardy. In addition to clinical considerations, there are also laws requiring certain actions be taken when the welfare of an individual is in danger. A clear example of this is child neglect or abuse. Child abuse reporting laws require therapists to inform authorities if they learn a child is suffering from neglect or being abused, regardless of the negative consequences likely to be incurred for future family treatment efforts.

Margolin (1982) summarized the complex responsibilities of therapists seeking to promote optimal client welfare from a system advocate's position:

> Attempting to balance one's therapeutic responsibilities toward individual family members and toward the family as a whole involves intricate judgments. Since neither of these responsibilities cancels out the importance of the other, the family therapist cannot afford blind pursuit of either extreme, that is, always doing what is in each individual's best interest or always maintaining the stance as family advocate. (p. 790)

Framo (1981) offered the commonsense, but perhaps understated conclusion that, "part of the skill of the therapist resides in finding the appropriate balance between the conflict of goals and expectations of all family members as well as those of the therapist" (p. 143).

CONFIDENTIALITY

The singularly most popularized ethical issue in the practice of psychotherapy is confidentiality. Confidentiality had its genesis in the physician-patient relationship in the 16th century. Physicians began to practice confidentiality when they realized contagious diseases were being spread by persons who feared detection of their affliction would remand them to social isolation (Slovenko, 1973). More recently, confidentiality has become intertwined with legal constraints dictated by state and federal legislation and court decisions regarding *privileged communication* and *privacy.* The terms *confidentiality, privileged communication,* and *privacy,* however, should not be used interchangeably because they have different meanings.

Shah (1969) defined confidentiality in stating: "Confidentiality relates to matters of professional ethics. Confidentiality protects the client from unauthorized disclosures of any sort by the professional without informed consent of the client" (p. 57). Confidentiality is a standard established and maintained by the ethical codes of professional organizations. Denkowski and Denkowski (1982) identified two reasons mitigating the need for confidentiality in psychotherapy: (a) confidentiality protects clients from the social stigma frequently associated with therapy; and (b) confidentiality promotes vital client rights, integral to therapists' professed concern for the welfare of clients. Standards from the codes of ethics of relevant professional organizations are stated in Table 1–5.

Little else in psychotherapy commands as much agreement as the belief that therapists have a responsibility to safeguard information obtained during the treatment process. Confidentiality is considered to be prerequisite for a satisfactory therapist-client relationship. Therapists' training in this matter has traditionally emphasized a stern but simplistic admonition as to the sanctity of psychotherapeutic confidentiality with references to principles stated in professional codes of ethics.

From the perspective of the legal system, confidentiality is generally viewed as a narrowly drawn exception to the principle that all relevant information should be available to judicial decision makers (Gumper & Sprenkle, 1981). Furthermore, state and federal legislation and court decisions have increasingly identified occasions mandating disclosure of information with penalties for failure to report, most notably in instances of child abuse. Likewise, procedures for disclosure of therapy information in educational settings must be determined in accordance with the Family Educational and Privacy Rights Act of 1976. Maintaining confidentiality relative to the treatment of minors with alcohol or drug abuse

---

Table 1–5   Ethical Considerations Relating to Confidentiality

American Association for Counseling and Development (1981)

  "The counseling relationship and information resulting therefrom (must) be kept confidential, consistent with the obligations of the member as a professional person."

American Association for Marriage and Family Therapy (1985)

  "Marriage and family therapists have unique confidentiality problems because the 'client' in a therapeutic relationship may be more than one person. The overriding principle is that marriage and family therapists respect the confidences of their client(s)."

American Psychiatric Association (1981)

  "A physician shall respect the rights of patients, of colleagues, and of other health professionals, and shall safeguard patient confidences within the constraints of the law."

American Psychological Association (1981a)

  "Psychologists have a primary obligation to respect the confidentiality of information obtained from persons in the course of their work as psychologists. They reveal such information to others only with the consent of the person or the person's legal representative, except in those unusual circumstances in which not to do so would result in clear danger to the person or to others. Where appropriate, psychologists inform their clients of the legal limits of confidentiality."

National Association of Social Workers (1979)

  "The social worker should share with others confidences revealed by clients, without their consent, only for compelling professional reasons."

---

problems may also not be possible subsequent to the first interview as mandated by the Confidentiality of Alcohol and Drug Patient Records Act of 1975 (DePauw, 1986). Hence, a thorough understanding of the concepts of privileged communication and privacy is prerequisite to offering and maintaining client confidentiality.

Privileged Communication

Privileged communication is "a legal right which exists by statute and which protects the client from having his confidences revealed publicly from the witness stand during legal proceedings without his permission" (Shah, 1969, p. 57). Where privileged communication laws apply, therapists are prevented from testifying in court about clients without their consent. If a client waives this privilege, a therapist has no grounds for withholding information. The privilege belongs to the client and is meant for the client's protection, not for the therapist's (Corey et al., 1984). It is important to note that privileged communication for the therapist-client relationship is *not* legally supported in a large number of states (Bray, Shepherd, & Hays, 1985). Furthermore, even where clients have not waived their right, privileged communication can also be subject to exceptions such as contained in Table 1–6.

Gumper and Sprenkle (1981) examined the potential repercussions of privileged communication laws for psychotherapy. They reported a wide variation in legal statutes, presenting particular problems for marriage

---

Table 1–6   Exceptions to Privilege

- When the therapist is acting in a court-appointed capacity—for example, to conduct a psychological examination (DeKraai & Sales, 1982)
- When the therapist makes an assessment of a foreseeable risk of suicide (Shultz, 1982)
- When the client initiates a lawsuit against the therapist, such as for malpractice (Denkowski & Denkowski, 1982)
- In any civil action when the client introduces mental condition as a claim or defense (Denkowski & Denkowski, 1982)
- When a client is under the age of 16 and a therapist believes that the child is the victim of a crime—for example, incest, child molestation, rape, or child abuse (Everstine, Everstine, Heymann, True, Frey, Johnson, & Seiden, 1980)
- When the therapist determines that the client is in need of hospitalization for a mental or a psychological disorder (DeKraai & Sales, 1982; Shultz, 1982)
- When criminal action is involved (Everstine et al., 1980)
- When information is made an issue in a court action (Everstine et al., 1980)
- When clients reveal their intention to commit a crime or when they can be assessed as "dangerous to society" or dangerous to themselves (DeKraai & Sales, 1982; Shultz, 1982)

Note. From *Issues & Ethics in the Helping Professions* (2nd ed.) (p. 172) by G. Corey, M.S. Corey, and P. Callanan, 1984, Monterey, CA: Brooks/Cole. Copyright © 1984 by Wadsworth Inc. Reprinted by permission of Brooks/Cole Publishing Company, Monterey CA 93940.

and family therapists. Specifically, Gumper and Sprenkle reemphasized that ownership of this privilege resides with the client, not the therapist. Dominant among the problems that arise is the question, "Who owns the right to waive privilege in marriage and family therapy?"

Margolin (1982) addressed this question in discussing the case of a New Jersey couple seen in conjoint marital therapy by a psychologist:

> When the couple, who were seen in marital therapy, decided to divorce, the psychotherapist was subpoenaed by the husband's lawyer to testify in court about statements made during the conjoint therapy sessions. Since the wife refused to waive privilege, the therapist refused to testify. On the basis of psychologist-patient privilege in New Jersey, the wife's confidentiality would not have been protected. The judge decided to rule to protect the wife's confidentiality, however, on the basis of laws in that state for marriage counselors. (p. 793)

Margolin went on to note similar cases involving psychiatrists. She reported courts in New York and Tennessee maintaining privilege, but a Virginia court denying the psychiatrist that protection. As reported by Herrington (1979), the Virginia judge ruled "when a husband and wife are in a counseling session with a psychiatrist . . . there is no confidentiality because statements were made not in private to a doctor, but in the presence of the spouse" (p. 1).

The model for statutory privilege provisions that apply in psychotherapeutic contexts was drawn from and has largely concerned one-to-one (i.e., attorney-client, husband-wife) relationships. Most privileged communication statutes tend to be ill-defined for situations in which two or more clients are seen simultaneously. In some states, for example, the presence of a third party is construed to mean that necessary confidentiality is lacking and the therapist-client privilege is accordingly deemed lost or waived (Gumper & Sprenkle, 1981). Questions also arise as to whether privilege applies to client-to-client communications. Since some states extend privilege to persons who aid in the delivery of personal services and are present during the uttering of confidential information (e.g., nurses, medical technicians), a liberal interpretation of privilege statutes can identify family members as agents of the therapist (Bersoff & Jain, 1980).

Gumper and Sprenkle (1981) argued that in states where statutory protection of communications in multiperson therapies is unclear, marriage and family therapists should put forth a position that the "client" is the couple or family as a unit. Rather than identifying family members as agents of the therapist, they recommended the contention that third party limitations on privilege do not apply because only one client (the couple or family) is present. Lacking definitive legislation on these issues, however, marriage and family therapists cannot comfortably assume that existing privilege statutes protect the confidentiality of communications in their work with couples and families.

Legal protection against court-compelled disclosure of therapy communications is thus qualified and particularly flawed with respect to marriage and family therapy. Given this cloudy mixture of protection and compelled disclosure, Gumper and Sprenkle (1981) offered several practical considerations for therapists to prepare themselves to confront this issue:

1. Whatever their credentials, therapists should acquaint themselves with the particular privilege provisions of their state. It is insufficient to simply know that "some kind of privilege statute" exists.
2. In marriage and family therapy, especially where divorce may be a real possibility, therapists would be wise to obtain a written agreement from all parties not to make or seek court disclosures of therapy communications. Courts may differ as to enforcement of such agreements, but efforts to obtain court disclosures will more likely be restrained.
3. If contacted by an attorney, a therapist should advise the attorney that a written release of information signed by the participating clients is necessary before being able to confer with him or her. The conversation should be one-way until such a release is obtained. Details about the pending proceeding and the attorney's plan for involving the therapist might be elicited. Such information may be helpful in arriving at a position on the disclosure issue.
4. A therapist who decides to assert a position of nondisclosure to an attorney should do so firmly and persistently, but without the loud indignance of a crusader seeking to protect therapist-client confidentiality. Most attorneys are conditioned to react to such a stance in an adversarial manner. A calm, reasoned approach, emphasizing the therapist's duty as opposed to the attorney's, is less likely to polarize the parties. This will allow the attorney to not lose face and potentially conclude the therapy information to be of insufficient worth to merit the effort necessary to obtain it.
5. Subpoenas should be viewed as the formal commencement, not the conclusion of any disclosure controversy. A therapist should not testify without a subpoena, but conversely, need not testify simply because a subpoena is present. When subpoenaed, a therapist should have, or can obtain, sufficient time to carefully consider ethical and legal obligations before making any decision regarding disclosure. Unless steps are taken to have a subpoena cancelled or limited by the court, the therapist must respond with his or her presence at the hearing in question. The therapist or his or her attorney can, however, still make arguments against testifying or providing records or reports. If a subpoena requiring court appearance is presented on short notice, the therapist should simply notify the court representative of when the subpoena was received and request time to consult legal counsel.
6. Ideally, therapists should maintain their own independent legal counsel. This is especially important when subpoenaed and the client is not represented by counsel in the proceeding, when the

therapist perceives his or her ethical or legal interests to be at odds with the client's, or when the interests of marital partner/family member clients are conflicting.

Privacy

Privacy with regard to psychotherapy has been defined as "the freedom of individuals to choose for themselves the time and the circumstances under which the extent to which their beliefs, behavior, and opinions are to be shared or withheld from others" (Siegel, 1979, p. 251). The concept of privacy is addressed by the Fourth Amendment to the United States Constitution, that portion of the Bill of Rights protecting a person's home against illegal search and seizure by the government. A rich tradition of case law exists in applying the basic principle of this amendment to a wide range of contemporary issues. In effect, persons are protected against invasion of their privacy by their government or by the agents of government. Everstine et al. (1980) raised two questions in preserving privacy:

— To what extent should psychological or emotional states be protected from the scrutiny of others?
— Who may intrude on persons' privacy; under what circumstances and how should this be decided?

Examples of pressing instances with regard to these questions include insurance companies' and other third-party payers' access to therapy information about clients, and circumstances wherein therapists are bound by law and/or professional codes of ethics to break confidentiality (e.g., child abuse, where clients pose a serious danger to themselves or others). Less pressing areas include professional consultation, tape recording, and third party observation/supervision of therapeutic activities. Still another area where privacy is an issue involves practitioners who also teach courses, offer workshops, write books and journal articles, and give lectures.

Therapists should maintain a current record of insurance and other forms of third-party reimbursement requirements to appraise clients of the kinds of information that will need to be released, particularly diagnostic labels, and who may have access to the information. Many clients choose to assume self-responsibility for therapy fees, for example, where employers have access to reimbursement requests. Therapists who seek professional consultation and supervision, or who utilize case examples from their clinical work in teaching and writing should obtain clients' consent beforehand and/or take adequate measures to ensure that clients' identities are disguised (Corey et al., 1984).

Shah (1970) addressed the question of "Whose agent is the therapist?" He noted in some governmental agencies and institutions, the therapist is *not* primarily the client's agent. In these situations, therapists are faced with conflicts between obligations to clients and obligations to their agency or institution. Shah maintained that potential conflicts should be clarified before beginning diagnostic or therapeutic relationships. Denkowski and Denkowski (1982) supported Shah's position in contending therapists must inform clients of potential breaches of confidentiality. They also asserted that therapists go further to assure "that all reasonable steps be taken to restrict the legally sanctioned dissemination to confidential client information to its bare minimum" (p. 374).

All of the professional organizations whose members practice psychotherapy have taken the position that certain information must be revealed when there is clear and imminent danger to an individual or to society: therapists have a "duty to warn." Consistent with this ethical position are legal mandates from legislation and court decisions (to be discussed in chapter 4).

Addressing therapists regarding their duty to warn, Knapp and Vandecreek (1982) wrote: "Psychotherapists need only follow reasonable standards in predicting violence. Psychotherapists are not liable for failure to warn when the propensity toward violence is unknown or would be unknown by other psychotherapists using ordinary skill" (pp. 514–515). These authors cautioned therapists not to become intimidated by potential client statements of hostility; every impulsive threat is not evidence of imminent danger. In their opinion, recent behaviors are the best predictors of future violence. In cases of likely danger, in addition to warning potential victims, Knapp and Vandecreek suggested therapists also consider alternatives that could defuse the situation and, simultaneously, satisfy their ethical and/or legal obligations. They particularly recommended consulting with professionals having expertise in dealing with potentially violent persons and documenting all steps taken.

Corey et al. (1984) offered a set of procedures for therapists to follow if they determine that a client poses a serious danger of violence to others:

1. Therapists should inform their clients of the possible action they must take to protect a third party where violence might be inflicted upon that party.
2. When a client makes threats against others, everything observed and stated in the session should be documented.
3. The therapist should inform his or her supervisor in writing of any serious threat.
4. The therapist should consult with colleagues qualified to offer opinions on how to proceed. This consultation should be documented.
5. The police and other proper authorities should be alerted.
6. The intended victim must be notified; in the case of a minor, his or her parents should also be notified.

Therapists have an obligation to inform clients that the duty to warn exists (Everstine et al., 1980). Clients should also be told that therapists also have a "duty to report" suspected instances of child abuse, incest, and other actions that constitute a threat to others as well as clients themselves. Everstine et al. (1980) aptly summarized therapists' overall obligations in matters of privacy: "Although a therapist, a person is still a citizen and he or she must protect and contribute to the common good. As a private citizen, the person of good conscience will not hesitate to warn an intended victim" (p. 836). Likewise, the person of good conscience would not hesitate to prevent a continuance of child abuse, incest, etc.

Confidentiality in Marriage and Family Therapy

Individual therapy clients must be informed of the limits of confidentiality. The same responsibility is present in marriage and family therapy, however the latter poses an additional obligation upon therapists vis-á-vis marital partners and/or other family members. Margolin (1982) identified two divergent but standard positions taken by therapists working with couples and families. One position calls for therapists to treat each marital partner or family member's confidences as though that person were an individual client. Information obtained during a private session, a telephone call, or from written material is not divulged to a spouse or fellow family member. Therapists adhering to this position often arrange for sessions with individual spouses and family members to actively encourage the sharing of "secrets" in order to better understand what is occurring within the relationship system. The therapist then works towards a goal of enabling that individual to disclose therapeutically relevant information in the marital or family session. Should that fail to occur, however, the therapist upholds the individual's confidentiality.

A second position adopted by marriage and family therapists is one of nonsecrecy. The therapist discourages the sharing of information that might lead to, or maintain, an alliance between the therapist and one family member or between individual family members. Therapists subscribing to this approach generally avoid receiving individual confidences by conducting only conjoint or family sessions. This safeguard can prove insufficient, however. Unless clients are informed of a nonsecrecy policy upon initiating therapy and are able to adequately consider its consequences, many will seek to influence the therapist.

Some therapists select an intermediate position falling between these two dichotomous stances. These therapists inform clients that information shared in individual sessions, by phone or written messages and the like, may be divulged as they see fit in accordance with the greatest benefit for the couple or family. They simply reserve the right to use their professional judgment about whether to maintain individual confidences (Corey et al., 1984). This intermediate approach creates greater responsibility for therapists who select it. Identifying information as ultimately helpful or hurtful places an increased burden on therapists' clinical abilities. The consequences of maintaining or divulging information in an untimely or what might be perceived as an inappropriate manner can cause an abrupt, premature termination of therapy as well as a souring toward future psychotherapeutic assistance of any kind.

Karpel (1980) critiqued a number of ethical and practical considerations confronting therapists seeking to select a position with regard to handling marital and family secrets. In doing so, he advocated a distinction between secrecy and privacy in terms of how relevant information is to those unaware of it. For example, a traumatic episode in one's childhood, now reasonably well resolved and not significantly affecting the present relationship, would be considered private. The client might at sometime decide to share this history with his or her partner or children, but does not *owe* it to them to do so. Similarly, intimate details of a marital partner's previous love relationships having no important implications for his or her current relationship are private, not secret. In contrast, a spouse engaged in an extramarital affair maintains a secret in the sense that it involves deception as well as a violation of reciprocity. Likewise, parents who withhold the fact a child is adopted violate that child's right to a complete self-definition and identity.

Karpel advocated a policy of "accountability with discretion." A therapist would share or withhold information based on his or her clinical judgment involving a consideration as to the relevance of the material for the unaware, an attempt to perceive this as much as possible from the unaware's perspective, and a sensitivity to the timing and consequences for the unaware.

> This means, to use an everyday expression, trying to "put yourself in the other person's shoes," trying to understand what they need and what they are owed. It also means that when a decision to share is made, it takes the other's situation and likely reactions into account. For example, one does not reveal a secret that is likely greatly to upset the other in the midst of his/her surprise birthday party or when s/he is already in crisis due to an unrelated situation. This stance clearly reflects. . . . a respect for individuation, an effort to maximize trust and trustworthiness in relationships, and an attempt to balance the two fairly. (Karpel, 1980, p. 298)

Karpel supported his accountability with discretion stance by arguing that therapists who agree to keep secrets collude with secretholders and betray the trust of unaware members while enhancing the potentially destructive power of secretholders. Karpel warned that while keeping secrets may be a well-intentioned attempt to protect the unaware members, this stance carries significant risk. The secret information may unexpectedly be revealed, resulting in negative individual, relationship, and therapeutic consequences. Karpel acknowledged therapists' need to know relevant information for diagnostic and treatment purposes and their obligation to maintain trustworthiness frequently come in conflict. He proposed a solution of discussing with the couple or family in the initial session the dangers posed by special confidences, asking them to agree on the direction the therapy will take.

The therapist might describe the likely decrease in effectiveness that occurs when something important is known in therapy that can't be discussed. Having explained this, s/he can ask how they would like this to be handled. It can also be made clear, if they sanction such confidences, that this arrangement may become unworkable at some point. If so, the therapist will tell them so and they will have to choose between disclosure and termination. (Karpel, 1980, p. 305)

Another situation that complicates confidentiality obligations is when a change in the format of therapy occurs, specifically when individual therapy is replaced by marriage or family therapy. Margolin (1982) raised a number of critical issues to address when considering such a change:

How does the therapist handle the information that he or she has obtained during individual therapy? One possibility is to obtain the individual client's permission to use such information, when necessary, in the conjoint sessions. If permission is not granted, however, that information must be kept confidential, a resolution far from desirable for the therapist who prefers not maintaining individual confidences in conjoint therapy. Even if the client permits the information to be shared, this permission has been granted *after* the information was obtained. Does the client remember all that she or he has confided under the previously assumed condition of confidentiality? Would that person have responded differently in individual therapy if it were known from the outset that such information would be available to the spouse? (p. 791)

Karpel (1980) utilized two case examples to illustrate what he referred to as "reparative strategies" for therapists to employ in responding to a change from individual to marriage and family therapy format.

Case 1. Mrs. T. is a 35-year-old, childless, married woman. She comes self-referred to an outpatient mental health clinic requesting an appointment for herself. She complains of some anxiety and depression, which she attributes to long-standing marital problems. She reveals that she has carried on a secret three-year affair with her husband's married brother. She is inflexible in her request for marital therapy, her insistence that the affair never be revealed to her husband, and her refusal to give it up. There are no indications of suicidal or homicidal ideation or intent. (Karpel, 1980, p. 303)

In this case, it was recommended the therapist communicate to the woman the extent to which her requests are incompatible. Improving her marital relationship requires building greater trust and reciprocity. She is unwilling to give up a competing relationship that violates both. She is also unwilling to discuss it. The therapist was advised to offer the woman additional individual sessions to explore her feelings about the situation with the hope this would help her decide on a course of action incorporating more realistic goals.

Case 2. Mr. and Mrs. L. seek psychiatric help for problems involving their 9-year-old son who is described as withdrawn and depressed, with a poor relationship with his father. Mr. L. is a successful architect who is heavily involved in community affairs. There are two teenage children. As part of a routine family evaluation, the parents are seen together and separately. In her individual meeting with the therapist, Mrs. L. impulsively discloses that in the past her husband has been involved in homosexual extramarital affairs. He has not done so for several years, although she says she remains somewhat jealous and anxious about this recurring. She immediately re-grets having disclosed this and asks the therapist not to reveal his knowl-edge to her husband. She makes a persuasive argument that her husband might be able to tolerate the therapist's knowing this once he knew and trusted the therapist more but that finding out at this early stage would almost certainly drive him and therefore the family from treatment. (Kar-pel, 1980, p. 303)

In this second case, it was recommended the therapist communicate the potential importance of informing the husband of the disclosure. Therapy may eventually reach a point where the therapist must revisit the issue with the wife unless she is able to inform her husband of her disclosure or he spontaneously discloses relevant facts in therapy. The therapist must clearly communicate treatment efforts can only go so far if significant information is withheld.

The circumstances present in this latter case allow for a gradual, less rigid approach. The therapist's insistence, for ethical and practical rea-sons, that the disclosure may need to be shared remains unchanged. The circumstances and timing of this sharing, however, are negotiable.

INFORMED CONSENT

Basic to ethical psychotherapeutic practice is assuring that clients are adequately informed of their rights and responsibilities. For most clients, the therapeutic setting is new. They present themselves for assistance and unquestioningly accept what the therapist says or does. Little thought is given to possible discomfort to be endured as well as considerable effort necessary to accrue therapeutic benefits. Clients need to know what will be expected of them, what they may expect from the therapist and ther-apy, and generally what their rights as clients are. It is ethically incum-bent upon therapists to inform and educate clients. Only when clients understand and act upon their rights and responsibilities can therapists facilitate positive movement within the therapeutic process.

The codes of ethics of all the major professional organizations whose members engage in the practice of psychotherapy require clients be given adequate information to make informed choices about entering and continuing a therapeutic relationship. The responsibility of thera-pists to educate clients in this regard is referred to as the ethical issue of *informed consent.* Relevant standards from these codes of ethics are identified in Table 1–7.

Table 1-7   Ethical Considerations Relating to Informed Consent

---

American Association for Counseling and Development (1981)

"The member must inform the client of the purposes, goals, techniques, rules of procedure, and limitations that may affect the relationship at or before the time that the counseling relationship is entered."

American Association for Marriage and Family Therapy (1985)

"Marriage and family therapists respect the right of clients to make decisions and help them to understand the consequences of these decisions. Marriage and family therapists clearly advise a client that a decision on marital status is the responsibility of the client."

American Psychiatric Association (1981)

"Psychiatric services, like all medical services, are dispensed in the context of a contractual arrangement between the patient and the treating physician. The provisions of the contractual arrangement, which are binding on the physician as well as on the patient, should be explicitly established."

American Psychological Association (1981a)

"Psychologists fully inform consumers as to the purpose and nature of an evaluative, treatment, educational, or training procedure, and they freely acknowledge that clients, students, or participants in research have freedom of choice with regard to participation."

National Association of Social Workers (1979)

"The social worker should provide clients with accurate and complete information regarding the extent and nature of the services available to them."

"The social worker should appraise clients of their risks, rights, opportunities, and obligations associated with social service to them."

Hare-Mustin, Marecek, Kaplan, and Liss-Levenson (1979) outlined three types of information clients should have to make informed choices about entering into and continuing therapy: (a) the procedures, goals, and possible side effects of therapy; (b) the qualifications, policies, and practices of the therapist; and (c) other available sources of help. Most therapists who recognize the need to educate clients regarding their rights and responsibilities employ some form of written document to introduce and record the implied contract that consent for treatment represents. Two such types of written communications include the therapeutic contract and the professional disclosure statement.

Therapeutic Contracts

The purpose of a therapeutic contract is to clarify the therapeutic relationship. Providing information and obtaining agreement through the use of a contract defines therapy as a mutual endeavor to which therapists contribute their professional knowledge and skills and clients bring a commitment to work. The development of a contract encourages all concerned parties to specify relevant goals, expectations, and boundaries (Hare-Mustin et al., 1979).

Most therapeutic contracts consider such issues as the specific therapeutic approach and procedures to be employed, the length and frequency of sessions, the duration of treatment, the cost and the method of payment, provisions for cancellation and renegotiation of the contract, the extent of each party's responsibilities, and the degree of confidentiality. Areas actually covered by any contract may vary according to a therapist's orientation and the inclination of the client. Most important, however, is the fact that concrete, identifiable ground rules are decided upon in advance and endorsed with signatures before the hard work of therapy begins.

Everstine et al. (1980) outlined a sample document incorporating the basic elements of informed consent in contract form. An adapted version of this document is illustrated in Figure 1–1.

Hare-Mustin et al. (1979) advocated contracts as an integral part of therapy. They cautioned, however, that therapists should first resolve certain questions before beginning this practice:

— How much should the contract specify?
— What if the therapist has personal or moral concerns about clients' goals?
— What should be done with clients who are unable to be specific about their goals?
— How should therapists respond to clients refusing to agree to a contract?

It is impossible to specify all that might occur during the course of therapy. Most therapists feel providing clients with an understanding of

---

Figure 1–1   A Therapeutic Contract

Mary E. Spates, Ph.D.
Licensed Psychologist (Connecticut No. 972)
62 Broadway, Suite 401
Bridgeport, Connecticut 06602
203/268-7899

PART I: *Your Rights as a Client*

1. You have a right to ask questions about any procedures used during therapy; if you wish, I will explain my usual approach and methods to you.
2. You have the right to decide *not* to receive therapeutic assistance from me; if you wish, I will provide you with the names of other qualified professionals whose services you might prefer.
3. You have the right to end therapy at any time without any moral, legal, or financial obligations other than those already accrued.
4. You have a right to review your records in the files at any time.
5. One of your most important rights involves confidentiality: Within certain limits, information revealed by you during therapy will be kept strictly confidential and will not be revealed to any other person or agency without your written permission.

6. If you request it, any part of your record in the files can be released to any person or agency you designate. I will tell you, at the time, whether or not I think releasing the information in question to that person or agency might be harmful in any way to you.
7. You should also know that there are certain situations in which I am required *by law* to reveal information obtained during therapy to other persons or agencies *without your permission*. Also, I am not required to inform you of my actions in this regard. These situations are as follows: (a) If you threaten grave bodily harm or death to another person, I am required by law to inform the intended victim and appropriate law enforcement agencies, (b) If a court of law issues a legitimate subpoena, I am required by law to provide the information specifically described in the subpoena, (c) If you reveal information relative to child abuse and neglect, I am required by law to report this to the appropriate authority, and (d) if you are in therapy or being tested by order of a court of law, the results of the treatment or tests ordered must be revealed to the court.

PART II: *The Therapeutic Process*

One major benefit that may be gained from participating in therapy includes a better ability to handle or cope with marital, family, and other interpersonal relationships. Another possible benefit may be a greater understanding of personal goals and values; this may lead to greater maturity and happiness as an individual. Other benefits relate to the probable outcomes resulting from resolving specific concerns brought to therapy.

In working to achieve these potential benefits, however, therapy will require that firm efforts be made to change and may involve the experiencing of significant discomfort. Remembering and therapeutically resolving unpleasant events can arouse intense feelings of fear, anger, depression, frustration, and the like. Seeking to resolve issues between family members, marital partners, and other persons can similarly lead to discomfort, as well as relationship changes that may not be originally intended.

PART III: *Fees and Length of Therapy*

1. I agree to enter into therapy with Mary E. Spates, Ph.D. for _____ one-hour sessions during the next _____ weeks.
2. I agree to pay _____ for each completed one-hour session. Payment may be made by me or by a third party when billed.
3. I understand that I can leave therapy at any time and that I have no moral, legal, or financial obligation to complete the maximum number of sessions listed in this contract; I am contracting only to pay for completed therapy sessions.

Client(s): _____

_____

_____

_____

Therapist: _____ *Date* _____

Note: From "Privacy and Confidentiality in Psychotherapy" by L. Everstine, D.S. Everstine, G.M. Heymann, R.H. True, D.H. Frey, H.G. Johnson, and R.H. Seiden, 1980, *American Psychologist, 35,* pp. 828–840. Copyright 1980 by American Psychological Association. Adapted by permission of the publisher and authors.

the broad outlines is sufficient. They seek to offer only the assurance of a degree of predictability as to potential process and procedures. Hare-Mustin et al. (1979) posited, however, that procedures at odds with clients' values should be specified. Clients should clearly be appraised of any aversive techniques or physical contact planned or if the use of medication is expected. Therapists who follow up on clients should secure their permission in the contract, even if this might bias future responses.

Practices such as sexual relations with clients are unethical and remain so even if agreed to by clients. Some have argued that treatments objected to by many therapists, such as primal scream or "tickle" therapy, should be permitted if clients freely agree to their use with full knowledge of potential risks and benefits. It must be remembered, however, that there is initial inequity in the bargaining power between clients and therapists in that many clients' vulnerability opens them to manipulation; thus, such contracts are likely unconscionable (Schwitzgebel, 1975, 1976).

Clients occasionally present goals neither appropriate nor desirable and detrimental to the best interests of the clients themselves or others. Halleck (1976) proposed that "therapists try to change behaviors they believe should be changed and be reluctant to change behaviors they view as understandable or socially acceptable" (p. 167). He cited the case example of a woman wanting to eliminate feelings of possessiveness and jealousy. Yet her current life circumstances suggested that these feelings were entirely appropriate and what she lacked was the ability to better cope with being oppressed.

Where clients' goals are at odds with therapists' professional values, the potential consequences of working towards goals sought by clients should be examined. If therapists feel they cannot agree with clients' expressed goals, they should not work with clients. Referral to another therapist or source of assistance should be offered (Hare-Mustin et al., 1979).

Therapists must negotiate with clients who are unable to be specific about their goals. These clients challenge therapists to help them translate vague complaints into concrete concerns. For such clients, an initial therapeutic goal might be to explore what prevents them from being specific about their desires with more definitive behavioral goal setting to follow. Outside-session tasks such as record keeping and diaries can encourage specificity. Time limits on therapy may also provide an incentive to set goals. Therapists who allow clients to stay in therapy without specific goals only increase the ambiguity of treatment efforts and deprive clients of the benefits inherent in pursuing a sought objective.

For some clients, negotiation and establishment of a therapeutic contract may be threatening. Certain clients may reject a contract because they suspiciously see it as benefiting only the therapist. For these clients, considerable orientation to the idea may be necessary. This orientation, however, must be presented in a manner that retains clients' right to refuse (Hare-Mustin et al., 1979). Rosen (1977) sampled over 900 clients in a study investigating reasons why clients relinquish their rights. He found when clients were not informed of their right to refuse, all signed away their rights to privacy; when informed that such an option existed, only 41% signed.

Professional Disclosure Statements

A number of authors have advocated a written *professional disclosure statement* as a means of meeting informed consent provisions of codes of ethics (Gill, 1982; Gross, 1977; Swanson, 1979; Winborn, 1977). Professional disclosure statements take many forms, but essentially entail a process of introducing prospective clients to a therapist's qualifications, the nature of the therapeutic process, and administrative procedures relating to time and money. An adaptation of Winborn's (1977) professional disclosure statement illustrated in Figure 1–2 provides a model.

While contributing to the ethical objective of gaining clients' informed consent, a professional disclosure also yields developmental benefits for practitioners. Creating such a statement clarifies professional practices and identity. Personal beliefs, values, strengths and weaknesses, and objectives pertaining to therapeutic relationships must be examined. By concisely stating who they are and what they are trained to do, therapists define a set of competencies and an approach identifying them as unique providers of beneficial human services. As Gill (1982) asserted:

Figure 1–2   A Professional Disclosure Statement

David Morgan, M.S.
Licensed Marriage and Family Therapist (Florida No. 475)
Child Guidance Clinic
181 Atlantic Avenue
Orlando, Florida 33310
904/342-7658

Some Things You Should Know About Your Therapist and Therapy

Since therapy is conducted in a number of different ways, depending on the therapist and his or her orientation, this description has been prepared to inform you about my qualifications, how I view the therapeutic process, and what you can expect from me as your therapist.

My Qualifications. I received my graduate degree from the Florida State University with a major in Marriage and Family Therapy. I have been employed as a therapist for more than 8 years, the past 6 years here with the Child Guidance Clinic. I am a licensed Marriage and Family Therapist in Florida. I am also a Clinical Member and Approved Supervisor in the American Association for Marriage and Family Therapy. I have written over 30 articles for professional journals and coauthored 2 books relating to marriage and family therapy.

The majority of my experience has been working with couples and families. While I do see individuals alone, especially children, I attempt to involve the entire family where appropriate and when possible. I have worked with individuals, couples, and families experiencing a wide range of problems. My training and experience provides me with the ability to assist with concerns that range from children's poor school achievement to marital problems and family hostility, as well as social skills training and alleviating fears, anxiety, and depression.

I am not a physician and cannot prescribe or provide any medication, nor perform any medical procedures. If medical treatment is indicated, I can recommend a physician and in certain situations, I have worked in concert with and under the supervision of a psychiatrist.

The Therapeutic Process. Marriage and family therapy is a learning process that seeks for you and your marital partner, parents, and/or other family members or significant persons to better understand yourself and others and the interactions that occur between and among you. Additional goals include achieving better functioning as a couple and/or family so that healthy interactions are established and greater satisfaction is attained. Further, by gaining a more harmonious relationship with significant persons around you, individual concerns can be more effectively and efficiently dealt with.

There are several steps in the therapeutic process. First, we will need to spend some time exploring the problems that have brought you to therapy. I need to get to know you, how you view yourself, and how you and significant persons in your life interact. You will likely come to understand your situation better as we proceed in this manner. Obviously, we need to discuss things openly and honestly. My responsibility at this point in the therapeutic process is to listen, to assist you to communicate with me and others who may take part in the therapy, and to provide an environment of trust so that all present can interact freely and speak what is on their mind.

All of our sessions will, of course, be confidential to persons outside of the therapy. Therapy will likely involve the participation of family members and/or other significant persons. I do not guarantee confidentiality among participants in the therapy, although I would use my professional discretion in disclosing communications related to me. My professional code of ethics prevents me from discussing what is said during sessions with anyone other than participants in the therapy or releasing any records without your/their permission. The only exceptions to this are if someone is in danger of being harmed or if the law explicitly states that confidentiality provisions do not apply.

After we have explored and developed sufficient background to proceed, we will decide upon specific goals and objectives. We will then develop a treatment plan outlining how these goals will be achieved. Such a plan will likely require strong efforts, and feelings of discomfort inherent in change will be experienced. We will regularly evaluate progress in terms of whether the plan is effective in attaining the desired objectives, comparing progress with the situation when therapy began. Treatment efforts will conclude when the sought-after goals are sufficiently achieved. This will be determined through mutual agreement among the participants, including myself as therapist.

Fees and Length of Therapy. Therapy sessions are normally for one hour. Depending upon the nature of the presenting problems, sessions are held one to two times per week. It is difficult to initially predict how many sessions will be needed. I will be better able to discuss the probable number of sessions after we have explored and gained some background into the situation—usually after two or three sessions. I will verbally discuss fees with you as the Child Guidance Clinic operates on a *sliding scale* fee structure, meaning the cost of sessions varies according to clients' yearly income.

Please Ask Questions. You may have questions about me, my qualifications, or anything not addressed in the previous paragraphs. *It is your right* to have a complete explanation for any of your questions at any time. Please exercise this right.

Note. From "Honest Labeling and Other Procedures for the Protection of Consumers of Counseling" by B.B. Winborn, 1977, *Personnel and Guidance Journal, 56,* pp. 206–209. Copyright 1977 by AACD. Reprinted by permission. No further reproduction authorized without permission of AACD.

Are we shrinks, faith healers, or gurus whose mystical understandings of the universe magically transform problems into solutions? Or, are we trained specialists who utilize a set of skills and a body of knowledge to help people cope with normal life problems? If we are the latter, we should be able to describe who we are and what we do. (p. 444)

Gill (1982) proposed writing a professional disclosure statement addressing one's approach to the therapeutic process to be a particularly demanding experience. As a way of facilitating therapists' preparation of this part, Gill synthesized a set of questions from the recommendations of a number of professional disclosure advocates (Gross, 1977; Swanson, 1979; Witmer, 1978):

— What do you believe is the purpose of psychotherapy?
— What do you believe helps persons lead more satisfying lives?
— What should clients expect as a result of engaging in therapy efforts?
— What is your responsibility during therapy?
— What are the responsibilities your clients can be expected to assume during therapy?
— What is your primary therapeutic approach and what are the general intervention strategies that emanate from that approach?
— What types of presenting problems have you been most effective in assisting clients with in the past?
— Under what circumstances might clients be offered referral to another source of assistance?
— How do you handle the confidential nature of the therapeutic relationship?

Informed Consent Concerns in Marriage and Family Therapy

A primary concern in marriage and family therapy is that procedures for informed consent be conducted with all persons who participate in treatment efforts, including those who may join therapy at a later time (Margolin, 1982). This is especially pertinent because risks and benefits for individuals tend to be much different in marriage and family therapy as opposed to individual therapy. Consider the following example:

A couple sought marital treatment. In the process that ensued, the wife recognized her unwillingness to expend the efforts necessary to eventually gain the satisfaction from the marriage she wanted and so stated her rational desire to seek a divorce. The husband reacted to his wife's statement with a verbal attack upon the therapist for allowing this to occur: "Therapy was supposed to save our marriage!"

Clients need to be prewarned that marriage and family therapy can lead to outcomes viewed as undesirable by one or another of the participants, for example, the wife's decision to divorce.

Somewhat similarly, marriage and family therapy may not always be in the perceived best interests of individual marital partners or family members. Priority placed upon the good of the couple or family as a whole calls for individuals to at times subordinate personal desires not congruent with the overall goals. The following case example illustrates this point:

> Parents with a 15-year-old son and a 17-year-old daughter complained of the teenagers' unwillingness to unquestionably follow their directives. Interaction during the initial evaluation session clearly indicated the parents as excessively authoritarian and the youths' actions as normal developmental strivings. As therapy progressed, the parents eventually came to realize how their "overparenting" was a major part of the presenting problem; they nevertheless experienced significant anguish in allowing their son and daughter to take on greater self-responsibility.

Family members can benefit unequally from therapy, at least in the immediate changes emanating from treatment efforts aimed at enhancing the overall family functioning.

Hare-Mustin (1980) asserted that therapists recognize their responsibility for minimizing the risks in marriage and family therapy and share this recognition with therapy participants. She suggested this is best accomplished by clearly stating goals the therapist wishes to pursue. Marital partners and family members should be encouraged to question these goals so they can better identify how their individual needs align or contrast with overall marital or family relationship goals. Therapists must be explicit about the extent to which individual goals are incompatible with the relationship goals, need to be subordinated to the relationship goals, or are simply unacceptable to their marital partner and/or other family members.

While general procedures for informed consent in marriage and family therapy appear rather basic, therapists need to carefully consider how their primary orientation interacts with their informed consent practices. This is most relevant in determining the degree of specificity in information presented (Margolin, 1982). Most marriage and family therapists offer an overview of objectives (e.g., more satisfactory family functioning, clearer communications) as well as the format sessions will take (e.g., length and frequency of sessions, approximate duration of treatment efforts). More concise information, however, may be detrimental to some types of treatment efforts. This might be particularly true for strategic therapists, for example, attempting to mobilize oppositional tendencies of participants through paradoxical interventions (Haley, 1976; Stanton, 1981).

Most marriage and family therapists advocate certain "maneuvers" that indirectly limit fully informed consent and free choice about therapy (Margolin, 1982). For example, in relating benefits to be expected from treatment efforts, therapists cannot ethically guarantee positive change. Most therapists, however, do express optimism about the potential outcome of treatment to reduce participants' anxiety, raise their expectations, and increase their persistence in pursuing agreed-to goals (Jacobson & Margolin, 1979).

Another such therapeutic maneuver involves certain explanations and interpretations offered marital partners and family members. Several major marriage and family therapy approaches advocate reframing or relabeling behaviors and interactions in ways that do not reflect a couple's or family's current reality but rather facilitate their interactions in more efficient and effective ways. Relabeling two marital partners' constant arguments as evidence of "your persistence in seeking to communicate clearly with each other" introduces a positive goal orientation where hostility is present. The likelihood of the couple pursuing a common course of future action will be greater if they accept the therapist's reframing of their interaction, even if seen by an objective observer as an inaccurate description of an actual occurrence.

Margolin (1982) aptly summarized marriage and family therapists' need for balance between informed consent and appropriate therapeutic action:

> Thus, even though clients deserve an accurate portrayal of therapy in informed consent procedures, complete objectivity and openness may not be possible. At the same time that families need factual information to make an informed decision about therapy, they also need the therapist's support, encouragement, and optimism for taking this risky step. An overly enthusiastic discussion of alternatives to therapy or overly detailed explanation of the risks of therapy may convince the client that the therapist does not want him or her in therapy. (p. 795)

SUMMARY AND CONCLUSIONS

Therapists must be well versed in the theory and procedures of the therapeutic approaches they advocate. They must also be able to recognize and respond to ethical issues directly affecting delivery of services and public acceptance of those services. One way of addressing such issues is through adherence to a professional code of ethics.

This chapter has emphasized the importance of adhering to a code of ethics; not as a means of procuring definitive guidelines for professional conduct, but rather as a way of becoming aware of options utilizing a paradigm for ethical decision making. Ethical dilemmas are infrequently simple choices between right and wrong, good and bad. They more often contain elements of both. The challenge is not only finding an ethical position to take but applying that position in specific instances.

Several major areas of ethical inquiry were presented and discussed. Within this discussion, the view was taken that ethical questions relating to client welfare, confidentiality, and informed consent in marriage and family therapy require specialized attention. It should be noted that these three issues, although predominent in all therapists' practices, represent only a sampling of the ethical issues therapists must address. Chapter 2 considers further ethical issues particular to the practice of marriage and family therapy. Chapter 3 provides an opportunity to gain greater expertise in offering case examples and critiques emanating from the American Association for Marriage and Family Therapy's *Code of Ethical Principles for Marriage and Family Therapists*.

2

Ethical Considerations in the Interactional Context of Marriage and Family Therapy

Marriage and family therapy is not simply a treatment approach. It is a way of understanding human behavior and conceptualizing problems—how symptoms develop and how they are resolved. Marriage and family therapy requires the *transactions between individuals* rather than the individual characteristics of given persons be the primary therapeutic focus (Sluzki, 1978). Even when attention is zeroed in on a single person, that person's actions are analyzed in terms of the power to affect and shape the actions of other members of the relationship system as well as how other members' actions reciprocally affect and shape the individual's original actions.

Marriage and family therapy contrasts with an individually oriented view of psychological dysfunction in adopting a systemic framework emphasizing interdependence between and among persons, information exchange, and circular feedback mechanisms. Individuals' symptomatic behaviors are viewed as actively maintained by the interpersonal context in which they currently function. Further, these symptoms are seen as serving a regulating, stabilizing, and communication function in that context (O'Shea & Jessee, 1982). When observing marital partners' and family members' interactions, marriage and family therapists consider effects rather than intentions. The effects of behaviors upon behaviors and the way interpersonal sequences are organized are the primary focus of observation, not the personal motivation of those parties. Thought given to individual motivation or intention is minimal, if existing at all (Sluzki, 1978).

Marriage and family therapists do not deny the existence of individual motivation or intention. Rather, the inferences that can be drawn from assertions about persons' intentions or inner motivations are simply of secondary importance for purposes of diagnosis and treatment. As occurs with the application of any coherent framework for conceptualizing human behavior, the utilization of a systemic perspective for understanding and modifying the way couples and families interact requires focusing on certain clinical considerations at the expense of others. Relevant variables are selectively attended to and acted upon while little regard is paid to less important variables.

The selective clinical attention and actions called for in adopting a systemic perspective immediately cause therapists to confront long-standing social, cultural, and religious assumptions. On a sociocultural level, marriage and family therapists are often at odds with North American ideology and legal tradition that emphasizes individual self-sufficiency, values individual responsibility and accountability, and sanctions individual rights over group preferences. On a religious level, Judeo-Christian tradition posits strong limits regarding the behavior of couples and families as well as profound assumptions about how marital and family organizations should proceed. Notable examples include "Honor thy father and thy mother" and "Thou shalt not commit adultery."

In proposing to see the couple or family unit as the focus for therapeutic efforts, therapists must consider the many deep-seated beliefs they may be confronting and the professional ethics involved in doing so. These confrontations create conflicts that are concrete manifestations of the clash among the practice of marriage and family therapy; individually oriented theories of psychological disturbance and treatment; and social, cultural, and religious standards espousing individualism and/or prescribing marital and family mores. Some major ethical dilemmas stemming from a therapeutic focus on the couple or family unit as the "client" include issues of problem definition; participation in therapy; the therapist as a direct, active change agent; the use of paradoxical procedures; and agency triangulation.

DEFINING THE PROBLEM

The typical interaction occurring in the opening phase of most marriage and family therapy efforts is one member of a dyad or family being presented as the "identified patient" or an individual coming alone requesting assistance. The therapist who defines the problem as a relationship problem makes an assumption that immediately raises an ethical issue (Fieldsteel, 1982). The therapist has taken on the obligation of imposing a new set of values and beliefs on the individual and/or members of the relationship system. The couple, family, or individual seeks therapeutic assistance for a specific concern; the therapist implicitly or explicitly informs them that they must put aside their beliefs and adopt those of the therapist.

Most therapists assume the right to define clients' presenting problems in terms of their own therapeutic orientation. They make this assumption with the belief that, as owners of greater psychological knowledge and professional qualifications, they have the prerogative to assert themselves without violating their clients' rights. Because of the perceived role inequality between patient and professional accepted by most clients, they tend to take on therapists' assertions as actual fact. While this redefinition of clients' problems is not limited to marriage and family therapy, it is more dramatic in this kind of therapy (Fieldsteel, 1982). Therapeutic definitions relative to the treatment of schizophrenic disorders, particularly the premise that weaning from both institutional and family caregiving will stimulate the "identified patient" to develop skills necessary for independent community living, illustrate this point.

Dincin, Selleck, and Streicker (1978) conveyed a common family therapy tack taken in the management of schizophrenia in their work with parents of schizophrenic offspring:

> The consistent message of the agency is that the greatest love parents can show . . . is to allow and encourage the child to separate from the parental home. We believe that living at home is usually counterproductive to long-

term growth and that psychological damage occurs when parents are unwilling or unable to "let go." (p. 599)

Madanes (1983) demonstrated a similar stance in her work using a Strategic Family Therapy approach:

> Parents typically avoid defining the family hierarchy as one in which they have power over their offspring. They do so because . . . they are afraid to do the wrong thing and harm the youth; because they are afraid they are to blame and wish to do no more harm. . . . The therapist must respond with various counteracting maneuvers to keep the parents in charge. (p. 216)

Terkelsen (1983), by contrast, asserted that family interaction contributes heavily to the etiology of schizophrenia, a position that has dominated contemporary family therapy even in the absence of solid empirical confirmation. He asserted as the conviction that sociogenic modeling of schizophrenia assumptions may not only be incorrect but even harmful to families. He proposed similar potential harm resulting in the relationship and families and clinicians and cited a need for research in this area.

Terkelsen described his own dilemmas encountered in 10 years of work with families having schizophrenic offspring. He related being trained in "a tradition that assumed madness to be an interpersonal affair" (p. 192). In early sessions with families, he had attuned himself to abstract from family members' reports only those interactional phenomena representative of parental pathogenicity that would "explain" the individual pathology. Treatment sessions constituted efforts to cloister the identified patient, to separate him or her from the rest of the family, with the belief that it was the family interaction maintaining the patient's pathology. The usual result was a sense of alienation as he found family members unwilling or unable to conform to his theoretical formulations.

Grunebaum (1984), in commenting upon Terkelsen's experience, proposed that therapists' first and foremost task is to understand and share the pain of parents and other family members who find themselves in such a predicament. He identified this as a precondition necessary for family members to open themselves to alternative explanations of their circumstances. Family members dealt with the identified patient because they did not know how to cope with the manifestations of mental illness in any other way. Grunebaum offered a case example involving a 25-year-old mildly retarded woman and her parents:

> Now it would appear to many clinicians that these parents needed to be reassured that their daughter was not suicidal, that she was highly unlikely to commit suicide, and that by responding to her slightest threats, they were responding to a manipulation on her part. In fact, the daughter would leave the community placements, wander around for a few hours and then call home. Her parents would then immediately come and get her. Reassurance about suicide had been given before and fallen on deaf ears. . . . The parents then left the room and the staff continued the discus-

sion. Present were the three nurses who had been on call for such cases. They included the two nurses responsible for community placements and one nurse from the ward from which the patient had been discharged. The latter, who knew the patient well, did not believe the patient was suicidal. She stated that she did not think the patient should have been readmitted. The other two nurses were equally clear that they were responsible for the patient and if she expressed suicidal thoughts or feelings, she had to be hospitalized. They were willing to delegate that responsibility to someone else but not to "take a chance." They turned to the ward nurse and asked, "Can you promise she won't kill herself?" (pp. 422–423)

These three nurses, trained mental health professionals, were unwilling to risk their role in interacting with the woman to allow her to assure her own well-being. Yet they had just posited the woman's parents should take that very risk and assume the responsibility of not being manipulated by their daughter's threats.

Grunebaum (1984) proposed that families appearing to interfere with attempts to foster the independence of the identified patient are sometimes making positive moral choices even though this involves capitulating to manipulation or intimidation at the hands of the schizophrenic member. It was his supposition that many of these individuals suffer from disruption of fundamental neurobiological processes. Their insistence on being taken care of by their family is often a "default position." Their experiences in the community have only been characterized by impossible challenges, humiliating failures, and rejection by others. Life with their family comes to be seen as the one respite from the continual agony of constant defeat.

Terkelsen (1983) summarized his own discussion and Grunebaum's comments in stating:

> If, under these circumstances, the family permits the patient to manipulate his or her way back into a dependent status, perhaps the family has come to feel that enough is enough. . . . If, . . . and I speak as a family therapist to family therapists—we lose sight of this sensibility, we will also have lost contact with the very people whose burden we seek to alleviate. (p. 427)

There is little doubt that couples, families, and individual clients present for therapy because they are experiencing a sense of distress and desire to gain relief. In seeking professional assistance, they attribute power to therapists on the basis of their clinical knowledge and skills. It is thus critical that therapists recognize the difference between appropriate professional judgment and biased personal power. By redefining presenting problems as relationship rather than individual issues, therapists ask members of relationship systems to sacrifice, at least temporarily, their autonomy. The therapist who imposes a specific problem definition upon a relationship system can only do so with the cooperation of the members of that system. There is often a question, however, as to whether this cooperation is attained under circumstances that could realistically be identified as containing clients' "informed consent."

Marriage and family therapists have an ethical obligation to help the members of a relationship system seeking treatment understand what is involved in the therapist's definition of their presenting concern. Reasons why such a definition is therapeutically beneficial and what it will demand of them should be provided (Fieldsteel, 1982). Couples, families, and individuals may be labeled "resistant" or "poor therapy risks" for many reasons. Therapists have a further ethical obligation to examine how their expectations and biases may lead to fulfillment of these prophecies (Hines & Hare-Mustin, 1978). This is not to suggest that empirical evidence and clinical experience should be ignored. Characteristics of certain clients, especially as they interact in relationship systems, are highly suggestive of a poor therapeutic prognosis. Rather, therapists must be cognizant of the long-term significance of the definitions they impose and the extent to which these definitions follow from an inability to deal with beliefs and value systems different from their own.

COMPLICATIONS IN CONVENING THERAPY

Only a small percentage of families seek therapeutic assistance by specifically requesting relationship therapy. While this may be changed as public awareness of marriage and family therapy as a treatment entity increases, typically one marital partner or family member seeks an appointment. Marriage and family therapists have as a critical task during this initial "presession" contact to promote the assembling or convening of significant familial or extrafamilial members for the upcoming first session. This is especially important because: (a) an adequate relationship assessment requires the presence of all significant members of that relationship; (b) convening as a marital dyad or total family symbolically accents the systemic or relationship nature of the presenting problem and its potential treatment; (c) it becomes increasingly more difficult to bring in absent members as therapy progresses; and (d) convening represents the first test of a therapist's ability and commitment to effectively manage relationship resistance (Teismann, 1980).

This desire by marriage and family therapists to engage all significant members of a relationship system raises the ethical issue of voluntary participation (Margolin, 1982). Obviously, coercion of reluctant members by their marital partner, family members, or the therapist is unethical. However, therapists should encourage reluctant members to participate in at least the initial evaluation session to investigate what therapy may entail. Therapists should also pay attention to what may be contributing to this reluctance: general anxiety, insistence on individual treatment for the identified patient, lack of effort on the part of the initiating members or the therapist, denial of any existing problem, or covert maneuvering by the participating member to exclude the reluctant member.

The most common ethical dilemma relative to convening complications surrounds the therapeutic policy put forth by many marriage and family therapists of refusing treatment unless all significant members of a relationship system become involved. Do willing members seeking assistance go untreated because one individual refuses to participate? This issue is particularly problematic for therapists employed in public agencies where such withholding of services is not only ethically but legally and politically questionable given that they are tax supported, legally mandated to serve those requesting help, and often funded on the basis of how many clients they serve (O'Shea & Jessee, 1982).

Napier and Whitaker (1978) referred to the convening process in marriage and family therapy as the "battle for structure." They saw the battle for structure as a couple or family's overt or covert attempt to control and resist change by dictating the terms of therapy. More often than not, the absent member or members are contributors to the symptom being presented and thus crucial to accurately identifying and intervening relative to the problem. Napier and Whitaker asserted therapists' ability to convene all significant relationship members as a necessary criterion to achieving successful treatment outcomes.

O'Shea and Jessee (1982) argued that withholding treatment in the battle for structure does not constitute a refusal to provide mental health services. They defined it instead as an "insistence on providing services appropriate to the nature of the difficulty, and thus, it is a responsible, competent, professional practice" (p. 6). They likened it to a physician in medical practice who orders tests and prescribes medication deemed as appropriate to a patient's illness or injury, not on the basis of what the patient wishes. Psychotherapy in general, and marriage and family therapy in particular, however, do not have the empirically established data base supporting the effectiveness of particular treatment for specific disorders (Gurman & Kniskern, 1981).

Teismann (1980) argued against the withholding of treatment in the battle for structure on the grounds that doing so denies services to motivated marital partners and family members and risks creation of an implicit alliance between the therapist and the nonparticipant. He identified two types of strategies for involving reluctant members of a relationship system short of refusing or withholding services: enforcing and enabling. He labeled as *enforcing* a strategy wherein therapists mobilize referral agents to exert pressure on relationship systems to convene for therapy as a total system. Enforcing, if utilized in an authoritarian manner, can be tantamount to coercion. Rather than therapists' directly requesting reluctant members to come to therapy, they indirectly do so through the referral source.

Enforcing done in a proactive as opposed to a reactive manner allows for greater free choice to all involved. Enforcing requires preplanning and prereferral agreement between therapists and referral agents. For example, a physician may make family therapy a prescribed part of medical treatment. Juvenile court services may offer family therapy as an alternative to prosecution or sentencing, with the stipulation of total family participation. Employee assistance program referral sources can similarly provide alternatives such as marital or family therapy as options for workers experiencing relevant personal problems affecting their jobs. It is recommended that referral agents be present at the initial evaluation session to explain the reasons for the referral and reconfirm marital partners' or family members' right to refuse treatment. Although potentially negative consequences may result, the understanding that there is an alternative course of action is critical to therapists' ethical practice.

Teismann (1980) explained *enabling* from two perspectives. The first manner of enabling involves the therapist working to increase the attractiveness of attending. Essentially, therapists utilizing this enabling strategy seek to decrease a reluctant member's perceived threat in participating in therapy while simultaneously persuading the member of attainable personal gain. The therapist must first make contact with the reluctant member, preferably a face-to-face meeting. In interacting with the reluctant member, the therapist should seek to increase the attractiveness of attending by appealing to and confirming the individual's strength and potential and focus on his or her position and special importance in the relationship system. For example, it can be pointed out to a reluctant father that his son needs a strong and able male model that only he can readily offer. Or a wife can be told that her husband needs someone with the courage and tenacity to temporarily, at least, take charge of the disorganization he is experiencing in his life. These types of proposals frequently provide reluctant members with a sense of purpose leading to participation in therapy.

To alleviate reluctant members' anxiety relating to the unknown that therapy represents, therapists might provide a verbal outline of the process, photocopies of relevant articles from popular magazines, or a referral to former clients willing to make themselves available to share their experience in marriage and/or family therapy. Frequently, a simple description of expectations, potential experiences, and probable effects offered directly by the therapist sufficiently relieves many reluctant members' anxiety.

The second form of enabling involves decreasing the attractiveness of being absent from therapy. Often a reluctant member offers rationalizations for declining to participate in therapy. Therapists can utilize the member's reasoning to emphasize the additional problems they potentially foster by their nonattendance. For example, one man believed his wife had "serious personal problems" that required individual attention. The therapist agreed and added that the husband may have underestimated the seriousness of the problems and that the help of both the husband and other family members would likely prevent the problem from worsening. In another case, a reluctant father voiced his concern that a family should not "hang out its dirty laundry" for all to see, directing this to mean the therapist. The therapist replied with full agreement and went on to note that therapy appeared to be a last resort to stop the trend since the dirty laundry was already visible at his son's school (truancy) and with the police (marijuana possession).

Wilcoxon and Fenell (1983) suggested a therapist-initiated letter for engaging a nonattending spouse in marital therapy. Given to the participating member as a homework assignment, the letter acts not only as an enabling strategy for engaging the reluctant member, but also offers a structured task for the couple to complete in their home. This task facilitates clarification of their intentions regarding their marriage as well as the marital therapy process. Figure 2–1 represents a sample of such a letter.

Another frequently suggested solution to the ethical dilemma raised by the potential withholding of treatment in the battle for structure is to offer brief, limited exploratory "presessions" to a marital partner or family member seeking assistance, although cautioning them that change is not likely to come about or endure unless all significant members of the relationship system participate. This practice, however, and those suggested by Teismann (1980) may only exchange one ethical dilemma for another. With the possible exception of conjoint marital therapy (Gurman & Kniskern, 1978), the rationale for the participation of all significant relationship system members is actually more a matter of clinical judgment and therapeutic orientation than empirically established fact (O'Shea & Jessee, 1982). Further, therapists who insist that all significant members of a relationship system attend therapy sessions may be making an error in presupposing that what may be beneficial for the relationship will be equally good for individual members, particularly the reluctant ones. The consequences of therapy are clearly unpredictable in certain cases, and not everyone can or should benefit from therapy (Silber, 1976). Additionally, this position implicitly promises the reluctant members enhanced well-being, something that therapists cannot assure (Hare-Mustin, 1980).

When enforcing or enabling efforts at convening all significant relationship members have been unsuccessful, therapists can still choose to treat the marital partner or family members who wish therapy rather than offer the ultimatum of no therapy. By identifying key relations and dynamics, and planning and executing interventions from a systemic perspective, change to the relationship is still possible. When a couple or family is resistant to convening together, the therapist can focus on individual change within the static relationship system to bring about change (Watzlawick, Weakland, & Fish, 1974).

For example, a very motivated 33-year-old woman, after gaining awareness that her unconditional caretaking perpetuated her husband's substance abuse, agreed to spend the night in a motel whenever he came home drunk. She left him a note explaining that she had been hurting him with her caretaking, that she wanted to stop doing so, and that she would return the next day. This strategy effectively interrupted a basic interaction sequence symbolic of the system's dysfunction. It further

---

Figure 2–1   Letter to Engage a Nonattending Spouse

(Date)

Mr. John Jones
111 Smith Street
Anytown, USA 00000

Dear Mr. Jones,

As you may know, your wife, Jill, has requested therapy services for difficulties related to your marriage. However, she has stated that you do not wish to participate in marital therapy sessions.

As a professional marriage therapist, I have an obligation to inform each of you of the possible outcome of marital therapy services to only one spouse. The available research indicates that one-spouse marital therapy has resulted in reported increases in marital stress and dissatisfaction for both spouses in the marriage. On the other hand, many couples have reported that marital therapy which includes both spouses has been helpful in reducing marital stress and enhancing marital satisfaction.

These findings reflect general tendencies in marital research and are not absolute in nature. However, it is important for you and Jill to be informed of potential consequences which might occur through marital therapy in which only your spouse attends. Knowing this information, you may choose a course of action which best suits your intentions.

After careful consideration of this information, I ask that you and Jill discuss your options regarding future therapy services. In this way, all parties will have a clear understanding of one another's intentions regarding your relationship.

As a homework assignment for Jill, I have asked that each of you read this letter and sign in the spaces provided below to verify your understanding of the potential consequences to your relationship by continuing one-spouse marital therapy. If you are interested in joining Jill for marital therapy, in addition to your signature below, please contact my office to indicate your intentions. If not, simply sign below and have Jill return the letter at our next therapy session. I appreciate your cooperation in this matter.

Sincerely,

Therapist X

We verify by our signatures below that we have discussed and understand the potential implications of continued marital therapy with only one spouse in attendance.

Attending Spouse   Date

Non-Attending Spouse   Date

Note. From "Engaging the Non-attending Spouse in Marital Therapy Through the Use of Therapist-Initiated Written Communication" by A. Wilcoxon and D. Fenell, 1983, *Journal of Marital and Family Therapy, 9,* 199–203. Copyright 1983 by American Association for Marriage and Family Therapy. Reprinted by permission.

redefined the problem as residing in the wife and thus opened the door for her to change and to simultaneously introduce change into the relationship.

In clarifying whether or not a marital partner or particular family member needs to participate in therapy efforts, therapists must be able to identify the extent to which each member of the relationship will be expected to participate. For example, some members may simply be able to attend sessions in the role of observer just to learn enough about the therapeutic process so they won't impede its progress. Therapists with a strong preference for convening all members of a relationship system should inform persons seeking assistance that other therapists do not necessarily share this view (Margolin, 1982). A list of competent referral sources should then be made available. The ethical issue is not so much the idea that therapists have a definition of what is conducive to optimal psychological functioning, but rather that they can acknowledge their professional views and be willing to be flexible in offering options to persons seeking help.

THE THERAPIST AS AGENT FOR CHANGE

All couples and families enter therapy with their own idiosyncratic styles of communicating with implicit patterns of meaning and relationship rules embedded in what can appear to an outsider an unimportant, insignificant, conventional interactions (Watzlawick, Beavin, & Jackson, 1967). Therapists beginning therapy with a couple or family are not privy to the special importance many of these interactions have within the relationship system. This puts therapists at an immediate disadvantage, not unlike that of a new member seeking entrance into a secret organization without benefit of the required password (O'Shea & Jessee, 1982). The therapist must decipher the relationship's communication style and gain access to the meanings and rules employed by the members of the system. Only then can the therapist accurately assess, intervene, and ultimately facilitate change within the couple or family.

The importance of marriage and family therapists functioning in an active, directive manner has been clearly indicated in studies of negative outcome of systems therapy (Gurman & Kniskern, 1978). To be effective, marriage and family therapists need to be influential. Although therapist influence and power are a recognized part of individually oriented therapies, the means by which marriage and family therapists achieve such a position characteristically stands in ready contrast. Consensus among most marriage and family therapists has concluded that this influence is best established by therapists assuming an active position of power early in therapy (Haley, 1976). Wachtel (1979), in describing the movement from an individual to marriage and family therapy perspective in her practice, suggested that the more reflective and insight-oriented stance common in individual therapy is influential only because of the traditional nature of the therapeutic contract and conferred largely as a result of clients' seeking to alleviate personally felt distress. She acknowledged her difficulty in sharing more control over the content and direction of sessions with family members, recognizing her position as one of less importance and centrality than with an individual client. The importance of assuming an active position of power to gain influence became readily evident as her experience with couples and families increased.

Marriage and family therapists recognize the necessity of assuming power. Most are direct about their role as agents of change. For example, family theorist and therapist Salvador Minuchin (1974) expressly described his own Structural Family Therapy as a "therapy of action." Minuchin wrote that families are organized around the specific functions of their members. The power of the therapist is seen as the primary means of bringing about change: "Change is seen as occurring through the process of the therapist's affiliation with the family and his restructuring of the family in a carefully planned way, so as to transform dysfunctional transactional patterns" (p. 91). Other marriage and family theorists and therapists convey similar messages as evident from the titles of their major writings (e.g., Virginia Satir's *Peoplemaking,* Jay Haley's *Changing Families*).

Corey et al. (1984) raised several ethical considerations relative to the power and action-oriented approach advocated by most marriage and family therapists:

— Should therapists impose their control upon couples and families?
— Should the primary responsibility for defining how change should occur rest with the therapist as opposed to the individual marital partners or family members?

Therapist power is a vital component in marriage and family therapy and in itself not inherently a negative force. It is when that power is misused that ethical misconduct comes into question. The major danger in misuse of therapist power is generally evidenced when it encourages client dependence. In their quest to establish their power and influence in a marital or family relationship system, some therapists do so at the expense of reducing adaptive autonomy of system members. Fieldsteel (1982) pinpointed the ethical dilemma confronting therapists who assume an inordinate share of responsibility for change in relationship systems: "There is a danger that the role of the therapist as a more active agent for change may shift the responsibility for the direction of change from the patient to the therapist" (p. 262).

A related issue involves marital partners and family members attributing magical qualities to effect changes in their marital or family functioning to therapists. This mystification process tends to intensify client dependence and reduces clients' ability to assert their rights in the therapy process (Hare-Mustin et al., 1979). Stensrud and Stensrud (1981) proposed that some therapists teach persons to be powerless instead of teaching them to trust themselves. They described this powerlessness as a "learned state of generalized helplessness in which clients (a) believe they are unable to have an impact on their environment, and (b) need some external force to intercede on their behalf" (p. 300). Stensrud and Stensrud cautioned that clients can develop self-fulfilling prophecies, whereby expectations of powerlessness evolve into regular experiences of powerlessness. They urged therapists to relate to clients in ways that maintain client self-responsibility—by regularly challenging clients to actively participate throughout the entire therapeutic process. Consider the following therapist's actions:

> A marriage and family therapist in a family services agency devoted many more hours to her position than she was expected to and overtaxed herself by taking on an inordinately large caseload. She frequently let sessions run overtime and encouraged clients to call her at home at any time. Couples and families were maintained much longer in therapy with her than her colleagues. Her former clients had a recidivism rate that was significantly larger than her colleagues' clients.

This therapist clearly has an obligation to examine the ways she established and misused her power base to keep clients so dependent.

Wachtel (1979) proposed that as the therapist's role is demystified, clients become more active. In discussing therapists' actions in this regard, he suggested that they openly and explicitly communicate their preferences. This leaves clients knowing more clearly what is going on and where they stand. They may still feel pressure and anxiety in response to therapists' expectations, but they are potentially in a much better position to differentiate their own preferences from the therapists. Fieldsteel (1982) affirmed the power of marriage and family therapists as agents of change. She advocated that they not delude themselves into thinking that therapy is an egalitarian, democratic relationship, especially at the outset. Rather Fieldsteel calls for this as a goal toward which therapists should work, much in the same manner that this becomes one of the major goals of child rearing.

Another major ethical dilemma confronting marriage and family therapists is occasioned by their allegiance to seeking relationship change as primary, and individual change as possibly equal, but likely secondary. O'Shea and Jessee (1982) suggested that therapists confront a central, ethical dilemma when they accept the notion that the symptomatic individual serves a homeostatic, protective, stabilizing function in his or her relationship system. They raised the question as to how much distress or risk one member should tolerate for the sake of long-term benefit to the greater marital or family relationship system.

It has been repeatedly recognized that many couples and families manifest a rigid scapegoating pattern toward one or more members and select specific members to bear the brunt of systemic discomfort. Therapists attempting to intervene can expect symptoms to escalate accordingly. In order to counteract this rigid homeostatic balance, it may be necessary to increase individual distress to a crisis level to facilitate a fundamental change in how the relationship system operates (Hoffman, 1981). O'Shea and Jessee (1982) asserted, however:

> The therapist who attempts to precipitate a structural shift in the system by tolerating or deliberately intensifying the distress in the system does so in opposition to the medical ethic and cultural expectation that helping professionals should relieve rather than prolong suffering. Clearly, a physician, despite the use of anesthetics, often inflicts immediate pain on the patient in the process of restoring a more global and long-term health. In systems therapy, however, the distress must at times be amplified before the family is motivated to change its dysfunctional avoidance behavior patterns. The therapist must, as it were, overcome the self-anesthetizing effect of the family's dysfunctional interactions by getting the family to experience the full thrust of anxiety and tension. (p. 12)

Several examples can serve to illustrate this ethical dilemma. The common and preferred legal response in cases of child abuse is to protect the victim by removing the abused or abusing member from the home. Marriage and family therapists are likely to view the abuser and/or abused member as actively fulfilling and maintaining a stabilizing, homeostatic function within the family system. This therapeutic perspective optimally calls for treating the family without removing the abused and/or abusing member for the sake of a more important and likely lasting change; that being change in the basic family functioning. The potential risks inherent in such a path are obvious.

The presenting of destructive behaviors such as suicidal potential make treatment decisions even more precarious. Therapists emphasizing the importance of primarily impacting on the relationship system face a trade-off between conservatively safeguarding the suicidal client through immediate hospitalization and thus reinforcing the system's scapegoating process or risking self-harm to the identified patient by negating the necessity of hospitalization in favor of outpatient treatment of the entire relationship system (Langsley & Kaplan, 1968). Marriage and family therapists prepared to accept this risk to the identified patient for the sake of a more meaningful and important relationship change should also be prepared to receive censure by individually oriented colleagues. However, precautions such as including all members of a relationship system in the evaluation and treatment of an identified patient exhibiting suicidal symptomatology may reveal that what appears as a mild suicidal risk when seen in isolation is actually more serious viewed within the context of a lethal relationship system (Richman, 1979).

Less dramatic ethical confrontations in this regard frequently occur within the confines of the therapy hour wherein marriage and family therapists encourage direct expression of negative feelings and evoke and escalate confrontations among members of relationship systems. Minuchin and Fishman (1981) offer a representative case excerpt:

> **Mother:** In the last five years I said to myself the only way not to be hurt is to try to be more like him, and I did. I tried to be like that. I tried to say, "I don't care. I don't need anybody." But I don't want to be like that any-

more! I really want to be like I used to be, and then I found that I couldn't, that I have really changed. It's hard when somebody reaches out to you. The normal thing would be to respond. I find that I'm not quite able to do that. It happened before: he touched me and I don't know what to do.

Minuchin: That is saying again that you want to sit on your shit!

> The therapist's pressure produces a response in the wife. . . . ("That is saying that you want to sit on your shit") is not a challenge to the dynamics of the wife but rather a reiteration of the demand for a transformation of the spouse subsystem.

Mother: But then he'll stick a knife in my back. (To husband.) If I drop my defenses when you feel like it, you'll withdraw and you'll start throwing little needles at me, and I don't know when it's going to happen.

Minuchin: Milt, she is throwing you a lot of nonsense. She is saying, "Love me, but don't do it because I will kick you in the balls." She is saying to you, "Hold me," and pushing you away. Don't listen to her.

Mother: Is that true? Is that what I have been doing all these years?

Father: Well, I felt that before, too.

Mother: Why didn't you tell me that?

Father: I'm not a talker, but you push yourself away. I know in the past I felt you preferred to be unhappy.

Mother: I don't know what to say. I don't know what to do next. I don't want to be unhappy like this.

Father: Well, the problem in the past—why I didn't tell you things—was because you get angry when you're criticized. Any kind of criticism on what you are or what you do gets a very strong reaction from you.

> The insistence of the therapist on stressing the system in the direction of changing the family members' perspective vis-á-vis each other produces a transformation of the spouse subsystem. The wife now takes the patient position, not as an isolating technique, but as a request for help. This change in the wife is complemented by the response of the husband.
>
> *Note.* From *Family Therapy Techniques* (pp. 188–189) by S. Minuchin and H.C. Fishman, 1981, Cambridge, MA: Harvard University Press. Reprinted by permission.

The degree of potential risk to an identified patient or to other members that should be tolerated in the service of seeking improved functioning for the total system also raises the problem of deterioration effects in marriage and family therapy. Gurman and Kniskern (1978) identified an important distinction between deterioration and relapse. They defined *deterioration* as a negative change or escalation of symptoms during treatment. *Relapse,* by contrast, was represented as a negative change occurring between posttreatment and follow-up in the direction of the pretreatment level of functioning. Thus, the risk of deterioration poses a more serious ethical dilemma for therapists than relapse, since relapse suggests that treatment was ineffective, but not necessarily harmful (O'Shea & Jessee, 1982).

Although deterioration effects are a concern for all therapists, individually-oriented as well as marriage and family, the latter garner a greater obligation because the scope of their responsibility must be expanded to include multiple members of a relationship system. Further, marriage and family therapists' position as active, directive agents of change increases the likelihood that they could precipitate deterioration. Gurman and Kniskern's (1978) review of research on deterioration in marriage and family therapy clearly indicated this. They identified variables relating to therapist functioning as dominant among those possibly contributing to deterioration effects. They stated:

> In summary, the available evidence points to a composite picture of deterioration in marital-family therapy being facilitated by a therapist with poor relationship skills who directly attacks "loaded" issues and family members' defenses very early in treatment, fails to intervene in or interpret intra-family confrontation in ongoing treatment, and does little to structure and guide the opening of therapy or to support family members. Such a style is even more likely to be counter-therapeutic with patients who have weak ego-defenses or feel threatened by the nature or very fact of being in treatment. . . . the therapist seems clearly to occupy a central role in most negative treatment outcomes. (p. 14)

Attempting to alter a couple or family's predominant mode of interaction, promoting change in one member of the system, or seeking change in an area of the total relationship's functioning is likely to evoke new or increased distress or dysfunction in the system, at least temporarily. Therapists who encourage enhancing of distress and intensification of symptomatology within the therapy hour must be concerned with the continued occurrence of these actions when the session ends. Marital partners or other family members may suffer from embarrassment, anxiety, and loss of respect in the eyes of their mate or other members of the system when they are pressured to make disclosures in session (Hines & Hare-Mustin, 1978). Angry outbursts and strong feelings may be provoked in marital and family sessions; if they are not resolved in the session, they can lead to increased hostility and bitterness.

Therapists who do not address this possibility run the risk of promoting premature termination from therapy, not to mention marital and family dissolution (Mace, 1976). Hines and Hare-Mustin (1978) suggested "innoculation" to guard against potential marital or family disintegration resulting from the direct facilitating of increased stress in the system; that is, alerting members during the initial stage of therapy to the stresses that can likely be expected in resolving their problems. This procedure also alleviates much of the ethical conflict occasioned in therapists' escalating symptomatology and distress in the interest of potential outcome. Therapists, however, must ultimately learn to balance the safety and immediate well-being of individual members of a relationship system with effective treatment considerations for the betterment of the overall system. Bosznormenyi-Nagy (1974) identified this ultimate goal as "a restoration of balanced reciprocity of fairness" in marriage and family relationships.

PARADOXICAL PROCEDURES

Haley (1976) posited two major types of interventions as possible in marriage and family therapy: (a) where therapists direct clients with the expectation of compliance, and (b) where therapists direct clients with the expectation of noncompliance. The latter intervention specifically suggests the purpose of a paradoxical procedure; the couple or family changes by rebellion or noncompliance. For example, Hoffman (1981) cited the case of a wife whose constant jealous questioning of her husband only reinforced the husband's reticence towards her. This in turn reinforced her jealousy. A paradoxical procedure was employed to disrupt this destructive sequence of behavior. The wife was directed by the therapist to redouble her jealous questioning. The expected result actualized wherein the wife rebelled against the task, leading to a resolution of the presenting problem.

The use of paradox has been a central and frequently controversial topic in marriage and family therapy. Proposing a couple or family continue dysfunctional patterns of behavior with the suggestion that these interactional sequences have a benevolent function comprises a therapeutic intervention that seems contradictory to the couple or family's expressed desire for problem resolution. Paradoxical procedures are designed to block or change dysfunctional sequences using indirect and seemingly illogical means. They "encourage" rather than attack symptoms and objectionable behaviors. They are used instead of direct attempts to introduce change when it is assumed that the couple or family cannot or will not comply with the therapist's advice or persuasion (Nichols, 1984). Paradoxical procedures can thus require selective disclosure to marital partners and family members by the therapist.

Regardless of their therapeutic orientation, all therapists selectively highlight certain facts and ignore, deemphasize, or avoid others. Although such behaviors constitute selective disclosure (or distortion) of information, the ethical issue that arises involves whether or not therapists are actually deceiving or harming clients (O'Shea & Jessee, 1982). Haley (1976) proposed that ethical prescriptions requiring therapists to disclose to clients everything they sense about them are naive and that therapists who are unwilling to draw a boundary between themselves and their clients and insist on sharing all not only risk failure but also risk doing harm. Haley maintained that the marriage and family therapist should function as a trained expert, not an equal partner.

In contrast, others (Fisher, Anderson, & Jones, 1981; O'Shea & Jessee, 1982) have stated that paradoxical procedures are effective precisely because they do represent the actual situation the couple or family is experiencing. These procedures embody each marital partner or family member's phenomenological experience of being involved in a dysfunctional system. Watzlawick et al. (1974) were quite explicit in this respect in defining change that occurs through *reframing*. They identified this process as an alteration in "the conceptual and/or emotional setting or viewpoint in relation to which a situation is experienced and to place it in another frame which fits the facts of the same concrete situation equally well or even better, thereby changing its entire meaning" (p. 95). In other words, the meaning attributed to the situation is altered or redefined and therefore its consequences change as well. Such a paradoxical directive brings covert patterns of interaction to the surface; the family responds by choosing either to continue or stop the problematic sequences. In either case, the problematic style of interaction now falls within the family's control.

Some paradoxical procedures, however, are directives given to clients without an explicit explanation or rationale. Hoffman (1981), for instance, described a therapist's telling a depressed wife to become more subservient to her husband. Not surprisingly, the wife rebelled in defiance of the therapist's directive. According to Hoffman, the paradoxical directive unbalanced a dysfunctional complementary balance in the marital relationship, which then became more functionally symmetrical. Previously the husband and wife were balanced in a relationship where he was one-up and she was one-down. By requesting that she put herself even further down (which she had been doing almost daily), the therapist provoked a rebellion, and the couple was able to establish a relationship characterized by greater equality. In discussing this case illustration offered by Hoffman, however, Nichols (1984) questioned why this should have happened as presented. Why didn't the couple simply reestablish the same complementary relationship?

This raises an added ethical concern as therapists can never be sure as to how a relationship system will absorb and respond to a given intervention (Selvini-Palazzoli, Boscolo, Cecchin, & Prata, 1978). O'Shea and Jessee (1982) proposed that out of the wide range of possible responses, the use of paradoxical procedures in particular "comes close to being based on faith" (p. 11). Gurman (1978) further asserted that paradoxical reframing and interactional tasks used without explanation or education may at times prolong the couple or family's dependence on the therapist, preventing the relationship system from developing its own coping mechanisms. O'Shea and Jessee differentiated between the appropriateness of paradoxical procedures that are factual from the couple or family's frame of reference and truly systemic, including and affecting all members of the relationship system, employing language or metaphor in harmony with members' subjective experience of their marital or family life. With such paradoxical procedures, the couple or family will more likely identify with the task, change in a more functional manner, and experience the change under their own direction (Selvini-Palazzoli et al., 1978).

Fraser (1984) made a strong case for the use of paradox as a primary procedure in marriage and family therapy. In doing so, he stated:

> For a therapist to look for "a paradox," and then decide whether to do or not to do the supposed paradoxical action is a contradiction in itself. Seeing an action as paradoxical implies that it is contradictory to an accepted body of beliefs. If these beliefs are the guiding premises of the therapist,

then choosing to perform the perceived paradoxical action implies the need to question or alter the very principles which guide the therapist's action. System-based intervention should ideally evolve from consistent employment of system theory and a subsequent description of system patterns. Consequent choice of therapeutic action should thus make "sense" to the therapist from within the theory. (p. 370)

Paradoxical procedures are clearly unethical if they are used as a spur-of-the-moment ploy based on limited data. Ethical, responsible use of a paradox requires therapist competency and experience gained from a thorough understanding of the role of the symptom within the relationship system, a theoretical/therapeutic approach conducive to the use of paradox, and sufficient clinical supervision and continuing consultation (Fisher et al., 1981). For example, Madanes (1980) concluded that certain steps were necessary for the use of paradoxical procedures in alleviating relevant psychiatric problems in children. She described a specific six-step process emanating from a Strategic Family Therapy orientation:

1. The problem should be clearly defined and specific goals set.
2. The therapist should conceptualize the problem (to him or herself only) as one in which the child is protecting one or both parents or a relative through his or her symptoms (emanating from the therapist's theoretical orientation).
3. The therapist must plan to intervene in offering the parents a directive that they will give their child; other family members potentially participate in auxiliary ways. The directive must include a prescription:
   a. To have the problem
   b. To pretend to have the problem
   c. To pretend to help the parents
4. The directive should be practiced in the session prior to being carried out at home.
5. In the session following the directive being given, the therapist must obtain a report on the performance of the directive and then continue to prescribe the same directive.
6. As change occurs and the presenting problem behavior begins to disappear, the therapist should drop the issue of the symptom and terminate therapy or begin dealing with other problem behaviors in the same or different ways. Credit should always be given to the parents for their child's improvement.

Madanes' six-step process encompasses a clear, conceptual rationale for choice of, as well as content of, a paradoxical procedure ethically considered and employed (Rohrbaugh, Tennen, Press, & White, 1981).

AGENCY TRIANGULATION

Triangulation as utilized in the marriage and family therapy literature has been defined as "the process by which a dyadic emotional system encompasses a third system member for the purpose of maintaining or reestablishing homeostatic balance" (Sauber, L'Abate, & Weeks, 1985, p. 172). Bowen (1978) asserted that two-person emotional systems become unstable in the face of conflict and stabilize by forming three-person systems or triangles. In general, the concept of triangulation has been used to describe interactional problems within the context of a marital or family system or within the therapy setting itself; for example, a therapist may become "triangulated" in a conflict between two marital partners as in this case illustration:

> A couple presented for therapy with increasing marital difficulties. Immense hostility was clearly evident between the pair almost immediately with the wife voicing her opinion that therapy "was a waste of time." The husband remained after the conclusion of the initial evaluation session to complain about his wife's unwillingness to "try." The therapist, a relative novice, felt good that the husband was open in confiding further with him and was reinforced in his fantasies about rescuing the couple; or at least the husband who was more open and accepting of the therapist's assistance.

The triangulation process emerging will be destructive to all three relationships: the therapist and wife, wife and husband, and the therapist and husband as well. Triangulation here represents two close and two distant poles (Figure 2–2). Sympathizing with the husband alienates the wife even further. It also makes it less likely that the husband will do anything to directly work out his complaints with his wife. Although this triangulation process may give the therapist the illusion of being close to the husband, it is at best a false intimacy. Defending the wife offers no better solution. That only moves the therapist from the husband to the wife and widens any gulf between them. As long as the triangulation continues, personal and direct one-to-one interactions cannot develop between the couple.

Even though marriage and family therapy approaches individuals displaying symptoms in the larger context of their marital or family system,

Figure 2–2   Therapist Triangulation

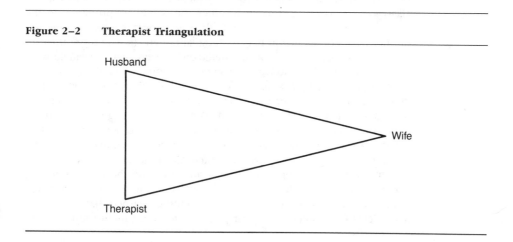

couples and families themselves are part of a larger social-cultural system. The concept of triangulation likewise can extend beyond the boundaries of the couple/family-therapist relationship system. This is a fact often neglected by marriage and family therapists even though they regularly address triangulation in the context of the couple or family relationship system. Unwittingly, many therapists become part of dysfunctional triangles created by the very sources that refer couples and families to them for help (Carl & Jurkovic, 1983). The ethical dilemmas presented can be most troublesome. Bowen (1978) addressed one part of this problem:

> In periods of very high tension, a system will triangle in more and more outsiders. A common example is a family in great stress that uses the triangle system to involve neighbors, schools, police, clinics and a spectrum of outside people as participants in the family problem. The family thus reduces the tension within the inner family, and it can actually create a situation in which the family tension is being fought out by outside people. (p. 479)

Therapists allowing themselves to become triangulated in such situations show little regard for the self-reliance of couples and families to grapple effectively with their own difficulties, raising the ethical issue of encouraging unnecessary client dependency.

Therapists must avoid assuming a superior position vis-á-vis couples and families in excessively helping them cope with service systems. Hoffman and Long (1969) asserted that therapists who act as "social brokers" or "advocates" in expertly mediating couple/family-agency relations may become "too omnipotent a figure" in the couple/family's affairs. Carl and Jurkovic (1983) offered a case illustration in this regard:

> Ms. James, a single-parent whose 6-year-old was not participating at school . . . complained that the teacher did not understand her daughter, Angela, and even feared that the teacher was physically abusing her. With mother's permission, the therapist visited the teacher at school where he learned that Angela was behaving in a listless and immature manner in the classroom. It was questionable whether she would be promoted to the next grade. Also of serious concern to the teacher was that Angela's mother did not have confidence in her teaching, although she had more than fifteen years' experience. All of the ingredients for an agency triangle were present: Both mother and teacher were complaining to the therapist about the other and clearly seeking a coalition with him. To avoid becoming part of the problem, the therapist "detriangulated" himself in a subsequent session in which he met with both the family and the teacher in the child's classroom. The strategy simply was to encourage mother and teacher to talk directly to one another and to agree on a plan for helping Angela. After a number of angry false starts in which Ms. Jones and the teacher attempted to speak through Angela first and then the therapist, which he stopped, they were able to make eye contact and to air their differences directly to each other. In the process, the mother learned that the teacher had Angela's best interests at heart, and the teacher came to some under-

standing of the mother's fears and stressful life situation. With additional prompting by the therapist, they clarified how each could appropriately help Angela in view of their different roles and also ways in which they could collaborate. (pp. 448–449)

The most respectful and productive stance by the therapist was to encourage Ms. Jones to directly deal with her daughter's teacher. Therapists can normally leave this task to a couple or family themselves or, if necessary, coach marital partners or family members on how to assert themselves when seeking services as well as protect themselves from unwarranted agency intrusions. By creating a context in which Ms. Jones was able to work out her concerns with the teacher in a one-to-one manner, the therapist not only aided her in resolving the current problems, but also prepared her to better cope with similar future difficulties.

Bowen's comments emphasize triangulation initiated by family members. Carl and Jurkovic (1983) also addressed the actions of helping agents who inadvertently triangulate families. They posited the addition of a corollary to Bowen's axiom concerning the instability of two-person system conflicts: "The relationship between an agency and a family is unstable under stress and will tend to form a three-party system, often with another agency, to diffuse the stress" (p. 442). Such interagency conflicts frequently develop after difficulty arises between an agency and a couple or family (as client). Some third agency is then pulled in as an attempt to divert the original conflict. Hoffman and Long (1969) termed this as a *systems dilemma,* describing it as follows:

> These systems seldom act collaboratively, and are more often than not in conflict with one another. As a result, a person may be caught in a paradoxical situation in a family which is in turn caught in paradoxical situations within the systems designed to help the family or person. (p. 241)

Couples and families enter therapy in many ways: referrals from family service agencies, schools, clergy, and courts; cross-referrals within mental health centers; and self-referrals. The kind of "paradoxical situation" alluded to by Hoffman and Long frequently develops when an agency refers a couple or family to another agency (i.e., a marriage and family therapist). The couple or family may have challenged the agency to be more helpful or act differently in some manner, or the agency may have felt the need for support services to carry out its functions, perhaps because its own efforts had been unsuccessful. The nature of this referral process can have a powerful effect on therapeutic process and outcome (Selvini-Palazzoli, et al., 1908).

Family service agencies, for example, may refer a family for therapy to "fix up" parents so that they can become "fit" to regain custody of their children. A court may refer a couple to therapy as a required precursor to potential divorce proceedings. Schools regularly refer children because they are acting out or doing poorly in the classroom in the belief that problems in their home environment constitute primary contributors. Carl and Jurkovic (1983) suggested that all of these situations have a common denominator: an "agenda" from the referral source that figures prominently in the development of agency triangulation. They illustrated this issue in discussing day treatment program referrals:

> Another intrasystem dilemma occurs when a day program in a mental health center refers a client family for treatment in the hope of making the client a "better-adjusted part" of the day program. Since many systems' interventions rely on reframing problems and inducing change in ways that make clients *less* dependent upon supporting agencies, conflictual program goals provide ample opportunity for a triangle. The day program wants a more cooperative "member." The systems therapist wants no "member" at all. The family can stay the same so that all concerned remain involved. These different "agendas" derive, of course, from the guiding philosophy, rules, procedures, and objectives of the agency. As stress develops between the agency and its charges (whether they be day program participants in a mental health center, students in the classroom, parolees, etc.), the agency may direct the client and his or her family to some other agency—often a therapist. The therapist's orientation frequently conflicts with that of the agency, and unless the two collaborate effectively, an agency triangle can result. (p. 444)

In accepting referrals from agency sources, therapists are immediately faced with an ethical dilemma. The couple or family as client is entitled to expect certain things from the therapist, particularly to put their interests above all others' interest. Couples and families as clients derive intrinsic benefits from the assurance that the therapist has an undivided commitment to helping them. All this changes when a third party enters the picture. The quality of the relationship between the therapist and a couple or family is irrevocably altered once that relationship is no longer encapsulated intact, which inevitably is the case when agency referrals incorporate agendas emanating from the referral source. Although the therapist-couple/family relationship is not necessarily invalidated nor will the couple or family stop receiving adequate services, the nature of the relationship is different.

Bourne (1982) summarized the ethical dilemma by stating, "No man can serve two masters." This is at the heart of the ethical issue therapists must confront in addressing agency triangulation. Carl and Jurkovic (1983) proposed a number of guidelines for therapists in preventing agency triangulation:

1. Therapists must include themselves and other nonfamily members, agencies, and institutions as parts of the presenting problem needing treatment. The unit of treatment thus becomes the larger "suprasystem" incorporating the couple/family-therapist-agency.
2. The identification of these parts requires an ecological assessment that extends beyond the boundaries of the immediate couple or family relationship system to include other interacting systems. Carl and Jurkovic (1983) proposed this being a point where potential agency triangulation can be detected.

3. After conducting such an assessment, therapists' further strategies should incorporate cooperation with relevant agencies. Successful collaboration that does not limit therapists' maneuverability calls for them to skillfully join with other helping agents without taking a one-up position and without implying that these agents are part of the unit of treatment. These collaborative efforts should begin early in the therapy process, preferably at the point of referral.

4. Although it is best if couples and families handle problematic agency contacts themselves, there will be times when therapists may wish to block or redirect subversive agency actions, especially if the couple or family is under significant stress. Particularly at a time of declining publicly funded services for the poor and needy, therapists working with such couples and families will have to resolve any quandary created by encouraging these relationship systems to be more self-reliant in the face of harsh economic realities.

5. Therapists should always be aware of their limited power to actually control other agency interventions and policies. At minimum, adverse agency actions can often be reframed in the interest of the couple or family. Or inventive therapists can seek out other facets of the agency operation that might offer therapeutic opportunities. For example, in special education settings, the development and updating of Individualized Educational Plans require that parents meet regularly with school staff. If not invited, therapists can ask to attend these meetings to offer input as a part of family therapy efforts.

6. Therapists must perceive themselves as active, not passive, participants in any agency triangulation process. They may even be the primary precipitators of such processes. Therapists who refer couples or families for other services—psychological testing, medication, tutoring, and so on—must be clear about the purpose of the referral. Is it to help the couple or family or to alleviate the therapist's own discomfort? If the former, then it is necessary to coordinate therapeutic efforts with other service providers, agreeing on areas of responsibility and control. Therapists' discomfort, on the other hand, is best addressed through consultation with a clinical supervisor or colleague.

SUMMARY AND CONCLUSIONS

Marriage and family therapy, as opposed to individually oriented psychotherapy, considers the couple or family as an active, whole unit. This represents a conceptual change in therapeutic thinking; relationship systems are seen as rule-governed, organic wholes, rather than as collections of individuals interacting according to the dictates of their separate personalities. This point of view—thinking about relationship systems instead of individuals—requires that special ethical as well as theoretical dilemmas be confronted. Such dilemmas are not necessarily derivable from individually-oriented psychotherapeutic experiences.

Marriage and family therapists are faced with the challenge of coping with a cornucopia of thorny ethical issues that impinge on their work; far more potential ethical conflicts in their clinical decision making than most individually oriented therapists because of the increasingly complex nature of their work (Morrison, Layton, & Newman, 1982). This chapter has addressed ethical concerns creating questions needing to be answered by marriage and family therapists. Can therapists automatically assume the right to define couples' and families' presenting problems in terms of their own therapeutic orientation? How much concerted effort (or pressure) can therapists exert in convening all significant familial or extrafamilial members for therapy sessions? Do willing individual marital partners or several family members seeking assistance go untreated because one individual refuses to participate? Should therapists impose their control on couples and families? If so, to what extent in seeking change in the relationship system? How much intrasystem stress should be engendered or allowed to actualize in the pursuit of change? What are the ethical implications inherent in employing paradoxical procedures? How can the impact of working with couples and families within the larger context of service agency impingements be ethically pursued?

Abroms (1978) asserted that ethical therapist behavior requires more than good intentions based on personal bias and subjectivity. If therapeutic ethics involves a determination of what therapists ought to do to provide maximum benefit for the greatest number of persons, then marriage and family therapy as a treatment of relationship systems instead of individuals in relative isolation would appear to be the most ethical and integrated of approaches (O'Shea & Jessee, 1982).

3

Ethical Accountability: A Casebook

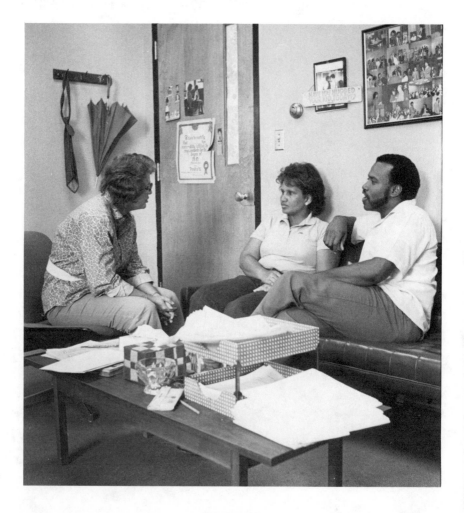

Several professional association ethics committees have published case-books of recommendations and interpretations of their respective codes of ethics as well as how the committee dealt with selected cases (e.g., American Association for Counseling and Development's *Ethical Standards Casebook* [Callis, Pope, & DePauw, 1982]; American Psychological Association's *Casebook on Ethical Standards of Psychologists* [APA, 1974]). Codes of ethics are, by nature, generalizable and often debatable. These casebooks represent a consensus from reputable professionals to assist practitioners to understand and best apply the principles the codes represent.

The primary professional affiliation for marriage and family therapists is the American Association for Marriage and Family Therapy (AAMFT). This organization has promulgated the *AAMFT Code of Ethical Principles for Marriage and Family Therapists* (AAMFT, 1985). The Association maintains a Committee on Ethics and Professional Practices. Operating under the AAMFT bylaws, the Ethics Committee interprets the Code of Ethical Principles, considers allegations of violations of this code made against AAMFT members, and, if the case is heard by Judicial Council, adjudicates the charges against the member (Engelberg, 1985).

AAMFT has not yet published a casebook to offer additional guidance to its members in adhering to the Code of Ethical Principles. This casebook chapter represents the authors' analysis of the selected standards within the AAMFT *Code of Ethical Principles for Marriage and Family Therapists* compiled through consultation with relevant professional colleagues. Actions recommended within each case illustration were also arrived at in a like manner. The Code of Ethical Principles and specific cases will follow an overview of the structure and functioning of AAMFT's Committee on Ethics and Professional Practices.

The Ethics Committee is composed of six members appointed by the president of AAMFT. Four are AAMFT members and two are "public members," representing consumers' interests. Normally, one of the two public members is an attorney. There is also an attorney retained by AAMFT to work closely with the Committee. The Committee meets regularly throughout the year to discuss cases brought before it. Engelberg (1985) outlined the Committee's procedures as follows:

> Cases consist of complaints brought against AAMFT members for violating the AAMFT Code of Ethical Principles. Complaints may be brought against an AAMFT member by another AAMFT member, or nonmember therapists, by clients, by members of the public, and by the Ethics Committee itself. Once a complaint is made, the AAMFT national office first determines whether the charged professional is an AAMFT member. If confirmed, the complaint is forwarded to the Chair of the Ethics Committee. The Chair then makes a determination whether the complaint, if proven, states a claim under the Code. If so, a case is opened and the complaint (if a client) is sent a waiver of the client-therapist privilege. Upon receipt of the signed waiver, a letter is written to the charged member, requesting a response. The case may be decided through further written communications between the Ethics Committee and the charged member. On occa-

63

sion, the Ethics Committee impanels an investigating subcommittee before which the charged member has a right to appear.

Cases are often disposed of through a process of agreement called "settlement by mutual consent." If settlement by mutual consent is unable to be agreed upon, the Ethics Committee can recommend to the AAMFT Judicial Council that final action be taken against a member. Any proposed settlement or final action recommended by the Ethics Committee can include a requirement that the charged member seek therapy or obtain supervision. The Ethics Committee is also authorized to propose revocation of a member's approved supervisor status and, in most serious cases, termination of membership. Charged members who wish to appeal Ethics Committee recommendations that final action be taken may do so to the independent Judicial Council. At that point, the Ethics Committee is, in effect, prosecuting the complaint, the Judicial Council making the final ruling on the matter.

The presence of the Ethics Committee exemplifies AAMFT's commitment to protect consumers of marriage and family therapy services from unethical practices without violating the rights of AAMFT members. The Ethics Committee, however, does not serve simply as a reactive body. Proactive functions are of equal importance. The Ethics Committee also serves as a consultation source for members of the Association for an opinion relative to a course of action; for example, a marriage and family therapist who is concerned with possible confidentiality violations in considering a request to appear on a television program aimed at common problems of couples in marital therapy. Thus, the actions of the Ethics Committee should be seen as primarily constructive, educational, and problem solving and only secondarily adversarial when the occasion arises.

PRINCIPLE 1: RESPONSIBILITY TO CLIENTS

Marriage and family therapists are dedicated to advancing the welfare of families and individuals, including respecting the rights of those persons seeking their assistance, and making reasonable efforts to ensure that their services are appropriately used.

1.1 Marriage and family therapists do not discriminate against or refuse professional service to anyone on the basis of race, sex, religion, or national origin.

1.2 Marriage and family therapists are cognizant of their potentially influential position with respect to clients, and they avoid exploiting the trust and dependency of such persons. Marriage and family therapists therefore make every effort to avoid dual relationships with clients that could impair their professional judgment or increase the risk of exploitation. Examples of such dual relationships include, but are not limited to, business or close personal relationships with clients. Sexual intimacy with clients is prohibited.

1.3 Marriage and family therapists do not use their professional relationship with clients to further their own interests.

1.4 Marriage and family therapists respect the right of clients to make decisions and help them understand the consequences of these decisions. Marriage and family therapists clearly advise a client that a decision on marital status is the responsibility of the client.

1.5 Marriage and family therapists continue therapeutic relationships only so long as it is reasonably clear that clients are benefiting from the relationship.

1.6 Marriage and family therapists assist persons in obtaining other therapeutic services if a marriage and family therapist is unable or unwilling, for appropriate reasons, to see a person who has requested professional help.

1.7 Marriage and family therapists do not abandon or neglect clients in treatment without making reasonable arrangements for its continuation.

CASE 1

A female client had been seeing the marriage and family therapist, a male, for over a year to resolve issues emanating from her divorce. When sexual desires between her and the therapist were mutually conveyed and then acted upon, the therapist immediately terminated the therapeutic relationship. No referral was recommended, nor was there any time spent addressing the termination. A socially and sexually intimate relationship continued for the next six months. The woman eventually broke off the relationship when she began to experience the same emotional difficulties that originally led her to initiate therapy following her divorce.

Analysis

Principles 1.2, 1.3, 1.5, 1.6, and 1.7 all come under consideration in this case. The therapist was correct in seeking to terminate the therapeutic relationship. However, by not assisting the client to obtain other therapeutic services when he decided he was no longer able to offer professional help, the therapist abandoned the client therapeutically. Further, his lack of cognizance relative to the influence he had with the client suggests an exploitation of her vulnerable position. The issue of sexual intimacy is a most flagrant ethical violation as was his use of their professional relationship to advance his own sexual interests.

CASE 2

A marriage and family therapist with a national reputation as an expert in the area of fathers who have sole custody of their children was recommended by a lawyer to a father engaged in a custody case. The father wrote to the therapist who resided in a neighboring state, requesting any relevant information that the therapist might have for distribution. The therapist replied that some materials could be sent for a specified fee. The therapist also offered his services as an expert witness to the father for a fee to include travel expenses. The father wrote back to the therapist, expressing anger at the therapist for "soliciting" him.

Analysis

Principles 1.2 and 1.3 are of primary consideration in this case. Although the father implied that the therapist sought to further personal financial interests, there is nothing stated to directly prove this allegation. Similarly, nothing is explicitly stated suggesting that the therapist sought to exploit the father's request nor create any dual therapeutic-business relationship, particularly since the former could not be considered as expressly present. The therapist clearly had an obligation to request reasonable compensation in offering services to the father.

CASE 3

A couple sought marital therapy from a female marriage and family therapist. The therapist saw the couple conjointly and also in concurrent individual sessions for several months. The couple eventually decided upon divorce and terminated their participation in therapy. Several months after the divorce was finalized, the wife discovered that her former husband and the therapist were seeing each other socially and had in fact become quite intimate. The wife confronted the therapist charging her actions to be unethical. The therapist replied that she had not entered into a social relationship with the woman's former husband until some time after professional contact between them had ended. The therapist further responded that she had sought peer consultation with two other marriage and family therapists immediately after meeting the husband at an open social affair; afterwards he had telephoned her in pursuit of further social contact. Both therapists consulted recommended a several month hiatus before accepting any social invitation from the husband. The therapist stated she had communicated this to the husband and followed through with her colleagues' recommendations.

Analysis

Principles 1.2 and 1.3 are of dominant concern in this case. Although the therapy had ended prior to the therapist and the husband socially entering a close personal relationship, concern must be raised in the case of a marriage and family therapist becoming socially and emotionally involved with a former client. Did the therapist exploit her professional position and enter into a dual relationship to further personal interests? Based on the therapist's pursuit of peer consultation and follow-through with regard to the professional cautions offered, it would appear that the therapist acted in a conscientious, ethically aware manner.

CASE 4

A 16-year-old sought the assistance of a marriage and family therapist working in a Catholic Services Center regarding her discovery that she was pregnant. The girl communicated her desire to obtain information and professional assistance in making a decision as to whether to terminate her pregnancy by abortion or offer the child for adoption. The therapist, a strong "pro-life" advocate, provided the girl with factual information and assisted her in contacting relevant referral sources to further investigate the available options. The therapist also, with the girl's permission, convened family therapy efforts to include the girl's parents and boyfriend in the decision making. At no time did the therapist personally advocate one option over the other.

Analysis

Principle 1.4 is of particular relevance in this case. The therapist displayed exemplary diligence in the respect shown this teenage girl. Despite strong personal views, the therapist sought only to assist the girl in arriving at a fully considered decision. Direct referral to both adoption and abortion services for concrete information and convening the boyfriend and parents in family therapy exhibited further evidence of the therapist's efforts to help the client fully comprehend the consequences of her options.

PRINCIPLE 2: CONFIDENTIALITY

Marriage and family therapists have unique confidentiality problems because the "client" in a therapeutic relationship may be more than one person. The overriding principle is that marriage and family therapists respect the confidences of their clients.

2.1 Marriage and family therapists cannot disclose client confidences to anyone, except:

1. As mandated by law.
2. To prevent a clear and immediate danger to one or more persons.
3. Where the marriage and family therapist is a defendant in a civil, criminal, or disciplinary action arising from the therapy (in which case client confidences may only be disclosed in the course of that action).
4. If a waiver is previously obtained in writing, and then such information may only be revealed in accordance with the terms of the waiver.

In circumstances where more than one person in a family is receiving therapy, each family member who is legally competent to execute a waiver must agree to the waiver required by subparagraph 4. A marriage and family therapist cannot disclose information from any family member without a waiver from each legally competent family member.

2.2 Marriage and family therapists use clinical materials in teaching, writing, and public presentations only if a written waiver has been received in accordance with Principle 2.1.4, or when appropriate steps have been taken to protect client identity.

2.3 Marriage and family therapists store or dispose of client records in ways that maintain confidentiality.

CASE 5

A marriage and family therapist working within an employee assistance program in a large company received a complaint from an employee who was being seen with his wife and children by the therapist. The

employee alleged the therapist had discussed aspects of
the employee's family life, as revealed during therapy
sessions, with the executive vice-president in charge of
the employee's department. He recalled signing a release
of information allowing the therapist and the department
vice-president to communicate about his progress, but
alleged that the information shared was of a strictly
personal nature and not job-related.

Analysis

Principle 2.1.4 is of primary concern in this case. Although the client had
signed a waiver, it is obvious that some misunderstanding was present as
to the exact terms of the waiver. Whether the therapist or the client was
unclear cannot be explicitly identified from the facts presented herein. It
is a therapist's responsibility, however, to provide clients a copy of and
fully explain the terms of any waiver, confirm their understanding, and
then act accordingly when communicating information.

CASE 6

A marriage and family therapist had received a referral
of a 19-year-old client who was a niece of the
referral source, a physician. The client's parents lived in
another city and the physician initiated the referral upon
the request of his brother and sister-in-law who were
concerned about their daughter's adjustment in
establishing herself away from home for the first time.
Some months later, the physician contacted the therapist
with the complaint that the therapist had refused to give
the client's parents any indication of her well-being
despite the fact that they had made phone calls and
written letters to the therapist, all of which had gone
unanswered. The therapist replied that the client was an
adult who requested that no information about her
participation in therapy be communicated to anyone.

Analysis

Principle 2.1 is of primary consideration in this case. It is clear that the
therapist was responding to the client's request accordingly, in line with

the identified ethical principle noted. The issue of the therapist's obligation to the client's family as well as to the referral source, however, is
raised in this case. The client specified that no information about her
participation in therapy be divulged. While it would have been prudent
for the therapist to have asked the client to consider communicating with
her parents, she still might have chosen not to do so. The therapist could
be considered to have some responsibility to the client's parents because
of their repeated attempts to contact the therapist. A brief return call or
letter might have been appropriate, simply explaining in a general sense
that no information about clients could be ethically communicated without their expressed permission; not even confirmation as to whether
their daughter is or is not a client. A similar stance might have been taken
with the referral source as well after the client had made her wishes
regarding strict confidentiality known to the therapist.

CASE 7

A new secretary was hired by a marriage and family
therapist. The therapist provided an orientation to
the position, addressing the importance of confidentiality,
but only in a general sense. A few days after the
orientation, an attorney contacted the office with regard
to a couple with whom the therapist had previously
worked. The attorney requested information about the
couple's participation in therapy efforts, indicating she
was representing one in a divorce suit. She further noted
that she would subpoena the records if she was unable to
get the information requested over the telephone. The
therapist was unavailable at the time and, deciding that
the information would eventually be available to the
attorney anyway, the secretary provided the requested
details.

Analysis

While Principle 2.1 is relevant, of dominant concern is Principle 2.3. The
therapist did not display sufficient attentiveness to the training of the
secretary concerning responsibilities for the maintenance and communication of client records. Support staff must be trained in the importance
of confidentiality and in the appropriate management of case files. The
secretary should have been explicitly instructed not to reveal information
regarding persons presently or previously receiving services nor the nat-

ure of any services they received in response to inquiries made by phone, letter, or in person. Such inquiries or related questions should always be reviewed by the therapist before final action is taken.

CASE 8

A marriage and family therapist received a telephone call from a husband whose wife and adult children were being seen together with him in family therapy relative to his alcohol abuse. The husband requested that information about his progress be communicated to his employer. The therapist was aware that the husband's job was in jeopardy, but declined his request, explaining that all family members must agree to the release of information on their mutual participation in therapy. The husband became angry, stating that his job was on the line and that he was the one with the problem, not his family. The therapist reiterated the ethical importance of mutual consent, requested that the husband gather the family members together, stop by the therapist's office and sign a waiver, and then the information might be forwarded as requested.

Analysis

Principle 2.1 is quite explicit in respect to the circumstances in this case. Without a waiver from each family member, the therapist is ethically obliged not to disclose the information. While the client made a logical argument for his request, marriage and family therapists must be attuned to the fact that the "client" in the therapeutic relationship is the family, calling for mutual consent for a waiver. The therapist acted in full ethical accord in this case.

PRINCIPLE 3: PROFESSIONAL COMPETENCE AND INTEGRITY

Marriage and family therapists are dedicated to maintaining high standards of professional competence and integrity.

3.1 Marriage and family therapists are subject to termination of membership or other appropriate actions under the following conditions:

1. Conviction of a felony

2. Conviction of a misdemeanor related to their qualifications or functions
3. Conduct that could lead to conviction of a felony or misdemeanor related to their qualifications or functions
4. Expulsion from other professional organizations
5. Suspension or revocation of licenses or certificates

3.2 Marriage and family therapists should seek appropriate professional assistance for their own personal problems or conflicts that are likely to impair their work performance and clinical judgment.

3.3 Marriage and family therapists, as teachers, are dedicated to maintaining high standards of scholarship and presenting accurate information.

3.4 Marriage and family therapists seek to remain abreast of new developments in family therapy knowledge and practice through both educational activities and clinical experiences.

3.5 Marriage and family therapists do not engage in sexual or other harassment of clients, students, trainees, or colleagues.

3.6 Marriage and family therapists do not attempt to diagnose, treat, or advise on problems outside the recognized boundaries of their competence.

3.7 Marriage and family therapists attempt to prevent the distortion or misuse of their clinical and research findings.

3.8 Marriage and family therapists are aware that because of their ability to influence and alter the lives of others, they must exercise special care when making public their professional recommendations and opinions through testimony or other public statements.

CASE 9

A marriage and family therapist had given court testimony contradicting the testimony of a second marriage and family therapist in a child custody action brought by one parent against the other. The marriage and family therapist hired by the father was upset and very concerned about the ethical implications of the testimony of the mother's marriage and family therapist. The therapist's concerns emanated from the fact that the therapist hired by the mother had seen the child alone during the actual therapy sessions, communicated with the mother only very briefly before and after those sessions, and had never met with the father yet testimony was given relative to the entire family's functioning. In contrast, the therapist hired by the father had seen the entire family together in therapy for several months.

Analysis

Principle 3.6 presents the primary ethical issue in this case. The marriage and family therapist hired by the mother appears to have based court testimony solely on hearsay. This therapist might have given reliable testimony relative to the child's current functioning. The ability to accurately evaluate total family functioning solely from the communications of the child or through brief encounters in a waiting room with the mother is a most questionable practice, however. This therapist should be strongly urged to seek supervision from a marriage and family therapist with significant experience in family evaluation, especially before agreeing to act as an expert witness to provide similar court testimony.

CASE 10

A psychiatrist raised questions about the ethical conduct of a marriage and family therapist employed by the clinical group to which he acted as psychiatric consultant. The psychiatrist alleged that the therapist's use of intensification procedures with the family of a young boy whom he was psychopharmacologically treating for hyperactivity was having a harmful effect on his client's condition. The psychiatrist portrayed the boy as experiencing undue harassment from his parents as a result of the family therapy sessions. The therapist responded by conveying to the boy's parents that the psychiatrist had some questions about the family therapy, requesting the parents' consent to communicate with the psychiatrist in this regard. With the parents' consent, the marriage and family therapist explained to the psychiatrist the specific nature of the procedure, anticipated side effects, and the likelihood of greater improvement as a result of its use.

Analysis

Principles 3.3 and 3.5 are of direct concern in the present case. The psychiatrist's inquiry was reasonable, given his apparent linear perception of his client's condition. The therapist responded conscientiously in asking the parents' permission to consult with the psychiatrist and then seeking to educate the psychiatrist on relevant ramifications of the procedures in question. The therapist presented not only the potential positive attributes of the procedures but also anticipated side effects. At no time, however, does it appear that the therapist engaged in any action that would encourage unwarranted harassment of the boy.

CASE 11

A marriage and family therapist had seen a client for a number of therapy sessions when he realized that his intimate feelings towards her were excessive and potentially harmful in their impact on the therapeutic relationship. He sought consultation from a senior colleague who recommended that the therapist refer the client and consider the probability of similar situations occurring in the future. The therapist followed through with the suggestions of the consultant and entered into personal therapy to address his own needs in more appropriate ways. Concurrently, he also contracted with the senior colleague whom he had consulted to provide regular supervision of his work until such time as his personal concerns were adequately addressed.

Analysis

Principle 3.2 states that marriage and family therapists seek professional assistance when personal issues might negatively impact on their clinical practice. The therapist in this case, upon becoming aware of his inappropriate feelings, acted with ethical promptness in consulting a senior colleague. His further actions of pursuing personal therapy and contracting for supervision are evidence of proper ethical practice.

CASE 12

A young woman requested of a marriage and family therapist to be able to attend a therapy session with her parents who were seeing the therapist to resolve their marital discord. The woman conveyed that she was feeling very depressed over her parents' conflicts and sought desperately to help them in any way. The parents had expressed strong feelings of anger and resentment about their daughter's continuing interference in their lives. Without considering the possible negative impact of the daughter's presence during a session or forewarning the daughter of her parents' intense hostility, the therapist agreed (with the parents' consent) to allow the daughter to attend the next session. The parents subsequently attacked her and she responded immediately by crying hysterically and running out of the session.

Analysis

This case highlights the importance of preparing family members who convene in the therapy some time after it has begun. Not doing so in this case suggests a violation of Principle 3.5. The daughter communicated to the therapist that she was in a depressed mental state when making her request to participate in therapy with her parents. This vulnerability, combined with the fact that the parents had been conveying intense hostility toward their daughter during sessions, should have been recognized as creating a context for harassment of the daughter. Although the harassment might be coming directly from the woman's parents, the therapist indirectly facilitated its occurrence, particularly by not preparing her for it.

PRINCIPLE 4: RESPONSIBILITY TO STUDENTS, EMPLOYEES, AND SUPERVISEES

Marriage and family therapists do not exploit the trust and dependency of students and supervisees.

4.1 Marriage and family therapists are cognizant of their potentially influential position with respect to students, employees, and supervisees, and they avoid exploiting the trust and dependency of such persons. Marriage and family therapists make every effort to avoid dual relationships that could impair their professional judgment or increase the risk of exploitation. Sexual harassment or exploitation of students, employees, or supervisees is prohibited.

4.2 Marriage and family therapists do not permit students, employees, or supervisees to permit or to hold themselves out as competent to perform professional services beyond their training, level of experience, and competence.

CASE 13

A licensed marriage and family therapist in private practice expanded her practice by opening satellite offices in a number of surrounding communities. She hired several school guidance counselors on a part-time basis to assist her in offering family therapy services.

None of the guidance counselors had any formal family therapy training. All listings and literature associated with these satellite offices identified them as belonging to and being staffed by a licensed marriage and family therapist. The therapist had, however, made arrangements to meet weekly with each of her employees.

Analysis

Principle 4.2 is a direct issue in this case. The marriage and family therapist appears to have sought to expand her practice more on an economic than an ethical basis. If the satellite offices are to be identified as offering services from a licensed marriage and family therapist, then the therapist should endeavor to employ licensed marriage and family therapists. Employing school guidance counselors to offer services relevant to their training and demonstrated competencies would be quite ethical and appropriate as an adjunct to family therapy services. Permitting these individuals to hold themselves as family therapy providers, even though under the supervision of a trained, experienced marriage and family therapist, represented unethical practice. It is therapists' ethical responsibility to clearly state the purposes of services being offered to prospective clients, being very careful to label providers appropriately so consumers can accurately acquire desired services, and said providers can be accountable for their professional activities.

CASE 14

A professor in a graduate marriage and family therapy training program maintained a part-time private practice in addition to his university responsibilities. The professor had a reputation among colleagues and students as an outstanding clinician as well as academician. Occasionally students in the program requested marital or family therapy services from the professor through his private practice. The professor was conscientious in explaining that such services could be obtained at the university's counseling center at very minimal cost for students and their families. Some students, however, insisted and the professor agreed to provide them the therapy services requested.

Analysis

It would appear that the therapist in this case is cognizant of his influential position with respect to students in the training program. His advocacy of the university's counseling center appropriately conveys this cognizance. However, he had obligations to his academic position that might create conflicts should issues of a problematic nature arise in therapy. For example, information might be shared in therapy suggesting that the student be prevented from pursuing an internship that incorporated direct client work. The student might seek to immediately pursue said internship, maintaining that information shared within the therapy be kept confidential. Or although the student might not be ready for an internship from an academic perspective, the therapist's sympathy for the student's family circumstances generated during therapy could encourage a biased academic assessment. Principle 4.1 calls for marriage and family therapists to avoid dual relationships that could impair their judgment. The therapist in this case seems to have entered such a dual relationship.

PRINCIPLE 5: RESPONSIBILITY TO THE PROFESSION

Marriage and family therapists respect the rights and responsibilities of professional colleagues to carry out research in an ethical manner and participate in activities that advance the goals of the profession.

5.1 Marriage and family therapists remain accountable to the standards of the profession when acting as members or employees of organizations.

5.2 Marriage and family therapists assign publication credit to those who have contributed to a publication in proportion to their contributions and in accordance with customary professional practices.

5.3 Marriage and family therapists who are authors of books or other published or distributed materials should appropriately cite persons to whom credit for original ideas is due.

5.4 Marriage and family therapists who are authors of books or other materials published or distributed by an organization should take reasonable precautions to ensure that the organization accurately and factually promotes and advertises the materials.

5.5 As researchers, marriage and family therapists must be adequately informed of and abide by relevant laws and regulations regarding the conduct of research with human participants.

5.6 Marriage and family therapists should recognize a responsibility to participate in activities that contribute to a better community and society, including devoting a portion of their professional activities to services for which there is little or no financial return.

5.7 Marriage and family therapists are concerned with developing laws and regulations pertaining to marriage and family therapy that serve the public interest, and with altering such laws and regulations not in the public interest.

5.8 Marriage and family therapists should encourage public participation in the designing and delivery of services and in the regulation of practitioners.

CASE 15

A couple participated in a research project conducted by a marriage and family therapy doctoral student. The couple filed a complaint with the university after their participation in the project stating that they were deceived by the student regarding the requirements of their participation and suffered undue stress as a result. The project did incorporate deception because participant couples were led to believe that the purpose was to rate a videotape of another couple's interaction, when the dependent variable was actually their reaction in having experienced a 2-hour delay before viewing the tape. The couple was thoroughly debriefed following their participation according to procedures incorporated in the project which had been previewed and approved both by the student's doctoral committee members and the university's Human Subjects Research Committee.

Analysis

Principle 5.5 maintains that marriage and family therapists doing human subjects' research must be adequately informed of and abide by established requirements regarding the conduct of this research. The student's preparatory actions in seeking the preview and approval of relevant bodies would suggest she took adequate precautions to minimize any stress reactions participant couples might experience. Were a significant number of the participant couples to complain that they had experienced excessive stress as a result of their participation, however, it would be ethically incumbent upon the student to consider revision of her procedures in consultation with her doctoral and university research committees. While the potential impact of the findings may be considerable, the welfare of participants must be the primary concern.

CASE 16

A marriage and family therapist discovered to his dismay that the publisher with whom he had contracted had changed the subtitle of his book to one that conflicted with AAMFT's Ethical Code. The subtitle was altered by the publisher during editing to promise "a guarantee of family happiness" to the reader. The therapist immediately contacted the publisher upon learning of the subtitle change and was informed that the first printing of the book would have to stand as is; no changes could be made until a second printing was initiated sometime in the future, depending upon the book's sales.

Analysis

Principle 5.4 is of direct concern to the author in this case. While it is not clear as to the relevant prepublication contact between the author and publisher, the author does appear to have taken timely and appropriate action upon learning of the subtitle change. Unfortunately, this case illustrates the limited control authors sometimes have with publishers and suggests a need for the marriage therapist to assume a more assertive stance with regard to editorial changes. Ethically, the author would best have sought to require his consent to any changes made prior to actual publication of the book to ensure its accuracy.

CASE 17

I n a graduate course in marriage and family therapy theory, the instructor assigned students as their major project an extensive analysis of dominant figures in the field. The instructor required that the projects become the permanent property of the department and asked that students desiring feedback attach a photocopy that was returned to them with comments. Later the instructor used the materials submitted by the students in preparing an article that was accepted and eventually published in a leading journal. No mention of the students' contribution was made.

Analysis

The instructor's actions in this case appear most questionable with re-gard to Principles 5.2 and 5.3. This is particularly true if the instructor utilized any students' original ideas in writing the article; if so, proper credit was ethically due to the students. Further, the students whose projects were utilized in the preparation of the article would have signifi-cantly contributed to its contents and thus publication credit was ethi-cally due them.

CASE 18

A marriage and family therapist employed by a county agency recognized understaffing as becoming a serious problem. As demands for services increased, therapists had been asked to carry an excessive caseload that caused the quality of services being delivered to deteriorate. Further, more and more student interns were being recruited by the agency's administration to meet new requests for services at a time when staff members' increased caseloads allowed less time for supervision of the interns' work. This was done in lieu of hiring additional full-time experienced professionals.

Analysis

Principle 5.1 is most relevant for the marriage and family therapist expe-riencing the dilemma. Although the therapist should expect the agency administration to recognize and appropriately respond to concerns about the quality of services, it is ultimately the therapist's responsibility to inform the administration and other relevant sources of the ethical stand-ards that apply. In this instance, the therapist would be ethically bound to pursue such a course of information-giving. Depending upon the re-sponse received, further action might include identifying relevant staff involved in the delivery of services and proposing that they organize in order to assess the present needs for direct client services, staffing, su-pervision, and the like and that they take an active stance in asserting that these needs be more adequately and ethically addressed.

PRINCIPLE 6: FEES

Marriage and family therapists make financial arrangements with clients that conform to accepted professional practices and that are reasonably understandable.

6.1 Marriage and family therapists do not offer or accept payment for referrals.

6.2 Marriage and family therapists do not charge excessive fees for services.

6.3 Marriage and family therapists disclose their fee structure to clients at the onset of treatment.

CASE 19

A family initiated therapy services with a marriage and family therapist. In completing a written intake form, the parents noted having mental health benefits as part of their insurance coverage. When they requested information with regard to the therapist's fees, they were told not to be concerned, as insurance will cover the costs.

Analysis

Principle 6.3 is of specific concern in this case. This principle clearly states that a therapist's fee structure be disclosed to clients at the onset of treatment. Adherence to this standard allows clients to make a fully informed choice regarding the pursuit of treatment. The "client" is not the insurance company or any other third-party payer. Consequently, the family (parents in the present case) must be informed of the session fees prior to being rendered services. This ethical obligation still stands, even though services are paid for by a third party.

CASE 20

A marriage and family therapist was frequently called upon by a group of pediatricians to provide family therapy services in cases wherein family dynamics appeared to be negatively impacting on children's physical conditions. In return, the marriage and family therapist regularly referred families to this particular medical group because of their enlightened position on the value of family therapy for their patients.

Analysis

Principle 6.1 appears to represent the major concern in this case. The primary ethical question revolves around the presence of any formal agreement regarding compensation for referrals. While the marriage and family therapist accepted referrals from the group and referred in turn, the facts suggest that this was done due to the professionals' mutual confidences in each other, not because a specific agreement had been made to offer remuneration in return for referrals. Thus, the marriage and family therapist's actions would represent appropriate ethical practice.

PRINCIPLE 7: ADVERTISING

The 1985 revision of the AAMFT *Code of Ethical Principles for Marriage and Family Therapists* incorporates a seventh principle—"Advertising." Regulation of professional advertising was previously addressed only by the separate *AAMFT Standards on Public Information and Advertising* (AAMFT, 1982b). Both of these guidelines are presently in effect and basically mirror each other. Professional advertising will be discussed in detail in chapter 8. Principle 7 and relevant case illustrations will be considered in that chapter and again in chapter 9.

PART TWO

Legal Issues in Marriage and Family Therapy

Law and therapy go hand in hand. What are some of the obvious areas in which legal input would be essential to the therapeutic or counseling process? When should the therapist be sensitive to legal issues? What problems exist where therapy and law must co-exist? Can a therapist afford to be ignorant of the law? Can such ignorance ever be excused?

(Bernstein, 1982, p. 90)

4

The Marriage and Family Therapist: Roles and Responsibilities Within the Legal System

Contemporary public policy has evolved from a progressive merger of legal principles and social science conceptualizations. As with most mergers, these two parties have come to pursue similar ends. For years the legal system has sought to maintain the family as the primary building block of the social order. Likewise, over the past century, mental health professionals became increasingly influential in legal assertions aimed at facilitating healthy, stable family functioning (Mulvey, Reppucci, & Weithorn, 1984). Today, the knowledge and assistance of both parties are inextricably linked to most aspects of public policy, so much so that there is presently an active use of the legal system to promote goals deemed desirable by the mental health profession and vice versa.

Because of this merger, there is clearly a need for marriage and family therapists to know the law. For instance, marriage and family therapists are regularly being called as expert witnesses to assist the legal system; effective testimony implies familiarity not only with marital and family understandings but also with the legal issues in question and the process by which they will be decided. Similarly, the principles upon which judgments of professional legal responsibility and liability are based have seen many changes in recent years. Marriage and family therapists must keep abreast of these changes to protect themselves and their clients. For example, familiarity with relevant law will allow them to make more sophisticated decisions about when confidentiality applies as opposed to circumstances mandating disclosure of information (e.g., child abuse, suicidal threat).

Involvement with the legal system calls for conceptual changes by many marriage and family therapists. In contrast with professionals from other disciplines, they may find movement into legal matters more difficult because of their philosophy and methods. Most marriage and family therapists' training is heavily influenced by goal-oriented notions of "what should be"; as a result, they are often unprepared for the "what is" emphasis of the courtroom. The legal system aims not at helping clients progress and become better but rather on reaching a fair decision that solves a practical problem in the here and now; one that can be applied to similar situations in the same way. The philosophy of the courtroom process frequently contradicts the therapy process (Woody & Mitchell, 1984).

Methodologically, marriage and family therapists' major therapeutic role is to facilitate individuals and families in functioning better. In legal proceedings, marriage and family therapists' primary role is simply to tell the truth. The attorneys' role is to promote their particular client's interest within the boundaries of the law and rules of the court. The attorney is not there to discover the truth; the court will determine the truth by weighing all evidence within the context of an adversarial struggle between attorneys. Marriage and family therapists are placed in the middle and sometimes mistakenly take an opposing attorney's activities as a personal attack against themselves or the best interests of their client. This creates a difficult dilemma in grappling with remaining objective in an atmosphere accentuating any tendency, conscious or unconscious, for personal bias as well as actual abuse of behavioral science data.

An understanding of the law and legal system as relevant to areas of merger with marriage and family therapy can relieve many of the pressures potentially confronting therapists in these circumstances. It is obviously not necessary nor possible for therapists to possess the knowledge of an attorney; rather, they should have a basic comprehension of legal processes and procedures as well as how to pursue elementary legal research efforts.

Ruback (1982) asserted that marriage and family therapists may assume three major roles within the legal system: that of a source of information leading to intervention by the state; that of a resource for therapy services; that of an expert witness. Following an introduction to the basics of legal education, this chapter will consider each of these roles as well as the increasingly critical issue of marriage and family therapists' professional liability under the law. A bibliography of recommended resources at the end of the chapter provides a more extensive exploration of the topics addressed.

LEGAL EDUCATION

Marriage and family therapists need to be familiar with the basics of legal research so they can educate themselves in matters relevant to their professional practice. Shea (1985) asserted that researching a particular point amid the expanse of the law is generally not beyond the ability of the competent layperson. For marriage and family therapists—legal "laypersons"—several distinctions are of particular concern.

Common Law

Common law is the fundamental law of the United States. Derived from the English Common Law, its authority stems from tradition and usage, not from legislation. Common law is regarded as expressing "the usage and customs of immemorial antiquity" common to the people of England. Conceptually, common law represents the belief that law does not have to be derived from only written sources (Reed, 1985). American law in the 1800s took pride in its common law arrangement. With acceleration into the 1900s, legislation has modified and often supplemented the common law.

Statutory Law

Statutory law consists of those laws passed by a legislative body, such as a state legislature or Congress, and signed into law. Statutory laws exist in each of the 50 states as well as on the federal level. The statutes are binding only in the jurisdiction where they are passed.

Administrative (Regulatory) Law

Administrative agencies have grown rapidly in this country beginning with the New Deal legislation of the 1930s. At that time it became clear that Congress and state legislatures could not effectively promulgate rules on all areas of government control. Highly specialized areas required knowledge and time beyond the limits of the average legislator. Consequently, Congress or state legislatures passed laws delegating broad rule-making authority to specialized agencies (Knapp, Vandecreek, & Zirkel, 1985).

Case Law (Court Decisions)

Case law is a body of legal decisions that, when taken collectively, creates rules for decision making. Typically, statutes prescribe certain legal principles. Legislation, however, is frequently written in broad terms, and thus courts apply, interpret, and fill in the interstices in the statutes. The court considers a statute and its legislative history and decides what the legislators actually intended. Court opinions take into account any bearing that higher laws (such as the state or federal constitution) may have on the interpretation of the statute in question (Knapp, Vandecreek, & Zirkel, 1985).

Many nuances enter the process. A determination must be made as to whether federal or state law applies. In general, state law must be considered first; if a federal issue, such as a constitutional right or a conflict between states, federal law will come into play. Depending on the nature of a case, a federal court may apply a state law, even when considering a federal issue (Woody & Mitchell, 1984).

Case law accumulates on the basis of stare decisis ("let the decision stand"). Under this doctrine, when a court interprets and applies common law, statutes, and/or regulations to the facts of a case, that court and lower courts in the same jurisdiction are bound to apply that precedent to future cases with similar facts (Kempin, 1982). Other courts may regard such decisions, depending on their number and reasoning as persuasive, albeit not binding. Reed (1985) described this process:

> The fashion in which one case governs another is elusive of description. In retrospect, the process is seen to constitute a form of logic, but a logic which often deals with principles that are imperfectly expressed, even in the court's opinion in the case at hand. Indeed, merely because a case has been decided in a given direction and because a legal principle applying to the case has been enunciated, the law on the point is, by no means, necessarily established. The saying, "Hard cases make bad law," illustrates a common failing of judges to overgeneralize a legal principle in rationalizing a case which, because of its one-sidedness, is easy to resolve. But one case does not establish the law; others come along which test declared legal principles and, consequently, lead to refinement.

> Typically, case law originates with a case, for example, in Oklahoma, the Supreme Court in that State formulates a legal principle that will be consid-

ered binding in Oklahoma (until it is successfully challenged). But the lawyers in an adjoining state might say that they are from Missouri and that they, themselves, have to test such a finding in their own courts. (A precedent in a neighboring state is bound to carry some weight in a jurisdiction, but it is not binding as precedent.) Missouri, with a somewhat similar fact situation as that in the Oklahoma case, will be likely to deal with the Missouri facts in the light of the decided case from Oklahoma, but may find different conclusions and somewhat different case law. Ultimately, several states, and perhaps even the courts of the Federal system, will formulate principles dealing with the same type of related cases, and a "weight of opinion" will have been achieved. The weight of opinion, expressed in differing ways and perhaps binding with somewhat differing nuances in different states, is considered to be the law. If the original decision on a case, as in Oklahoma, should, in retrospect, be seen as countering the trend of opinions, it is likely that that viewpoint will be challenged in the original state. The highest appellate court may overrule its original opinion, usually in some face-saving manner, or the state may continue in a maverick status with respect to that particular legal point. The trend is for some homogeneity to evolve over the various states and over Federal jurisdictions. The process of this evolution takes place over time and over several regions. (pp. 4–5)

Cases may be decided in the trial, intermediate, appellate, or highest court levels within the state or federal system. Although the nomenclature may vary from one jurisdiction to another, the typical designations for various court levels are listed in Figure 4–1.

Trial courts determine facts in disputes and apply appropriate rules of law. In the trial court, parties first appear, witnesses testify, and other evidence is presented. The losing party on the trial level may appeal the decision to an appellate court. Appellate courts do not hear new testimony, but rather decide whether the law was properly applied at a lower level in the court system. A higher level of appeal is typically available, depending on the issue as a matter of right or as a result of an upper court's discretion. Important to reiterate is that even a minor change in the facts can change the decision of the court.

An understanding of five component parts is helpful in interpreting court decisions (Shea, 1985):

1. **Facts.** The facts of a case form the basis for a court's decision. In a jury case, it is the jury who decides what are the facts; in a nonjury case, it is the trial judge who makes these determinations.
2. **Issue.** An issue of a case is its decisional focus. The parties attempt to focus a judge's attention on the issues of a case most favorable to their position. Ultimately, the judge decides what are the issues of a case regarding his or her decision.
3. **Rule.** A rule is a statement of the law which is applied to the facts. Often rules are incomplete or ambiguous, requiring the court to interpret them. Such an interpretation is also a rule as also may be a statement of the common law developed by the court. The rule of a decision, especially of an appellate court, serves as a precedent. Once a rule is stated in a decision, only that court or a higher court may alter it.

Figure 4–1   Typical Court Names in Federal and State Systems

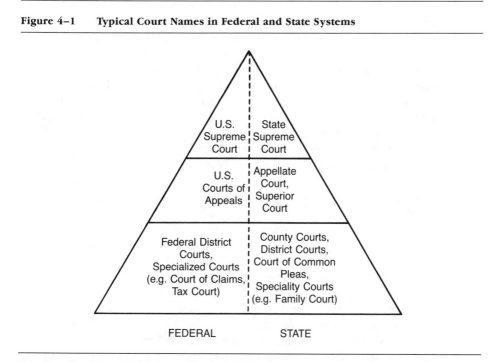

FEDERAL   STATE

Note. From "Legal Research Techniques: What the Psychologist Needs to Know" by S. Knapp, L. Vandecreek, and P. Zirkel, 1985, *Professional Psychology; Research & Practice, 16,* pp. 363–372. Copyright 1985 by American Psychological Association. Reprinted by permission of the author.

4. **Holding.** The holding of the decision is its outcome, the result of the rule applied to the facts, and who wins or loses.
5. **Dicta.** In a decision, a court may discuss rules which are not directly related to the facts of present case. When a court states a rule that is not necessary for deciding a case, the rule is referred to as an "obiter dictum." Dicta (plural) serve as guidance, but do not constitute binding precedent for lower courts.

Criminal vs. Civil Law

Although their basic purposes are similar, that is, to promote social order and to provide a system of dispute resolution, civil and criminal law differ in one significant way. *Civil law* pertains to acts offensive to individuals, *criminal law* to acts offensive to society in general. The ultimate remedy for harms inflicted in violation of criminal laws is punishment of the violator in the name of the state. Civil law provides a framework within which claims by one party or parties against another are adjudicated before a court. In civil law, the remedy is some compensation to the victim (Keary, 1985).

Marriage and family therapists who seek to supplement their therapeutic expertise with specific legal understandings should become familiar with the major types of legal sources. Woody and Mitchell (1984) offer an orientation for doing so in Figure 4–2. This information should provide sufficient information to enter a law library. Law libraries are maintained by law schools whose official policies vary; however, most will give permission for legal research by professionals such as marriage and family therapists. State, county, and city law libraries, although intended for judges and lawyers, are generally available to the public. While their collections are probably less extensive than a good law school library, most are quite willing to provide assistance to nonlawyers. Local bar associations can be contacted for the location of these libraries. Private law libraries provide another research source. Larger law firms and office complexes catering to attorneys often have fairly good libraries. Access may prove more difficult, however (Shea, 1985). Finally, many university, college, and public libraries have good legal collections.

In most locations, law librarians are available to assist researchers, including marriage and family therapists. Furthermore, many attorneys typically welcome giving "free advice" for bona fide research efforts; such contacts frequently facilitate future referral relationships. Lastly, seminars, symposia, and workshops on relevant legal issues are regularly sponsored by colleges and universities, public and private agencies, and various professional organizations.

Of special note is the AAMFT Legal Consultation Plan, a service available to members of the American Association for Marriage and Family Therapy. For an annual fee, the plan offers consultation on legal issues relating to the professional and business aspects of marriage and family therapy. (Information on the plan can be obtained from Grove, Engelberg and Gross, P.C., 2033 M Street, N.W., Suite 404, Washington, D.C. 20036.)

THE MARRIAGE AND FAMILY THERAPIST AS SOURCE OF INFORMATION

As a source of information, marriage and family therapists have an obligation to provide information leading to intervention by the state. The two most frequently encountered situations calling for therapists to serve as sources of information involve their "duty to warn" and statutes requiring the reporting of child abuse and neglect. Both of these requirements can pose painful professional dilemmas for therapists as discussed in earlier chapters on ethical obligations. The present discussion, however, will highlight only the legal obligations.

The "Duty to Warn"

In 1976, the California Supreme Court handed down a decision in *Tarasoff v. Board of Regents of the University of California* that signaled a

Figure 4–2   An Orientation to Legal Research Sources

It would be unrealistic to expect the human services professional to acquire the same facility at locating and understanding legal information as would be commonplace for the legal scholar. On the other hand, the human services professional can supplement his or her behavioral or health science expertise with legal ideas, albeit in a somewhat rudimentary fashion. The human services professional can achieve an adequate orientation by becoming familiar with the major types of legal sources. This fundamental orientation can be augmented by guidance from a professional legal librarian.

United States Supreme Court decisions are reported by official and unofficial reporters. The official reporter, created by statutory authority, is the *United States Supreme Court Reports* (cited as U.S.). The unofficial reporters, products of commercial publishers, are the West Publishing Company's *Supreme Court Reporter* (S. Ct.) and the Lawyers Co-operative Publishing Company's *Lawyers' Edition of United States Supreme Court Reports* (L. Ed. or L. Ed. 2d). All these editions are authoritative as to text, but the unofficial versions may also contain supplemental information (such as summaries of the attorneys' arguments or abstracts on specific legal points). If a Supreme Court case has not yet appeared in these publications, it might be found in *United States Law Week* (U.S.L.W.), a looseleaf service.

Decisions on cases from the U.S. Courts of Appeals appear in the *Federal Reporter* (F. or F.2d). U.S. District Court decisions appear in the *Federal Supplement* (F. Supp.) and *Federal Rules Decisions* (F.R.D.).

State court decisions (except in a few states) are disseminated by an official state reporter, such as *Michigan Reports* (Mich.) or *California Reports* (Cal., Cal.2d, or Cal.3d). There will also be a regional reporter, such as *Northwestern Reporter* (N.W. or N.W.2d), which includes important cases from Michigan, Wisconsin, Minnesota, Iowa, North Dakota, South Dakota, and Nebraska.

Contrary to popular belief, not all court cases are published. That is, most cases at the federal level are published (especially those decided by the U.S. Supreme Court or a U.S. Court of Appeals); at the state level, most jurisdictions publish appellate decisions, but other cases (for instance, those decided at the trial level) may not be published unless they have special legal importance. Cases that are unreported elsewhere (as well as recent cases that have not yet appeared in the various reporters) may sometimes be found in separately paginated "advance sheets," in "looseleaf services" (such as the *Criminal Law Reporter,* the *Family Law Reporter,* or the *Labor Law Reporter*), or in legal periodicals.

Federal statutes appear, among other sources, in the *Statutes at Large* (these "session laws" are arranged in the order in which they are enacted); this source (cited Stat.) also includes congressional resolutions, select presidential proclamations, and treaties and other international agreements. The *United States Code* (U.S.C.) is published by the U.S. Government Printing Office and is the primary authority on final legislative law.

Federal administrative rules and regulations appear in the *Federal Register* (Fed. Reg.). The *Code of Federal Regulations* (C.F.R.) cites (by title and section) all federal administrative rules and regulations, except Treasury materials. Federal administrative decisions are published by various agencies, such as the Federal Trade Commission and the National Labor Relations Board.

State statutes—for example, the *Arkansas Statutes Annotated* (cited Ark. Stat. Ann.)—are published in bound volumes periodically. In between issues, a statute may be eliminated, amended, or added, and will be found in supplemental editions. It is always necessary to check in the back of a bound volume to see whether a "pocket supplement" reflects any revision of a statute.

Municipal and county ordinances appear in many forms but are usually confined to local distribution. The variations in form preclude detail herein. In general, however, these ordinances are similar in form to the statutes.

Legal research is blessed with encyclopedic sources. For example, the *American Law Reports* (A.L.R., A.L.R.2d, or A.L.R.3d) include selected cases and annotations on specific subjects, along with historical background, current law, and probable future developments. Similarly, the *Corpus Juris Secundum* (C.J.S.) series cites case authority, presents a researched summary of the law, and so on. *Words and Phrases* contains more descriptive and extensive definitions than the well-known *Black's Law Dictionary*.

An often-used legal research method is to "Shepardize" a case—that is, to use *Shepard's Case Citations* to follow the judicial history of a targeted case, learn the contemporary status of the case, locate other cases that have cited it, and acquire research leads (such as where to look in *American Law Reports*). The *Shepard* volumes are divided by jurisdiction. Statutes may also be researched in *Shepard's United States Citations,* and law review articles may be located in *Shepard's Law Review Citations*. Municipal charters and ordinances may be cited in *Shepard's Ordinance Law Citations*.

Legal materials follow a special referencing or citation system. For example, cases are cited as follows (with minor variations in type style used in different publications):

Tarasoff v. *Regents of the University of California,* 17 Cal.3d 425, 551 P.2d 334, 131 Cal. Rptr. 14 (1976).
("Cal.3d" is the third series of *California Reports,* the state reporter for California Supreme Court cases; "17" is the volume where the *Tarasoff* case is reported, and "425" is the first page where the case appears. "P.2d" is the *Pacific Reporter,* the regional reporter for California state court cases; and, again, "551" is the volume number and "334" the first page where the case appears. "Cal Rptr." is *West's California Reporter,* an unofficial reporter for California court cases.)

Muller v. *Oregon,* 208 U.S. 412, 415 (1908).
("U.S." is *United States Supreme Court Reports,* and "415" is the page where a specific quoted passage, presumably just cited in the text, appears. If the case has previously been cited, this citation may appear as "*Muller* v. *Oregon,* 208 U.S. at 415.")

Driver v. *Hinnant,* 356 F.2d 761 (4th Cir. 1966).
("F.2d" is *Federal Reporter,* publisher of U.S. Court of Appeals cases; "4th Cir." indicates that the case was heard by the U.S. Court of Appeals for the Fourth Circuit.)

Greenberg v. *Barbour,* 332 F. Supp. 745 (E.D. Pa. 1971).
("F Supp." is the *Federal Supplement,* reporter for U.S. District Court Cases; "E.D. Pa." indicates that the case was heard by the U.S. District Court for the eastern district of Pennsylvania.)

In addition, books, periodicals, newspapers, statutes, legislative materials, and other specialized materials are cited in prescribed ways. An authoritative source for learning legal citations is *A Uniform System of Citation* (12th ed., 1976), created by law review groups at Columbia, Harvard, Pennsylvania, and Yale (distributed by the Harvard Law Review Association, Gannett House, Cambridge, Massachusetts 02138).

Note. From "Understanding the Legal System and Legal Research" (pp. 30–33) by R.H. Woody & R.E. Mitchell. In *The Law and the Practice of Human Services* by R.H. Woody (Ed.), 1984, San Francisco; Jossey-Bass. Reprinted by permission.

trend toward protection of the public's safety in preference to client confidentiality in psychotherapy. The case involved a client who threatened during therapy to kill his girlfriend and did so two months later:

> In August 1969, Prosenjit Poddar, a voluntary outpatient at the student health service on the Berkeley campus of the University of California, informed his therapist, a psychologist, that he was planning to kill a young woman. He did not name the woman, but as was established later, the psychologist could have easily inferred who she was. The murder was to be carried out upon the woman's return to the university from her summer vacation. Following the session during which this information was given, the therapist telephoned the campus police, requesting that they observe Poddar for possible hospitalization as a person who was "dangerous to himself or others." The therapist followed up his telephone call with a formal letter requesting assistance from the chief of the campus police. The campus police did take Poddar into custody for the purpose of questioning, but later released him when he gave evidence of being "rational." Soon afterward, the therapist's supervisor asked the campus police to return the letter, ordered that the letter and the therapist's case notes be destroyed, and directed that no further action be taken to hospitalize Poddar. No warning was given to the intended victim or her parents. The client, understandably, did not resume therapy. Two months later Poddar killed Tatiana Tarasoff. Her parents filed suit against the Board of Regents of the university, several employees of the student health service, and the chief of the campus police plus four of his officers for failing to notify the intended victim of the threat. A lower court dismissed the suit, the parents appealed, and the California Supreme Court upheld the appeal and later reaffirmed its decision that failure to warn the intended victim was irresponsible.

In *Tarasoff* the court held that a therapist who knew, or by the standards of his profession should have known, that his client posed a threat to another, had a duty to warn the intended victim. Several other courts in jurisdictions outside California have since adopted the *Tarasoff* reasoning, subsequently further narrowing and refining it.

Three factors emanating from the *Tarasoff* decision have come to embody these findings regarding therapists' duty to warn. First, the court noted that generally one person does not have a duty to control the conduct of another. However, an exception to this was established for instances wherein one person has a "special relationship" either to the person whose conduct needs to be controlled or to the foreseeable victim of that conduct. This special relationship must be found to exist in the factual context of the case. In *Tarasoff* the court held that the therapist-client relationship met the test of being a special relationship.

The second condition required to create a duty to warn is a determination that a client's behavior "needs to be controlled." Again, in the factual context of *Tarasoff,* the court found that the client, Prosenjit Poddar, was a threat. It was noted, however, that determining whether an individual's conduct needs to be controlled is frequently a difficult prediction to make. The court identified a "reasonableness" test as the standard for determining if a client's conduct could result in a threat to a third person. In determining reasonableness, the court considered within the context of the specific case "that reasonable degree of skill, knowledge, and care ordinarily possessed and exercised by members of (that professional speciality) under similar circumstances" (*Tarasoff v. Regents of the University of California,* 1976, p. 345). The court further pointed out within that standard, opinions might differ and thus therapists are free to exercise judgment without fear of liability: "Proof aided by hindsight, that he or she judged wrongly is insufficient to establish negligence" (p. 345).

The third and final condition that gave rise to the duty to warn was a "foreseeable" victim. Tatiana Tarasoff, while not specifically named, was readily identifiable as the proposed victim. Thus, the facts of *Tarasoff* satisfied the three conditions creating a duty to warn for the therapist: a special relationship, a reasonable prediction of conduct that constituted a threat, and a foreseeable victim.

In *McIntosh v. Milano* (1979), a New Jersey court ruled on a factual situation similar to *Tarasoff* and similarly addressed a therapist's duty to warn:

> In this case, the client was an adolescent boy referred by a school counselor to the therapist, a psychiatrist. The boy informed the therapist of several fantasies he had including a fear of others, being a hero or important villain, using a knife to threaten those who might intimidate him, and having sexual experiences with Kimberly, the girl living next door to him. The boy also informed the therapist of having shot at Kimberly's car with a BB gun when she left for a date and showed the therapist a knife he had bought. The therapist was well aware of the boy's possessive feelings for Kimberly. The boy further told the therapist that he wanted Kimberly "to suffer" as he had and showed anger when Kimberly moved out of her parents' home. He was hateful toward Kimberly's boyfriends and upset when he could not obtain her new address. The boy killed Kimberly. Although the therapist had spoken to his client's parents on a number of occasions about their son's relationship to Kimberly, he never addressed the issue with either Kimberly or her parents.

Lane and Spruill (1980) asserted that dangerousness cannot be accurately predicted and that errors in this direction are likely. The prediction of dangerousness in *Tarasoff* did not seem to be a questionable factor. Based on the testimony of another psychiatrist, dangerousness was not a question in *McIntosh v. Milano* but rather considered a fact based on a violent act (firing a weapon at Kimberly's car) and on the therapist's statement that his client had admitted fantasies of violence and feelings of retribution. The client had also verbalized threats toward Kimberly and her boyfriends. The court pointed out that "a therapist does have a basis for giving an opinion and a prognosis based on the history of the patient and the course of treatment" (*McIntosh v. Milano,* 1979, p. 508).

Thompson v. County of Alameda (1980) represented a case in which the court was asked to decide if there was a duty to warn the parents of a child who was murdered by a released juvenile offender. The juvenile had been in the custody of Alameda County and confined to an institution. He was known to have "latent, extremely dangerous and violent propensities regarding young children and that sexual assaults upon young children and violence connected therewith were a likely result of releasing (him) into the community" (p. 72). Within 24 hours of his temporary release to his mother, the boy killed a child who lived a few doors away. The foreseeability of the victim was the predominant question. The court referred to the language of *Tarasoff* and held that although the victim need not be directly named, he or she must be "readily identifiable." The court thus refused to impose liability on the involved county officials for failing to give a blanket warning to all neighborhood parents, the police, or the juvenile's mother.

Although generally no legal obligation is imposed on a person to control the conduct of another, there is an exception. When an individual has a special relationship to either the one whose conduct needs to be controlled or to the intended victim of that conduct, the law imposes a duty to warn the victim. This is particularly relevant for marriage and family therapists because their relationship with their clients fulfills this "special relationship" condition. Given this, marriage and family therapists will be expected to apply a standard of reasonableness in determining a threat posed by clients' conduct. It is important to remember that reasonableness is not a fixed concept but a standard comparing an individual therapist to others in the same profession with similar knowledge, skills, and training. Finally, when these two conditions occur and there is an intended victim who is foreseeable, the marriage and family therapist has a duty to warn that victim or be liable under the law for negligence.

Child Abuse and Neglect

There are no reliable statistics regarding the exact extent of child abuse and neglect in the United States. This uncertainty is likely caused by inconsistencies in definitions of what child abuse and neglect represent, variations in reporting laws from state to state, and the different methods of data collection commonly utilized. Nevertheless, it was estimated that during one recent two-year period (1982–83), close to two million cases of child abuse and neglect were reported to child welfare agencies (National Center on Child Abuse and Neglect, 1983).

The United States Department of Health, Education, and Welfare (now Health and Human Services) Regulations on Child Abuse and Neglect (Bureau of National Affairs, Inc., 1977) define *abuse* and *neglect* as follows:

> Child abuse and neglect means harm or threatened harm to a child's health or welfare . . . Harm or threatened harm can occur through: Non-accidental physical or mental injury; sexual abuse as defined by State law; or negligent treatment or maltreatment, including the failure to provide adequate food, clothing, or shelter. (p. 101:0063)

Although a clarifying definition, because child abuse is not a federal crime, federal law does no more than make money available to the states that meet its reporting guidelines and other qualifications such as agreeing to set reporting standards. Thus, state definitions become very important as they provide the basis for abuse and neglect as a crime within a particular jurisdiction. Although state laws vary, most use a combination of two or more of the following elements in defining child abuse and neglect: physical injury, mental or emotional injury, and sexual molestation or exploitation. Fischer and Sorenson (1985) noted that while some states have separate definitions for abuse and neglect, others do not. They asserted it is unimportant to be able to distinguish between abuse and neglect.

> The time and effort spent in trying to distinguish between abuse and neglect serves no useful purpose. A child may suffer serious or permanent harm and even death as a result of neglect. Therefore, the same reasons that justify the mandatory reporting of abuse require the mandatory reporting of child neglect. (p. 183)

All states require that child abuse and neglect be reported to the proper authorities, particularly if physical injury is present. Some states do not require the reporting of emotional or mental injury and others do not explicitly mandate the reporting of sexual abuse, although this is changing. Marriage and family therapists should check with appropriate agencies in their respective states to identify relevant statutes.

In order to be eligible for federal funds under the Child Abuse and Treatment Act, states must grant immunity to reporters. All states have complied with this request and therefore provides immunity by law from civil suit and criminal prosecution that might arise from the reporting of suspected child abuse or neglect. Such immunity applies to all mandatory or permissible reporters who act "in good faith." In many states, good faith is presumed; therefore, the person seeking to sue a reporter has the burden to prove that the reporter acted in bad faith. Clearly, any marriage and family therapist who, mandated by law, acts in good faith in reporting suspected cases of abuse or neglect is immune from suit.

No state requires that the reporter be absolutely certain before filing a report of abuse or neglect. It is sufficient that the reporter have "reason to believe" or "reasonable cause to believe or suspect" that a child is subject to abuse or neglect. As noted with respect to the duty to warn, the standard applied is what the reasonable person (professional) would believe under similar circumstances. As abuse rarely occurs in the presence of witnesses and because the protection of children is the primary purpose of reporting laws, reporters are not held to unduly rigorous standards as long as they act in good faith. Some states even require one to report when he or she "observes the child being subjected to conditions or circumstances which would reasonably result in child abuse or neglect" (Fischer & Sorenson, 1985, p. 184).

Marriage and family therapists are trained observers of children and their interactions with significant adults. There are, however, various symptoms that should alert therapists that some form of abuse or neglect is taking place. Table 4–1 lists in chart form some of the most common indicators of child abuse and neglect.

Table 4–1   Physical and Behavioral Indicators of Child Abuse and Neglect (CA/N)

Type of CA/N	Physical Indicators	Behavioral Indicators
PHYSICAL ABUSE	Unexplained Bruises and Welts: —on face, lips, mouth —on torso, back, buttocks, thighs —in various stages of healing —clustered, forming regular patterns —reflecting shape of article used to inflict (electric cord, belt buckle) —on several different surface areas —regularly appear after absence, weekend, or vacation Unexplained Burns: —cigar, cigarette burns, especially on soles, palms, back or buttocks —immersion burns (sock-like, glove-like, doughnut shaped on buttocks or genitalia) —patterned like electric burner, iron, etc. —rope burns on arms, legs, neck or torso Unexplained Fractures: —to skull, nose, facial structure —in various stages of healing —multiple or spiral fractures Unexplained Lacerations or Abrasions: —to mouth, lips, gums, eyes —to external genitalia	Wary of Adult Contacts Apprehensive When Other Children Cry Behavioral Extremes: —aggressiveness, or —withdrawal Frightened of Parents Afraid to Go Home Reports Injury by Parents
PHYSICAL NEGLECT	Consistent Hunger, Poor Hygiene, Inappropriate Dress Consistent Lack of Supervision, Especially in Dangerous Activities or Long Periods Unattended Physical Problems or Medical Needs Abandonment	Begging, Stealing Food Extended Stays at School (early arrival and late departure) Constant Fatigue, Listlessness, or Falling Asleep in Class Alcohol or Drug Abuse Delinquency (e.g., thefts) States There Is No Caretaker

Table 4–1   (Continued)

Type of CA/N	Physical Indicators	Behavioral Indicators
SEXUAL ABUSE	Difficulty in Walking or Sitting	Unwilling to Change for Gym or Participate in Physical Education Class
	Torn, Stained, or Bloody Underclothing	Withdrawal, Fantasy, or Infantile Behavior
	Pain or Itching in Genital Area	Bizarre, Sophisticated, or Unusual Sexual Behavior or Knowledge
	Bruises or Bleeding in External Genitalia, Vaginal or Anal Areas	Poor Peer Relationships
	Veneral Disease, Especially in Preteens	Delinquent or Run-Away
	Pregnancy	Reports Sexual Assault by Caretaker
EMOTIONAL MALTREATMENT	Speech Disorders	Habit Disorders (sucking, biting, rocking, etc.)
	Lags in Physical Development	Conduct Disorders (antisocial, destructive, etc.)
	Failure to Thrive	Neurotic Traits (sleep disorders, inhibition of play)
		Psychoneurotic Reactions (hysteria, obsession, compulsion, phobias, hypochondria)
		Behavior Extremes: —compliant, passive —aggressive, demanding
		Overly Adaptive Behavior: —inappropriately adult —inappropriately infant
		Developmental Lags (mental, emotional)
		Attempted Suicide

Note. From *The Educator's Role in the Prevention and Treatment of Child Abuse and Neglect* by D.D. Broadhurst, 1979, Washington, D.C.: National Center on Child Abuse and Neglect, U.S. Department of Health, Education and Welfare, Publication No. 79–30172.

These signs are, of course, only indicators that should alert marriage and family therapists to the *possibility* of abuse or neglect. They do not *prove* the existence of abuse or neglect. The therapy setting provides further clues to confirm suspicions or present satisfactory explanations for a child's condition.

Marriage and family therapists have criminal liability for failure to report suspected abuse or neglect in the overwhelming majority of states. Failure to report is a misdemeanor in most states. The penalty might range from a 5–30-day jail sentence and/or a fine of $10–$100, to as high as a fine of $1000 and a year in jail. This may be a paper tiger, however, as "reported" cases of criminal prosecution for failure to report a case of child abuse or neglect are rare.

Fischer and Sorenson (1985) attributed this lack of enforcement to the fact that state laws usually require a "knowing" or "willful" failure to report. They noted the difficulties involved in proving, beyond all reasonable doubt, that someone knowingly or willfully failed to report; therefore, cases have tended not to be prosecuted. Instead, they identified a trend among states enacting laws imposing civil liability (liability in money damages) for failure to report. Some states in this regard require proof of willful misconduct while others utilize a lesser standard for establishing liability, namely the standard of negligence.

THE MARRIAGE AND FAMILY THERAPIST AS REFERRAL RESOURCE

As a referral resource, marriage and family therapists are called upon by the courts for informational as well as therapeutic intervention assistance. Primarily within the juvenile justice system and in civil actions addressing issues ranging from adoption to divorce to child custody, marriage and family therapists assume the role of referral resource. This referral resource role reflects a growing recognition of their expertise in offering preventative as well as rehabilitative services to youthful offenders and their families. Likewise, it has long been recognized that every civil action reflects the failure of a relationship. The parties involved are not capable of satisfactorily resolving their own disputes. All things considered, it is almost always more advantageous for two disputing parties to come to their own resolution rather than run the risk of losing control of their situation by having a third party (judge or jury) decide for them. This is in addition to the costs and time involved with a court encounter (Sidney & Petrila, 1985). Marriage and family therapists have thus taken on the roles of treatment specialist, particularly within the juvenile justice system, and mediator in averting civil court actions.

The Treatment Specialist

Evans (1983) described the role of mental health professionals aiding the courts within the criminal justice system as that of treatment specialist. Marriage and family therapists have the clinical and academic training as well as the experience and are currently acting in some capacity as a treatment specialist predominantly within the juvenile justice system. Their functions are described in the following paragraphs.

Diagnostician

The first funciton of marriage and family therapists within the juvenile system is to provide diagnostic evaluations for rehabilitative decisions. Although judges make the final decisions about what will happen to a youthful offender, information made available through evaluations of identified youth and their families has a heavy impact upon those decisions.

Initially the court must decide whether it has jurisdiction to act; that is, it must decide if the youth falls within a prescribed statutory classification. Although there is variance from state to state, typical statutory classifications and dispositional alternatives that marriage and family therapists can provide diagnostic input toward are discussed in the paragraphs that follow (Kissel, 1983).

Juvenile delinquency. Juvenile courts generally have jurisdiction over youth accused of committing a crime if they are under 18 years of age on the date of the commission of the act. Relatively recent changes in the law have introduced some exceptions to jurisdiction over children age 13 or older charged with murder, forceable rape, robbery while armed, first-degree burglary, or assault with intent to commit any of the aforementioned (Guggenheim, 1979). Juveniles age 15 and over at the time of the offense who are charged with a felony may be transferred to the appropriate criminal division for trial, as well as juveniles age 16 or over who have previously been committed to an institution and are charged in a new delinquency petition for any offense.

The court's relationship to youthful offenders is a meld of providing for "the best interests of the child" along with protection for the community. The court can decide to dismiss a youth; that is, grant an outright dismissal of the charge. This motion might be considered where a minor offense is charged against a first offender and court supervision of the child is perceived as unnecessary. A consent decree can also be granted by the court and may be entered if the youth has not been previously adjudicated a delinquent by the court, or if such adjudication has been sealed (is not available to the court). Under a consent decree, a juvenile is put on probation for up to 6 months without a finding of guilt. Thus, the court provides supervision without stigmatization. After successful completion of the specific terms of the decree (therapy, community work hours, restitution, etc.), the original petition is dismissed. If the conditions of the decree are violated, the original petition may be reinstated and the juvenile forced to stand trial.

Person in Need of Supervision (PINS). A PINS is typically a youth who is habitually truant from school without justification or is habitually disobedient of the reasonable and lawful commands of his or her parents, guardians, or other custodians and is thus ungovernable and in need of care and supervision. When parents and social agencies are unable or unwilling to find a solution for a troubled or troublesome child, it is in society's interest to try, through its legal system, to *prevent* crime and delinquency via an attempt at rehabilitation rather than wait to punish its occurrence.

The court normally has at its disposal an array of social services as well as traditional judicial remedies. Referral to court is not meant for children with inconsequential discipline problems at home or minor school difficulties. Only when youth are at risk of becoming delinquent should this step be taken. The court has considerable leeway when fashioning a plan for disposition. Youth typically are placed in facilities for delinquents only if they have been adjudicated a PINS more than once.

Child abuse and neglect. The primary aim of the court is to preserve the family bond unless such preservation endangers the welfare of a child. Consequently, the court attempts to arrange dispositions when abuse and neglect allegations are brought before it that permit parents to maintain custody of their children unless such custody is harmful to the child. The judge can also order families to seek medical, psychiatric, or other treatment services if parents want to maintain custody of their child.

If the court finds that placement with the parents is not possible, then relatives, other qualified individuals, or commitment to that agency charged with foster placement will be sought. When more than one child is involved, courts generally prefer to keep siblings together to preserve whatever family bonds remain as well as to ease the transition to an alternative home environment. The court can also free a child for adoption by termination of parental rights in severe cases. It is important to know, however, that unless abused/neglected children are also found to be delinquent, they cannot be committed to or confined in an institution for delinquent children.

Resource Expert

The second major function of marriage and family therapists serving in the role of treatment specialists is that of resource expert. The court is continually in need of information regarding referral resources for use in the disposition of youth and their families. Identification and categorization of referral resources require knowledge of treatment modalities and a constant updating of information on the facilities providing treatment. To the court, it is the quality of the information and the credibility of the treatment specialist that are crucial. Evans (1983) asserted that the following information regarding referral resources should be submitted to the court.

"Primary" program characteristics. The treatment specialist should be prepared to offer his or her "primary" recommendation given the circumstances of the case and his or her understanding of the way the recommendation will fit with available referral resources. This includes the services offered by the recommended program, clients served, referral procedure, cost and duration of structured programs, funding sources and location, director or contact person, and telephone number.

The relationship of the facility to the courts. It is important that it be clear whether there can be an ongoing contact with the probation department or other court personnel. Is the program willing to accept court referrals requiring reports back to the court and possible court appearances? There may also be questions of payment, the acceptance of juvenile offenders, and the ethical implications of accepting a court-ordered referral.

An inventory of other available programs. This up-to-date list should include some subjective and evaluative comments regarding reputation, outcome of program involvement, and treatment modality used, in addition to the typical objective data as just outlined. The court, with some youthful offenders, may be highly sensitive to security issues, for example. Thus, the presence of a secure facility that is fully accredited and licensed may be of paramount importance and override the recommendation for an innovative drug program that may appear ideal as a primary recommendation to the treatment specialist.

Treatment Provider

The third function of marriage and family therapists as treatment specialists is that of providing direct treatment services to youth and their families at various points during the court process. Shrybman and Halpern's (1979) summarization of the hearing process in juvenile court illustrates these intervention times:

> Utilizing the instance of a complaint of abuse and neglect, said complaint can be initiated by the filing of a petition (written complaint) in the juvenile court alleging that a child has been abused or neglected. The petition may be written and filed by the county attorney, the juvenile probation officer, and/or county social worker according to state law and local court procedures. (Some states allow anyone to file a petition alleging a child has been abused or neglected.)
>
> In emergency situations where there is imminent danger to the child in remaining with the parent(s), the child may be removed from the custody of the parent(s) and placed in protective custody pending the outcome of the juvenile court proceeding. This decision may be made by the police, juvenile probation, child protective services, and/or a physician, depending on state law. Whenever a child is placed in protective custody, a petition must be filed in juvenile court, usually within 24 to 48 hours, and a hearing must be held soon thereafter (usually within 48 to 72 hours, depending upon state law), to allow a judge to review the decision.
>
> There must be an evidentiary trial in which the state must prove to a judge that a child has been abused or neglected. Unless the parent(s) admit to abusing or neglecting their child, it is necessary to call witnesses to substantiate the allegations of abuse or neglect. This is called an *adjudicatory hearing* and normally occurs from two to six weeks after the initial petition is filed. Because dependency (the idea that the child is in need of

services that the parent(s) cannot provide and therefore is dependent upon the state to see that they are provided) is technically a civil rather than criminal issue, the state need not prove abuse or neglect beyond a reasonable doubt, only by a preponderance of evidence, a somewhat lower standard of proof.

Child abuse and neglect proceedings are usually "bifurcated proceedings," meaning the decision as to what should be done with child occurs in a separate hearing from that which determines whether the child is, in fact, abused or neglected. A dispositional hearing, analogous to the sentencing hearing in a criminal case, may occur on the same day as the adjudication hearing or be held at another time, sometimes weeks later. The dispositional hearing generally focuses on those recommendations made to the judge regarding the appropriate order for the child. An important point to understand regarding the disposition order is that the court has leverage over parents only by its jurisdiction over their child. Thus, the court cannot directly enforce its orders against parents of a child by fines, imprisonment, or threats of either. The court can, however, after finding that a child has been abused or neglected, order that the child remain in the home of the parents on the provision that the entire family participate in therapy efforts. If the parents fail to comply, the court can then order the child removed from the home and placed in a foster home or other care setting.

In some states, no review hearings are held. In others, they are an integral part of the hearing process. After a child has been declared dependent by the court, the court retains jurisdiction over that child until the child reaches adulthood or until the dependency status is ended by the court. In order to measure the progress of the case and determine any need to modify a previous order, courts will generally hold periodic hearings to review the case every six months to a year.

In their function as treatment providers, marriage and family therapists work closely with the court and associated state social service personnel to formulate and facilitate families' follow-through on treatment plans designed to protect their children and improve the family situation with the primary purpose of preserving the family system. Intervention can come at any point in the process beginning with the initial petition and concluding with successful treatment outcome culminated with dependency status being terminated by the court at a follow-up hearing sometime subsequent to the disposition order.

Mediation

In recent years, fundamental questions about the legal system's response to families experiencing divorce have been a major focus of concern by marriage and family therapists. Therapists who have seen family conflicts exacerbated by courtroom experiences have wondered whether there are better alternatives to the current procedures for legally dissolving marriages. The central issue raised has been the adversarial orientation embedded within the very structure of the court system.

Trained to operate within this adversarial system, divorce lawyers typically see their job as getting the best possible settlement for their particular client, while remaining relatively unconcerned about the impact of the settlement on the entire family system. Nor do they see their role as including helping a family to negotiate the emotional minefield of divorce. Law schools do not pretend to prepare their students to appreciate the psychological dilemmas divorcing families must face. While family law constitutes a primary component of most law programs, there is rarely more than a passing reference to the personal and family trauma involved or to the effect of divorce on children (Vroom, 1983).

Mediation is an increasingly utilized alternative to court action. A cooperative dispute resolution process in which a neutral intervener helps disputing parties negotiate a mutually satisfactory settlement of their conflict, mediation stresses honesty, informality, and open and direct communication. It also facilitates emotional expressiveness, attention to underlying causes of disputes, reinforcement of positive bonds, and avoidance of blame (Deutsch, 1973; Felstiner & Williams, 1978).

According to proponents, mediation relieves court dockets that are clogged with divorce and child custody actions, reduces the alienation of litigants, inspires durable consensual agreements, and helps families to resume workable relationships even though legally divorced (Herrman, McHenry & Weber, 1979; Milne, 1978; Spencer & Zammit, 1976). Comparisons of mediation and court adjudication have shown that mediation encourages settlement, generates a higher degree of user satisfaction, improves communication and understanding in families, results in more cooperative coparenting, reduces the incidence of divorce relitigation, and translates into savings of time and money (Pearson & Thoennes, 1982). Conciliation courts in many states offer mediation as a court-related service for families seeking divorce. The family sits down with a mediator to resolve disputed areas rather than have a judge impose a resolution. For years, the Family Court System in Australia has used such court-related mediation services as the primary method of working out visitation, child custody, spousal maintenance, and child support questions (McKenzie, 1978).

In actual practice, divorce/family mediation can look much like couples counseling or family therapy. As in family therapy, husband and wife sit together in a room with a third person who facilitates their communication (although some mediators may see each party separately and perform a kind of "shuttle diplomacy"). When appropriate, children are brought into the decision making. There are some differences however, the primary one being that the mediator begins with the understanding that it is the clear intention of the family to physically break up (Vroom, 1983). The task of the mediator is then to create an environment where productive negotiation in areas of conflict can occur.

Generally, mediation is viewed as progressing in stages. These include:

1. Setting the stage by providing a neutral setting, introducing oneself

as a mediator, establishing ground rules, and gaining the disputants' commitment to mediation

2. Defining the issues by eliciting facts and expression of needs, desires, and feelings
3. Processing the issues by managing emotions, encouraging empathy, narrowing differences, exploring solutions, and maintaining positive momentum
4. Reaching a settlement and assuring its implementation (Felstiner & Williams, 1978; Gulliver, 1979)

This stage conceptualization is utilized by all the practitioners who have developed and published model approaches to divorce/family mediation. For example, Kessler (1978) emphasized the need to systematically progress from Stage 1 to Stage 4. Rules need to be established at the beginning to create a secure atmosphere and avoid the violation of "unspoken" rules by either party at critical moments later in the mediation. Processing and resolving issues prior to their proper definition may result in wasted energy. Kessler clearly defined specific mediator goals, focuses, and techniques appropriate to each mediation stage.

Black and Joffee (1978) outlined a stage approach to mediation comparable to Kessler's, although they also delineated a division of labor for attorney-mental health professional teams. With the attorney focusing on settlement details and the mental health professional dealing with emotional and communication issues, the team helps families to simultaneously achieve a legal and psychological divorce.

Milne (1978), a social worker, outlined a very specific procedure that involves extensive information gathering and emotional ventilation prior to the generation of a mediation settlement. Believing that emotional issues are at the root of most custody battles, Milne instructs each disputant to prepare an autobiography and spend one mediation session reviewing the marriage and decision to divorce. During following sessions, the parties describe existing and desired custody and visitation arrangements. The mediator also meets with the children and communicates the information to the parties. The mediator then solicits resolution proposals from the parties and helps them combine these proposals and/or generate new ones.

In contrast, Coogler (1978), a lawyer with training as a therapist, identified economic issues as underlying most custody battles. His model calls for extensive information gathering on financial matters and property issues. After an orientation to the mediation process, the disputants work out a temporary arrangement regarding child and financial issues. Next, they do homework that involves identifying assets and preparing budgets and income statements. Subsequent sessions are devoted to dividing property and generating acceptable maintenance and child support arrangements. Custody and visitation matters are tackled last. Each party submits two property settlement plans: one in the event they receive custody, the other in the event they do not. The goal of the process is to prevent children from becoming pawns in their parents' financial battles. The resolution of financial issues is believed to lead to resolution of emotional issues.

Another mediation model was developed by Haynes (1981), a social worker with experience in labor mediation. Haynes also offered a stage approach. Initially, the process is explained and basic data on the marriage and impending divorce collected. The parties then meet with the mediator individually to assess their areas of agreement and disagreement, power relationship, communication style, and potential divorce adjustment. At this time too, the mediator seeks to balance their power relationship by educating the weaker party about negotiation strategies, divorce finances, and the adjustment process. The mediator then meets with the parties jointly to identify points of agreement and narrow the issues in dispute. The parties are then separated and the mediator uses shuttle diplomacy techniques to relay trial proposals, encourage trade-offs, and suggest compromises. The parties are brought together when it seems they have reached a settlement.

A number of organizations offer training, certification for competence, and consultation to assist marriage and family therapists in establishing expertise in mediation methodologies. The Divorce Mediation Research Project (1720 Emerson Street, Denver, Colorado 90218) publishes a directory of providers in this area.

THE MARRIAGE AND FAMILY THERAPIST AS EXPERT WITNESS

Recognition by the courts that family influences play a significant part in determining litigants' behavior has expanded the role of marriage and family therapists to encompass that of expert witness. For many marriage and family therapists, however, the courtroom may be an unfamiliar environment with different ground rules and basic assumptions. Testifying as an expert witness may call for a reconsideration of those situational role demands normally encountered in usual therapeutic settings.

Brodsky and Robey (1972) identified the ideal role of the expert witness as "that of a detached, thoroughly neutral individual who simply and informatively presents the true facts as he sees them" (p. 173). Likewise, others have asserted that the position of the mental health professional as expert witness should be to strive to be impartial, free from prejudice, and not act as an advocate for either side (Bromberg, 1979; Macdonald, 1969; Slovenko, 1973).

The Rules of Evidence

Understanding the rules of evidence employed in the courtroom is the most fundamental issue marriage and family therapists must consider. These rules have evolved to promote the goals of the law; specifically, to facilitate a fair trial. The marriage and family therapist can tailor a therapeutic plan to the needs of clients; if one intervention does not produce the desired results, intervention efforts can be redirected. The court cannot afford this luxury. It must solve the presenting problem in a timely manner and its solution must be applicable to persons with similar problems. The court reaches its solution to the problem on the basis of presented evidence. The rules of evidence are, therefore, of utmost importance because they determine what will be allowed to come before the court. No professional function in the legal system can occur without an allegiance to the rules of evidence (Woody & Mitchell, 1984).

Almost anyone who is "professionally acquainted with, skilled, or trained in some science, art, trade, and thereby has knowledge or experience in matters not generally familiar to the public" can serve as an expert witness (Schwitzgebel & Schwitzgebel, 1980, p. 238). The expert witness may offer opinions or inferences and may respond to hypothetical questions. The lay witness must have had direct contact with the action or expression—otherwise, the testimony would be hearsay and not admissible.

The expert witness may be allowed to offer testimony based on indirect observation. For example, many jurisdictions will allow a professional to testify about data collected by another professional who is part of a team effort; in a child custody case, for example, a marriage and family therapist may be allowed to cite a home visitation report made by a child services worker. Usually, however, any source of information, such as the child services worker, is expected to be personally available for testimony to accommodate cross-examination by the attorney for the party being testified against (Woody & Mitchell, 1984).

Opinion testimony must be directly aligned with the issue in question. There must also be a concrete description of facts. Opinion evidence must also be such that the state of the present scientific body of knowledge permits a reasonable opinion to be asserted by an expert (Cleary, 1972). Examining attorneys will frequently preface or summarize their questioning of an expert witness by asking, "Have you derived or formed an opinion based on your professional knowledge and with a reasonable degree of professional certainty?" Since expert opinions must be qualified, expert witnesses are usually asked to cite their qualifications relevant to their professional knowledge on the subject and to enter a copy of their professional credentials into the court record.

Hypothetical questions comprise another area where experts may be allowed to testify without firsthand, observation-based knowledge of the parties involved (Woody & Mitchell, 1984). Judges are free to decide whether to allow testimony based on hypothetical facts (which closely parallel the characteristics of the parties or circumstances of the current case). If such testimony was erroneously admitted, however, it would present the probable basis for an appeal. For example, a judge could be lead to believe that certain data were obtained through normally accepted data collection methods of a profession and therefore qualified as an exception to the hearsay rule. If the methods were not commonly used, the information would definitively be hearsay. Were the case determined by that evidence, an appeal would be in order.

Some jurisdictions allow reports to be submitted as evidence, whereas others will not allow reports unless the author is available for in-court cross-examination (or is available for cross-examination under oath via a deposition). There are some exceptions, such as illness, incapacitation, and death. Cross-examination, however, maintains strong traditional importance:

> For two centuries, common law judges and lawyers have regarded the opportunity of cross-examination as an essential safeguard of the accuracy and completeness of testimony, and they have insisted that the opportunity is a right, and not a mere privilege. . . . And the premise that the opportunity of cross-examination is an essential safeguard has been the principal justification for the exclusion generally of hearsay statements, and for the admission as an exception to the hearsay rule of reported testimony taken at a former hearing when the present adversary was afforded the opportunity to cross-examine. Finally, state constitutional provisions guaranteeing to the accused the right of confrontation have been interpreted as codifying this right of cross-examination. (Cleary, 1972, pp. 43–44)

Courtroom Testimony

An expert witness generally testifies at the request of a representative attorney, although an expert can be requested to give testimony by both attorneys or by the court. Irrespective of the basis of the expert's entry into a case, however, testimony should reflect expertise, preparation, and perhaps most importantly, complete candor. Sidney and Petrila (1985) outlined a slate of strategies applicable to marriage and family therapists serving as expert witnesses.

Preparation

The successful presentation of testimony depends to a large degree upon the willingness of the witness and requesting attorney to prepare for court. There are a number of preparatory steps that expert witnesses should concern themselves with.

1. Provide the requesting attorney with a written list of qualifications; for example, education, years in practice, publications, and other pertinent information that demonstrates familiarity with the subject of the upcoming testimony.
2. If the testimony will involve a particular client, review and become familiar with the client's records. Particularly be aware of the frequency of sessions with the client.
3. Acquire at least a rudimentary understanding of the legal issues involved in the case. This information can be most readily obtained from the requesting attorney.

4. Insist that the requesting attorney take the time to prepare and discuss the questions he or she intends to ask on direct examination. The attorney should also assist in anticipating and discussing questions that are likely to be asked on cross-examination. Issues of information protected by confidentiality or privilege particularly need to be addressed at this time.

5. If about to testify for the first time as an expert witness, visit a court in session in advance and observe the examination and cross-examination of a number of witnesses.

Direct Examination

The requesting attorney presents his or her side of a case through direct examination of the expert witness. The goal of the requesting attorney and expert witness on direct examination is to present the technical aspects of the case in layperson's terms so that the judge and where present, jury, may understand. In direct examination, the attorney cannot "lead" the witness; that is, the witness must testify without the aid of suggestions from the attorney conducting the examination. The value of pre-court preparation becomes increasingly obvious. In-court considerations are also of paramount importance as well.

1. The expert witness must remember that the judge or jury is the ultimate decider of what is "fact" in a given case. Thus, in presenting testimony to the fact finder, the witness may enhance effectiveness and credibility by carefully attending to his or her courtroom image.
   a. Arrive on time.
   b. Concentrate on courtroom etiquette, especially in addressing the judge as "Your Honor."
   c. Dress conservatively and neatly.
   d. Maintain a generally serious demeanor; not talking about the case in hallways, restrooms, or other public places.
   e. Avoid displaying nervous mannerisms (e.g., wringing hands or pencil tapping).

2. The manner in which the expert witness listens and responds to the requesting attorney's questions is similarly important.
   a. Listen carefully to each question and be certain that the question is understood. If necessary, request that the question be repeated.
   b. Directly and simply, in appropriate layperson's language, answer the question asked and then stop. Do not volunteer information.
   c. Address the judge or jury when responding, rather than the attorney asking the question. Never forget that it is the jury or judge who weigh the testimony.
   d. Speak clearly, slowly, and sufficiently loud so all present can hear, remembering that the court reporter is recording the pro-

ceedings. "Yes" and "no" responses must be verbalized, not
simply head shakes.
e. Questions should never be answered in a joking or arrogant
manner.
f. Pointedly avoid exaggeration and misrepresentation in answering.
g. Answers should be given as confidently as possible.
  1. Language such as "perhaps" or "possibly" presents problems.
    a. Mere speculation or possibility is usually not relevant to a
    legal decision, which demands at least a preponderance of
    the evidence; that is, that any proposition presented is
    more probably true than not. Therefore, in any situation
    involving less than certainty in an expert witness's testi-
    mony, the expert must be prepared to give a reasonable
    appraisal of how probable the proposition is. The usual,
    still ambiguous standard sought is "to a professional cer-
    tainty."
    b. Qualifying words like "possibly" suggest uncertainty and
    lack of confidence.
h. If the answer to a question is unknown or can only be estimated, this should be clearly stated. The expert witness is only
human and fact finders appreciate an honest recognition of this
point.
i. Avoid looking at the examining attorney or judge in a manner
that suggests seeking their assistance.
j. When an objection is made by the nonexamining attorney, stop
until the court or that attorney indicates it is acceptable to continue.

Cross-examination

After direct examination, in which the expert witness has usually been
questioned in a sympathetic manner by the requesting attorney, the opposing attorney cross-examines the witness. During cross-examination,
the opposing attorney will attempt to pigeonhole the expert witness by
asking leading questions and framing questions in a manner that requires
a "yes" or a "no" answer favorable to that attorney's position on the
case. The opposing attorney will generally seek to test the credibility of
both the substance of the expert's testimony and the expert as well.

1. Common methods of attempting to discredit the expert witness
include:
  a. Challenging the thoroughness of an evaluation by asking
  whether the examiner was aware of certain facts when performing an evaluation. Sometimes, certain facts that may bear on the
  expert's opinion surface only during the court proceedings. It is,

of course, perfectly reasonable on cross-examination to ask if those facts change the expert's opinion, as indeed they might. The requesting attorney calling the expert should apprise him or her of those facts; otherwise, the opposing attorney may take the expert by surprise, with potentially disastrous consequences for the requesting attorney's case.

b. Challenging the witness by the use of treatises giving an opinion contrary to that of the witness.

c. Challenging the witness by attempting to demonstrate that his or her viewpoint, as presented on direct examination, is either internally inconsistent or has changed over time.

d. Challenging the expert by attempting to show that he or she is incompetent because of a lack of necessary training or experience. While this will not serve to disqualify the expert after having been qualified earlier, it may reduce the value in the fact finder's eyes of any testimony given. For example, the cross-examiner may deliberately ask obscure questions from the witness's field.

e. Challenging the expert by attempting to show that he or she has a financial interest in the outcome of the case.

2. The opposing attorney may ask one or more "trick" questions in an effort to discredit the expert witness. Examples are:

a. "Have you talked to anyone about this case?" A response of "no" is easily disproved, because inevitably the witness has discussed the case with others, normally including the requesting attorney for whom he or she has already testified. A response of "yes" may lead the opposing attorney to suggest that the witness was told what to say. The best response is to simply acknowledge that the case was discussed. If the cross-examiner persists, the witness can mention that he or she was advised only to tell the truth.

b. "Are you being paid to testify in this case?" This question implies that the expert's testimony is for sale. An appropriate answer to this question is, "I am not being paid to testify. I am being compensated for time I have spent on this case and for my expenses associated with it."

3. The expert who is undergoing cross-examination must remember that his or her demeanor and style of presentation are even more important on cross-examination than on direct examination. Further considerations in this regard include:

a. Above all, remain calm and answer the opposing attorney's questions in a courteous manner. Nothing is worse than emotionalism on the witness stand. A cross-examiner able to provoke an expert to an emotional display has scored a major triumph.

b. Ask to have a question repeated if it is not clearly understood.

   c. Indicate when a "yes" or "no" answer is insufficient and that an explanation is necessary by answering, "That requires more explanation than a simple 'yes/no' answer." (Remember that the cross-examiner will attempt to restrict the witness to "yes" or "no" answers.)

   d. Refrain from asking the judge if an answer must be given to a question. If the question is improper, the requesting attorney should object to it. Remember that the court proceedings are primarily orchestrated by the attorneys. If the attorney who requests the expert's presence is at all competent, he or she will know better than the expert whether to object to a question or allow it to be presented to the expert without challenge. It is advisable for the expert and the requesting attorney to discuss in advance how to deal with such questions on cross-examination.

Redirect Examination

After cross-examination is concluded, the requesting attorney who originally called the expert witness will have the opportunity to *redirect examination*. This gives that attorney and the witness the opportunity to offer clarification on any points made by the opposing attorney during cross-examination. A further round of cross-examination may follow the redirect examination.

Systemic Understandings and Expert Testimony

Meyerstein and Todd (1980) asserted that marriage and family therapists who can transfer their systemic understandings from the therapy context to the courtroom significantly enhance their effectiveness as expert witnesses. These authors paralleled the courtroom context with a family environment. For example, they noted the unique physical arrangement seen upon entering a courtroom that graphically conveys the hierarchy of positions and nature of the contest. Likewise, the activities of the courtroom are governed by rules that possess their own internal logic and order; a system based on a theory predicating that the truth will emerge from the oppositional presentation of the best arguments that can be made for each side of the conflict.

Meyerstein and Todd (1980) proposed that marriage and family therapists enter the courtroom and redefine the setting as simply a different kind of system. Although different, it is still a system where certain predictable phenomena occur. The therapist's task is to apply available information and transfer it to the interactional skills within the court context. Particularly valuable strategic suggestions in this regard included redefining the problem and dealing with resistance.

Redefining the Problem

Perhaps the key technique of a skilled marriage and family therapist is the art of redefining the problem or *reframing* (Watzlawick, Weakland, & Fish, 1974). The therapist challenges the couple or family's view of a problem and presents an alternative explanation of the same set of facts in a way that facilitates change through a shift in context. In utilizing reframing, the witness should feel free to engage in a persuasive teaching and advocacy of his or her position (Brodsky & Robey, 1972). This will often entail elaboration, systematic repetition, and intensification of ideas using commonsense examples familiar to laypersons to clearly illustrate concepts.

Meyerstein and Todd (1980) described the case example of a marriage and family therapist called upon to give testimony as an expert witness in a civil commitment suit filed against an adult male by his parents. The prosecutor portrayed the defendant as insane and beyond rehabilitation. His advocating for an indefinite commitment to a state institution suggested a belief that contextual family and community factors were irrelevant both to the defendant's emotional disturbance and his treatment. The therapist as expert witness sought to provide a clearer, more encompassing contextual view:

> **Question:** Are you saying that the blame can't really be placed on either side?
>
> **Answer:** All of them participated in this situation and the outcome was a result, but it's not really one party's fault. The parents have a good deal of love for both their boys, but in their parenting approach they had been so lenient with them that they never put any regulation on them, and they were so worried about their welfare that they could never leave them alone. If he was six or eight I would say that he was a bad boy, that he was disobedient, stubborn and childish. He's not six or eight or 10, but 29. Perhaps he should be seen as an ungrateful son. No doubt, in recent events the defendent equally participated in maintaining the closeness in the family which became detrimental to his and the parents' growth. The defendant has continued to reinvolve his parents and they comply. There is no question . . . the difficulty separating has been a two-sided thing. (p. 47)

The therapist viewed her task as one of illustrating an interactional picture of the problem by highlighting, in a sympathetic manner, participation of family members in maintaining the defendant's problem. Furthermore, the witness utilized developmental analogies to reframe the behavior in question from "sick" to "immature" and "disobedient," to construct a more normalized and, thus, treatable view of the disability.

Dealing with Resistance

The marriage and family therapist is no stranger to the strategic handling of resistance in therapy situations. The most effective path is to initially go with and then redirect the resistance. This skill is particularly relevant during cross-examination in the courtroom setting as well. The cross-examining attorney ordinarily has a well-practiced repertoire consisting of clever phrasings. The grammatical logic of these phrases intend to create doubt and rejection of the expert witness' testimony in the minds of the judge or jury. Any discrepancy uncovered in the testimony given may cause the witness to redouble efforts at explaining apparent inconsistencies. Backtracking and correcting misimpressions may leave the witness looking flustered and defensive.

A common tack used by cross-examining attorneys in this regard is: "Would you be surprised if I were to tell you that. . . . ?" Meyerstein and Todd (1980) offered the following example taken from a right to treatment suit on behalf of mental hospital patients:

> **Question:** So, would you assume that the people in the higher staff positions are basically unfamiliar with the community based programs, that sort of orientation?
>
> **Answer:** I would suspect that, yes.
>
> **Question:** Would it surprise you if I were to tell you that [the hospital superintendent] is a former Executive Director of [a] community mental health center?
>
> **Answer:** Yes, that would surprise me.
>
> **Question:** Would it surprise you to know that he was a consultant to the Department of Health, Education, and Welfare, in community mental health, from 1970 to '74?
>
> **Answer:** Based on the operation he's running at [the mental hospital], that surprises me a great deal. (pp. 49–50)

Being opaque and calling the questioner's bluff with a calm "Yes, that would surprise me" is obviously preferable to equivocating and attempting to reconcile apparent inconsistencies. And, if the cross-examining attorney does procure contradictory evidence to compromise the witness, it is still possible for the witness to have an opportunity to explain on redirect examination. The expert witness should pursue proper preparation to be sure of his or her facts and conclusions.

PROFESSIONAL LIABILITY UNDER THE LAW

Always implicit, and frequently explicit, in legal discussions regarding the practice of marriage and family therapy is the concept of therapists' responsibility and professional liability. Most legal authorities agree that if a therapist is to act legally, then he or she must behave responsibly. Responsible behavior would seem clearly to be at least a necessary, if not a sufficient, condition for legal behavior (Widiger & Rorer, 1984). Legally, therapists have a responsibility to communicate to their clients an honest representation of their skills and methods, along with the conditions of treatment, fees, appointment schedules, and any special obligations incumbent upon either the therapist and client. Clients' informed consent should always be obtained. The understanding that develops during the initial contacts becomes, in effect, an unwritten agreement. (The terms of therapy may be agreed to in a written document as well.) Each party has a responsibility to abide by the agreement. If the agreement is breached, the remedy may be legal action (Van Hoose & Kottler, 1985). Marriage and family therapists' major areas of legal responsibility and thus liability are centered on civil liability, including contract law, unintentional torts or malpractice, and intentional torts (Schultz, 1982).

Contract Law

Contractually, marriage and family therapists' legal responsibility to their clients and thus their liability comes from a conception of the therapist-client relationship as a fiduciary one. *Black's Law Dictionary* (1968) defines a *fiduciary* relationship as: "It exists where there is a special confidence reposed in one who in equity and good conscience is bound to act in good faith and with due regard to interests of one reposing the confidence" (p. 753).

A fiduciary relationship is, in essence, based on trust; the therapist, as fiduciary of the client's trust, cannot serve his or her own needs in preference to those of the client. Schultz (1982) stated that a therapist is not strictly a fiduciary because the commonly called-for requirement of absolute candor is normally not present: "The therapeutic privilege—instances where the therapist withholds information in the interest of the patient and the treatment—may contraindicate it; and the maintenance of early rapport, so that later confrontations may be handled, also cuts into the degree of candor that best serves the patient" (pp. 12–13). On the other hand, since the therapeutic relationship is also a fee-for-services relationship, it has implied contractual elements and legal responsibility and thus liability is present through contract law.

Schultz (1982) raised a number of situations in which therapists might be liable under contract law. For example, the fee-for-services aspect of the therapeutic relationship can be conceived as creating circumstances wherein the therapist has a compelling personal interest taking precedent over the client's; namely preserving his or her income. Marriage and family therapists could be open to a charge of fiduciary abuse in recommending that a couple or family not terminate treatment or that the frequency of sessions be increased without a sound therapeutic rationale. Likewise, the therapist who tells clients that treatment will be successful can be sued for breach of warranty if the predicted outcome does not occur. Reassurances should always be couched in probabilistic terms. Therapists who hold themselves out as guarantors of success can be held to that, even though it is not a normally expected responsibility.

Marriage and family therapists can more definitively carry out their legal responsibilities by the use of explicit, written contracts specifying roles and duties. They can shape such contracts to accurately reflect what they can provide for a fee. At the same time, however, precisely because of their clarity, expressed contracts can make breach of contract or warranty easier to prove. Moreover, reducing the complexity involved in the therapeutic enterprise to the confined context of an explicit contract may reinforce clients' tendency to view the relationship solely in terms of the conditions described in the contract, therefore increasing the likelihood of litigation (Schultz, 1982). The contract can be pointed to, noting, "We didn't get what we paid for."

Although contractual liability is a potential source of litigation, it has been a relatively infrequent approach to legal liability for psychotherapeutic dissatisfaction (Hendrickson, 1982; Schultz, 1982). Primary liability has been through tort liability.

In general, *tort liability* is a civil wrong that does not arise out of contractual liability (Hendrickson & Mangum, 1978). Torts arise out of a responsibility to protect individuals from harm resulting from socially unacceptable behavior. A *tort* is a type of harm done to an individual in such a manner that the law orders the person who inflicts the harm to pay damages to the injured party. Torts may be intentional or unintentional.

Unintentional Torts: Malpractice

Corey et al. (1984) defined *malpractice* as "the failure to render proper service, through ignorance or negligence, resulting in injury or loss to the client" (p. 229). In order to prove malpractice, four key elements must be shown to be present (Schultz, 1982):

1. That a therapist-client relationship was established
2. That the therapist's conduct fell below the acceptable standard of care
3. That this conduct was the cause of an injury to the client
4. That an actual injury was sustained by the client

Professional Relationship

The existence of the therapist-client relationship is usually the easiest of the four elements to prove; normally, a bill for the therapist's services is sufficient evidence.

Standard of Care

Establishing the acceptable standard of care in a given case is a more difficult undertaking. First, there are numerous "schools" within the psychotherapeutic community advocating different treatment approaches to the same presenting problem. With the variety of schools in existence, almost any treatment activity will probably be endorsed somewhere. Prosser (1971), in writing on tort liability, clarifies this however, in stating:

> A "school" must be a recognized one with definite principles, and it must be the line of thought of at least a respectable minority of the profession. In addition there are minimum requirements of skill and knowledge as to both diagnosis and treatment, particular in light of modern licensing statutes which anyone who holds himself out as competent to treat human ailments is required to have, regardless of his personal views. (p. 163)

Schultz (1982) cautioned of two situations where therapists might *not* be judged according to the tenets of a particular school: (a) if the therapist does not profess membership (if, for example, he or she advocates a professional eclecticism), he or she will then be held to the standard of care of a therapist "in good standing" who will be called upon to testify as an expert witness in the case; and (b) if the approach is so innovative that the therapist is the only person capable of expert testimony, then his or her testimony will be held to a general standard of reasonableness, as evaluated by the judge and/or jury. Obviously marriage and family therapists who adhere to a particular school carry less liability in that the scope of a standard of care is clarified. Such clarity will aid those therapists falling within the scope, but it may hurt when practices employed are at odds with the school's principles or with commonsense expectations; innovation *could* appear as negligence.

Traditionally, the standard of care for psychotherapeutic practice has been based on what other practitioners in the same geographical area would do under similar circumstances. This is still the predominant frame of reference, however, with knowledge increasingly more accessible, this "locality rule" is being replaced by national standards of practice. In addition to expert testimony, published professional standards are allowed as a yardstick in a number of states, particularly if they are standards of a school or group with whom the therapist identifies.

Once a standard of care has been determined, the plaintiff must show that a breach of this standard occurred in that the therapist did not exercise (a) the minimally accepted degree of knowledge or skill possessed by other practitioners, or (b) the minimally accepted degree of care, attention, or diligence exercised in the application of that knowledge or those skills.

Proximate Cause

Once a breach of standard of care has been shown to have occurred, then that breach must be proven to be the proximate cause of the injury. *Proximate cause* is considered to be a cause that produces the injury in question in a natural and continuous sequence, unbroken by any independent intervening causes. Thus, the breach must be the direct cause of the injury.

Proximate cause is easiest to prove if the acts and the injury in question are closely related in time. As the time draws on from act to injury, the opportunity for intervening variables to intercede increases. States arbitrarily set statutes of limitations on negligence cases, thereby setting a limit on liability. It is important to know the statute of limitations in one's own jurisdiction and whether it is dated from the day of the actual injury or of the *discovery* of the injury. It should also be noted that a minor's right to sue begins when he or she comes of age, so that a therapist might be sued by a child's parents, or, depending upon the age of the child and statute of limitations, some years later by the child, now an adult.

The major defense against allegations of malpractice is the concept of contributory negligence on the client's part as an intervening cause, breaking the chain of causality between the therapist's acts and the injury. What must be proven is that the client's acts fell below the level of self-care that the average person would have exercised under the same or similar circumstances. This defense is not normally applicable to children or to clients whom a judge has declared as mentally incompetent.

Injury

If proximate cause is proven, an injury must have resulted from it. Strupp, Hadley, and Gomes-Schwartz (1977) offered a partial list of negative effects:

1. Exacerbation of the presenting symptoms (including increased depression, inhibitions, extension of phobias; increased somatic difficulties; decreased self-esteem; paranoia; obsessional symptoms; guilt; decrease in impulse control)
2. Appearance of new symptoms (including severe psychosomatic reactions, a suicide attempt, development of new forms of acting out, disruption of previously perceived stable relationships)
3. Client misuse or abuse of therapy (settling into a dependent relationship, increased intellectualization with concomitant avoidance of action, therapy as a place to ventilate and rationalize hostility, increased reliance on irrationality and "spontaneity" to avoid reflection on real-world limits)
4. Clients' overextending themselves in taking on tasks before they can adequately achieve them, possibly to please the therapist or due to inappropriate directives, leading to failure, guilt, or self-contempt
5. Disillusionment with therapy, leading to feelings of hopelessness in getting help from any relationship

Other negative effects often cited by plaintiffs as injuries emanating from psychotherapeutic malpractice include damages due to reliance on a therapist's directives, leading to divorce, job loss, economic loss, emotional harm, suicide or death of a third party, self- or non-self-inflicted injuries (Schultz, 1982).

Damages

If the four key elements of malpractice are proven, then damages will be awarded to the plaintiff. The standard of proof in civil cases is a "preponderance of the evidence." Numerically, this may be conceived of as at least a 51–49 split of the evidence, a lower standard than the criminal one of "beyond a reasonable doubt." Damages can be of two types, either compensatory for the injury, or punitive as a punishment for wanton or reckless acts. Compensatory damages generally consider past earnings lost, future earnings lost, pain and suffering, restitution to undo the damage, and/or the cost of the therapy itself (Schultz, 1982).

Intentional Torts

A number of difficulties arise when plaintiffs seek to prove the four elements in a malpractice action. These difficulties center primarily upon the inherent vagueness in the elements of standard of care and proximate cause. Barring gross misconduct, the large range of treatment options allows for great latitude in acceptable care. Also, since the "natural" course of "mental illness" is a still uncertain conception, it is difficult to prove that a therapist's action or inaction caused an alleged injury; the injury might just as easily be explained as a natural consequence of the illness. This vagueness of the elements of proof in negligence cases invites more suits than other tort actions but, at the same time, makes them harder for plaintiffs to win. In contrast, the relative clarity of the elements of proof for intentional torts makes them easier to prevent but harder to defeat in court when reality-based allegations are made (Schultz, 1982).

Generally, expert testimony is not required in cases involving intentional torts. The questions raised are more clear-cut "yes" or "no" as opposed to variable assessments of acceptability or proximate causation. The major intentional tort actions normally filed are discussed in the following paragraphs.

Battery

Schwitzgebel and Schwitzgebel (1980) stated with regard to *battery*:

> The unconsented touching of a person gives rise to a legal action in tort, even though that touching as a treatment is for the welfare of the patient and actually benefits the patient. . . . If the person consents to the touching, then there is no battery. (p. 274)

The standard of care is not a question in battery. While the act must be willful on the part of the therapist, it does not have to be based on proving intent to harm the client. Proximate cause, injury, and most importantly, lack of informed consent are the elements needed to be proven in this tort. It should be noted, however, that consent obtained without imparting adequate information nullifies the consent. Therapists must fully explain their particular treatment procedures and any possible adverse or negative consequences that may result from clients' participation. The reasoning of this requirement is that clients who know the risks involved in certain procedures would elect not to participate. Sex therapy represents an area of potential liability of particular relevance for marriage and family therapists.

Defamation

Black's Law Dictionary (1968) defines *defamation* as: "The offense of injuring a person's character, fame, or reputation by false and malicious statements" (p. 505).

Defamation may be oral, as in slander, or written, as in libel. It must be made public, and it must be injurious to the reputation of the plaintiff. There are three avenues of defense in this tort (Schultz, 1982): (a) An absolute bar to liability is that the statement is true; (b) An informed consent to release the information would indicate that the plaintiff had no reason to bar the information from being made public; and (c) The defendant can invoke the doctrine of "qualified privilege," or overreaching social duty to release the information. *Berry v. Moensch* (1958) elaborated on this latter point in setting forth the following four conditions:

1. The information must be presented in good faith and not in malice.
2. There must be a legitimate social duty to release the information.
3. The disclosure must be limited in scope to what is necessary to discharge the duty.
4. The disclosure must be only to the appropriate parties with a right to know.

Invasion of Privacy

Invasion of privacy is a violation of the right to be left alone. It requires that private facts be disclosed to more than a small group of persons and that the information must be offensive to a reasonable person of ordinary sensibilities (Schultz, 1982). Invasion of privacy can be distinguished from defamation in that even complimentary statements can be considered an invasion of privacy and such invasion need not require publication of the information, only an intrusion into an individual's private spheres. It is the fact of the invasion itself that is the question in this tort, regardless of the intent or negligence. The certain defense in this tort action is informed consent by the client.

Invasion of privacy requires unreasonable or offensive conduct. Schultz (1982) identified a number of examples in this regard:

> A therapist who makes phone calls to a patient's place of work, identifying himself as a therapist, or who sends bills and correspondence to a patient, with an identification of his relationship to the patient, might give grounds

for an invasion of privacy action. The presence of nonessential staff in treatment settings has been viewed as an intrusion on the patient's seclusion. The patient has an absolute right to refuse to be interviewed as a "case conference." (p. 11)

It is obviously important from not only an ethical but also a legal standpoint that client confidentiality be carefully maintained. The implications for this tort reach into office practices such as record keeping as well as the professional realms of research, training, and supervision.

Infliction of Mental Distress

The tort of *infliction of mental distress* normally requires outrageous conduct by the defendant. The harm done is the infliction of emotional pain, distress, or suffering. Schwitzgebel and Schwitzgebel (1980) noted that most cases have required the existence of physical injury resulting from the distress as well.

Malicious Prosecution and False Imprisonment

The tort of *malicious prosecution* is relatively difficult to prove, as it requires the plaintiff to prove malicious intent on the part of the defendant. Even grossly destructive behavior can occur without the requisite malice (Schultz, 1982). *False imprisonment* normally is brought as an action when the sufficiency of an examination or treatment are questionable, particularly in cases of involuntary commitment (Schwitzgebel & Schwitzgebel, 1980). The injury in both of these torts is usually deprivation of liberty.

Diligence and a reasonable belief on the part of the therapist that a client may be harmed or harmful should serve as adequate protection against this tort action. Completeness in examinations and regular evaluations should be standard procedure so any necessary confinement is kept to a required minimum.

Professional Liability Insurance

Therapist-client relationships resulting in court action are on the increase, with subsequent risks to the contemporary marriage and family therapist. Certainly such risks can be minimized by acting responsibly and in concert with the ethical standards of the profession and accepted practices within the field. While risk can be minimized, however, it cannot be eliminated and insurance coverage is therefore advisable (Hendrickson, 1982).

Professional liability insurance will be necessary for most marriage and family therapists to afford to pay the costs of litigation, should they be sued, as well as pay any damages, should a court find liability. Some states have indemnification statutes that provide that state or private institutions pay for damages and legal fees of employees at the end of litigation. Insurance is also advisable for these professionals as well. Since litigation may be frequently drawn out over several years, professional liability insurance will prevent these therapists from having to utilize their own personal assets to pay legal expenses *during* the litigation.

Unfortunately, "selective" and "expensive" are two adjectives that are coming to describe professional liability insurance. In 1984 property and casualty insurance companies paid out $116.10 for every $100 received in premiums with the average medical malpractice award for the same year being $950,000 ("Professional Liability," 1985). For policies already written, many companies are decreasing policy limits or setting deductibles on the coverage. Others are discontinuing coverage or continuing to write coverage only for present clients with a good claims history. The American Association for Counseling and Development's professional liability policy, for example, formerly offered coverage to all members. In 1985, members who identified themselves as psychologists in private practice were excluded from the coverage.

Professional liability insurance is available through most national and regional professional associations. The American Association for Marriage and Family Therapy, American Psychological Association, American Association for Counseling and Development, and others offer a group liability insurance plan for members. As with any insurance, the policy should be studied and exclusions recognized; for example, the just-noted American Association for Counseling and Development's 1985 policy changes relating to member psychologists. The American Psychological Association's policy was changed a few years ago to no longer cover sexual contact between clients and therapists. Other forms of legal liability may not be covered as well. There can be no coverage for intentional torts that are also crimes. It is against public policy to insure for the commission of a crime, even if the act was not intended as such.

SUMMARY AND CONCLUSIONS

Legal roles and responsibilities have become more persuasive in the practice of marriage and family therapy as consumer advocacy and stress on accountability have grown along with changes in judicial attitudes toward mental health professionals. These roles and responsibilities influence every aspect of practice and must be addressed by all marriage and family therapists.

The courts are finding an increasing number of uses for the opinions, recommendations, and therapeutic resources offered by marriage and family therapists—as a source of information leading to needed intervention by the state, as a resource for therapy services and as an expert witness. It is clear that training in this psycholegal interface must be a significant part of marriage and family therapy training. Relative to other participants in the courtroom drama, marriage and family therapists will otherwise be underprepared, however expert they are in clinical confines. The legally naive therapist will likely experience frustration and embarrassment at the hands of a skilled and well-prepared attorney within the adversarial system of the court. Moreover, his or her responsibility to best serve clients' welfare may be seriously compromised in the process because of improper preparation.

Chapters 1, 2, and 3 of this book addressed ethical responsibilities incumbent upon marriage and family therapists. There is a strong relationship between ethics and the law. Codes of ethics reflect statements by professions with respect to acceptable standards of practice; they outline members' basic responsibilities. Ethically responsible therapist behavior relating to client welfare, confidentiality, and especially informed consent not only maintain professional standards but help avoid unnecessary legal actions.

Van Hoose and Kottler (1977) asserted one major reason for the professional codes of ethics is to protect the profession from governmental regulation. Ethical codes foster professions' internal regulation of themselves rather than risk being regulated by governmental bodies. A therapist's failure to follow the published code of his or her primary professional association may result in disciplinary action and/or expulsion from that group. Van Hoose and Kottler (1985) noted, however:

> Professional societies have no legal power per se, and their standards, however, appropriate, may be unenforceable without statutes to back them up. Thus, laws may become necessary to prevent practice by unqualified persons, to prevent abuses, to protect the general public and the professions from charlatans and quacks, and to discipline offenders. (p. 70)

Ultimately, ethical responsibilities thus equate with legal responsibilities; neither can be ignored. Marriage and family therapists need to educate themselves with regard to both. Chapter 5 will look specifically at family law while chapter 6 will provide case examples and critiques offering further opportunities to expand one's knowledge base in this area.

RECOMMENDED RESOURCES

Cohen, R. J., & Mariano, W. E. (1982). *Legal guidebook in mental health.* New York: The Free Press.
Coogler, O. J. (1978). *Structured mediation in divorce settlement.* Lexington, MA: D.C. Heath.
Haynes, J. M. (1981). *Divorce mediation: A practical guide for therapists and counselors.* New York: Springer.
Reppucci, N. D., Weithorn, L. A., Mulvey, E. P., & Monahan, J. (Eds.). (1984). *Children, mental health, and the law.* Beverly Hills: Sage Publications.
Schultz, B. M. (1982). *Legal liability in psychotherapy.* San Francisco: Jossey-Bass.
Sidley, N. T. (Ed.). (1985). *Law and ethics: A guide for the health professional.* New York: Human Sciences Press.
Woody, R. H., & Associates. (1984). *The law and the practice of human services.* San Francisco: Jossey-Bass.

5

Family Law

The life circumstances confronting all couples and families and their thoughts and feelings concerning these circumstances must be considered in light of reality. Legal issues represent a major portion of that reality. When legal problems arise within the therapeutic context, clients are usually advised to consult with an attorney. Yet there can be several significant stumbling blocks in gaining meaningful assistance in the "this is a legal problem—see a lawyer" approach. Some lawyers may not be aware of, understand, or even care about relevant psychosocial or psychiatric difficulties underlying any legal problems. Consulting an attorney could initiate the involvement of marital partners or family members in a bitter adversary process, resulting in the downfall of therapeutic efforts. Once begun, litigation could become difficult to directly channel or impact on in a manner conducive to originally sought-after treatment goals (Bernstein, 1982).

Marriage and family therapists need to be familiar with these stumbling blocks and the law that affects couples and families if they are to effectively work with cases requiring the input of both legal and therapeutic objectives. Many problems that couples and families present for therapy have legal implications that cannot be ignored. Therapists must be able to effectively address both legal and therapeutic problems when they exist in tandem. Marriage and family therapists should recognize and understand relevant legal issues; not to practice law, but rather to provide basic, therapeutically relevant information; and to refer or seek appropriate consultation. Bernstein (1982) summarized this position most aptly:

> Ignorance of the law may be an excuse in the malpractice area in the sense that therapists are not liable for failure to offer legal advice nor would they be liable for failure to refer a client to an attorney. But, certainly, effective therapy must at least consider the options that are allowable and involve these options in the therapeutic process. (p. 100)

This chapter presents an overview of relevant issues in family law. However, contemporary family law in the United States is far too complex a subject to detail in depth in a single chapter. Changes in the law are constantly occurring, individual states have different rules and procedures, and courts can interpret the meaning of the law in contrasting ways. Where applicable, the primary references employed for the information presented in this chapter are "uniform" acts put forth by professional bodies for the purpose of providing common provisions for state legislatures. For example, the Uniform Marriage and Divorce Act was promulgated by the National Conference of Commissioners on Uniform State Laws in 1971. The American Bar Association approved this Act and recommended it for passage by the states in 1974. Acceptance by the American Bar Association does not imply that the Act has been equally accepted by all state legislatures; however, it does provide the model most frequently used by states to revise or prepare their own statutory provisions. To clarify specific laws in their own state, marriage and family therapists must consult that state's statutes and cases. With regard to particular legal problems, therapists are urged to consult an attorney with a reputation of specializing in family law. For a more thorough presentation of the issues addressed in this chapter, a bibliography of recommended resources concludes the chapter.

MARRIAGE AND COHABITATION

The two major forms of legal marriage are ceremonial marriage and common law marriage. *Ceremonial marriage* is performed in a ceremony before a religious or civil authority, while *common law marriage* results from partners living together as husband and wife for a specified minimum period of time without having participated in a marriage ceremony. For both forms of marriage, partners must have the legal capacity to enter into a contract and actually have made an agreement to marry (Clark, 1974).

Most marriages are ceremonial marriages. In the majority of states, there is no specified procedure for the ceremony, although most require witnesses (normally at least two) and that a marriage license has been obtained and recorded in the appropriate civil office. Section 203 of the Uniform Marriage and Divorce Act (Bureau of National Affairs, Inc., 1982) outlines this licensing procedure:

> When a marriage application has been completed and signed by both parties to a prospective marriage and at least one party has appeared before the (marriage license) clerk and paid the marriage license fee of ($ . . . . .), the (marriage license) clerk shall issue a license to marry and a marriage certificate form upon being furnished:
>
> (1) satisfactory proof that each party to the marriage will have attained the age of 18 years at the time the marriage license is effective, or will have attained the age of 16 years and has either the consent to the marriage of both parents or his guardian, or judicial approval; (or, if under the age of 16 years, has both the consent of both parents or his guardian and judicial approval); and
>
> (2) satisfactory proof that the marriage is not prohibited; and
>
> (3) a certificate of the results of any medical examination required by the laws of this State.

Requirements relating to Subsection 2 prohibiting marriage have been the subject of significant judicial scrutiny. The Supreme Court has established persons' marital choice as a fundamental right: "The freedom to marry has long been recognized as one of the vital personal rights essential to the orderly pursuit of happiness by free men" (*Loving v. Virginia*, 1967). The Supreme Court held in *Loving* that the state of Virginia could not prohibit interracial marriage between whites and members of other races because such racial classifications violated the equal protection clause of the Fourteenth Amendment and because marriage is a basic right:

> Marriage is one of the "basic civil rights of man," fundamental to our very existence and survival. To deny this fundamental freedom on so unsupportable a basis as racial classification embodied in these statutes, classifications so directly subversive of the principle of equality at the heart of the Fourteenth Amendment, is surely to deprive all the state's citizens of liberty without due process of law. The Fourteenth Amendment requires that the freedom of choice to marry not be restricted by insidious racial discriminations. Under our Constitution, the freedom to marry, or not to marry, a person of another race resides with the individual and cannot be infringed by the state.

Given that the right to marry is fundamental, the extent to which states may infringe upon that right has been incorporated in a number of judicial decisions. For example, in *Zablocki v. Redhail* (1978), the Supreme Court held a Wisconsin statute as unconstitutional. The statute required state residents who were under a court order to support minor children not in their custody to prove, before being permitted to marry, that the children were not likely to become public charges. In a similar stance, the Court of Appeals of California ruled against prison officials who sought to prevent prisoners from marrying (*In re Carrafa*, 1978). *In re Carrafa* affirmed the right to marry as a fundamental one, especially considering that many of the civil rights normally available to citizens convicted of criminal action may be curtailed.

Because the right to marry is a basic one, states can significantly interfere with this right only in the presence of a "compelling state interest" (Glendon, 1976). Prohibitions against bigamy and close incestuous marriage have been consistently upheld. Less clear is the constitutional status of restrictions against homosexual marriages, although every state that has considered this issue has ruled that such unions can be prohibited (Ruback, 1984).

Weyrauch and Katz (1983) asserted, however, that "since the courts seem to rely more on traditional community values on homosexuality than on exhaustive exploration of the underlying issues in given cases, constitutional attacks on prohibitions of homosexual marriages are likely to continue" (p. 431). They further proposed in such situations that marriage and nonmarriage not be the only alternatives considered. They identified contractual cohabitation (a partnership providing for equal division of mutually acquired property) as one likely alternative to be recognized, sooner than homosexual marriage.

Clearly the structure of the family in America has dramatically changed within the past few decades. In a parallel process, the nature and functions of marriage as a legal and social institution have seen a similar evolution. Although this evolution is ongoing, particular patterns can be discerned. A family based on marriage is still perceived as the most desirable and productive unit of society, although no longer necessarily the most stable. While procreation may continue to be a pre-dominant purpose of marriage, other forms of productiveness are being increasingly recognized; for example, the financial or educational ad-vancement of both partners by joint effort. With such ends in view, parties to a marriage are paying closer attention to the economics of the relationship than they might have in the past. Thus, marriage can be seen as acquiring many of the characteristics present in a pooling of resources for speculative investment, or as a co-ownership in gaining present and future property similar to a business partnership for profit (Weyrauch & Katz, 1983).

As a result, prenuptial agreements have taken on increased importance and recognition. A *prenuptial agreement* is a contract made by a couple before their marriage in order to modify certain legal repercussions that would otherwise occur as a result of marrying (Krause, 1977). In the past, such agreements were a rare practice confined to the elderly and rich who sought to preserve their assets. Prenuptial agreements today are being entered into by many young couples attempting to articulate their mutual expectations. Reversing earlier patterns, courts are tending to ac-cept their validity even if they contemplate and regulate the possibility of future divorce or dissolution of a marriage. The courts are increasingly leaving the nature and terms of marriage to the parties themselves rather than imposing restrictions by a formal pronouncement of policy by the state (Weyrauch & Katz, 1983).

This increased acceptance of prenuptial agreements by the courts has particular relevance for marriage and family therapists. Religious man-dates frequently call for couples contemplating marriage to seek premari-tal counseling from the clergy. Likewise, many couples considering marriage, especially for a second or third time, sensibly seek therapeutic input (from marriage and family therapists) prior to entering into mar-riage to address potential problems they may encounter. In this era of the blended family, while an early marriage was likely entered into basically unencumbered, second or third relationships should be entered only with reasonable caution regarding legal and property rights before, dur-ing, and perhaps even following the marriage, should it end in divorce. Bernstein (1982) characterized these possible circumstances in stating:

> One can easily picture the typical American family of "your" children, "my" children, and possibly "our" children. Then there is your property before marriage, my property before marriage, and our property during marriage. Then, in a later marriage, there are children and grandchildren as well, often former spouses, and business or financial arrangements and obligations of various degrees of complexity. Likewise, there might also be items of inheritance from either side of the family that can cause owner-ship problems. One can easily envision two parties immediately prior to marriage who have real and personal property, children, insurance, family obligations, and perhaps properties secured by substantial debts. (p. 96)

Couples entering into marriage should be forewarned about the legal complexities and potential consequences arising from their union in the same manner as they need to understand and address emotional and developmental tasks. Therapists who participate in premarital therapy efforts with couples should present legal issues that may impinge upon their emotional well-being. The possibility of preparing a prenuptial agreement should accompany such a discussion. Each party may clearly desire the marriage. One or both partners, however, may fear the real or imagined hazards inherent in negotiating finances and other sources of contractual conflict during this sensitive time. One or both partners may be so enamored; emotion overrules thought that should be given to realistic, concrete planning for the future.

Bernstein (1982) proposed that, at minimum, each party entering into marriage should prepare an inventory of their present assets. He recommended an accompanying prenuptial agreement that can then provide that in the event of divorce, each partner will leave the marriage with the property they brought into it. Further, the ownership, control, and characterization of property gained during the marriage can also be fixed. Thus, each partner can be secure in understanding that the interest in his or her property and monies earned from that property during the marriage remain personal, individual, and apart from that of his or her spouse. Finally, a full review of each party's insurance and estate plan should be made so each party can be comforted by the knowledge that loved ones will not be isolated and that prior family expectations and obligations will be respected.

Most states require that prenuptial agreements be in writing. Ruback (1984) reported that prenuptial agreements that concern the transfer of property before a marriage have generally been considered valid, although federal tax consequences were applicable. Similarly, agreements relating to the distribution of property on the death of one spouse have also been generally validated, assuming there was full disclosure of the spouse's financial circumstances at the time of the contract and the other spouse was fairly provided for. Ruback cautioned, however, that prenuptial agreements relating to the distribution of property and support obligations that a partner would receive in the event of a divorce have been struck down by the courts as being against the public policy of state. This suggests that such agreements encourage divorce.

Weyrauch and Katz (1983) nonetheless advocated the increasing importance and acceptance of prenuptial agreements relating to potential divorce settlements. They cited *Posner v. Posner* (1979) as a leading case in support of the proposition that parties should be able to regulate incidents of marriage breakup. According to the viewpoint alluded to as background for the case, such regulation was traditionally identified as against public policy; the conception of marriage as a personal relationship entered into for life made any contemplation of divorce seem an impairment to the marital intent. Also noted was the traditional notion of the state as a third party to the marriage contract, intervening with party autonomy. In its final decision the court stated:

> We cannot blind ourselves to the fact that the concept of the "sanctity" of a marriage—as being practically indissoluble, once entered into—held by

our ancestors only a few generations ago, has been greatly eroded in the last several decades. This court can take judicial notice of the fact that the ratio of marriages to divorces has reached a disturbing rate in many states; and that a new concept of divorce—in which there is no "guilty" party—is being advocated by many groups and has been adopted by the State of California in a recent revision of its divorce laws providing for dissolution of a marriage upon pleading and proof of "irreconcilable differences" between the parties, without assessing the fault for the failure of the marriage against either party. With divorce such a commonplace fact of life, it is fair to assume that many prospective marriage partners whose property and familial situation is such as to generate a valid antenuptial agreement settling their property rights upon the death of either, might want to consider and discuss also—and agree upon, if possible—the disposition of their property and the alimony rights of the wife in the event their marriage, despite their best efforts, should fail.

Prenuptial agreements concerning obligations and duties during marriage are also increasingly being prepared. These agreements attempt to regulate areas such as sexual practices, finances, and religious upbringing and education of children. These latter agreements, however, have been rarely enforceable because of courts' increasing reluctance to intrude in ongoing marriages (Ruback, 1984).

Given this shifting emphasis toward marriage as a legal partnership with a corresponding acceptance of prenuptial agreements, marriage, except in the formal legal sense as a symbol, is becoming decreasingly necessary. While the practice of living with someone of the opposite sex without being married is old, it appears to be more common today (Glendon, 1980). A number of reasons have been offered to explain this increase in cohabitating couples (Lavori, 1976):

1. The desire by couples to avoid the sex-stereotyped allocation of roles associated with marriage
2. The feeling that unless children are involved, marriage is unnecessary or irrelevant
3. A lack of readiness to commit oneself completely
4. The idea that one cannot predict how he or she will feel in the future and so promises should not be made that potentially cannot be kept or may not promote desirable outcomes
5. The desire to avoid the legal involvement and expense inherent in a possible divorce
6. A conscientious objection to marriage on the part of some couples
7. The belief that legal sanction of a relationship is irrelevant and meaningless

Corresponding to this increase in cohabitation among couples has been a trend for individuals to seek court action when the relationship ends to divide property that was obtained during the period of cohabitation (Cruchfield, 1981). This was exemplified in the well-publicized case of *Marvin v. Marvin* (1976) in which the California Supreme Court held that the cohabitating couple, actor Lee Marvin and his partner, could make an express contract affecting their property rights as long as sex was not part of the consideration for the agreement. In responding to the question of precedence in legal theory and practice set by *Marvin v. Marvin,* Weyrauch and Katz (1983) concluded:

> An express contract of cohabitation is not likely to raise serious problems; courts will be increasingly inclined to enforce well-drafted ones. Since one of the many functions of express contracts of cohabitation is to refute any presumption of marriage, as well as limit judicial discretion, express contracts may become an alternative available to the literate American middle classes. That is, if they choose not to protect themselves by formal marriage, they will be able to protect themselves through written contractual stipulation. (p. 204)

Not all states have followed the decision handed down in *Marvin v. Marvin.* Where not, however, the general trend has been to incorporate concepts from other areas of the law to address the obvious fact that a legal remedy is often needed to divide property obtained by couples cohabitating without being married. Such borrowed concepts include implied contract, implied partnership, and constructive trust (Douthwaite, 1979; Hennessey, 1980). The position of the prudent practitioner of marriage and family therapy in all of these instances is a recommendation to formalize relationship interests whether through ceremonial marriage or legal contract. Still, equitable legal remedy is likely available, although more questionable in its ultimate outcome as well as the effort necessary to secure a successful decision.

PARENT-CHILD RELATIONSHIPS

Ruback (1984) identified five frames of reference for considering parent-child relationships under the law: legitimacy, paternity, adoption, surrogate parenthood, and abortion.

Legitimacy and Paternity

Legitimate children are those who are held as having a "full legal relationship" with both of their parents (Krause, 1977). Generally, the marital status of the parents determines legitimacy of children. Because of the importance of identifiable and stable family relationships for society, the law presumes that children born to married women are the offspring of their husbands (Rauch, 1984).

Children identified as illegitimate were, until relatively recently, denied benefits relating to such things as support, inheritance, and wrongful death claims. While discrimination is still present to some degree in cases of legitimacy determination, the Supreme Court has offered judicial opinions that have struck down most legislation denying benefits to nonmarital children. For example, the Supreme Court found in *Weber v. Aetna Casualty & Surety Co.* (1972) that there is no justifying state interest for denying workers' compensation benefits to the dead father's un-acknowledged, illegitimate children. Likewise, in *Gomez v. Perez* (1973), the Supreme Court decided that illegitimate children are guaranteed a right of support from their father.

The different states vary in the types of proceedings used to make paternity determinations. Some states settle paternity issues in civil pro-ceedings. Other states determine paternity as an adjunct to a criminal proceeding. As a result of contrasting types of proceedings, various standards of proof and presumptions of paternity are employed. Section 4 of the Uniform Parentage Act (Bureau of National Affairs, Inc., 1976) is that portion of the Act dealing with the ascertainment of parentage and provides a common statutory framework that has been presented to the states by the National Conference of Commissioners on Uniform State Laws:

(a) A man is presumed to be the natural father of a child if:

(1) he and the child's natural mother are or have been married to each other and the child is born during the marriage, or within 300 days after the marriage is terminated by death, annulment, declaration of invalidity, or divorce, or after a decree of separa-tion is entered by a court;

(2) before the child's birth, he and the child's natural mother have attempted to marry each other by a marriage solemnized in appar-ent compliance with law, although the attempted marriage is or could be declared invalid, and,

(i) if the attempted marriage could be declared invalid only by a court, the child is born during the attempted marriage, or within 300 days after its termination by death, annulment, declaration of invalidity, or divorce; or

(ii) if the attempted marriage is invalid without a court order, the child is born within 300 days after the termination of cohabi-tation;

(3) after the child's birth, he and the child's natural mother have mar-ried, or attempted to marry, each other by a marriage solemnized in apparent compliance with law, although the attempted mar-riage is or could be declared invalid, and

(i) he has acknowledged his paternity of the child in writing filed with the (appropriate court or Vital Statistics Bureau),

(ii) with his consent, he is named as the child's father on the child's birth certificate, or

(iii) he is obligated to support the child under a written voluntary promise or by court order;

(4) while the child is under the age of majority, he receives the child into his home and openly holds out the child as his natural child; or

(5) he acknowledges his paternity of the child in a writing filed with the (appropriate court or Vital Statistics Bureau), which shall promptly inform the mother of the filing of the acknowledgment, and she does not dispute the acknowledgment within a reason-able time after being informed thereof, in a writing filed with the

(appropriate court or Vital Statistics Bureau). If another man is presumed under this section to be the child's father, acknowledgment may be effected only with the written consent of the presumed father or after the presumption has been rebutted.

(b) A presumption under this section may be rebutted in an appropriate action only by clear and convincing evidence. If two or more presumptions arise which conflict with each other, the presumption which on the facts is founded on the weightier considerations of policy and logic controls. The presumption is rebutted by a court decree establishing paternity of the child by another man.

Section 12 of this same Uniform Parentage Act identifies evidence courts can be expected to employ relating to paternity cases:

(1) evidence of sexual intercourse between the mother and alleged father at any possible time of conception;

(2) an expert's opinion concerning the statistical probability of the alleged father's paternity based upon the duration of the mother's pregnancy;

(3) blood test results, weighted in accordance with evidence, if available, of the statistical probability of the alleged father's paternity;

(4) medical or anthropological evidence relating to the alleged father's paternity of the child based on tests performed by experts. If a man has been identified as a possible father of the child, the court may, and upon request of the party shall, require the child, the mother, and the man to submit to appropriate tests; and

(5) all other evidence relevant to the issue of paternity of the child.

In paternity suits, a judgment that a man is a child's father normally incorporates an order that the father pay periodic support for the child. Also included may be an order for the father to pay the mother's expenses for the pregnancy and birth, as well as expenses incurred in prosecuting the paternity suit (Krause, 1977).

Adoption

Adoption is the legal process by which children acquire parents other than their natural parents and parents acquire children other than their natural children (Clark, 1968). In the event of adoption, the rights and duties between a child and his or her natural parents are ended and replaced by rights and duties between the adoptive parents and the child. All states permit adoption of children and minors (Krause, 1977).

Most adoptions of children by nonrelatives are supervised and take place through adoption agencies. Private adoptions are legal in certain states; however, some contact with a public child welfare agency is still required before a legal adoption can occur. The extent of this required contact varies. Some states merely require that parents provide notification of the prospective adoption to the appropriate regulatory agency. In other states, the agency investigates the prospective parents, and in still others it totally controls the adoption process. Criminal prosecution is possible in some states if an adoption takes place without the requisite agency involvement, particularly if the natural parents receive compensation beyond what is required for medical, legal, and appropriate administrative expenses (Krause, 1977).

Despite the threat of criminal prosecution, there is an extensive black market in "desirable" (usually meaning healthy and white) babies. Likewise, independent adoptions where available are also steadily increasing. It is often more advantageous for natural mothers to participate in a private as opposed to public adoption. The former process is often viewed as less demeaning and mothers who give their children up for public adoption are not likely to be reimbursed for medical and living expenses as they are with private adoptions. Further, the natural parent can occasionally meet the adopting parents, a practice that is almost impossible in public adoptions (Ruback, 1984).

A point currently lacking clarity with regard to adoption relates to the right of a nonmarital father in proceedings by others to adopt his children. The Supreme Court in *Stanley v. Illinois* (1972) held that an unwed father was entitled to notice and a hearing concerning the disposition of his children. A major factor in this decision, however, was the fact that the father had lived with the children in a *de facto* family unit (Krause, 1977). Although many state courts have interpreted *Stanley v. Illinois* to mean that an unmarried father's consent is needed for a valid adoption, two more recent Supreme Court decisions (*Caban v. Mohammed,* 1979; *Quilloin v. Walcott,* 1978) identified limits to the power of unmarried fathers over an adoption procedure. These limits refer to unmarried fathers who have never had or sought custody or did not maintain frequent contact with their children.

Surrogate Parenthood

Recent years have seen a pronounced increase in the number of instances where only one member of a marital dyad is the natural parent of their child (Ruback, 1984). With regard to artificial insemination of the mother from a donor who is not the husband, presumptions as to legitimacy and paternity are relatively clear. Section 5 of the Uniform Parentage Act (Bureau of National Affairs, Inc., 1976) precisely specifies:

(a) If, under the supervision of a licensed physician and with the consent of her husband, a wife is inseminated artificially with semen donated by a man not her husband, the husband is treated in law as if he were the natural father of a child thereby conceived. The husband's consent must be in writing and signed by him and his wife. The physician shall certify their signatures and the date of the insemination, and file the husband's consent with the (State Department of Health), where it shall be kept confidential and in a sealed file. However, the physician's failure to do so does not affect the father and child relationship. All papers and records pertaining to the insemination, whether part of the permanent record of a court or of a file held by the supervising physician or elsewhere, are subject to inspection only upon an order of the court for good cause shown.

(b) The donor of semen provided to a licensed physician for use in artificial insemination of a married woman other than the donor's wife is treated in law as if he were not the natural father of a child thereby conceived.

A situation with relation to surrogate parenthood that is less clear is the use of a surrogate mother to bear the child of a father whose wife is unable to. Major questions regard financial considerations, possible criminal penalties, and the unenforceability of the contracts between the parties (Ruback, 1984). Financial considerations involve the surrogate mother's medical expenses (including prepregnancy, medical, and psychological screening) and compensation to her for the pregnancy. Paying the surrogate mother for her services can make the procedure a crime in some states where statutes have been enacted outlawing payments to parents for their consent to an adoption of their children. Handel and Sherwyn (1982) have asserted that these statutes are likely unenforceable because of their vagueness and the fact that they may violate constitutional guarantees of privacy.

A potentially more volatile concern is the question of surrogate mothers who ultimately decide to keep their children. To overcome this possible circumstance, prospective parents and surrogate mothers often sign contracts prior to the pregnancy designed to allay this problem. Handel and Sherwyn (1982) cautioned, however, that such contracts are likely unenforceable.

Abortion

Roe v. Wade (1973) represented a landmark Supreme Court decision on the subject of abortion. In it, the Court examined the state's interests in regulating abortion. The Court held that during the first three months of pregnancy, a mother's right to privacy is paramount and the state has no compelling interest that outweighs this right; during the second three months, the state has a compelling interest in the mother's health and therefore can establish reasonable regulations for the abortion procedure; during the last three months, the state has a compelling interest in safeguarding the life of the fetus. Thus, the Supreme Court asserted that the state can regulate and even ban abortion. However, in *Doe v. Bolton* (1973), a companion case to *Roe v. Wade*, the Court declared unconstitutional a Georgia statute that was too restrictive of abortion. Among other things, this law required that abortions be performed only in accredited hospitals and only after approval by a hospital abortion committee.

The Supreme Court addressed the issue of whether consent from a woman's husband or parent is required prior to an abortion being performed in *Planned Parenthood of Central Missouri v. Danforth* (1976). The Court held that both adult and minor women have a constitutional right to reproductive privacy; no spousal or parental consent thereby being necessary for an abortion to be procured. However, the Court also suggested that the constitutional right may be restricted with less justification than adults. Justice Blackman, writing for the Court, described the right as extending to the "competent minor, mature enough to have become pregnant." Shortly thereafter, however, he further noted that "not every minor regardless of age or maturity may give effective consent for the termination of her pregnancy."

Thus, the extent to which a state might involve parents in their child's reproductive decision was left unsettled in *Planned Parenthood of Central Missouri v. Danforth*. In *Bellotti v. Baird (II)* (1979), the Supreme Court held that while a state may require parents' consent as one form of access to abortion, an alternative, either a judicial or administrative proceeding, must be available to the minor woman who is reluctant to approach her parents. If she demonstrates that she is "mature and competent to make the abortion decision," to the satisfaction of a judge or other state decision-maker, she must be allowed to act independently. Even if she fails to establish her capacity to make a mature decision, the abortion should be authorized if it is determined to be in her best interest.

Although the ruling in *Bellotti v. Baird (II)* represents an avenue to abortion for the minor woman who does not want to seek parental permission, it still presents a forbidding path to the teenager lacking experience or knowledge of legal procedures. A requirement that minors pursue a legal remedy to prove their ability to make an abortion decision can potentially lead to delayed decisions (and hence more risky abortions), illegal abortion, and an increased incidence of unwanted childbirth (Torres, Forest, & Eisman, 1980). The necessity for marriage and family therapists to provide basic information relative to these legal issues, along with traditional therapeutic assistance, is obvious in working with a pregnant teenager and/or her family.

These Supreme Court decisions have established that states may not require that minor woman must have parental consent to obtain an abortion. Notice to parents of any abortion, however, may be an acceptable restriction. In *H. L. v. Matheson,* (1981), the Supreme Court held constitutional a Utah law requiring physicians to give notice to parents when performing an abortion on a minor. The Court suggested several significant state interests were served by the statute. These included encouraging pregnant minors to seek advice from their parents, preserving the integrity of the family, and protecting the adolescent. The assumption that all informed parents will respond in a manner beneficial to their daughter's interests has been questioned. While many parents may be supportive, it would seem equally plausible that others will respond negatively (Scott, 1984). Marriage and family therapists' understanding of this legal dilemma confronting involved parties is obviously critical in carrying out effective counseling as well as potential crisis intervention efforts.

PARENTAL RIGHTS AND RESPONSIBILITIES

That area of primary legal impact upon parents' rights and responsibilities relative to their children are those state statutes addressing child maltreatment: neglect and abuse. Rosenberg and Hunt (1984) characterized legal issues in cases of child maltreatment as "an evolving attempt to balance the often competing interests of state, parent, and child" (p. 83). They described the interests of the state and the child as requiring that children be protected from serious harm, such as might result from abuse or neglect. Parent and child interests require that the family be free from unnecessary intrusion by the state. In circumstances where parents act in ways inconsistent with their children's best interests, the state can assume the role of parent in protecting children's welfare, thereby overriding parental authority. There has been ongoing debate, however, as to the state's ability to provide alternatives that are as good or better than children's own family situation (Mnookin, 1973; Wald, 1976, 1982).

The state's right to intrude upon a family derives from two distinct sources: its police power and the concept of parens patriae. The *police power* is the state's inherent power to prevent its citizens from harming one another, as well as its mandate to promote all aspects of the public welfare. *Parens patriae* is the limited paternalistic power of the state to protect and promote the welfare of certain individuals (e.g., children) who lack the capacity to act in their own best interests (Rosenberg & Hunt, 1984). The state's exercise of parens patriae over children, however, is limited: it is used solely to further the best interests of children. Before intervening, the state must show that children's parents or guardians are either unfit, unable, or unwilling to care for them (Mnookin, 1973).

This latter point has been most controversial, becoming associated and further delimiting parens patriae by the "void for vagueness" doctrine. As applied herein, this doctrine concerns potential infringement of parents' due process rights and is composed of three distinct, yet related, components providing the basis for judicial consideration (Day, 1977). The concept of "fair warning" comprises the central component of the doctrine and requires that a statute be worded clearly so that parents are given adequate notice of what behaviors are considered illegal. The second component, an antidiscretionary element, concerns the potential for arbitrary judicial enforcement of ambiguously worded statutes. The third component considers whether a component is too broad; that is, there is a strong potential that legal as well as illegal behavior might be prosecuted.

Alsager v. District Court of Polk County, Iowa (1975) was a precedent-setting family law case that illustrated the importance of the void for vagueness doctrine as well as the tension between the state's parens patriae interests and parents' autonomy. In this case, the Supreme Court of Iowa acted "in the best interest of the child" to terminate the parents' rights with respect to five of the six Alsager children. The stated grounds for doing so were that the parents "substantially and continuously or repeatedly refused to give the child necessary parental care and protection" and that they were "unfit parents by reason of . . . conduct . . . detrimental to the physical or mental health or morals of the child."

The parents successfully appealed this initial decision; the appeals court held that the evidence presented in the termination proceeding was insufficient to warrant severing the parent-child relationship. For example, evidence entered into the proceedings identified that the parents "sometimes permitted their children to leave the house in cold weather without winter clothing on, allowed them to play in traffic, to annoy neighbors, to eat mush for supper, to live in a house containing dirty dishes and laundry, and to sometimes arrive late at school." The decision to order the initial temporary removal of the children from the home was based on a 20-minute visit by a probation officer who found that the only occupants at that time included the mother and her youngest child, who was less than a year old. Further, following the children's removal from the home, they spent the next 5 years in a total of 15 separate foster homes and 8 juvenile home placements. The decision to terminate the parental rights was determined to have failed to provide the children with increased stability or improved lives.

While few would argue that severe, purposefully inflicted physical injury or a clear diagnosis of failure to thrive constitutes abuse in the first instance and neglect in the latter, the majority of reported abuse and neglect cases fall somewhere along a continuum of "potential" child maltreatment. The importance of clearly defining and delineating instances of abuse and neglect was aptly noted by Wald (1975) in considering psychological harm to children emanating from abusive and neglectful caretaker behaviors:

> While emotional damage to a child should be a basis for intervention in some cases, it is essential that laws be drafted in a manner consistent with our limited knowledge about the nature and causes of psychological harm. Intervention should not be premised on vague concepts like "proper parental love" or "adequate affectionate parental association." Such language invites unwarranted intervention, based on each social worker's or judge's brand of "folk psychology." Although such language might clearly apply to parents who refuse to hold, talk to, or engage in any contact with their children, it could also be applied to parents who travel a great deal and leave their children with housekeepers, who send their children to boarding school to get rid of them, or who are generally unaffectionate people. (pp. 1016–1017)

Ruback (1984) proposed that court procedures are usually in the best interests of allegedly abused or neglected children. In child protective court proceedings in most states, involved children are provided representation by an independent agent, an attorney or lay guardian ad litem ("in a law suit") appointed by the court. This party represents the child's interests as opposed to the parents or the state. Prior screening tends to eliminate the majority of those cases that do not belong in court and often acts as a precipitant for families to seek therapeutic assistance and/ or change their potentially destructive interactions. Court proceedings are generally dismissed when there is insufficient evidence of abuse or neglect, the child is in no danger of further harm, the harm from potential state intervention outweighs any dangers posed by the parents, a mature child asks that a petition be dismissed, and the parents voluntarily accept treatment (Besharov, 1982).

The latter "voluntary" acceptance of treatment services is frequently the result of pressures from professionals to "take advantage" of these services in lieu of threatened court action (Rosenberg & Hunt, 1984). Further, most families who proceed through court action will find participation in treatment to be embodied in consequent court orders, particularly in cases where children are temporarily removed from their parents' custody. Thus, these families' contact with marriage and family therapists is common.

If a court does find that parents have abused or neglected their children, several options are available. The children may be temporarily or permanently removed from the custody of their parents. If so, a temporary or permanent guardian (an individual or a state or private agency) is appointed to take responsibility for the child's well-being. While it depends upon the facts present in individual cases, parents do not necessarily lose their parental rights (e.g., visitation) when a guardian is appointed. In severe cases of abuse or neglect, however, the state may initiate proceedings to terminate parents' rights to the custody of their children and permit the children to be adopted (Chemerinsky, 1979).

ANNULMENT AND DIVORCE

Unless a partner dies, most marriages are terminated by divorce. They may also, however, end through the process of annulment. Because the overwhelming majority of unsuccessful marriages are dissolved through divorce as opposed to annulment, the former will be given the greatest emphasis.

Annulment

Annulment is a declaration by the court that *for reasons existing at the time of a marriage,* the marriage was invalid from its inception. Common grounds for annulment include factors affecting parties' ability to enter a legal contract (such as fraud, duress, insanity, and immaturity) and factors about the parties' marriage proscribed by law (such as incest or bigamy). The traditional difference between court actions initiated for annulment and those initiated for divorce is that the grounds for annulment must have occurred prior to the marriage, such as preexisting insanity or fraud, usually combined with an allegation that marital consent had been impaired as a result. In contrast, divorce conceptually requires grounds that occurred after the marriage.

Weyrauch and Katz (1983) reported that requests for annulment today are rare and frequently involve cases in which one party, because of strong feelings, is particularly aggrieved. Allegations necessary to obtain an annulment can be difficult to adequately prove to a court's satisfaction. For example, in *Larson v. Larson* (1963), the Appellate Court of Illinois ruled that the plaintiff, the husband, had not clearly and definitively satisfied the burden of proving that his wife was insane at the time of their marriage even though she had numerous inpatient hospitalizations during their 10 years of marriage. In commenting on this case, Weyrauch and Katz (1983) emphasized that insanity as used for purposes of an annulment action is not necessarily identical with common psychiatric conceptions of mental illness. Specific complications in this case surrounded the psychiatric classification of schizophrenia.

Because of the difficulty in obtaining annulments and to avoid the need for filing new complaints, many attorneys are inclined to combine requests for annulment with alternative requests for divorce. There are situations, however, wherein obtaining of an annulment as opposed to a divorce can be critical. Examples include efforts to receive a pension or Social Security benefits from a preexisting marriage.

Divorce

Many couples originally seek therapy in the hope of preserving and enhancing their marriage. The result of therapeutic efforts is often a more vibrant, healthier marriage. By contrast, however, therapeutic efforts also can create an increased awareness in one or both partners that the costs of maintaining the marriage greatly outweigh the potential benefits. Should this be the case, the therapist involved with the couple leading up to their decision to divorce is then often excluded from the divorce proceedings as the couple seeks legal assistance. It is important that marriage and family therapists work with couples past the point of deciding to divorce; a couple must be prepared to deal with the win-lose legal process they are about to enter.

Most couples, particularly those seeking an amicable divorce, seldom consider in advance that they might be thrust into a bitterly competitive struggle. While they have heard stories of divorce and custody battles, they may have agreed not to let it happen to them. After all, "We've gone through enough pain" or "We've got to work things out peacefully for the children's sake." They might even have worked out an agreement in advance on everything they thought was necessary. What they did not realize is that the legal system they are entering is by its nature adversary and can work against their well-intentioned, cooperative endeavors.

Coogler (1978) addressed this issue:

> The lawyer, as an advocate, is required to represent, or advocate, *solely* the interest of his client. *He cannot represent both parties,* as is commonly supposed. The lawyer represents his client within the "light of his profes-

sional judgment." But the client's interest is always perceived as being in opposition to the interests of the other party. The lawyer cannot and does not regard the parties as having a common problem which he or she will help resolve. (p. 7)

Lawyers are ethically bound to represent their own particular client to the best of their abilities, regardless of the effect it might have on the other party. As a result, each tends to push his or her own client to win every possible advantage (Haynes, 1981). Thus, the retaining of one attorney leads to the retaining of a second for the unrepresented partner. These circumstances certainly do not support the give and take required to gain a mutually satisfying settlement. Further, much of the decision making is taken out of the couple's hands.

The battle between attorneys normally occurs outside of the courtroom. However, if attorneys cannot agree on an out-of-court settlement, the matter goes before a judge who makes the final decision. Unless they are prepared to individually and assertively push for a concerted and active involvement, neither husband nor wife will have much of an effect on the outcome. This lack of involvement often leaves both partners dissatisfied and angry at the court, the attorneys, and even more antagonistic toward each other. These potentially bitter and hostile responses frequently continue long after the marriage is legally ended, not because of the fact that it did end, but because of the way it ended. The resulting negative effects can be devastating, especially for children (Hammond, 1981; Schoyer, 1980).

Traditionally, obtaining a divorce required that one party be at fault. The original "fault" grounds were adultery and physical cruelty. These were later expanded to include habitual drunkenness, willful desertion, mental cruelty, and conviction of a felony. Since the assumption was that only the innocent party was entitled to a divorce, if it could be proven that both parties were at fault, neither one could receive a divorce. This reasoning, called the *doctrine of recrimination,* made contested divorces difficult to win. Proof of collusion between the two parties was also sufficient to bar the action for a divorce. This action was based on the state's interest in protecting marriages (Ruback, 1984).

In recent years, there has been a significant trend away from requiring fault in divorce actions. Almost every state allows for some type of "no-fault" divorce, although traditional fault grounds may still be alleged. The grounds in these no-fault actions are best represented by Section 305 of the Uniform Marriage and Divorce Act (Bureau of National Affairs, Inc., 1982):

(a) If both of the parties by petition or otherwise have stated under oath or affirmation that the marriage is irretrievably broken, or one of the parties has so stated and the other has not denied it, the court, after hearing, shall make a finding whether the marriage is irretrievably broken.

(b) If one of the parties has denied under oath or affirmation that the marriage is irretrievably broken, the court shall consider all relevant factors, including the circumstances that gave rise to filing the petition and the prospect of reconciliation, and shall:

(1) make a finding whether the marriage is irretrievably broken; or

(2) continue the matter for further hearing not fewer than 30 nor more than 60 days later, or as soon thereafter as the matter may be reached on the court's calendar, and may suggest to the parties that they seek counseling. The court, at the request of either party shall, or on its own motion may, order a conciliation conference. At the adjourned hearing the court shall make a finding whether the marriage is irretrievably broken.

(c) A finding of irretrievable breakdown is a determination that there is no reasonable prospect of reconciliation.

While finding fault is no longer required, in most states, divorce is not immediately granted merely on the parties' filing a petition. Many states have a mandatory minimum waiting period after the action is filed before the court may grant a divorce. Further, there normally must be some evidence to support the finding that the marriage is irretrievably broken (Freed & Foster, 1981). In addition, in many states, courts have at their discretion the ability to require couples to attend counseling and conciliation sessions. The stated purpose of these barriers to automatic divorce is to avoid hasty dissolution of marriages. For liberalized divorce procedures, the barriers might also still be viable and remain intact (Ruback, 1982). Such statutes that delay but do not deny access to divorce have been ruled as constitutional, the assumption being that the delay is reasonable and the state has legitimate interests protected by the requirements (Strickman, 1982). For example, in *Sosna v. Iowa* (1975), the Supreme Court upheld Iowa's requirement of a year's residency in the state for a divorce action. This requirement could be justified in several legitimate ways, other than budgetary considerations or administrative convenience (e.g., confirming that the party seeking divorce had sufficient contact with the state before important questions such as child custody were decided by the courts) (Ruback, 1984).

The requirement of counseling and conciliation sessions prior to the granting of divorce has obvious implications for marriage and family therapists. For example, an Iowa statute allows judges the power to require parties to participate in conciliation efforts conducted by the domestic relations division of the court or its representative. Orlando (1978) reported in those areas where required conciliation counseling outcome has been studied, a majority of participating couples reconcile and stay together for at least a year. Even when reconciliation was impossible, however, the required counseling was successful in reducing the number of custody disputes and contested divorces. Others have disputed the value of required conciliation efforts, suggesting them to be expensive, to have a low probability of success, and to generate overexpectations due to the shortage of trained personnel (Krause, 1977).

Given that no-fault divorce is the avenue of choice for most divorcing couples, problems relative to divorce tend to center almost completely on matters relating to property and children. Thus, marriage and family therapists seeking to prepare couples to amicably, yet assertively, address issues relative to their divorce proceedings need to be aware of matters relating to spousal maintenance (alimony) and the division of property as well as custody and support of dependent children.

Spousal Maintenance

Although newspaper headlines are sometimes made by alimony awards, about 86% of all divorces do not involve alimony (U.S. Bureau of the Census, 1981). Moreover, the amount of alimony awarded is relatively small. Statutory guidance is provided in most states for awarding alimony; however, some states provide no clear guidelines beyond considering the "wife's needs" and the "husband's ability to pay" (Ruback, 1984). Section 308 of the Uniform Marriage and Divorce Act (Bureau of National Affairs, Inc., 1982) offers a common denominator for marriage and family therapists to consider concerning alimony awards:

(a) In a proceeding for dissolution of marriage, legal separation, or maintenance following a decree of dissolution of the marriage by a court which lacked personal jurisdiction over the absent spouse, the court may grant a maintenance order for either spouse, only if it finds that the spouse seeking maintenance:
   (1) lacks sufficient property to provide for his reasonable needs; and
   (2) is unable to support himself through appropriate employment or is the custodian of a child whose condition or circumstances make it appropriate that the custodian not be required to seek employment outside the home.
(b) The maintenance order shall be in amounts and for periods of time the court deems just, without regard to marital misconduct, and after considering all relevant factors including:
   (1) the financial resources of the party seeking maintenance, including marital property apportioned to him, his ability to meet his needs independently, and the extent to which a provision for support of a child living with the party includes a sum for that party as custodian;
   (2) the time necessary to acquire sufficient education or training to enable the party seeking maintenance to find appropriate employment;
   (3) the standard of living established during the marriage;
   (4) the duration of the marriage;
   (5) the age and the physical and emotional condition of the spouse seeking maintenance; and
   (6) the ability of the spouse from whom maintenance is sought to meet his needs while meeting those of the spouse seeking maintenance.

Required alimony payments generally end with the death of the supporting ex-spouse or with the remarriage of the supported ex-spouse. In some states, alimony can be discontinued with the submission of proof that the supported ex-spouse is cohabitating with a person of the opposite sex. Further, permanent or open-ended alimony awards are significantly declining, likely reflecting the belief that alimony should be used to obtain education and training leading to self-sufficiency (i.e., rehabilitative alimony). Increasingly, however, the trend among states is away from alimony and toward a division of property. Alimony is being seen as a supplement to the division of property occurring upon divorce (Ruback, 1984).

Division of Property

One of two basic systems of marital property rights are normally operational in divorce proceedings: common law and community property (Krause, 1977). In those states where common law property rights laws are present, each spouse separately owns the property that he or she brought into the marriage and that came to him or her during the marriage by personal income, interest, or dividends from separate property; by inheritance; or through gifts. Problems arise in deciding upon the division of property primarily in regard to property bought during the marriage with money from both spouses but with the title taken in the name of only one spouse or when property is purchased with money from only one spouse but title is taken in the name of both. Courts frequently have difficulty deciding who owns what property. They attempt to answer this by reconstructing the parties' intent at the time the property was purchased (Ruback, 1984).

As is the case with spousal maintenance, statutory guidelines available to judges with regard to the division of marital property have been relatively unclear. Most often those factors taken into account relate to an evaluation of marital assets (Connell, 1981). Section 307, Alternative A of the Uniform Marriage and Divorce Act (Bureau of National Affairs, Inc., 1982) provides a common set of considerations for adoption in this regard:

> (a) In a proceeding for dissolution of a marriage, legal separation, or disposition of property following a decree of dissolution of marriage or legal separation by a court which lacked personal jurisdiction over the absent spouse or lacked jurisdiction to dispose of the property, the court, without regard to marital misconduct, shall, and in a proceeding for legal separation may, finally equitably apportion between the parties the property and assets belonging to either or both however and whenever acquired, and whether the title thereto is in the name of the husband or wife or both. In making apportionment the court shall consider the duration of the marriage, any prior marriage of either party, any antenuptial agreement of the parties, the age, health, station, occupation, amount and sources of income, vocational skills, employability, estate, liabilities, and needs of each of the parties, custodial provisions, whether the apportionment is in lieu of or in addition to maintenance, and the opportunity of each for future acquisition of capital assets and income. The court shall also consider the contribution or dissipation of each party in the acquisition, preservation,

depreciation, or appreciation in the value of the respective estates, and as the contribution of a spouse as a homemaker or to the family unit.

(b) In the proceeding, the court may protect and promote the best interests of the children by setting aside a portion of the jointly and separately held estates of the parties in a separate fund or trust for the support, maintenance, education, and general welfare of any minor, dependent, or incompetent children of the parties.

In contrast to states where common law property statutes operate, courts in states emphasizing community property rights rule that all property coming to spouses during their marriage belongs equally to the husband and to the wife. Upon divorce, community property is divided equally between the two spouses. Courts are, however, free to divide the community property as they see fit (Ruback, 1984). Section 307, Alternative B of the Uniform Marriage and Divorce Act (Bureau of National Affairs, Inc., 1982) seeks to offer a set of common considerations relative to the division of marital property where community property laws are in effect:

In a proceeding for dissolution of the marriage, legal separation, or disposition of property following a decree of dissolution of the marriage or legal dissolution by a court which lacked personal jurisdiction over the absent spouse or lacked jurisdiction to dispose of the property, the court shall assign each spouse's separate property to that spouse. It shall also divide community property, without regard to marital misconduct, in just proportions after considering all relevant factors including:

(1) contribution of each spouse to acquisition of the marital property, including contribution of a spouse as homemaker;
(2) value of the property set apart to each spouse;
(3) duration of the marriage; and
(4) economic circumstances of each spouse when the division of property is to become effective, including the desirability of awarding the family home or the right to live therein for a reasonable period to the spouse having custody of any children.

Ruback (1984) reported two important recent developments regarding the division of marital property. The first relates to property "earned" but not received during the marriage; this includes pensions and training, the latter especially through a formal education. With regard to pensions, particularly in states with community property laws, the trend has been to give the spouse (generally the wife) a property interest in the husband's pension proportional to the amount of the pension earned during the marriage (Krause, 1977). An exception has been made for military pensions. In *McCarty v. McCarty* (1981), the Supreme Court held that these pensions are controlled by federal law, not state property laws.

The second type of property earned, but not received, during the marriage is a professional degree, normally obtained by one spouse while the other works to pay for the education and support the dyad during the schooling period. Several state courts have held that the spouse who worked has an equitable interest in the value of the professional degree. For example, in *Reen v. Reen* (1981), a Massachusetts probate and family court held that a wife who sacrificed her own education and the prime child-bearing years of her life to put her husband through dental school and orthodontic training was entitled to part of the value of the degree in orthodontia.

CHILD CUSTODY AND SUPPORT AFTER DIVORCE

Parents have traditionally entered divorce proceedings believing that single-parent custody with tightly regulated visitation rights was the only option. Parents, angry with each other given the potential hostility emanating from the adversial legal process, frequently used custody controversies over children to provide a structure for dealing with their anger. Most states gave physical custody only to mothers and put sole responsibility for child support upon fathers. Times are changing, however. Mothers are working and fathers are mothering. Parenting roles have lost their gender identity as parents are increasingly becoming equally involved in raising their children, though their children are likely spending greater amounts of time in the care of others. Likewise, the male's image as "breadwinner" has been considerably blemished by the developing evidence that women have been and are providing substantially to the support of the family. These developments have had a significant impact upon child custody and support determinations in divorce proceedings.

Child Custody

Ruback (1984) proposed that child custody after divorce is best seen as a continuing problem rather than a one-time determination. He partitioned the issue initial determinations and changes in custody.

Traditionally, initial custody decisions have been based on a conceptualization termed the *tender years doctrine*. The tender years doctrine was an assumption that preadolescent children benefit most from being with their mother because only their mother could provide the particular nurturance they needed during their "tender years." Mothers were generally awarded custody of younger children unless ruled by the court to be "unfit." The term *unfit* referred to moral fitness. It was and occasionally still is an attack on a mother's morals and represented the only successful way of overcoming the tender years presumption. Children beyond their tender years were presumed to benefit more from being in the custody of their same-sex parent, thus fathers were awarded custody of sons and mothers the daughters. Exceptions usually occurred only in cases where courts were reluctant to separate siblings (Krause, 1977).

In the past two decades, the tender years doctrine has been officially discarded by the courts or legislatures in most of the states (Freed & Foster, 1981). Replacing it is the "best interests of the child" standard.

Section 402 of the Uniform Marriage and Divorce Act (Bureau of National Affairs, Inc., 1982) offers guidelines delineating the best interests standard:

> The court shall determine custody in accordance with the best interest of the child. The court shall consider all relevant factors including:
>
> (1) the wishes of the child's parent or parents as to his custody;
> (2) the wishes of the child as to his custodian;
> (3) the interaction and interrelationship of the child with his parent or parents, his siblings, and any other person who may significantly affect the child's best interest;
> (4) the child's adjustment to his home, school, and community; and
> (5) the mental and physical health of all individuals involved.
>
> The court shall not consider conduct of a proposed custodian that does not affect his relationship to the child.

Although the tender years doctrine has been superceded in most states by the best interests standard, judges still tend to have a bias that childrens' best interests are served by awarding custody to their mother. Other problems that arise in the application of the best interests standard include childrens' natural unwillingness not to want to express a preference for one parent and thereby offend the nonchosen parent, and judges' subjectivity and/or lack of professional training regarding adjustment, interactional, and mental health variables. The best interests standard also requests that judges ignore conduct of a parent that does not affect his or her relationship with the child. This provision was included to discourage parties from spying on each other to prove marital misconduct (usually sexual) for use as evidence in a custody case. Some authors have suggested, however, that marital misconduct is very often paralleled by poor parenting practices. Such misconduct might include serious emotional problems, habitual drunkenness, adultery, and gross immorality (Weiss, 1979).

In determining child custody under the best interests standard, judges often need to rely on the advice of experts. Marriage and family therapists' testimony in this regard can be very persuasive. Very frequently, parents seek the services of marriage and family therapists as do the courts themselves. For example, were testimony to be rendered by a marriage and family therapist asserting that a child's emotional needs were best met by one parent over another or that the parent's marital behaviors did not affect his or her parenting practices, that parent will obviously have a stronger case. This would be particularly so if the testimony was perceived to be objective. In fact, expert testimony regarding the emotional needs of a child is generally superior to the expressed wishes of the child (Kazen, 1977).

In initial custody determinations, four forms of custody are available today: sole custody, split custody, divided custody, and joint custody (Folberg, 1984).

1. *Sole Custody* is still the most common form of custody determination after divorce. One parent is awarded sole legal custody of the

child with visitation rights allowed to the noncustodial parent. The noncustodian, by informal agreement, may have a voice in important decisions affecting the child, but ultimate control and legal responsibility rest with the custodial parent.

2. *Split Custody* is a custody award of one or more of the children to one parent and the remaining children to the other. Courts tend, however, to generally refuse to separate siblings unless for compelling reasons. Intense hostility or competition between siblings may be one such reason. Another reason might be the inability of either parent to care for all of the children at once.

3. *Divided Custody* allows each parent to have primary custody of the child for a part of the year or every other year. This form of custody is also referred to as *alternating custody.* Each parent has reciprocal visitation rights under this arrangement, and each exercises exclusive control over the child while the child remains in his or her custody. Courts tend to most often award divided custody that provides for residence with one parent during the school year and the other during vacations. When parent's homes are separated by greater geographical distances, making frequent visitation impossible, divided custody is generally an approved award. In contrast, courts have also tended to award divided custody on the grounds that both parents live in close proximity. In these cases, this proximity was seen as minimizing the strains that divided custody might place upon children (Folberg & Graham, 1979).

4. *Joint Custody* goes beyond the concept of divided custody and may also be referred to as *shared parenting, shared custody,* or *concurrent custody.* Both parents retain legal responsibility and authority for the care and control of their child, much as in an intact family unit. The parent with whom the child is residing at a specific moment must make immediate, day-to-day decisions regarding discipline, diet, emergency care, and so on. Both parents in joint custody awards have an equal voice in their child's education, upbringing, religious training, nonemergency medical care, and general welfare. Joint custody is most often applicable where parents are able to give priority to their children's needs, are willing to negotiate differences, and can arrange their life-styles to accommodate their children's needs.

How children and their parents react to the aftermath of divorce and initial custody determinations is relevant to the law in that any problems that children experience may initiate and thus affect judgments concerning modifications of custody. The primary consideration in calling for a custody change is proof that there have been substantial changes in the custody situation that affect the welfare of the child and that have arisen subsequent to the initial award of custody (Ruback, 1984). What constitutes sufficient evidence to justify a decision to alter an initial custody determination varies from state to state. Further, changing societal values have created a mirroring change in what constitutes an unfit parent. For example, although the appeals court in one state approved a change in custody because the mother was cohabitating with a man who was not her husband (*Sims v. Sims,* 1979), in other states, such behavior is not likely to result in a change in custody. Correspondingly, a parent's homosexuality has traditionally been a bar to custody. More recently, however, many courts are requiring evidence confirming a connection between the parent's homosexuality and likely harm to the child before deciding custody (Guernsey, 1981).

Interstate custody disputes are more common. Direct attempts to alter custody decisions by seeking proof that substantial changes have occurred following the initial award emanate from violations of prior determinations of custody. Increased mobility in American society has resulted in over 47% of the population moving at least once within the past 5 years (U.S. Bureau of the Census, 1981). Thus, many divorced parents are moving to different states. Noncustodial parents have kept their child after a visitation period has ended, or simply snatched their child from the custodial parent's home and taken him or her to a second state and entered a court action there to change custody.

Prior to the adoption of the Uniform Child Custody Jurisdiction Act (UCCJA) by the vast majority of the states, it was relatively easy for an abducting parent to find a court in a second state that would not enforce a first state's custody decree. The reasons for this were based in states' sovereignty issues, judicial jurisdictional contradictions, and the fact that child custody decrees are never final (Katz, 1981). The UCCJA was designed to prevent conflicting custody decrees in two or more states. To ensure that only one state makes an official custody determination, the Act requires that parties notify the courts of any pending custody proceeding in another state and that the courts involved determine the more appropriate forum, so that the actual custody determination will be made in only one court. Thus, the predominant emphasis of the UCCJA is that only one state and one court will make a final judgment.

Child Support

Section 15 of the Uniform Parentage Act (Bureau of National Affairs, Inc., 1976) summarizes major factors to be considered by judges in deciding upon child support awards:

> In determining the amount to be paid by a parent for support of the child and the period during which the duty of support is owed, a court enforcing the obligation of support shall consider all relevant facts, including:
>
> (1) the needs of the child;
> (2) the standard of living and circumstances of the parents;
> (3) the relative financial means of the parents;
> (4) the earning ability of the parents;
> (5) the need and capacity of the child for education, including higher education;
> (6) the age of the child;
> (7) the financial resources and earning ability of the child;
> (8) the responsibility of the parents for the support of others; and
> (9) the value of services contributed by the custodial parent.

Child support awards remain in effect until a child reaches the age of majority. Complete and continued follow-through on payment of support obligations, however, represents a major problem. This is particularly the case where the parent making support payments remarries and becomes obligated to provide support to a second family. Generally, support obligations can be enforced through either civil or criminal contempt proceedings. *Contempt proceedings* call for the parent seeking support payments to show that the supporting parent has not complied with the support order and that this failure was intentional and without justification (Harp, 1982). Given evidence of willful contempt, the amount of money owed must be proved. The court will then order some method of repayment and pronounce a penalty of a fine and/or jail sentence.

Ruback (1984) suggested that although an available remedy, it makes little sense to impose a fine if a defaulting parent could not make the original support payment. Neither is it sensible to put the offender in jail, where he or she will be unable to earn the money needed to pay the support and will be costing the state money, in addition to the money the state might have to pay to support the family. Of course, these latter caveats are likely to become secondary in circumstances where a supporting parent arrogantly refuses, overtly or covertly, to comply with a court order. Aimed at motivating rather than seeking revenge, a judicial penalty may be most appropriate.

In cases where a supporting parent has remarried and has taken on obligations to a second family, an issue often arising is whether obligations to the first family should be reduced because of the new obligations to the children of the second family. The courts have generally not found such changes in circumstances to justify a reduction in previously ordered child support awards (Ruback, 1984). Further, many state courts maintain priority for the children of a first marriage, although it has been strongly suggested that all the children involved should be considered on an equal basis (Krause, 1982).

The majority of states have tended to enforce support obligations ordered in another state. The primary means of enforcing out-of-state support obligations is the Uniform Reciprocal Enforcement of Support Act (URESA) and its later revision, the Revised Uniform Reciprocal Enforcement of Support Act (RURESA). All of the states have adopted URESA in some form. Under the provisions of this Act, the parent claiming support can bring an action in a court in his or her state of residence. The action is then forwarded to a court located in the supporting parent's home state, under whose law the case will be tried. The case is heard and a judgment rendered and enforced in this second court. Monies collected under the judgment are sent to the first court and disbursed to the claimant.

The federal government is also involved in the problem of nonpayment of child support by a parent who resides in a different state or whose whereabouts are unknown. Under legislation passed in 1975 and amended in 1984, the Office of Child Support Enforcement operates as an agency within the Department of Health and Human Services. This agency assists states to find absentee parents, establish paternity, and obtain child support from the absent individuals. In the 1980 fiscal year alone, the agency collected almost $1.5 billion, about half of which was obtained on behalf of welfare families (White, 1982).

SUMMARY AND CONCLUSIONS

Family law matters account for over 50% of civil law filings in this country (Hennessey, 1980). Families are increasingly turning to the legal system for help in their problem-solving processes. Part of this willingness can be explained by the confidence expressed towards that system. Yet this often tends to be a false confidence, frequently shattered within the confines of the adversarial system of legal actions. Judges and attorneys are increasingly realizing that many of the problems presented to them are often more likely within the province of mental health rather than the law (Ruback, 1982). Thus, marriage and family therapists are being called upon to assist legal professionals.

More pressing from marriage and family therapists' perspective, however, is the need of their clients to understand and prepare for potential legal interventions into their personal problem-solving processes. For therapeutic efforts to be effective, questions of psycholegal interface must be addressed. As is evident in this chapter, family law encompasses a number of extensive and fluctuating topics. It is vital that marriage and family therapists gain some knowledge in family law to adequately assert themselves, and therefore allow their clients to do so in this regard.

The following is a list of recommended resources for marriage and family therapists. Chapter 6 provides several case examples and critiques that show how family law issues affect therapeutic experience.

RECOMMENDED RESOURCES

Areen, J. (1978). *Cases and materials on family law.* Mineola, NY: Foundation Press.

Clark, H. (1974). *Cases and problems on domestic relations.* St. Paul, MN: West Publishing.

Krause, H. D. (1977). *Family law in a nutshell.* St. Paul, MN: West Publishing.

Ploscowe, M., Foster, H., & Freed, D. (1972). *Family law: Cases and materials.* Boston: Little, Brown.

Statsky, W. T. (1978). *Domestic relations law and skills.* St. Paul, MN: West Publishing.

Waddington, W., & Paulson, M. (1978). *Domestic Relations: Cases and Materials* (3rd ed.). Mineola, NY: Foundation Press.

6

Legal Considerations

Marriage and family therapists need to be sensitive to basic legal issues inherent in their professional practices. They need to understand general guiding principles and the processes whereby our legal institutions address and resolve controversies. They should then know when to seek the advice of attorneys.

This chapter is structured to further sensitize marriage and family therapists to the legal dimensions affecting their work and to make them more aware of the legal environment in which they function. Case illustrations involving guiding legal principles are presented and explained with reference to leading laws and cases. There is no effort, however, to present an exhaustive analysis of all relevant laws and cases. Practicing attorneys may have need for all such cases, but marriage and family therapists do not.

Although this sampling represents a cross section of cases, individual state laws may differ. In addition, these cases can contain complex issues, especially as related laws and court case findings are changing. New laws are passed, regulations change, courts are persuaded by novel legal arguments, and the Supreme Court can declare a policy or law unconstitutional. Therefore, no writing related to the law is a final, definitive word at the time of its publication or a substitute for competent legal advice when specific considerations arise.

CASE 1
Divorce Mediation

A s a marriage and family therapist, Mary E. all too often had observed the negative results for families traveling through the emotional grinder of divorce and child custody court battles. Having read about divorce mediation as a potentially more positive alternative, she considered seeking training for the purpose of offering this service as a part of her practice. In discussing this pursuit with several attorneys, however, questions of significant concern arose for her. "Isn't divorce basically a legal process involving the application of legal rules and principles to the facts of the parties' lives?" She wondered. "If so, then how appropriate is it for a marriage and family therapist to offer such services?"

Considerations

The basic issue confronting Mary E. appears to revolve around the belief that divorce is first and foremost a legal event. It has become increasingly evident over the past decade that mental health professionals are taking a more active role in helping families resolve the personal and financial issues incidental to divorce. In doing this, they have found themselves moving into an area once occupied exclusively by attorneys. Marlow (1985), an attorney, argued that viewing divorce as a legal event ignores the fact that it is more importantly a personal event in a family's life. His major points are summarized in the following paragraph as an alternative for Mary E.

In What Real Sense Is Divorce a Legal Event?

The decision to divorce, like the decision to marry, can be viewed as primarily a personal as opposed to a legal decision. Many couples seek premarital counseling from marriage and family therapists; very infrequently do they consult attorneys when deciding to marry (unless legal rights and obligations between them are created). If the parties treat such matters as personal at the time of their marriage, deciding on them without resorting to legal counsel, can they not continue to do so when divorcing? This is not to mean that there are no legal implications whatsoever, simply that personal aspects of the event should take precedence.

What Has Prevented This "Personal Event" Concept of Divorce from Becoming the Dominant View?

Marlow (1985) asserted that the idea that divorcing parties must seek legal counsel, first to determine their legal rights, and then to protect those rights—that this is a prerequisite to any resolution of their dispute—is a myth. The divorce process has mistakenly been represented to be more than the resolution of a dispute between a couple; divorcing couples are erroneously perceived to be unable to protect their respective rights and obligations without resorting to the law.

How Does the Law Offer This Protection?

One partner is told by the other that she is considering divorce and has consulted an attorney. He immediately assumes that his wife and her attorney are planning to get him for everything they can (a reasonable assumption, given the adversarial structure of the legal system). These concerns are further fed by the fact that legal ethics demand that he and his wife cannot be represented by the same attorney; she meets with her attorney "in confidence." To protect himself, he too retains an attorney and thus feeds the adversarial cycle. This phenomenon is referred to as a *self-fulfilling prophecy* in psychology.

Doesn't a Divorcing Family Need Attorneys to Advise Them of Their Legal Rights?

Again, the very idea that the determination of the couple's respective legal rights is an issue in the divorce is more myth than fact. This myth has stemmed from a failure to distinguish between two types of laws. The first type is usually constitutional in nature and guarantees such rights as voting, free speech, and practicing the religion of one's choice. Such laws can appropriately be labeled *legal rights*. The second type, however, contains those laws that regulate society's conduct or simply resolve personal disputes. While these laws may embody society's conception of what is fair and appropriate at any given time, to speak of them as legal rights is to endow them with exaggerated significance.

Most people want their disagreements to be resolved in a fair manner, to represent what is just. Those rules society adopts in the form of laws to resolve disputes between people are just "rules" and no more. Legal rules are applied by society, not because they do justice, but because they are a means of ending disputes that parties are unable to end themselves. The prevailing belief, although a mistaken one, is that divorcing families must use a dispute resolution procedure that emanates from traditional legal regulation, whether they need this regulation or not. That couples may ultimately be required to resort to the law and the application of legal rules to resolve personal disputes does not change them into legal disputes. They remain personal problems that are still best resolved by relevant personal decision-making strategies, not necessarily by the application of legal rules.

Are There Times When Legal Rules Should Legitimately Take Priority in a Divorce Dispute?

Primary legal intervention would be relevant in one situation: if one or both partners wish to use the agreement to divorce, not as a vehicle to resolve their mutual problems, but rather as a means for venting hurt and anger. If one partner seeks to discredit the other from what is rightfully his or hers, then quite obviously both need to be appraised of legal rules and equally may need to have those rules applied to their dispute.

There is an important point to further consider, however. Families in the process of divorce generally have little accurate understanding of why and how they have gotten to this point in their lives. Frequently both partners tend to idealize themselves as victims; they want the other to pay and look to the divorce agreement as the vehicle to accomplish this. Divorce offers an opportunity to help them put their pasts behind them and to get on with the important business of their future. Divorce agreements that seek to correct past wrongs, whether real or imagined, block this potential opportunity.

Conclusions

Divorce, like marriage, is an important transitional event in the life of a family. As such, it concerns issues that are primarily personal and not legal. What the law only offers is a procedure for resolving a family's dispute if all other dispute resolution mechanisms fail. Given this fact, and contrary to a self-perpetuating myth, the law has little to contribute to the resolution of disputes between divorcing families.

After consulting with attorneys on the relevance of divorce mediation for the practice of a marriage and family therapist, Mary E. saw that the mental health community has not overstepped its boundaries and entered into the legal world in assisting divorcing families to resolve their disputes through mediation. Rather, the legal profession has for years taken mostly personal decisions in the lives of divorcing families and, by the blanket imposition of legal rules and principles, converted them into legal problems.

Mary E. can equally assert that divorce mediation represents more than an alternative procedure to help families resolve issues in a less destructive manner. She can affirm a view of divorce as a personal, not a legal, problem to which mediation represents a better means of dispute resolution. What keeps divorcing families from resolving their disagreements is their fear, hurt, and anger; the adversarial procedures inherent in legal rules almost guarantee an exacerbation of these. If families are to experience a psychological as well as a legal divorce, they must be helped to put these destructive emotions into proper perspective and resolve them.

Mary E. might be more accurate in generally viewing divorce mediation based on her own understanding of family functioning. The specialized training she is considering will add to these understandings by offering pragmatic procedures to aid divorcing families in making concrete decisions after they have been helped with their emotional confusion.

CASE 2

Liability in Crisis Counseling

L ou was a 16-year-old who had been seen together with his parents in family therapy for a few sessions over a year ago. Originally therapy was initiated because Lou had been experiencing problems with regard to peer pressure to engage in drug use. The family prematurely terminated therapy efforts after some early positive changes. More recently, feeling alienated, Lou had turned to drugs to alleviate his anxiety and provide himself with a greater sense of belonging. Paradoxically, he developed a barbituate dependency, creating depression and feelings of isolation. After an especially hostile interchange with his parents over his drug use, Lou, in a hysterical frenzy, telephoned the therapist, crying that he was going to kill himself. The therapist remembered Lou and attempted to calm him, but Lou responded negatively, perceiving the therapist as preaching to him like his parents. The therapist had taken Lou's call between sessions and had someone waiting to see him. Feeling rushed, impatient with Lou, and not accurately perceiving Lou's desperation, the therapist lashed out at Lou, telling him to "grow up," whereupon Lou hung up. Feeling further rejected, Lou took an overdose of barbituates and died. Later that day, feeling guilty about his response to the situation, the therapist called Lou's parents, hoping he might get the family to come in for further therapy. The parents were enraged that the therapist had reacted in a way that added to their son's problems. They accused the therapist of "killing" their son and filed suit against the therapist, claiming negligence that resulted in wrongful death.

Considerations

The law of negligence, which comprises a large part of the law of torts, includes various kinds of wrongful acts that result in injury or damages. As a general rule, liability for negligence will accrue if one person causes damage to another through a breach of duty owed to that person. To hold a therapist liable in a tort action for negligence, the court must find the following:

1. A duty was owed by the therapist to the client; that a therapist-client relationship had been established.
2. The duty was breached; that the therapist's conduct fell below an acceptable standard of care.
3. There was a sufficient legal causal connection between the breach of duty and the client's injury.
4. There was an actual injury sustained by the client.

As there had been a previous therapist-client relationship, the first major point of inquiry in the present case seeks to determine if the therapist's conduct fell below an acceptable standard of care. Concurrently, does the fact that this was a "crisis or emergency" situation have additional bearing on the issue? What standard of care does the law require of therapists in such special situations?

Fischer and Sorenson (1985) quoted former Supreme Court Justice Oliver Wendell Holmes, Jr. in this regard, "Detached reflection can not be expected in front of an uplifted knife" (p. 48). What Holmes sought to convey is that in emergency situations, the same degree of care and thoughtful action cannot be expected as would be in ordinary affairs. This principle particularly applies to telephone crisis counseling where the therapist does not typically have real control over the client or the situation. The guiding legal principle in such situations has tended to be this: A person is responsible for harm to another only if failure to exercise reasonable care increases the risk of harm to that other person (57 American Jurisprudence 2d Negligence * 1). A failure in crisis counseling would require that the therapist reject the client's cry for help in a way indicating that the therapist did not exercise reasonable care in doing so. If the therapist so acted, the next major question to consider would be whether such action by the therapist had indeed increased the risk of harm to the client.

Conclusions

Clearly, a crisis was at hand when the therapist received Lou's phone call. Lou was in an extremely distraught emotional state. It might still be argued his emotional state was not sufficiently dangerous that, considered alone, it could be construed as the cause of his death. It could be asserted, however, that the last straw for Lou was the therapist's rejection of his cry for help. Taken in that light, the therapist not only failed to alleviate an impending crisis, he actually made it worse.

An added factor in the therapist's scope of liability was the fact that Lou had been a client and the therapist was aware of his problems. Because the therapist was better informed about Lou's situation than a professional Lou might have selected from the Yellow Pages, a higher standard of care would be expected. The presumption is that increased knowledge about a situation renders an increased capability to give real assistance. As a result, it is likely that a court might well find that the therapist's actions did constitute negligence that resulted in wrongful death.

CASE 3

Informed Consent?

A husband initiated individual therapy to resolve a number of personal conflicts, of which the state of his marriage was only one. The man reported having had a number of extramarital affairs during the past 4 years over which he was experiencing significant guilt as they were unknown to his wife. The therapist suggested the potential value of pursuing a number of conjoint sessions to generate the husband's motivation toward finding greater fulfillment within his marital relationship. The therapist did not explicitly take any stance regarding confidentiality of the information shared in individual sessions in the upcoming conjoint sessions. The therapist did bring up the issue of the husband's affairs during an early conjoint session whereupon the wife, outraged by this disclosure, left the session and later initiated a divorce action. The husband asserted that the facts of the affairs were confidential to the individual sessions, should have remained separate from what was discussed during the conjoint therapy, and sought legal action against the therapist.

Considerations

Basic to all treatment is professionals' and clients' discussion of the nature of the problem and possible treatments for it. Before treatment begins, the client must consent to it, thus giving the therapist power to act. Two notable cases are relevant in this regard. In the 1957 case of *Salgo v. Leland Stanford, Jr., University Board of Trustees,* tort liability was established for the failure of a physician to explain the risks and benefits of a medical procedure. The court declared that not all risks need be explained, but that the practitioner should use discretion in explaining risks based on each person's mental and emotional status. Initiation of the doctrine of informed consent has been attributed to the 1960 case of *Nathanson v. Kline.* Negligence in informing the client of possible risks was the basis for the tort liability. Further, this case changed the standard for assessing liability from the "reasonable person doctrine" to the doctrine of deviation from the standard of conduct of a reasonable and prudent medical doctor of the same school of practice as the defendant under similar circumstances (Foster, 1978). This distinction between the "reasonable person" and "reasonable medical doctor" standards was an important one for establishing evidence and proof in a malpractice action. The conduct of a marriage and family therapist would be measured against the standard of the average, reasonable person who is a marriage and family therapist (i.e., the average, reasonable person who has superior knowledge and skills as a result of training and experience and whose knowledge and skills are commonly possessed by members in good standing of the profession).

Consent to act is simply willingness that treatment can occur and will prevent liability in a tort. Consent is manifested by words or actions that "reasonable person" would understand to be consent. Silence or inaction have been held to be consent in cases in which a reasonable person would have spoken if he or she objected. In legal actions seeking damages, the principle of informed consent of the person damaged will ordinarily void liability for intentional interference with a person or property (Prosser, 1971). Typically consent is usually implied in clients' initiation of therapy. Such a general consent may, however, have no legal force if a client had no opportunity to compare the risks of participating in therapy with the dangers of foregoing it (Dooley, 1977).

Systemically oriented marriage and family therapists maintain an assumption that any procedures they employ may have an impact well beyond the identified client. The work they might do with individual clients is likely to affect not only the client but also those persons in contact with him or her. The legal requirement of obtaining informed consent before beginning actual treatment applies, however, only to those persons who have direct contact with the therapist. Further, *legally adequate consent* of those in direct contact with the therapist has been defined as "consent by a person who has the following characteristics: legal capacity, comprehension of information, and voluntary agreement" (Bray, Shepherd, & Hays, 1985, p. 54). *Legal capacity* means that the person giving consent is of minimum legal age and has not been adjudicated as incompetent to manage his or her affairs. *Comprehension of information* means that the person giving consent must have been given information relating to the risks and the benefits of the procedure, the risks of forgoing the procedure, and the procedures available as an alternative to the proposed treatment.

The type and amount of information to discuss with clients has been a subject of controversy. Johnson (1965) suggested that the only potential risks needing to be disclosed are those that would cause the client to forgo therapy. Yet Oppenheim (1968) argued for the disclosure of any risk that might influence, however slightly, the clients' decision to accept therapy. In general, therapists need not disclose every risk. In deciding what risks to discuss with clients, therapists should balance clients' desires and the right to make their own decisions regarding therapy with the therapist's own desire to withhold information about potential risks when disclosure might harm a client's well-being. This balancing calls for an exercise of professional judgment that is an exception to the basic principle of disclosure of all potential risks (Waltz & Scheuneman, 1969). Waltz and Scheuneman expressed their belief that the ideal informed consent rule calls for risks being disclosed when a client would find them important in deciding whether or not to consent to therapy. In resolving the question of what to disclose, the therapist can apply the standard of the reasonable person who finds himself or herself in the position of the client. The value of the "Professional Disclosure Statement" presented in chapter 1 is most relevant regarding this.

Given the legal requirements for informed consent, it has been recommended to ensure proof of such procedures by having clients sign a form during an initial session, indicating that appropriate information was provided and consent is thus given for treatment (Cohen, 1979). An example of such a form is the "Therapeutic Contract" discussed in chapter 1. Failure to obtain informed consent leaves therapists liable and subject to legal action. The proof required to show consent when not in written form is unclear. In many cases, practitioners have been asked to prove that the client consented, while in others, the issue of consent was so vital to the case that the *lack* of consent must be proven by the client (Prosser, 1971).

Conclusions

Three possible legal actions can be taken in cases of informed consent. The first and most common is *negligence*. In this instance, the failure to make a complete disclosure can result in a judgment of negligent practice (*Cobbs v. Grant,* 1972). The second potential legal action is *battery*. If the client's bodily integrity is invaded without consent, battery occurs. Cases of this nature are characterized by absence of informed consent and do not require proof of negligence. The reasoning of this rule is that, had the client known about the risks involved, he or she would not have agreed to the procedure. A third type of possible liability is *breach of contract*. If a marriage and family therapist guarantees that a certain treatment will "cure" the client and it does not, the therapist is liable for breach of contract (Slovenko, 1978). As in battery complaints, proof is not needed because it is in the domain of contractual law and not a breach of tort liability.

In the present case, it may well be that the therapist's failure to fully inform the client of the possible risks in the conjoint therapy would provide reasonable cause for a negligence suit to be pursued by the client, given the outcome of the conjoint therapy. This is particularly true, given the client's apparent expectation that confidentiality of what was discussed during individual sessions would be maintained. Further, the four criteria for proving therapist negligence appear to be met: (a) there was a therapeutic relationship established; (b) the therapist's conduct fell below the acceptable standard of care by not obtaining informed consent of the client; (c) this conduct was the proximate cause of injury by the client; and (d) an actual injury was sustained by the client (divorce).

CASE 4

Criminal Liability

Melissa J. is a novice marriage and family therapist employed by a community-funded child guidance clinic. Cindy is a 15-year-old client Melissa has been seeing because of family conflicts. Cindy's parents were recently divorced and she was having problems coping with their breakup. Neither parent was willing to

participate in therapy with their daughter, seeing her
concerns as "things she needs to work out on her own."
Cindy confides to Melissa that she and her boyfriend had
stolen a car the past weekend. They still have the car.
Having no one else to turn to, Cindy asks Melissa's help
in returning the car to the owner without involving the
police.

Considerations

Marriage and family therapists such as Melissa J. who work with minors
can encounter situations that might cause the therapist to incur criminal
liability. Therapists must be aware of areas of possible danger. Two particular areas to consider include contributing to the delinquency of a minor
and being an accessory to a crime before or after the fact (Fischer &
Sorenson, 1985).

Contributing to the Delinquency of a Minor

Each state defines the meaning of "minor" for purposes of its own
laws. Although there are variations among states, a *minor* is generally
defined as a youth subject to the control of a parent or guardian or under
a specified age (usually 16). Likewise, individual states have their own
laws concerning what constitutes contributing to the delinquency of a
minor. There are several common elements, however. The generally
cited purposes of such laws are to protect minors from the negative
influence of adults who might lead them astray and to prevent conduct
that would lead to delinquency. Massachusetts law is typical, providing
in part, that:

> Any person who shall be found to have caused, induced, abetted, encour-
> aged or contributed toward the waywardness or delinquency of a child, or
> to have acted in any way tending to cause or induce such waywardness or
> delinquency, may be punished by a fine of not more than five hundred
> dollars or by imprisonment for not more than one year, or both. (Massa-
> chusetts General Laws, ch. 119, *63)

Contributing to the delinquency of a minor is frequently associated by
the general public with sexual interactions. The law identifies a much
broader range of actions that might adversely affect the welfare of the
public or the healthy development of a minor. Consequently, the meaning of contributing to the delinquency of a minor could encompass a
wide variety of behaviors that injure the morals, health, or welfare of
minors, or encourage their participation in activities that would lead to
such injury.

Fischer and Sorenson (1985) offered case examples of therapists found
facing a charge of contributing to the delinquency of a minor:

The therapist who chaperoned a school-sponsored weekend trip and helped students procure beer and wine for the cookout.

The therapist who chaperoned a Friday-evening party and was aware of several youths smoking marijuana but did nothing about it.

Even though there may be no intention to commit a crime, a marriage and family therapist could still be found guilty of contributing to the delinquency of a minor. In general, for a person to be guilty of a crime, there must be a concurrence of an act and an intent. The law generally requires mens rea (guilty intent) for an act to be a crime. For example, if a pedestrian is hit by an out of control car because of a tire blowout, the driver has not committed a crime. If it can be proven that a driver intentionally sought to run down a pedestrian, a crime would have been committed.

In cases involving delinquency, however, individual states differ with regard to proof of guilty intent. Some states require proof of guilty intent while others do not require the presence of such intent. It is important that marriage and family therapists know the specific provisions in the laws of their respective states to adequately address activities that might be construed by their state courts as contributing to the delinquency of a minor.

Accessory to a Crime

Marriage and family therapists can be in a difficult position if their clients discuss either a plan to commit a crime or a crime they have already committed. Therapists' duty to warn probable victims of a crime resulting in danger to the victims supercedes any claim of confidentiality or privilege. Therapists' obligations are fairly clear in such instances. There is less clarity, however, when a client seeks a therapist's help after a crime has been committed.

Not all crimes involve danger to persons; some crimes are against property. For example, a client might confide a plan to destroy some equipment or building related to racist or antireligious activities. The mere knowledge that a crime will occur, if there is no special duty to prevent it, does not incur guilt. However, if a therapist were to accompany a client to the scene of a crime with knowledge that it likely will be committed, or assist a client in getting away from committing the crime, he or she will become culpable in the eyes of the law (Fischer & Sorenson, 1985). Any person who aids in the commission of a crime, even if he or she is not present when it takes place, may be as guilty as the instigator or an accessory before the fact. This will depend on the laws of the particular state.

An accessory after the fact is generally a person who, knowing that a crime was committed, receives, relieves, comforts, or assists the perpetrator or somehow aids the perpetrator in escaping arrest or punishment. Thus:

1. A crime must have been committed.
2. The accessory must know that the perpetrator committed the crime.
3. The accessory must harbor or protect the perpetrator.

If, during a session, the therapist learns that the client committed a crime, and if, thereafter, the therapist helps the client hide or otherwise offers protection from law enforcement authorities or assists the client in escaping detection, the therapist is guilty of being an accessory to a crime after the fact (Fischer & Sorenson, 1985).

It is important to note that there may be differences relative to whether the crime is a felony or misdemeanor. Common law identifies no accessory to the commission of a misdemeanor. Individual states, however, may create such a category.

Conclusions

Marriage and family therapists who act with a reasonable degree of care should have few occasions to be concerned about criminal liability. This is not to say, however, that marriage and family therapists are immune from criminal prosecution. Intentional actions or even some careless, unintentional behaviors may constitute contributing to the delinquency of a minor or being an accessory to a crime. Burgum and Anderson (1975) described an illustrative case relating to criminal liability of a school counselor that somewhat parallels Melissa J.'s situation.

> A boy in the custody of a juvenile court had developed a good relationship with his school counselor. The boy, with two companions, robbed a service station and then, realizing the gravity of his actions, went to the counselor for help. The counselor convinced the boy that he should turn himself in to the police. It was late at night, however, so they agreed he would go to the police the next day. Meanwhile, the counselor committed a series of acts that made him an accessory to a felony. He denied to the police that the boy was in his home. He gave the boy money, which was found in the youth's possession when he tried to skip town the next morning rather than reporting to the police. The counselor would have been well-advised to have reported the matter to the boy's juvenile court representative and/or the police. Instead, he inadvertently helped the boy avoid arrest.

In this case illustration, the school counselor was clearly an accessory after the fact: (a) a crime was committed; (b) the counselor knew that the boy committed the crime; and (c) the counselor harbored and protected the boy from police.

It would seem most prudent that Melissa J. discuss the potential ramifications of not involving the police with Cindy and strongly urge her and her boyfriend to do so. Melissa might offer Cindy further support and services in acting as her advocate with police and her parents. Should Cindy decide not to turn herself in, Melissa might not be criminally liable as an accessory to a crime after the fact unless it became known that she was aware of the theft and harbored and protected Cindy in some manner (e.g., denying knowledge of the theft if questioned by police). Depending upon the laws of the state, however, Melissa might still be charged with contributing to the delinquency of a minor were it to become known that she was aware of the theft even though she might not have harbored and protected Cindy (e.g., Cindy's parents learned of the theft and turned their daughter in to the police. The police, in questioning Cindy, learned that Melissa had been aware of the theft and had not reported it to anyone).

CASE 5
The Buckley Amendment

A aron M. is a marriage and family therapist who regularly receives referrals from public school personnel. He works with families where the children are experiencing emotional difficulties affecting their ability to perform adequately in the classroom. His common practice has been to provide written reports to the referral source (with the child's and parents' permission) at regular intervals and upon completion of therapy efforts.

The Kent family was initially referred to the therapist because their 13-year-old son David was displaying significant acting-out behaviors with both peers and school personnel. In consultation with David's teacher, the school guidance counselor suspected that David was having these behaviors modeled at home and thus the referral was made to Aaron M. The therapist structured the therapy so that total family sessions would be alternated weekly with individual sessions for David (primarily because the parents were unable to participate every week because of work schedules). In discussing the therapist's latest report with the parents, David's teacher made particular reference to the therapist's notation that "David perceives his parents' general hostility toward each other as the way all people are." The parents became incensed as they had not heard their son say this in their presence, assumed that he had done so during an individual session, and demanded that Aaron M. share all information from the individual sessions. The therapist politely declined, explaining the therapeutic need to allow David the opportunity to feel safe in sharing himself. The parents sought the aid of their attorney who telephoned the therapist requesting that the parents be allowed to review the therapist's session records, citing the Buckley Amendment.

Considerations

It had long been common practice among mental health personnel to clearly mark or otherwise indicate that all client notes, reports, letters, and charts are "confidential." Access to or communication of the materials is generally shared only with relevant professionals directly concerned with the client. Thus, such materials are typically not intended to be seen or used by clients themselves. Such materials are often subject to misinterpretation and misunderstanding by clients and therefore could possibly have negative or harmful effects.

The Family Educational Rights and Privacy Act of 1974 (The Buckley Amendment) and the regulations promulgated for its implementation guarantee to parents and to "eligible students" (18 and over) certain rights with regard to the inspection and dissemination of educational records. Because it is a federal law, it applies to all school districts and schools that receive federal financial assistance through the U.S. Department of Education. While state departments of education, at least theoretically, can decide not to accept federal money, the guarantees of the Buckley Amendment are not really rights in the fullest sense. As one court noted however, the Buckley Amendment is not necessarily binding on a particular school district, but because federal funding might otherwise be discontinued, the court decided to go along with the spirit of the law (*Sauerkof v. City of New York,* 1981). Pragmatically, the Buckley Amendment does create rights for parents and students, that most, if not all, schools will be responsible for ensuring (Fischer & Sorenson, 1985). Further, this law is quite consistent with current legislative trends in other areas and thus grants legal support to persons (parents') right to know and to challenge personal and evaluative material maintained by various agents of society (McGuire & Borowy, 1978).

The minimum requirements of the law call for the adoption of policies and practices that meet the following criteria (*Federal Register,* 1976):

1. Parents and eligible students be informed of their rights.
2. Parents and eligible students be permitted to review educational records, request changes, request a hearing if changes are disallowed, and add their own statements by way of explanation, if necessary.
3. Insure that the institution does not give out personally identifiable information without prior written, informed consent of a parent or eligible student.
4. Maintain and allow parents and eligible students to see the institution's record of disclosures.

5. Facilitate parents' and eligible students' access to records by providing information on the types of educational records and the procedures for gaining access to them.

Educational records under the law are defined as those records that (a) are directly related to the student, and (b) are maintained by the educational agency or institution or by a party acting for that agency or institution (*Federal Register,* 1976). Although educational records that must be made available upon parents' request include a wide variety of materials, some exceptions are especially relevant to the present case. One record not subject to disclosure is that made by a relevant professional remaining in "the sole possession of the maker thereof" and is not "accessible or revealed to any other individual except a substitute" (*Federal Register,* 1976). The legislative history of the Buckley Amendment makes clear that educational records do not include the "personal files of psychologists, counselors, or professors if these files are entirely private and not available to other individuals" (*Congressional Record,* 1974). However, Senator James Buckley, for whom the law is named, stated that this "memory aids" exception was not intended to allow either regular school personnel or a variety of substitutes to "rotate through courses and classes . . . for the purpose of effectively gaining access to another's notes and evaluations" (*Congressional Record,* 1974). This is reinforced by the definition of *substitute*: "An individual who performs on a temporary basis the duties of the individual who made the record and does not refer to an individual who permanently succeeds the maker of the record in his or her position" (*Federal Register,* 1976).

Conclusions

What constitutes eligible educational records appears to represent the primary issue in this case. The definition hinges not so much on the nature of the material as on the primary purposes of the material and who may have access to it. Aaron M.'s personal session notes are likely *excluded* from the definition of educational records, provided he prepares and maintains them solely for his own purposes; for example, the session notes themselves are not available to the referral source to review. The letters communicating feedback to the referral source are a different matter. Materials accessible to other personnel (i.e., the referral source) would be considered part of David's educational record and must be made available to his parents upon their request.

One path that David's parents do have access to, however, regards the contents of the therapist's report. Several provisions in the law guarantee the right to challenge information that parents or eligible students believe is "inaccurate or misleading or violates the privacy or other rights of the student" (*Federal Register,* 1976). If the school personnel decline to change the records, there is a further right to a hearing, where parents or eligible students are allowed to bring an attorney or other representative. If, after this hearing, the school still declines to change the record.

the complaining party is permitted to add a statement to the record explaining the disagreement. The school is then obliged to give out this explanation any time the part of the record it refers to *is* disclosed to anyone, including other school personnel.

CASE 6
The Premarital Agreement

Jan and Howard have lived together for the past 11 months. Both are divorced and have children by previous marriages. Jan's daughter lives with her and Howard. Howard's son and daughter live with their mother. The couple initiated therapy efforts to attempt to work out several problems they are experiencing between themselves and Jan's daughter. A dominant difficulty revolves around Jan's guilt feelings over the "negative" role model she sees herself as providing by living with Howard without benefit of formal marriage. Howard clearly states his love for and desire to marry Jan, but equally identifies his fear that, should the marriage fail, he would be overwhelmed if he had to pay support for Jan and any children they might have, in addition to the support he pays his first wife and two children. The issue of a premarital agreement to circumvent this concern was raised.

Considerations

The number of marriages between persons previously married is steadily increasing. For this and other reasons, it is becoming more common for couples contemplating remarriage to attempt to resolve by premarital agreement specific issues created by their forthcoming marriage. Despite a lengthy legal history of premarital agreements, however, there is still substantial uncertainty as to the enforceability of all, or a portion, of the provisions of such agreements. Further, there has been a significant lack of uniformity in the treatment of these agreements among the various states. The problems caused by this uncertainty and nonuniformity are exacerbated even more by the mobility of today's population. Nevertheless, this reflects not so much basic policy differences among states but rather spontaneous and reflexive responses to various factual circumstances at different times (Bureau of National Affairs, Inc., 1984).

Accordingly, the Uniform Premarital Agreement Act was adopted by the National Conference of Commissioners on Uniform State Laws in

1983 and was approved by the American Bar Association in 1984. It was felt that the Act would provide a model for state governing bodies to conform to modern social policy, providing sufficient certainty yet flexibility to accommodate different circumstances. (As of this writing, the Act has yet not been adopted by any state. However, its derivation from a consensus of state laws suggests it as utilitarian model for the purposes of the present case.)

Comprised of 13 sections, the Act is relatively limited in scope. Section 1 defines a premarital agreement as "an agreement between prospective spouses made in contemplation of marriage and to be effective upon marriage" (Bureau of National Affairs, Inc., 1984). Section 2 requires that a premarital agreement be in writing and signed by both parties. Section 3 provides an illustrative list of those matters that may be properly dealt with in a premarital agreement. Section 4 states that the premarital agreement becomes effective upon the marriage of the parties. Sections 1, 2, and 4 in particular establish significant parameters. The Act does not deal with agreements between persons who live together but who do not marry or contemplate marriage. Nor does the Act provide for postmarital, separation, or oral agreements.

Section 5 prescribes the manner in which a premarital agreement might be amended or revoked. Section 6 is the key operative of the Act and sets forth the conditions under which a premarital agreement is not enforceable. Such an agreement is not enforceable if the party against whom enforcement is sought proves that he or she did not enter the agreement voluntarily or that the agreement was one-sided, oppressive, or unfair when it was entered. Also, before the agreement was entered, he or she (a) did not have access to a fair and reasonable disclosure of the property or financial obligations of the other party, (b) did not voluntarily and explicitly waive, in writing, any right to the disclosure of property or financial obligations, and (c) did not have, or reasonably could not have had, an adequate knowledge of the property and financial obligations of the other party. Even if these conditions are not proven, if a provision of a premarital agreement modifies or eliminates spousal support, and that modification or elimination causes a party to be eligible for public assistance should a future separation or divorce occur, the court is authorized to order the other party to provide support to the extent necessary to avoid that eligibility (Bureau of National Affairs, Inc., 1984).

Sections 7 and 8 address more tangential issues. Section 7 provides for very limited enforcement where a marriage is subsequently determined to be void. Section 8 tolls any statute of limitations applicable to an action asserting a claim for relief under a premarital agreement during the parties' marriage. Sections 9, 10, 11, 12, and 13 simply address very minor points such as the Act's "short title," "time of taking effect," and "repeal."

Of the greatest relevance to the present case is Section 3 relating to areas of contract in a premarital agreement. These include:

1. Rights and obligations of each party in any of either or both the property whenever and wherever acquired or located.
2. The right to buy, sell, use, transfer, exchange, abandon, lease, consume, expend, assign, create a security interest in, mortgage, encumber, dispose of, or otherwise manage and control property.
3. Disposition of property upon separation, marital dissolution, death, or the occurrence of any other such event.
4. Modification or elimination of spousal support.
5. The making of a will, trust, or other arrangement to carry out the provisions of the agreement.
6. Ownership rights in and disposition of a death benefit from a life insurance policy.
7. Choice of law governing construction of the agreement.
8. Any other matter, including personal rights and obligations, not in violation of public policy or a statute imposing a criminal penalty.
9. The right of a child to support may not be adversely affected by a premarital agreement. (Bureau of National Affairs, Inc., 1984)

Conclusions

Section 3 permits parties to contract in a premarital agreement on any matter listed and any other matter not in violation of public policy or imposing a criminal penalty. Point 4 specifically deals with spousal support obligations.

Remember that this Act is a model advanced by the National Conference of Commissioners on Uniform State Laws and the American Bar Association for states to adopt. States have differed as to whether a premarital agreement may control the issue of spousal support. Some states have not permitted a premarital agreement to control this issue (e.g., Iowa: *In re Marriage of Winegard,* 1979; Wisconsin: *Frick v. Frick,* 1950). The more common and growing trend, however, has been to permit premarital agreements to govern this matter if such agreements and the circumstances of their execution satisfy certain standards (e.g., Colorado: *Newman v. Newman,* 1982; Connecticut: *Parniawski v. Parniawski,* 1976; Massachusetts: *Osborne v. Osborne,* 1981). Thus, it is likely that the couple in the present case, Jan and Howard, might enter into a premarital agreement, eliminating spousal support should their marriage ultimately end in divorce.

Point 9, by contrast, makes clear that any premarital agreement may not adversely affect what would otherwise be this couples' obligation to children born of their marriage. This latter point of concern will not be resolved through any premarital agreement.

CASE 7
Child Custody and Privileged Communications

A couple had been seeing a therapist for the marital discord during the fourth year of their marriage. The couple met with the therapist for five conjoint sessions. During these sessions, the wife was open in sharing her self-perceived faults. The husband was rather guarded. The husband's lack of commitment to the therapy added much to create a context wherein the couple was unable to accommodate their differences and thus led to a decision to divorce. Some months after the last session with them, the therapist received a subpoena to appear in court to testify relative to the custody of the couple's daughter. In contacting both parties, who were now living separately, the therapist learned that the husband was seeking to have the therapist testify to what his wife had shared about herself. The therapist was requested by the wife to keep what she had stated confidential, recognizing that revealing it might adversely affect her custody chances.

Considerations

According to common law, courts should have broad access to evidence. Citizens should present their evidence to the court because all of society benefits from the proper administration of justice. Privileged communication laws run contrary to common law in this respect because they exclude evidence from the courts. Yet the need for a therapist-client privilege is an obvious one. Successful therapy efforts require the establishment of trust between therapists and clients. Fear of potential disclosure before a court would obviously deter many persons from seeking needed treatment, impair the course of therapy, or foster premature termination when issues of risk arose (Foster, 1976; Kennedy, 1973).

State legislatures have consequently enacted privileged communication laws to protect consumers of psychotherapy. The application of such privileges vary from state to state or even within the same state according to the professional training or credentials of the therapist. Generally speaking, however, courts tend to strictly interpret privileged communication laws. The traditional view holds that the statutes must specify any exception to the common law duty to provide testimony to the court. The privilege has existed only for clients of professionals specifically named in the statutes. Hence, the definition of the terms *psychologist, social worker, marriage and family therapist,* or *counselor* in statutes will determine whether a specific therapist is included. In the absence of a statute, courts have tended to refuse to extend the privilege (e.g., social workers: *State v. Driscoll,* 1972; unlicensed psychologists: *State v. Vickers,* 1981).

Several states extend privileges to associates working under the direction of a protected professional. For example, Wisconsin law holds that the privilege extends to persons "who are participating in the diagnosis and treatment under the direction of the . . . psychologist" (*Wisconsin Statutes Annotated,* 1981–1982). This would cover marriage and family therapists, social workers, unlicensed psychologists, and other relevant professionals working with the protected therapist. Of course, the courts have the discretion of interpreting the words "under the direction" (Knapp & VandeCreek, 1985). Further, the privilege applies only to psychotherapy and not to court-ordered evaluations. When the court orders parents to undergo psychiatric or psychological evaluation, the results are always available to the court (e.g., *New Mexico ex rel. Human Services Department v. Levario,* 1982). The failure of parents to comply has severely damaged their position in court (e.g., *In re Marriage of Gove,* 1977).

Courts have always valued the welfare of children very highly and attempt to include all testimony that may help them make a proper placement in custody cases. As a whole, courts value the welfare of children more than the privacy of their parents (Foster, 1978). Unless a statute clearly protects the privacy rights of parents, courts tend to rule in favor of admitting testimony. The ruling judge in *Atwood v. Atwood* (1976) reflected this most explicitly in writing: "Regardless of the desires of the parents in making an award of custody, the polar star is to determine what is for the best interest of the child."

Even in the presence of a privileged communication statute, the court may obtain a therapist's testimony in four ways:

1. A client may waive the privilege and permit testimony in court.
2. The court may nullify the privilege for communications made in the presence of third parties.
3. The wording of the state statutes may allow for waiver of the privilege in certain cases.
4. The privilege may be waived if clients introduce their mental condition into the court proceedings.

Knapp and VandeCreek (1985) offer an analysis of each of these waivers.

Client Waiver

Traditionally the right to waive the privilege belongs to the client. The therapist has no independent right to invoke the privilege against the wishes of the client. Other interested parties, including payers for the therapy of another, have no right to the privilege. For example, in *Bieluch v. Bieluch* (1983), a father tried to prevent the testimony of a psychologist who was treating his wife and children. Although the father had paid for many of the sessions, he was not allowed to invoke the privilege because he had no professional relationship with the therapist.

The waiver may be implied or expressed. In an *implied waiver,* the actions of the client imply that the communications were not confidential. For example, in *In re Fred J.* (1979), a mother requested that two psychiatrists examine her children and report the findings to a social service agency. In a later custody hearing, the court concluded that the psychiatrists' evaluations were not privileged because the reports had been divulged earlier to the agency. In an *expressed waiver,* the client explicitly allows the testimony of the therapist. Waivers are absolute; the client may not selectively agree that only one portion of communications be open and another portion withheld.

Third-Party Rule Waiver

Most privileged communication controversies have dealt with situations in which only one person was the client. There have been substantially fewer cases where families or couples were being treated together and disagreement about the waiver emerged in court. No consistent principles have been established as a result. In a number of jurisdictions, however, the privilege has been waived in such cases, not because one party or the other controls the waiver, but because the presence of a third person in therapy was alleged to indicate that the communications were not intended to be confidential or privileged.

The privilege has thus been waived or maintained according to a court's interpretation of the "third-party rule." Common law tradition holds that the presence of third persons suggests that communications were not intended to be confidential. This rule is obviously reasonable when applied to casual conversations made in public places. Not so obvious, however, is its applicability to communications made during therapy in the presence of a marital partner or family members (Meyer & Smith, 1977).

The application of the third-party rule has tended to depend on the wording of specific state statutes. For example, a Delaware statute states that "A communication is 'confidential' if not intended to be disclosed to third persons except persons present to further the interests of the patient in the consultation . . . including members of the patient's family" (*Delaware Rules of Evidence,* 1981). When the statutes fail to specify any rule for marital or family psychotherapy, some courts have ruled on therapist-client privilege using the attorney-client model (DeKraai & Sales, 1982). Communications between therapists and clients are placed on the same legal ground as communication between attorneys and clients. According to this model, when two or more persons consult the same attorney about a common matter, communications made by them are not privileged among themselves (*American Jurisprudence,* 1976). Applying this principle, the Arizona Supreme Court ruled in *Hahman v. Hahman* (1981) that the communications made to a psychologist by a husband and wife were not privileged.

In other states, court decisions have reflected a mixture of findings. Some courts upheld the privilege when parents have been present in therapy with their children (*Grosslight v. Superior Court,* 1977), and when spouses have been seen together (*Yaron v. Yaron,* 1975). Some courts have, however, held otherwise and waived the privilege because a spouse was present (Herrington, 1979). In summary, no consistent judicial trend has emerged in this area. Where there is no protective legislation, the ruling will depend upon the interpretation of the court and/or on the unique circumstances of the case (Knapp & VandeCreek, 1985).

Statutory Waiver

The most common statutory waiver relating to child custody cases is when suspected child abuse is a factor in the proceedings. Almost all states have child abuse reporting laws that waive the privilege in court cases that arise out of reports of suspected child abuse.

A number of states have waiver rules that apply particularly to child custody cases. Massachusetts law, for example, specifically allows a waiver if the judge, upon a hearing in chambers, "determines that the psychotherapist has evidence bearing significantly on the patient's ability to provide suitable custody, and that it is more important to the welfare of the child that the communications be disclosed than the relationship between the patient and psychotherapist be protected" (Massachusetts General Laws, 1980).

Several other states, including New York, New Hampshire, and Virginia allow judges to waive the privilege when they believe that the interests of justice outweigh clients' need for privacy (DeKraai & Sales, 1982). New York state courts have specified, however, that privileges may not "cavalierly be ignored or lightly cast aside" (*Perry v. Fiumano,* 1978). To permit the waiver, the mental health of parents must be raised as a relevant issue in a child's placement, and that this information is unavailable from other sources (*State ex rel. Hickox v. Hickox,* 1978). Also, the courts must attempt to look for a less intrusive means of acquiring the information, such as requesting the parents undergo an evaluation, or by viewing relevant records in the privacy of the judge's chambers to first determine its relevance to the case.

Mental Health as a Condition Waiver

Clients waive the privilege when they enter their mental health into the proceedings. States have disagreed, though, on whether or not the mental condition of parents is automatically entered into litigation in child custody cases. Most states have held that the privilege is maintained and the mental condition of parents does not automatically enter in such cases (e.g., Florida: *Kristensen v. Kristensen,* 1981; Michigan: *Matter of Atkins,* 1982; Texas: *Gillespie v. Gillespie,* 1982).

Courts in Kentucky (*Atwood v. Atwood,* 1976) and Delaware (*Shipman v. Division of Social Services,* 1981), however, have ruled that parents automatically enter their mental health into litigation in child custody cases. In the *Atwood* case, the mother had been awarded custody of her three children. She remarried and later obtained therapy with her children and new husband. Her first husband then sought custody. The Kentucky Supreme Court refused to exclude the testimony of the therapist, concluding that custody investigations needed to be extensive and acute and that the mental condition of the parties involved must be considered an issue.

Conclusions

The application of privilege varies greatly according to the wording of state statutes, the common law traditions within each state, and the interpretations made by courts; prime illustrations being the *Atwood* and *Shipman* cases. The decisions in these cases are binding only in Kentucky and Delaware, respectively. Most states will not automatically waive privileges in child custody cases. A specific response herein therefore cannot do justice to the myriad nuances of laws among the states. Consequently, the therapist in question must of necessity consult a local attorney.

Depending upon the state in which they practice, most marriage and family therapists will likely find themselves operating under a patchwork of existing laws and judicial interpretations. Therapists subpoenaed to court to provide testimony they believe could ultimately harm a child or family or represents an unreasonable waiver of privilege, need not passively submit to the subpoena. Instead, they may ask the court to pursue a less intrusive means of acquiring the information. They may suggest that the judge require a court-ordered examination. Or, if the therapist's records are deemed important, the therapist can request that the judge screen the records privately in chambers before allowing them into the court proceedings. Obviously there are no guarantees that the court will be amenable to a therapist's proposals. Nonetheless, such initiatives may create a context wherein judges will be able to more prudently balance the need for information in court with the need to protect the confidentiality of therapeutic efforts.

CASE 8
Legal Responsibility of Clinical Supervisors

O ne state's licensure for marriage and family therapy requires that unlicensed graduates of marriage and family therapy training programs complete 2 years of clinically supervised postdegree experience. Part of the position agreement for entry-level therapists at a Family Services Agency is that they receive regular supervision by the senior level therapist at the agency. The designated supervisor has not been able to provide what he considers to be adequate supervision. He has had to leave two entry-level therapists mainly on their own with rather difficult caseloads. The staff members at the agency are all overloaded; the supervisor is feeling overburdened by his supervisory responsibility in addition to his regular heavy caseload. Thus, quality supervision time is rare. The supervisor is preparing to bring the situation to the agency's Board of Directors and seeks to identify his legal liability as one justification for a reduced client caseload so he can adequately attend to his supervisory responsibilities.

Considerations

Recent years have seen a gradual and profoundly important change in the attitudes of clients toward helping professionals. Clients have become more consumer-oriented with respect to accountability; this has become a critical concept for both marriage and family therapists and supervisors. From the supervisory standpoint, the legal doctrine of respondeat superior (also known as vicarious liability) has consequently become of significant relevance (Cohen, 1979). According to this doctrine, someone in a position of authority or responsibility, such as a clinical supervisor, is responsible for acts of those individuals under his or her supervision. Stated another way, supervisors are ultimately legally responsible for the welfare of clients seen in therapy by their supervisees (Cormier & Bernard, 1982).

There are a number of implications inherent in this principle as applied to clinical supervision. The first demands that supervisors ensure that supervision actually occurs. Supervisors must avoid delegating all responsibility to a supervisee because negligence may occur. Therefore, a supervisor must be familiar with each case of every supervisee. This can be established by conducting (and documenting) that face-to-face contacts with supervisees regularly take place.

Cormier and Bernard (1982) reported an attorney's advice that supervisors also conduct one face-to-face meeting with each supervisee's clients sometime during the initial stages of therapy. Such a contact allows clients the opportunity to meet the supervisor and discover how their therapist is being supervised. This information can assist clients in providing informed consent to their therapist for his or her services. Also, a face-to-face contact with clients allows supervisors to gain additional information about them, the possible management of their case, and to better determine the amount of supervision needed. Slovenko (1980) restated a comment made by the attorney in the Tarasoff case:

> It is my view that if the supervisor of the clinic had personally examined the patient Poddar and made an independent decision that the patient Poddar was not dangerous to himself or his victim, Tatiana Tarasoff, there would be no cause of action based on foreseeability. However, the supervisor never saw the patient Poddar and ignored the medical records developed by his staff. (p. 468)

Thus, it may be of significant importance from a legal standpoint for supervisors to make contact with supervisees' clients.

Van Hoose and Kottler (1985) identified failure to supervise a therapist working with a disturbed client as one of the leading causes of psychological malpractice suits. The supervisor is legally responsible to know when supervisees are insufficiently prepared to deal with certain situations and need assistance. Knowledge that a supervisee is having difficulties in working with particular clients may call for closer supervision, cotherapy, or possibly reassigning the case to a more experienced person.

A further implication of the respondeat superior doctrine addresses supervisees' competence to provide adequate services. Some formal assessment of competence should be conducted prior to assuming an independent caseload. If a supervisor has reservations about a supervisee's clinical abilities, supervision should not be agreed upon until remedial training activities are undertaken and completed and/or the supervisor seeks to protect him or herself from liability by stating reservations about the supervisee in writing to relevant parties (Cormier & Bernard, 1982).

Finally, the respondeat superior doctrine also suggests certain responsibilities supervisors have to clients to ensure appropriate referral and termination procedures. Dawidoff (1973) noted that supervisors are liable if treatment is terminated or a referral is made without due cause. Referrals and terminations must be handled in a way that meets the recognized standard of care.

Although the respondeat superior doctrine creates legal liability for the supervisor, the supervisee is not necessarily absolved. Clients have the option of bringing action against the supervisor, the supervisee, or all parties. Cohen (1979), for example, reported the case of a supervisee, who away from the formal clinical setting and without the supervisor's knowledge, allegedly engaged in sexual relations with a client. Under the doctrine of respondeat superior, a lawsuit was brought against the supervisor rather than the supervisee. The plaintiff claimed that the supervisor was negligent by allowing an unlicensed person, not competent of providing due care, to treat her.

In a contrasting case, a supervisee rather than the supervisor was sued for failure to more closely monitor a client who committed suicide. The supervisee, a student intern, was found to be negligent (*Eady v. Alter,* 1976). Exactly who is named as defendant in such cases obviously depends on the circumstances, setting, alleged acts, plaintiff, and perhaps above all, who is seen as having the most to lose (Cormier & Bernard, 1982).

Conclusions

Slovenko's (1980) warning that "litigation involving supervisors may be the 'suit of the future' " (p. 468) can be best addressed by well-informed and conscientious supervisors. The supervisor in the present case should assert the need for regularly scheduled supervision based on a careful assessment of the needs of both supervisees and their clients. The amount and frequency of the supervision will be best determined by an accurate knowledge of the supervisees' strengths and deficits, as well as the difficulties likely to be presented by their caseloads. The supervisor should be careful to document how supervision is scheduled and what occurs during supervisory sessions.

Beyond this, the supervisor must actually provide the supervision. Negligence is based on the idea that the professional has departed from what is considered acceptable in terms of the standards of the profession. Consultation with professionals in similar situations and professional association standards can provide a recommended minimum; anything above that can take place as warranted by the results of the supervisor's assessments.

Professional liability insurance is a further consideration for the supervisor to consider. The agency should provide such coverage. It will be important to identify in advance of purchase, however, what a policy actually covers. Occasionally, policies will not cover damages from either negligent supervision or acts of supervisees with less than a master's degree.

Finally, if the supervisor is not able to provide adequate supervision or if some undesirable consequences befall clients being seen by a supervisee, the supervisor must take appropriate action. Although an important goal of providing supervised practice is to produce more effective practitioners, the supervisor must protect his or her own welfare, and most importantly, the welfare of clients.

PART THREE

Professional Issues in Marriage and Family Therapy

The counselor needs to develop a sense of unique personal identity, and with it an awareness and appreciation of the meaning of a profession with all the specific guidelines, regulations, and policies that define the practice of the speciality.

(Tolbert, 1982, p. 292)

7

Valuing: Basis for Professional Therapeutic Practice

Rokeach defined a *value* as "an enduring belief that a specific mode of conduct or end-state of existence is personally or socially preferable to an opposite or converse mode of conduct or end-state of existence" (1973, p. 286). Anthropologists (e.g., Kluckhohn & Strodtbeck, 1961) identified a great similarity among predominant values orientations found in diverse cultures, suggesting a universal dimension in all human efforts to cope with life's events. These broadly accepted values address a belief in the desirable, an effective component elicited when this belief is accepted or challenged, and an action component that signals behaviors considered congruent or incongruent with the belief (Stuart, 1980).

All human events are guided by the interaction of the values of the parties concerned. This interaction of values determines those aspects of human experience labeled as events, the significance ascribed to those events, the ways plan for goal selection and pursuit emanate from events, and the manner in which goal attainment is evaluated. People cannot interact independently of their values, even if those values are not explicit. Professional therapeutic practice is particularly shaped by value interaction among therapists, societal institutions, and clients.

Institutional representatives of society, including governmental bodies, clinics, hospitals, social agencies, insurance companies, academic and training facilities, and professional associations, formally and informally hold out values for professional therapeutic practice. These values define professional therapeutic services, who is eligible to receive them, and who is qualified to offer them. They also decide the conditions under which such services will be financed, whether through direct fee payments, insurance coverage, tax deductions, or other subsidies and which professionals will be approved for these remunerations. In making these determinations, societal representatives assert their values about the nature of mental illness, marital and family problems, and treatment alternatives (Aponte, 1985).

Values can describe either means or ends to actions. In each case values determine efforts to make discriminations among alternative courses of actions. Values that prescribe ends contribute to attitudes about all facets of society (Rokeach, 1968). Values that prescribe means provide the basis for professional norms (Williams, 1968). Professional norms are hierarchically organized (Maslow, 1959) and relate to a series of beliefs about all phases of therapeutic practice (Stuart, 1980).

Therapists' values thus provide the basis for their professional practice. Values gained from personal life experiences and professional training interact with, and filter societal values about, professional therapeutic practice to influence every therapeutic decision. These decisions may govern who will be offered services, the goals of those services, the procedures used to achieve identified goals, and the criteria by which therapeutically mediated changes are evaluated. A further interaction with clients' values (the therapeutic process) is framed by the parameters of therapists' values. Thus, in the consideration of values interaction, valuing is the most essential issue in the professional practice of marriage and family therapy.

185

After a brief introduction to values clarification, this chapter will address the importance of delineating between a linear and systemic epistemology. It will proceed by expounding a systemic approach to valuing and then emphasize several practice implications of systemic valuing for marriage and family therapists. The chapter will conclude by directing attention to specific valuing components that have an effect on marital and family therapy efforts.

VALUES CLARIFICATION

In an article appropriately entitled, "Counselor: Know Thyself," Hulnick (1977) posited the inescapable need for therapists to clarify their own values if they are to assume a distinct professional identity. Similarly, Pell (1979) concurred with an earlier position asserted by Bergantino (1978) that lack of self-awareness by therapists represented a "fatal flaw." Such self-awareness must entail a clear understanding of why therapists choose to assume their professional identity.

Values clarification has been suggested as a means for therapists to clarify their professional position (Glaser & Kirschenbaum, 1980). Inherent in the values clarification perspective is the assumption that thoughtfully reflecting on one's beliefs is better than not doing so, that considering alternatives and their consequences is better than not considering them; and that acting consistently with one's most cherished beliefs—one's values—is important.

Values clarification represents a consideration of the *process* of valuing as opposed to simply identifying the *content* of values. It is an active process composed of seven subprocesses, each eliciting questions needing to be answered in a developmental sequence (Glaser & Kirschenbaum, 1980):

Choosing Basic Beliefs

1. Choosing from alternatives:
   Have a number of alternatives been considered? Has sufficient time been given to identifying possible alternatives?
2. Choosing after considering consequences:
   What are the most valuable aspects of the belief? What if everyone held the belief?
3. Choosing freely:
   How was the belief first procured? How freely is it now being chosen?

Prizing Basic Beliefs

4. Prizing and cherishing:
   Does the belief hold significant importance? Is it one to be proud of?

5. Publicly affirming, when appropriate:
   Is there a willingness to share the belief with others? Who would it be appropriate to share the belief with?

Acting On Beliefs

6. Acting:
   Is the belief one that can be readily acted upon? Is there a willingness to act upon it?
7. Acting with a pattern of consistency:
   Is the belief one that is typically acted upon? Is there a willingness to consistently act upon the belief?

Seymour's (1982) injunction identifying regular values clarification as essential to professional therapeutic practice aptly addresses the importance of this process:

> We do become emotionally invested in our values, we do hold some of them to be unquestionably right, and we do act in counseling in accordance with what we believe. We, as counselors, must be aware of the emotional investment, admit to, and hopefully question those values that have been previously unquestioned, and then examine closely how what we believe influences how we act as counselors. If our values are, in fact, the lenses through which we view the world, then we need to have our vision checked as a part of the selection and training process, and at regular intervals thereafter. (p. 45)

Within the profession many hold the very essence of marriage and family therapy depends upon a therapist choosing, prizing, and acting upon certain predominant beliefs of a systemic nature. They posit a systemically oriented epistemology as delineating the difference between doing marriage and family therapy and simply seeing marital partners and family members in the same room and dealing with their individual concerns.

AN EXPANDING EPISTEMOLOGY

Epistemology is a branch of philosophy that investigates the origin, nature, methods, and limits of human knowledge. For the profession of marriage and family therapy, the term has come to mean a formal world view—a framework for thinking and conceptualizing (Sauber, L'Abate, & Weeks, 1985). Anthropologist Gregory Bateson first addressed epistemology as a professional issue within marriage and family therapy and others have built upon his work. Bateson saw epistemology as rules for making sense out of the world, and identified two particular villains (Hoffman, 1981). One was any form of *dualism.* Bateson expressed this concern in discussing one of the most dominant products of dualism, the idea of the self:

> To draw a boundary line between a part which does most of the computation for a larger system and the larger system of which it is a part, is to

create a mythological component, commonly called a "self." In my episte-mology, the concept of self, along with all arbitrary boundaries which delimit systems or parts of systems, is to be regarded as a trait of the local culture—not indeed to be disregarded, since such little epistemological monsters are always liable to become foci of pathology. The arbitrary boundaries which were useful in the process of analyzing data become all too easily battlefronts, across which we try to kill an enemy or exploit an environment. (Bateson, 1977, p. 53)

Bateson took pains to stress his emphasis on the larger context. Hoff-man (1981) interpreted this stance in stating:

To "chop up the ecology" is what one does when one takes the parts and pieces of what one is describing and decides that one part "controls" another or one part "causes" another. (pp. 342–343)

Hoffman's interpretation represents Bateson's second villain, *linear thinking,* that assigns causality (often seen as blaming). Becvar, Becvar, and Bender (1982) expounded on this supposition in stating:

Previously we studied and treated the person in isolation. Our inquiry, consistent with the theoretical models then in use, was concerned with the nature of the individual's pathological condition and, in a wider sense, with the nature of the human mind. Consistent with our new models de-rived from ecology, ethology, cybernetics, systems theory, and structural-ism, our inquiry is now extended to include the effects of an individual's behavior on others, their reactions to it, and the context in which all of this takes place. Our focus has shifted from the isolated monad to the relationship among the components or members of a system. We have turned from an inferential study of the mind to a concern with the observ-able manifestations of relationships. (p. 386)

Linear epistemology focuses predominantly on the individual. It pro-vides a framework for processing information about individual dynamics and actions. Linear epistemology resembles, however, a pair of binocu-lars that a spectator at a sporting event uses to observe only one player on the field. The spectator can see the player's movements and expres-sions in fine detail. Yet the drawback of using binoculars eventually be-comes clear: the interaction between one player and the others on the field is screened out. The spectator fails to take in the overall action among all participants, particularly important when the primary action of play occurs away from the single player.

While linear epistemology acknowledges that individuals react to out-side events, it sees order, pattern, and predictability as being essentially within the individual. All critical motivating and determining forces are likewise seen as within. Left unaddressed are the motivating and deter-mining forces as well as the order, pattern, and predictability of the larger social systems in which the individual is embedded (Karpel & Strauss, 1983). This oversight is well recognized by systemic epistemology that calls for widening the spectator's field of vision, so to speak, in an effort to consider the total context.

A central concept of this expanding epistemology is the idea of *circularity*. Mental illness has traditionally been perceived in linear terms, with historical, causal explanations given for the distress. Etiology was conceived primarily in terms of prior events—disease, emotional conflict, or learning history—that caused symptoms in the client. Using circularity as a core concept, systemic epistemology views mental illness not as something that is caused, but rather part of ongoing, circular fit. Dell (1982) described this in stating:

> Without reference to etiology or causation, fit simply posits that the behaviors occurring in the family system have a general complementarity; they fit together. *Causation,* on the other hand, is a specified type of interpretation of fit that considers the observed complementarity to have the form: A causes B. For instance, bad parents make their children sick. (p. 25)

Of those who have addressed the professional impact of an expanding epistemology that includes a circular understanding of behavior, Gregory Bateson's work again is most relevant. Bateson (1979) made an important distinction between the world of physical objects and the world of living forms. Linear causality applied to the physical world assumes that the world is like a billiard table in which the balls go in one direction when hit. Bateson believed that the world of living things is poorly represented by such a model because it neglects to account for communication and relationships; simple force alone is not enough.

Hoffman (1981) illustrated the difference between these two viewpoints in describing what may occur as a result of kicking a stone and kicking a dog. In the case of a stone, the energy transmitted by the kick will move the stone a certain distance, depending upon the force of the kick and the weight of the stone. But in kicking a dog, the outcome is not so simply predicted. What happens will depend upon the relationship between the person and the dog. The dog may respond in any number of ways. It may cringe, run away, or bite the person, depending upon how the relationship is defined and how the dog interprets the kick. Moreover, the behavior of the dog will send back information that may modify the person's subsequent behavior. If the dog bites, the person will give greater thought before he kicks the dog again.

The circular emphasis within systemic epistemology recognizes that individuals are not unrelated atoms motivated only by internal urges and instincts; rather, they are parts of larger systems that exert considerable influence on their thoughts, feelings, and actions. Nonetheless, couples and families are composed of individuals, an understanding sometimes minimized or ignored by systemic writers in their zealousness to assert their perspective. Such is not a fully systemic epistemology; therein again is raised Bateson's villain of dualism. Language emanating from systemic epistemology identifies individuals as whole systems themselves whose internal dynamics play roles in mediating their reactions with other system forces. No systemic epistemology can ever adequately explain the dynamics of a relational system without reference to individual dynamics (Karpel & Strauss, 1983).

Inherent in any discussion considering the problems occasioned by dualistic thinking is also the issue of *evolution*. The belief that patterns of connectedness are dynamically unfolding rather than structurally based is at the heart of the matter (Taggart, 1982). Linear epistemology uses a world view marked by a structural rather than an evolutionary orientation. This structural orientation advances an ultimate objective perspective. In contrast, systemic epistemology asserts an evolutionary perspective emphasizing that no living system can ever be permanently stabilized. The dynamics of living systems prescribe no output beyond self-organization and self-renewal.

Brown (1977) proposed the only permanent aspect of science as being the process of research, and it is only the current consensual agreement of the scientific community that determines the research findings that have validity, not the findings themselves. Thus, reductionism and separatism are transcended as one discovery sets the stage for another, like the ever-widening ripples occasioned by the proverbial pebble thrown into the pond. In the same manner early marriage and family therapists who expanded their focus of observation to bring clients' family members into the process occasioned developments that lead to an appreciation of the dynamic connectedness of all things within an openly unfolding world (Jantsch, 1980).

Taggart (1982) summarized the importance of this expanding epistemology for marriage and family therapists:

> Family therapy may be viewed as a "research program" (Brown, 1977) that came into being because existing research programs in psychotherapy failed to find adequate solutions to their own problems. No matter how previous research programs seemed to differ from each other, they all developed in the context of an already developed view of reality. The advent of family therapy, in effect, was a turning away from this customary epistemology. Instead of relegating "family" to what happened in the gaps between the substantial attributes of isolated entities, the new model viewed the family as a "system in process." (p. 25)

This premise is a research realization that finality is nonexistent and provides the basis for professional therapeutic practice. The context of new discovery must be deemed as equally important as the context of verification.

NEGOTIATION: THE NATURE OF VALUING

The negotiation of values is increasingly central to the professional practice of marriage and family therapy. Today less is accepted on the strength of tradition and precedent and more is open for debate. Technological and social changes are occurring at a greater rate today than at any previous period. Moreover, people are actively seeking ways to determine the terms of these changes.

One major reason for this progressive acceleration of change has been an explosion in the amount and quality of information available through the media and increased opportunities for education, communication, and travel. All this has led to an escalation in the rate of change among traditional racial, socioeconomic, transgenerational, sex role, and other social network relationships. Traditions, customs, and roles within relationships must contend with mounting pressures to change. They resist, accommodate, mutate, or vanish in this swirl of social movement. Currently people have gained greater autonomy, flexibility, and power over their own lives and in relation to the rest of society. This phenomenon, while resulting in more choice, has also created more sources of stress. Marriage and family therapy is one of the means societal institutions have identified to assist people more successfully negotiate this social evolution (Aponte, 1985).

Traditional linear epistemology promotes a profound disinterest in connectedness and process and virtually insists that values be viewed as rules for behavior intended to promote the welfare and development of individuals. Traditional approaches to values exhibit a view of reality marked by a content rather than a process orientation. Put in its most basic terms, there is a "right" way advocated for individuals' conduct that is normally presented as contrasting to a "wrong" way. The only legitimate response to such an approach is adaptation (Taggart, 1982). A more modern variant of this position is the view that social change is permitted only within the restraints of unchanging social values; the institutions that support and promote these unchanging values must themselves survive without changing (Jantsch, 1980).

Taggart (1982) posited that nowhere is this linear focus on values more apparent than in the contemporary concern for individual rights. He took particular issue with the work of Hare-Mustin (1978, 1980; Hines & Hare-Mustin, 1978) who introduced that concern into the marriage and family therapist's office. Hare-Mustin discussed the risks inherent in giving priority to the good of the family as a whole over individual member's rights. She listed a number of these rights: the right not to be treated, the right to individual confidentiality, the right to privacy (not to be exposed, embarrassed, and the like), and the right of women to equal treatment. Taggart asserted raising questions "about rights—understood as inalienable, individual, and axiomatically supreme—at the logical level of family or system may be no more than the same epistemological error which insists that a family member's 'schizophrenia' be treated as an entity distinct from the family's pattern" (p. 30).

This individualistic rights paradigm calls for a distinction of opposites resulting in stabilization and rigidification of existing professional practice. Values within this perspective are often seen as the only things that last; to tamper with the methods embedded within those lasting values is to risk being accused of seeking to overturn them (Taggart, 1982). Thus an unnecessary dichotomy is created. Systemic epistemology suggests that values need not be static entities denoting a right or wrong way; rather, there exists a continuing negotiation of values resulting in an evolving valuing process that operates like any system—in a balance between confirmation and novelty. Total confirmation identifies a system in equilibrium; for living systems, this equals death. Total novelty, by contrast, identifies a system in chaos; in living systems, this heralds disintegration. Life is a dance between the two (von Weizsacker & von Weizsacker, 1974).

Watts (1961) used language as a metaphor for the continuing negotiation between novelty and confirmation. A language that becomes too innovative in either time or space is at risk of losing its coherence. A language that stops growing is in danger of becoming a relic. Likewise, valuing from a systemic perspective suggests a process of unfolding within the context of negotiating older beliefs, thus ensuring both debate and a common task.

A particularly cogent concern emerging from traditional individual rights discussions is the notion of a therapeutic opposition known as resistance. Linear, individually oriented, therapeutic modes reflect a view wherein the client is seen as an external object operated upon by the therapist using therapeutic procedures as instruments of change. Client and therapist represent two distinct and opposed entities. The term *resistance* represents a conceptual wall between the client and the therapist. The view is held that this wall must be broken down for change to occur (Searight & Openlander, 1984).

Resistance represents a logical outgrowth of the duel between client and therapist of linear epistemological values between opposing forces. Erickson (1967) described resistance as a stance taken by a therapist in which the client is allowed to maintain only certain values. Resistance is located within and emanates from the client. A systemic valuing perspective recognizes that when therapist and client come together, they negotiate a new, common system containing elements of both subsystems as well as unique properties arising from their interaction. Thus, resistance would also represent a product of mutual client-therapist negotiation (DeShazer, 1982).

Dell (1982), in questioning the epistemological relevance of the resistance concept, noted how resistance is most often used as an explanatory device to account for situations in which clients do not respond to therapeutic interventions in a manner desired by their therapists. Resistance represents attributions made by therapists to account for this "difficulty." Dell (1982) saw this notion as epistemologically mistaken: "People and systems do not resist; they simply are what they are" (p. 22). In considering valuing from a systemic perspective, the client's current values are not right or wrong, correct or incorrect; they simply *are*.

As strategically oriented systemic therapists have noted, clients traditionally seen as "resistant" will come to generate a different orientation when therapists "go with reality." Therapists accept clients' values as they are and negotiate within clients' construction of them. Andolfi, Angelo, Menghi, and Nicolo-Corigliano (1983) emphasized a somewhat similar negotiation process resulting in clients evolving a different "script." In their valuing process, a therapist negotiates with a client in emphasizing certain values previously deemphasized, while at the same time relegating other values to the background. With the context of the therapist-client negotiation, the client's values change; behavioral changes are compatible with value changes. Essentially, the therapist and client come together in negotiating a common world of less pain and conflict.

Valuing essentially consists of negotiating the context that surrounds clients' and therapists' values. The therapist and client work together in changing their conceptual frameworks. This process is similar to *reframing,* which is defined as follows:

> [Changing] the conceptual and/or emotional setting or viewpoint in relation to which a situation is experienced and to place it in another frame which fits the "facts" of the same concrete situation equally well or even better, and thereby changes its entire meaning. (Watzlawick, Weakland, & Fish, 1974, p. 95)

Reframing reflects a systemic valuing process to negotiate a frame close enough to the client's so the client can meaningfully associate a new, better-fitting frame. The blended frame consists of the client's original frame, the therapist's contributed frame, and a unique new frame resulting from the melding of these views (DeShazer, 1982). The therapist does not become entangled in discussing motives and rightness or wrongness or seeking to stop the client from holding certain values. The client is not confronted, but rather encouraged to negotiate in the context of the client-therapist interaction. Thus, a systemic valuing process is less culture-bound and also offers greater likelihood of change because it presents a new perspective aimed at catching clients' attention while remaining congruent with their present reality.

THE PRACTICE IMPLICATIONS OF VALUING

There has been ongoing debate for years as to whether professional psychotherapy represents art or science. Many marriage and family therapists' opinion is on the side of art, yet their terminology often suggests science. To measure human exchange, marital and family systems have been compared to the cybernetic working of machines, the organization of solar systems, the interplay of chemical compounds, mathematical equations, and more. The language of science offers a definitive way to describe human functioning. It eliminates, however, many of the political and psychological interchanges in human systems as well as peculiarly human qualities—imagination, creativity, and unpredictability (Papp,

1984). It also represents a static value, rather than a valuing process mode of addressing therapeutic change.

As art, the major goal of marriage and family therapy is to negotiate basic perceptions so that participants see differently. Through the introduction of the novel or unexpected, a frame of reference is broken and the content of reality is rearranged. This artistic focus does not represent a solely creative act. Something is not created from nothing; rather, there is an uncovering, selection, reshuffling, combination, and synthesis of already existing facts, ideas, and skills (Papp, 1984). Valuing as presented in this chapter mirrors the idea of psychotherapy as an artistic endeavor.

The predominant implication of valuing for marriage and family therapists is its affirmation of marital and family relationships as pluralistic and multidimensional. As Lewis, Beavers, Gossett, and Phillips (1976) state, however:

> Historical preference for research in the pathological as well as the relative ignorance of the functional is, of course, common in research processes in all health fields . . . (the) focus is invariably on the dysfunctional. (pp. 3–4)

Valuing calls for the addition of positive interpretations of symptomatic behaviors to the usual negative ones, not just as a strategy for change, but because doing so generates a greater complexity that guards against linear thinking. Instead of solely assuming that a symptom is a minus sign indicating a dysfunctional marital or family relationship, the therapist can also regard symptoms as factors that affect a couple or family in moving toward a new and different state (Hoffman, 1981).

All mental health professionals have had to address in their academic preparation the questions of "What is normal?" and "What is abnormal?" Valuing posits that seeking answers to such questions is of little avail. Dell (1983) stated that boundaries of health and pathology do not actually exist. He proposed that professionals normally act as if pathology is objective and obvious when pathology is actually only a projection of their own values and intentions. He noted in this regard:

> When we "see" pathology as having an objective existence in the world, then we are projecting our values about how we think the world ought to be. We have shifted from, "I don't like it to be that way" (an explicit statement of personal values) to, "That's sick; that shouldn't be that way" (a statement that implies that the sickness is objective—independent of the observer's values). (p. 30)

Dell (1983) discussed five implications for clinical practice emanating from his assertion that objectively there is no pathology in the universe—"the universe simply is how it is." These five implications likewise mirror those implications emanating from a valuing perspective and include living without objective knowledge, taking personal responsibility, taking responsibility for pathologizing, doing therapy without pathology, and accepting what is.

Living Without Objective Knowledge

Dell (1983) asserted that objectivity is impossible. This is not to say, however, that human beings are passive, innocent recipients of information about the world. Rather, "the world bumps up against us and we each have our own reaction to it" (p. 31). Absolute, static values do not objectively exist. A person does not simply receive a system's values; he reacts to those values. Even if values did represent an objective, absolute reality, a person could not attain objective knowledge of them. Interaction can only provide one with his or her reaction to them, not how they objectively exist (Maturana, 1978). Thus, valuing represents the "bumping" together of values, the outcome always a negotiation around any reactions to that collision. The absolute adoption of "a" value is virtually impossible.

Taking Personal Responsibility

If other systems' values cannot be taken as absolutes, then persons must realize some responsibility for their own values. Systems cannot completely determine each others' values and the manner they are acted upon. For example, who is responsible for the reader's reaction to a book? The reader or the author? Does a book determine what a reader's reaction to it will be? Both contribute, but ultimately as the age-old adage suggests, "Beauty is in the eye of the beholder." Dell (1983) referred to this as an *epistemological responsibility.*

This epistemological responsibility must be contrasted, however, with a more familiar kind of responsibility that occurs in the everyday give-and-take of human interaction. This social form of responsibility is also more active: people hold each other responsible for many different things. Valuing is an epistemological process that posits the fruitlessness of therapists' thinking that they can take total responsibility for clients' changing their values. Both therapists and clients can present and be presented with alternatives, with their ultimate adoptions being a reflection of both; in the final analysis, they will be personal positions. However, both therapists and clients have to be held responsible for their alternatives and ultimate adoptions.

Taking Responsibility for Pathologizing

A primary illustration of the implications inherent in therapists' epistemological responsibility is the matter of "seeing pathology." If, as Dell (1983) proposed, there is no objective pathology in the world, then therapists who "see" pathology are projecting certain values. He further asserted:

> We are attached to pathology, I think, because it allows us to disown responsibility for our values. We wish to imply *our* values are really objective

or universal. I believe that many of the protests to my de-construction of pathology originated in peoples' unwillingness to substitute the personal, "I don't like that," for the objective, "That is sick." (p. 31)

Any conceptualization of objective pathology represents a linear epistemology. Systemic epistemology as a manner of "seeing" is represented by, "I don't like that behavior, view, emotion, and so on"—a personal reaction, rather than asserted "fact."

Doing Therapy Without Pathology

If there is no objective pathology, then therapists who take a professional position of seeking to identify and intervene regarding clients' pathology encounter problems. Most professional therapeutic training affirms the importance of therapists' acceptance of their clients. Yet acceptance cannot actually occur if therapists believe there is something wrong with the client (i.e., pathology). Dell (1983) declared that therapists who project pathology onto their clients while trying to accept them are in essence saying, "I accept part of you, but there is a part of you that i do not accept. That latter part needs to be fixed first before I can accept it." When this occurs, therapists are therefore claiming there is something objectively wrong with the client and thus one-sidedly postulating therapeutic goals.

One-sided postulation of therapeutic goals represents subtle, and not-so-subtle paternalistic social control, not therapy. "We know what is best for you" maneuvers represent social control. In contrast, therapists who do not maintain a concept of pathology likewise do not assert any right to singularly establish therapeutic goals. Decentralizing the concept of pathology results in professional therapeutic practice being guided by negotiation between therapists *and* clients.

Accepting What Is

In his fifth implication for professional therapeutic practice, Dell (1983) referred to the idea of "what is, is." He took pains to assert that he was not alluding to an overly optimistic "everything is fine because everything is the way it should be," nor any fatalistic, ideological brainwashing to take no action because "what is, is." Instead, Dell described a distinction many marriage and family therapists already recognize—the difference between Murray Bowen's "taking an I-position" and not doing so. Dell described this, stating:

> If I say that I dislike something—and explicitly base my dislike on my own values (i.e., take an I-position—then I am taking responsibility for my disliking. I am not blaming my dislike on an intrinsic wrong or sickness in the object of my dislike. By taking responsibility for my disliking, I am simultaneously accepting myself, i.e., admitting that my feelings are *mine,* and accepting that the disliked thing is the way it is. Conversely, if I were to

refuse to take responsibility for how I should feel by saying, "That's sick," or, "That shouldn't be that way," then I would be refusing to accept both myself and the disliked thing. (p. 64)

From a valuing perspective, "what is, is" does not mean therapists should take no action. It means that when marriage and family therapists do seek to change something they don't like, they should take that position from an I-position (i.e., "I don't like that") as opposed to a stance advocating pathology (i.e., "You're sick"). Further, "what is, is" means that upon taking a position, therapists should seek to observe what happens. If the position fails to achieve the intended result, they must identify and accept what has happened: a particular action did not achieve the desired result. For a therapist to refuse to accept "what is, is" is to blame the thing (which he or she tried to change) for the *therapist's* difficulty in changing it.

VALUING COMPONENTS

Valuing as an evolutionary process has seldom been a direct subject of discussion in marriage and family therapy literature (Nichols, 1984). The majority of writers have addressed the content of specific values, particularly therapists' values relative to families and family functioning. For example, Seymour (1982) urged marriage and family therapists to be intimately aware of problems surrounding values associated with divorce, dual careers, birth control, sexual dysfunction, abortion, child rearing, and child and spouse abuse. Margolin (1982) strongly recommended that therapists examine their values regarding divorce, extramarital affairs, and sex roles.

Likewise, the matter of gender bias in marriage and family therapy has received significant attention, particularly from the feminist perspective. Hare-Mustin (1978) declared that "unquestioned reinforcement of stereotyped sex roles takes place in much of family therapy" (p. 181). Because of value biases, Hare-Mustin questioned the ability of male therapists where gender issues are in question. She suggested an abnormal frequency of alliances between male therapists and male clients because of similar values; such alliances negatively affect female clients.

These and other authors have tended to take predominantly linear epistemological positions in focusing on content as opposed to process in their presentations. The content of these values is obviously important and cannot be ignored. Values need not, however, represent static stances construed as right or wrong. Rather, they encompass beliefs and resultant actions best regularly reconsidered, reclarified, and renegotiated.

In contrast to authors addressing the content of values in marriage and family therapy have been Ivan Boszormenyi-Nagy and his colleagues. They have framed their process-oriented discussions in the context of ethical accountability, stressing that satisfying family relationships require ethical behavior among family members, that is, consideration of each other's welfare and interests. In describing a type of therapy, Contextual Family Therapy, family members are facilitated in addressing relational commitments and balances of fairness (Boszormenyi-Nagy & Ulrich, 1981) The aim of the approach is a loosening of static values so family members become better able to shift their intentions and interactions toward more satisfying life experiences. What occurs is the development of a greater balance of fairness.

The ethical dimensions centering Contextual Family Therapy represent process-oriented elements of equal utility. Employed as *valuing components,* general issues can be facilitated. Regardless of the content of values, the use of these process-oriented components allows valuing to generalize to any specific issue arising in marriage and family therapy.

Obligation and Entitlement

Valuing as a process begins with a recognition of two primary valuing components: the mutual obligations and entitlements within all relationships. These components have been frequently minimized, overlooked, or contested in the professional literature. For example:

> I do my thing and you do your thing.
> I am not in this world to live up to your expectations.
> And you are not in this world to live up to mine.
> You are you and I am I.
> And if by chance we find each other, it's beautiful.

This "Gestalt Prayer" originated by Frederick Perls represents an overt statement of a value that permeates much of professional therapeutic practice. It is derived from a recognition that many personal and interpersonal problems appear to emanate from destructive and unrealistic obligations in relationships. Consequently, freedom from obligations is sought. While the intention may be freedom from only *destructive* obligations, the implication in practice has often resulted in encouraging persons to free themselves from all obligations (Karpel & Strauss, 1983).

This focus on retreating from relationships with destructive obligations offers little to describe how persons might move back into more or less satisfying, nondestructive relationships. Persons should take responsibility for themselves instead of trying to get others to take responsibility for their lives, but much of what individuals find important in their lives depends upon the willingness of people to assume some responsibility for one another.

Karpel and Strauss (1983) expounded upon the work of Boszormenyi-Nagy and his colleagues in describing a vocabulary to better comprehend the underlying structure of balanced, fair, mutually satisfying, growth-producing relationships. Karpel and Strauss asserted the inherent presence of obligations in relationships, emphasizing that not all obligations are destructive. They further offered the following illustrations:

> A wife is grateful for her husband's having gone out of his way to purchase something she wanted. She, in turn, offers to make a phone call both of them have been avoiding.

> An adolescent boy feels sad at having made fun of his younger sister in front of her peers. He apologies to her and offers to let her use his previously off-limits record player.

> A young man with severe diabetes feels indebted, literally for his life, to his sister who donated one of her kidneys for a transplant operation.

> A man feels a sense of debt to his parents for the physical and emotional support they offered him in building the satisfying, productive life he has come to enjoy.

These illustrations all involve at least one person's obligation based either on the *merit* of the other person (depending on his helpful actions or sacrifices) or the *debt* of the person (contingent on his actions having in some way harmed the other). This valuing component for achieving a balance of fairness relative to obligation is *entitlement.* Obligation and entitlement represent two ends of a valuing continuum. If it is agreed that one is obliged to another, there follows an agreement that the other is entitled to something.

In any relationship, recognition of obligations and entitlements constantly fluctuates. Fulfilling obligations results in decreasing one's own obligations, yet simultaneously increasing one's entitlement as well the obligations of others. Ignoring obligations tends to increase one's obligations as well as others' entitlement. "Give and take" underlies most of the valuing process.

Acknowledgment and Claim

Closely related to obligation and entitlement are acknowledgment and claim. *Acknowledgment* refers to "the willingness of one party in a relationship to recognize and 'give credit for' the entitlement of the other" (Karpel & Strauss, 1983, p. 34). Acknowledgment calls for a willingness to seek a balance of fairness in a relationship. Withholding acknowledgment in a relationship creates an imbalance. this is so even when such withholding is preceded by a refusal to provide acknowledgment. This second refusal only compounds the initial imbalance. Two examples illustrate withholding of acknowledgment:

> An elderly couple anticipate and make daily reference to their son's upcoming visit from his distant home. The weekly visits of their daughter who lives locally, however, are ignored or minimized.

> Two young children's efforts to clean up the kitchen receive ridicule and rebuke from their parents when some dishes are accidentally broken in the process.

Resentment and bitterness tend to be evoked by withholding acknowledgment. The likelihood of an in-kind response (concurrent withholding of acknowledgment by the opposite party) is thus increased. Mutual accusation, deafness, mistrust, and stagnation characterize such situations.

The opposite of acknowledgment on a valuing continuum for seeking a balance of fairness is claim. *Claim* refers to "one person's asking for something from the other" (Karpel & Strauss, 1983, p. 35). Examples of claims include:

> A woman postpones completing her graduate degree program so she can work to provide income for the family while her husband pursues his professional education. She now requests that the husband assume a greater child-rearing and breadwinning burden so she can complete her own professional educational objectives.

> A single parent, who has provided well for her two teenage children in the past, is temporarily unemployed. She asks that they contribute a portion of their earnings from part-time jobs to support the running of the household during this time of financial crisis.

Claims are not inherently valid. Persons frequently do make unwarranted claims in relationships. Therefore, the willingness of one party to capitulate to unilateral, excessive claims can be as harmful to a relationship as an unwillingness to consider any claims (Karpel & Strauss, 1983).

Balance of Fairness

In an ideal sense, effective valuing within, between, or among persons is that outcome wherein entitlement and obligation, acknowledgment and claim stand in relative balance with each other. There is a balance of fairness. Of course, no perfect, static balance can exist. Any balance of fairness achieved through valuing efforts can and will be altered by a variety of factors. One person may momentarily refuse to acknowledge the contributions of others. His or her entitlement to an acknowledgment may have been inadvertently ignored. Involved parties may have to redefine what they consider a balance of fairness if circumstances drastically alter the entitlement of one or more of them, for example, one family member becomes seriously injured in an auto accident.

Pursuing a balance of fairness through valuing involves ongoing efforts to consider mutual obligations and entitlements and to make realistic acknowledgments and claims. There is no perfect continuing parity. Seeking a balance of fairness thus requires commitment by all involved to try to correct imbalances. Boszormenyi-Nagy and Ulrich (1981) referred to this as *rejunction*—persons connecting with each other for the purpose of rebalancing fairness in their relationships. This may take the form of willingness to sit in a room together to reassess their certain values, to surface claims, and to hear one another's sides. This may also call for an acknowledgment of the sacrifice or merit of others, admitting to an obligation (and therefore acknowledging the legitimacy of others' claims), or taking the factors that may limit others' ability to acknowledge certain claims more seriously (e.g., a strong obligation to another relationship, such as a newly married child's significant obligations to his or her new spouse).

In seeking a balance of fairness through valuing, the question often arises, "Who is to say what is fair and what is unfair?" The answer is rarely simple. Karpel and Strauss (1983) suggested several guidelines to make this determination more manageable. They first asserted the importance of accepting that final word on what constitutes fairness and unfairness in a particular relationship comes from those who are directly involved in the relationship. There are no objective, external criteria to compare against. The only factor that might be introduced is an asserted effort to reassess the balance of fairness. This is not a fixed code with universal application; rather, it is an interchange during which involved members can seek movement toward in the context of the specifics of their relationship. This process is facilitated by asking questions that encourage the consideration of obligations and entitlements and statements of acknowledgment and claim.

The process of give-and-take that this common examination requires— asserting and considering claims, seeking to see another's side, and presenting one's own side—marks the beginning and the most important part of valuing aimed at achieving a balance of fairness. Frequently, this balance is gained in ways quite different from what might have been expected. This is natural since only the participants can truly gauge the weight and meaning of events and considerations for themselves and even these assessments may significantly change as new factors are introduced into ongoing interactions (Karpel & Strauss, 1983).

A second guideline identified by Karpel and Strauss (1983) for arriving at a balance of fairness involves what they referred to as *realistic accountability.* This concept suggests the greatest benefits for all members in a relationship as being derived from mutual efforts to carry out reasonable obligations without either shortchanging others or paying excessively or destructively. Realistic accountability encourages persons neither to ignore their entitlement nor tolerate unreasonable obligations, but rather to look for ways to balance entitlement and obligation. In this sense, realistic accountability proposes that people face obligations in relationships, but also puts some ceiling on how much they will ask of themselves and how much they will tolerate being asked by others. The "height" of the ceiling will be determined by involved members' consideration of obligations and entitlements in the context of their present situation.

Realistic accountability applies equally to all members in a relationship. Thus, a ceiling also exists on the extent to which others can be held accountable. An elderly parent may, for example, desire perfect or total accountability from his or her adult children, but should also consider the limitations, lack of resources, and other problems the children face. Put simply, there needs to be a recognition of the importance of judging others' beliefs and actions by the same standard of accountability by which one judges one's own.

SUMMARY AND CONCLUSIONS

This chapter examined some implications of valuing for the professional practice of marriage and family therapy. Valuing was described as emanating from the "expanding epistemology" of a systemic perspective. Valuing as evolutionary and unfolding within the context of negotiation around older beliefs was contrasted to linear notions of values as static entities. The practice implications of valuing, as well as specific valuing components, were considered.

Efran and Lukens (1985) asserted that marriage and family therapists do not give "treatment"—something applied like a mudpack—to a waiting, passive organism. They referred to George Kelly (1955) who warned against the term "patient," implying someone who sits patiently, waiting for something to happen or something to be done to him or her. Efran and Lukens stated:

> Families do not *start* changing at the therapist's office. They are always changing, and the visit to the therapist's office is simply the next step in their process. . . . It is arrogant of us to think that we "control" other people's lives. Even court-adjudicated cases and other so-called "unwilling" clients, cannot be sold anything against their will. Because people's structures keep changing as we spend time interacting with them, it seems to us as though they bought something from us that was incompatible with their beliefs. What was bought may have originally been incompatible, but at the point of sale, by definition, there could not have been an incongruity. Neither salespeople nor therapists *ever* sell their customers anything they do not want. To buy is to want. (p. 72)

Valuing as a process represents an approach similar to that suggested by students of ethnicity: respect for ethnicity involves initial acceptance of cultural differences, polite exploration of those differences, and subtle explanations of how a given ethnic group's customs differ from the larger culture. The therapist assumes the role of "culture broker," helping couples and families negotiate the traditional values they wish to retain and discard (McGoldrick, Pearce, & Giordano, 1982). With respect to gender issues, Pittman (1985) advocated marriage and family therapists assume a parallel role as "gender brokers":

> As a gender broker, I show initial respect for each person's efforts in playing out the gender role they have been taught, as well as sympathy for the difficulties and limitations they encounter in doing so. I try to make these people aware that they have choices about how and whether they will play out their gender stereotypes, and I am determined that they will get an equal voice in that choice. While I am personally uncomfortable with some of the arrangements my patients choose, I try to make sure that gender issues will never again go unquestioned in their relationship. And, I

try to help them realize that whether someone is male or female, does not mean that they must be Masculine or Feminine. (p. 31)

The essence of professional therapeutic practice from this perspective is to participate with persons in relationships so that their interactions within themselves and with each other can move in directions they prefer. The focus of marriage and family therapists is to find out what their clients are trying to conserve, and participate in their attempts to conserve it while seeking to maintain that balance of fairness necessary for more satisfying experiences.

8

Professional Identity as a Marriage and Family Therapist

For many years, individual psychotherapy was the only model of treatment for psychological ills. While different approaches to individual therapy existed, all therapists shared certain basic assumptions. Rogerians and Freudians may have disagreed about the root cause of psychopathology being, respectively, low self-esteem or repressed drives, but they never disagreed in accepting the primary forces shaping and maintaining behavior as being "within the individual." The resulting treatment focus required only the presence of the therapist and client.

The advent of marriage and family therapy was initially viewed as simply another means of treating the same problem. The individual was still the client. Marital partners, for example, were seen separately to deal with their *individual* concerns. The rationale put forth by individually oriented therapists reasoned that marital partners or other family members' direct participation (interaction during sessions) was potentially destructive to the necessary confidentiality and supportiveness needed for a meaningful therapeutic relationship. This point of view emanated from the therapists' linear epistemology.

It soon became clear that marriage and family therapy was more than just another way to treat individual clients. It was a new way of defining the problem. The "client" was not the individual alone, but included the client's marital or familial (or social) context. This more comprehensive concept called for a redefinition of fundamental beliefs (Nichols, 1984), as well as an expanded epistemology to consider the dynamics of evolving systems, not simply the vicissitudes of individual rights (L'Abate, 1982).

With regard to direct clinical practice, marriage and family therapy has come of age; theoretical assumptions have been identified and research has increased in both volume and sophistication (Russell, Olson, Sprenkle, & Atilano, 1983). While a number of various schools advocate their own approaches to clinical practice of marriage and family therapy, they agree on core components. They generally give attention to similar relationship dynamics in diagnosis and share similar therapeutic goals (Olson, Russell, & Sprenkle, 1980).

PROFESSION OR PROFESSIONAL SPECIALIZATION?

Especially in its infancy and still today, marriage and family therapy has been considered by some to be an area of specialization within other professional disciplines. This is reflected vividly in professional association membership. Therapists who practice marriage and family therapy subscribe their primary allegiance to professional associations representing psychiatry, psychology, social work, and counseling: the American Psychiatric Association, the American Psychological Association, the National Association of Social Workers, and the American Association for Counseling and Development. The prevailing perception is that marriage and family therapy is a therapeutic modality, a professional specialization, within psychiatry, psychology, social work, or counseling.

Marriage and family therapy has, however, clearly acquired those characteristics that are hallmarks of a profession unto itself (Winkle, Piercy, & Hovestadt, 1981). As Ard and Ard (1976) maintained:

> Marriage and family counseling is a profession . . . with a scientific body of knowledge, some relevant theory, a code of ethics, and some specific techniques. (p. xv)

Marriage and family therapy is an independently identifiable entity, a peer to psychiatry, psychology, and social work. The growth in membership and influence of the American Association for Marriage and Family Therapy as well as concurrent legislative efforts to create government-regulated licensing offer ample evidence. As Haley (1984) asserted:

> The issue of whether to organize the family therapy field has been resolved. This organization [AAMFT] has accomplished that and is working on the difficult problem of setting standards for membership and training. The power of the state is being brought to bear on who shall and who shall not be licensed to do therapy with families. All of us face the accomplished fact that the field is organized and ready for the benefits that follow to those who belong to the club. A certain point is reached, as in nuclear fission, when the outcome is inevitable. As therapists join an organization and are licensed, other therapists must do the same to compete. The supervisors and teachers come under pressure to be properly approved, or their trainees cannot share in the financial benefits of membership. (p. 12)

This chapter will examine several major issues relating to professional identity as a marriage and family therapist: professional affiliation, the legislative regulation of marriage and family therapy, potential interdisciplinary difficulties, and associated pragmatic concerns such as public relations, continuing education, and intraprofessional communications.

PROFESSIONAL AFFILIATION

One criterion for a profession is that it be self-regulating. Established professions are identified as such because they have developed standards and policies that, to some degree at least, control entry into the profession, prescribe training standards, and establish procedures and requirements for membership and practice. Professions develop ethical codes that outline standards of service, prescribe members' appropriate relationships to each other and the general public, and identify proper and improper practice. The primary organization for marriage and family therapists is the American Association for Marriage and Family Therapy (AAMFT).

The AAMFT

The AAMFT had its beginnings in 1942. Originally called the American Association of Marriage Counselors, it was renamed the American Association of Marriage and Family Counselors in 1970 and then in 1979 became the American Association for Marriage and Family Therapy. During most of its existence, the AAMFT has consisted primarily of psychiatrists, social workers, psychologists, and counselors who received degrees in their own specific discipline and then sought masters or doctoral training in marriage and family therapy. More recently, however, an increasing number of members have received terminal degrees specifically in marriage and family therapy (Kosinski, 1982).

From its inception, the AAMFT has been active in promoting rigorous standards for gaining and maintaining professional affiliation. Clinical membership calls for the completion of a master's or doctoral degree from a regionally accredited educational institution, or an equivalent course of study. This has been interpreted to mean the completion of a course of study substantially equivalent to the courses described here (AAMFT, 1983):

—*Human Development* (Three courses minimum). Human development, personality theory, human sexuality, psychopathology-behavior pathology.
—*Marital and Family Studies* (Three courses minimum). Family development; family systems; marital, sibling, and individual subsystems.
—*Marital and Family Therapy* (Three courses minimum). Major marital and family therapy treatment approaches, such as systems, neoanalytic (object relations), communications, behavioral, structural.
—*Research* (One course minimum). Research design, methodology, statistics, research in marital and family studies and therapy.
—*Professional Studies* (One course minimum). Ethics, family law.
—*Supervised Clinical Practice* (One year minimum). Fifteen hours per week, approximately 8–10 hours in direct contact with individuals, couples, and families.

This course of study can be completed with or after obtaining a master's or doctoral degree.

Clinical membership also calls for 2 calendar years of supervised work experience in marital and family therapy. This experiential requirement is in addition to the supervised clinical practice secured as part of the academic requirements. It requires at least 1,000 hours of direct clinical contact with couples and families and 200 hours of supervision of that work, at least 100 of which shall be in individual supervision. Also, this supervision must be provided by AAMFT approved supervisors or supervisors acceptable to the AAMFT Membership Committee. Students completing AAMFT accredited degree programs may identify up to 100 hours of supervision toward their required 200 hours for membership. Not more than 50 of these hours, however, may be in group supervision.

Finally, written endorsement by two clinical members of the Association, attesting to suitable qualities of personal maturity and integrity for the conduct of marriage and family therapy, are further necessary to complete the basic clinical membership requirements. The Association also maintains associate and student membership categories with lesser requirements for individuals pursuing clinical membership.

Concurrent with a focus on maintaining high standards for membership, the AAMFT has emphasized the importance of quality training and supervision opportunities in marriage and family therapy. To this end, the AAMFT Board of Directors established standards for marriage and family therapy supervision in 1971. The Commission on Supervision, established in 1983, regulates requirements for approved supervisor designation within the Association. The approved supervisor is one who has received advanced recognition for clinical skills, special training, and experience in the supervision of prospective marriage and family therapists, and who meets the highest standards of clinical education and practice. Approved supervisors are recognized as competent to provide supervision to students and potential members of the Association as they seek to fulfill their clinical member requirements.

Two tracks are available to gain an approved supervisor designation, each with specific requirements (AAMFT, 1984):

Track I:
1. Has been in clinical practice as a marriage and family therapist for at least 5 years.
2. Has at least 2 years of experience supervising marriage and family therapy.
3. Has received at least 36 hours of individual supervision. An approved supervisor observes the candidate's supervision of at least two supervisees who meet minimum qualifications for student or associate membership in AAMFT. This is usually for a period of 1 year and shall not exceed 2 years. Observation should customarily be scheduled once a week; once every other week is considered minimum. Up to 18 hours of the noted individual supervision may be earned through group supervision at the ratio of 3 hours of group supervision to 1 hour of individual supervision. Therefore, a maximum of 54 hours of group supervision may replace 18 hours of individual supervision. Group size should not exceed six candidates. The candidate for appointment as an approved supervisor must complete the training for supervision with an AAMFT approved supervisor.
4. Has attended and participated in a workshop on supervision issues. Presented by the Commission on Supervision at an annual AAMFT conference, this workshop is required for non-AAMFT members.

Track II:
1. Has had at least 10 years of experience in specialized therapy and supervision within the marriage and family therapy field.
2. Has written documentation of a systemic orientation in any published materials and in the written materials provided to the Commission in support of the application.
3. Has prominence in one's community or the nation as an educator/trainer in marriage and family therapy.
4. Has letters of recommendation from two AAMFT approved supervisors attesting to competence in the supervision of marriage and family therapy trainees and to adherence to a systemic orientation and prominence in the field.
5. Has attended and participated in a workshop on supervision issues. Presented by the Commission on Supervision at an annual AAMFT conference, this workshop is required for non-AAMFT members.

In addition to the Commission on Supervision regulating approved supervisors, the AAMFT sponsors the Commission on Accreditation for Marriage and Family Therapy Education that establishes standards for training programs in marriage and family therapy and identifies institutions and programs promoting and maintaining these standards. The Commission maintains several purposes in performing its functions (Commission on Accreditation for Marriage and Family Therapy Education, 1981):

1. To stimulate the improvement of professional marriage and family therapy education, including helping training institutions/agencies develop quality programs by fostering ongoing self-study and development.
2. To establish and maintain programs to ensure that institutions/agencies meeting such standards provide students with appropriate learning resources so they have the opportunity to acquire the requisite skills, knowledge, and ethical sensitivity to be professionally competent.
3. To provide an authoritative guide to programs in the field of marriage and family therapy that deserve public and professional confidence and support, to provide prospective students with a dependable basis for the selection of educational programs, and to provide state boards that license or certify marriage and family therapists with a list of accredited graduate degree and postdegree programs.

The Commission on Accreditation reviews programs seeking accreditation, trains representatives to conduct site visits, and conducts workshops for leaders of developing programs. In 1978, the Commission gained official recognition as an accrediting agency for graduate degree and postdegree clinical training programs in marriage and family therapy by the United States Office of Education, Department of Health, Education, and Welfare. This recognition was renewed in 1980 by the new United States Department of Education.

The Commission's accrediting role is unique among bodies recognized by the Department of Education in that it accredits not only university-based degree granting programs but also "free-standing" postdegree training centers (Shalet & Everett, 1981). These postdegree programs have a unique roll in offering an alternative entry into the marriage and family profession. Ordinarily, the master's degree program is recognized as the entry level into the profession by providing broad theoretical knowledge, basic applied skills, and professional attitudes. The doctoral degree is viewed as offering mastery of further comprehensive theory, advanced supervised practice, basic skills and practice in research, and potential experience in teaching and supervision. The postdegree programs have traditionally offered intensive supervised practice with ongoing didactic seminars for individuals who have already attained allied clinical degrees and are seeking specialized training in marriage and family therapy. As of August 1985, 21 university programs and 8 postdegree programs had been awarded accreditation by the Commission (Commission Releases '85 MFT Program Roster, 1985). These programs are listed in Table 8–1.

Shalett and Everett (1981) asserted that the accreditation process provides needed linkages for adequate geographical licensure within the profession. In their view licensure basically functions to offer the public minimal protection against untrained practitioners; it identifies minimal qualifications for the practitioner, but neither ensures competency nor addresses the quality of the individual education and training. They identified accreditation as the primary way to establish standards for practitioners' educational and training experiences, since licensure is essentially meaningless in the absence of accreditation. The AAMFT has been recognized as the focal point for the marriage and family therapy profession by several states whose licensing boards have incorporated major aspects of AAMFT membership standards and its Commission on Accreditation's program standards into their licensing laws. Further, the

---

Table 8–1   AAMFT Accredited Programs

Accredited Graduate Programs		
ABILENE CHRISTIAN UNIVERSITY Marriage and Family Institute Abilene, TX 79699 *DEGREE:* M.A. Paul B. Faulkner, Ph.D. (915) 677-1911 BRIGHAM YOUNG UNIVERSITY Dept. of Family Sciences Marriage & Family Cslg. Clinic Provo, UT 84602	*DEGREES:* M.S., Ph.D. Dr. D. Eugene Mead (801) 378-3888 EAST TEXAS STATE UNIVERSITY Dept. of Counseling and Guidance Commerce, TX 75428 *DEGREE:* Ed.D. Patricia Lutz-Ponder, Ed.D. (214) 886-5631, 5637 FLORIDA STATE UNIVERSITY Department of Home and Family Life Tallahassee, FL 32306	*DEGREE:* Ph.D. Craig A. Everett, Ph.D. (904) 644-1588 FULLER THEOLOGICAL SEMINARY 135 North Oakland Avenue Pasadena, CA 91101 *DEGREES:* M.A., M. Div. Dennis B. Guernsey, Ph.D. (818) 449-1745 GEORGIA STATE UNIVERSITY Dept. of Psychology Clinical Child, and Family Psy. University Plaza Atlanta, GA 30303

DEGREE: Ph.D.
Luciano L'Abate, Ph.D.
(404) 658-2283
HAHNEMANN UNIVERSITY
Mental Health Sciences Dept.
230 North Broad Street
Philadelphia, PA 19102
DEGREE: M.A.
Lee Combrick-Graham, M.D.
(215) 448-7261
KANSAS STATE UNIVERSITY
Dept. of Family and Child Guidance
Justin Hall
Manhattan, KS 66506
DEGREES: Ph.D., M.S.
Candyce S. Russell, Ph.D.
(913) 532-5510
LOMA LINDA UNIVERSITY
Dept. of Social Relations
Loma Linda, CA 92354
DEGREE: M.S.
Antonius Brandon, Ph.D.
(714) 824-4547, 0800 ex. 4547
NORTHERN ILLINOIS UNIVERSITY
Dept. of Home Economics
Human Family Resources
Dekalb, IL 60115
DEGREE: M.S.
Connie Salts, Ph.D.
(815) 753-1196
PURDUE UNIVERSITY
Marriage and Family Therapy
Center
CDFS Bldg.
Lafayette, IN 47907
DEGREE: Ph.D.
Wallace Denton, Ed.D.
(317) 494-2940
SOUTHERN CONNECTICUT STATE
UNIVERSITY
Counseling and School Psychology
Dept.
501 Cresent Street
New Haven, CT 06515
DEGREE: M.S.
Rocco Orlando, Ph.D.
(203) 397-4574, 4580
ST. MARY'S UNIVERSITY
Marriage and Family Counseling
Program
1 Camino Santa Maria
San Antonio, TX 78284
DEGREE: M.A.
Grace Luther, Ph.D.
(512) 436-3133
TEXAS TECH UNIVERSITY
Dept. of Home and Family Life
P.O. Box 4170
Lubbock, TX 79409
DEGREE: Ph.D.
William H. Quinn, Ph.D.
(806) 742-3000
UNIVERSITY OF BRIDGEPORT
Counseling and Human Resources
College of Health Sciences
Bridgeport, CT 06601
DEGREE: M.S. in MFT
Gerald Arndt, Ed.D.
(203) 576-4173
UNIVERSITY OF HOUSTON AT
CLEAR LAKE
Behavioral Sciences Program
2700 Bay Area Blvd.
Houston, TX 77058

DEGREE: M.A.
Linda Bell, Ph.D.
(713) 488-9236
UNIVERSITY OF CONNECTICUT
School of Family Studies
Storrs, CT 06268
DEGREE: M.A.
Robert G. Ryder, Ph.D.
(203) 486-4633
UNIVERSITY OF MARYLAND
Dept. of Family and Community
Development
College Park, MD 20742
DEGREE: M.S.
Ned L. Gaylin, Ph.D.
(301) 454-2142
UNIVERSITY OF SOUTHERN
CALIFORNIA
Dept. of Sociology
J.P. Human Relations Center
725 West 27th Street
Los Angeles, CA 90007
DEGREE: Ph.D.
Carlfred Broderick, Ph.D.
(213) 743-2137
UNIVERSITY OF
WISCONSIN-STOUT
School of Education and Human
Services
Menomonie, WI 54751
DEGREE: M.S.
Charles Barnard, Ed.D.
(715) 232-2404
VIRGINIA TECH UNIVERSITY
Marriage and Family Therapy
Program
Dept. of Family and Child
Development
Blacksburg, VA 24061
DEGREES: M.S., Ph.D.
James F. Keller, Ph.D.
(703) 961-7201

**Accredited Post Degree
Programs**
ACKERMAN INSTITUTE OF FAMILY
THERAPY
148 East 78th Street
New York, NY 10021
Robert Simon, M.D.
(212) 879-4900
BRISTOL HOSPITAL
Marriage and Family Therapy
Program
Bristol, CT 06010
Thomas C. Todd, Ph.D.
(203) 589-2000 ex. 206
CALIFORNIA FAMILY STUDY
CENTER
4400 Riverside Drive
Burbank, CA 91505
Edwin S. Cox. Ph.D.
(213) 843-0711
FAMILY AND CHILDREN SERVICES
OF GREATER ST. LOUIS
Family Therapy Institute
2650 Olive Street
St. Louis, MO 63103
Paul K. Reed, M.S.W.
(314) 371-6500
FAMILY INSTITUTE OF
WESTCHESTER
147 Archer Ave.
Mt. Vernon, NY 10550

Elizabeth A. Carter, A.C.S.W.
(914) 699-4300
KANTOR FAMILY INSTITUTE
THE FAMILY CENTER
385 Highland Ave.
Somerville, MA 02144
David Kantor, Ph.D.
(617) 628-8815
MARRIAGE COUNCIL OF
PHILADELPHIA
Division of Family Studies
4025 Chestnut Street
Philadelphia, PA 19104
Ellen M. Berman, M.D.
(215) 382-6680
FAMILY SERVICE OF MILWAUKEE
The Milwaukee Psychotherapy
Training Inst.
Box 08434
Milwaukee, WI 53208
Russell Brethauer, Psy.D.
(414) 342-4560

MFT PROGRAMS IN PROCESS
Graduate Degree Programs
Auburn University (M.S.)
Dept. of Family & Child. Dev.
School of Home Economics
203 Spidel Hall
Auburn, AL 36849
Dr. Marilyn Bradbard
(205) 826-4151
PRESBYTERIAN COUNSELING
SERVICE
564 NE Ravena Blvd.
Marriage & Family Therapy Training
Seattle, WA 98115
Barbara J. Fischer, M.S.W.
(206) 527-2266
UNIVERSITY OF RHODE ISLAND
Marriage and Family Counseling
Program
College of Human Science and
Services
Kingston, RI 02881
DEGREE: M.S.
Peter E. Maynard, Ph.D.
(401) 792-2440

Post Degree Programs
FAMILY INSTITUTE OF
PHILADELPHIA
P.O. Box 15825
Middle City Station
Philadelphia, PA 19103
Alfred S. Friedman, Ph.D.
(215) 567-1396

Note. From "Commission Releases '85 MFT Program Roster," 1985, *Family Therapy News, 16,* p. 11. Copyright 1985 by AAMFT. Reprinted by permission.

AAMFT's methods of giving credentials have provided recognition for practitioners in those states with no licensure, particularly with regard to insurance reimbursement for services.

American Family Therapy Association (AFTA)

A second organizational affiliation for the marriage and family therapy profession is the American Family Therapy Association (AFTA). Founded in 1978, its stated objectives include:

1. Advancing family therapy as a science, which regards the entire family as the unit of study;
2. Promoting research and professional education in family therapy and allied fields;
3. Making information about family therapy available to practitioners in other fields of knowledge and to the public;
4. Fostering cooperating among those concerned with medical, psychological, social, legal, and other aspects of the family and those involved in the science and practice of family therapy. (Sauber, L'Abate, & Weeks, 1985, p. 180)

Membership in the AFTA is open to individuals who have been teachers in family therapy for at least 5 years and made a thoughtful contribution to the profession. The membership numbers approximately 500 family therapy teachers and researchers who meet once a year to share ideas and develop common interests. It is a "think tank" whose annual meeting brings together professionals to address a variety of clinical, research, and teaching topics. In 1981, a joint liaison committee of representatives from the AAMFT and the AFTA was formed to take up the issue of the respective roles of the two organizations within the profession. The AFTA was identified as an academy of advanced professionals interested in the exchange of ideas; the AAMFT retained recognition by the government as providing credentials to marriage and family therapists (Nichols, 1984).

LEGISLATIVE REGULATION OF MARRIAGE AND FAMILY THERAPY

Established professions are self-regulating, and through self-regulation, gain public acceptance and respectability. Professions are also regulated, however, through legal processes assigning licensure as a symbol of competence to practice the profession. Statute law in all states controls the practice of medical and legal professionals. Since the 1970s, the licensing of psychologists, clinical social workers, counselors, and marriage and family therapists has aroused intense professional interest, primarily because licensure has become synonymous with professionalism. As Davis (1981) stated:

> Licensure . . . seems to furnish an objective positive personal identification ("I am a member of a legally recognized, and therefore valuable, group in our society"). There is reflected public agreement that a licensed person must possess unusual, scarce skills to qualify for licensure. The status by association with institutions wielding the power of social control—that is, to other licensed professionals and to government itself—cannot be overlooked. (p. 84)

Fretz and Mills (1980) defined *licensure* as "the statutory process by which an agency of government, usually of a state, grants permission to a person meeting predetermined qualifications to engage in a given occupation and/or use a particular title and to perform specified functions" (p. 7). Unlicensed practitioners in most states with licensing laws are subject to legal penalties should they misrepresent themselves. Thus, licensure can restrict entry into the profession and those denied entry who persist in their activities can be prosecuted (Davis, 1981).

Most professional mental health literature has been opposed to licensure, yet licensing legislation has continued to accelerate (Fretz & Mills, 1980). In their work examining this paradox, Fretz and Mills identified five major premises supporting licensure efforts. Corey, Corey, and Callanan (1984) expounded upon these five premises in addressing other writers' views.

Fretz and Mills' posited that licensure is designed to protect the public by establishing minimum standards of service. They contended consumers would be harmed by the absence of such standards; incompetent practitioners would have the potential to cause long-term, negative consequences. Their position was further developed by Phillips (1982):

> For all that can be said about legal constraints on practice, one thing is most important: Their purpose is to promote the public's welfare by improving and maintaining the quality of training and practice, maximizing benefits-to-cost service delivery outcomes, and protecting the public from gross incompetence. (p. 924)

Others have challenged the position that licensure protects consumers. Gross (1978), for example, cited substantial evidence that existing licensure practices have been a confused array of policies that promise protection but actually serve to institutionalize a lack of public accountability. Citing problems in the medical and legal professions as representative, Gross pointed out that licensing a profession is no guarantee of quality or responsible behavior. He noted that in 38 of the 50 states that license physicians, professional incompetence is not specified as a reason for disciplinary action. Bernstein and Lecomte (1981) asserted the protection offered the public by licensure is more fiction than fact. They found little objective data to support the claim that licensure regulations have prevented abuse or assured more than minimal professional competence. Bernstein and Lecomte pointed to the increasing number of malpractice suits occurring along with the increase of licensure regulation as evidence that licensure in its present form does not guarantee clients' welfare.

Fretz and Mills (1980) secondly proposed that licensure is designed to protect the public from ignorance about mental health services. They based this assumption on the belief that consumers in need of mental health services typically do not know how to choose an appropriate practitioner or how to judge the quality of services rendered. Gross (1978), with a contrary opinion, contended licensure tends to mystify the therapeutic process by reducing the amount of information actually provided to consumers. Gill (1982) questioned how licensure by itself provides information. He pointed to the general public's ignorance of differences among licensed mental health professionals, such as psychologists, social workers, and counselors.

Fretz and Mills (1980) thirdly advanced that licensure increases the likelihood that practitioners will be more competent and their services better distributed and thus more available. Hogan (1979) disagreed with the latter portion of this view, noting that when a group becomes licensed, it gains increased status, privileges, and income. Services usually cost more after licensure; the profession tends to be less willing to provide services to the poor and lower income public most likely to need its services.

Fretz and Mills (1980) fourthly offered that licensure upgrades a profession. They proposed a licensed profession will have more practitioners committed to improving and maintaining the highest standards of excellence. Van Hoose and Kottler (1977) criticized this position, writing that licensure tends to make training curricula and definitions for service too rigid. Rogers (1980) concurred, contending that a profession becomes frozen as soon as criteria are set up for licensure.

Finally, Fretz and Mills (1980) posited licensing allows a profession to define for itself what it will and will not do. Accordingly, a profession is assumed to be more independent, since other professions or the courts cannot specify its functions. On the other hand, Fretz and Mills themselves noted licensure frequently incites challenges to a profession that makes definite claims, particularly in cases involving the right to offer certain services or to obtain payments from insurance companies. Thus, licensure can protect a profession's domain but at the risk of inviting increased attacks.

In summary, this seeming ambivalence raises a question about the dominant benefits of licensure. The mental health professions overtly assert public welfare as primary; but perhaps more self-serving interests are of equal importance. Writings in the professional mental health literature would suggest so. For example:

> For the past several years, psychologists have been debating the effects of licensure . . . on the development of psychology as a profession. . . . Two dominant themes have emerged from the discussion: ensuring psychology's place within the third-party reimbursement system and excluding

other professions (e.g., social work and marriage and family counseling) from such a system. (Danish & Smyer, 1981, p. 13)

The time has come for all professional counselors to face the following fact: Either we (all of us) get serious, unite, and fight for our professional right to provide mental health services to the public; to regulate our own profession; to eliminate any unfair trade practices by insurance companies and our peer professionals or we may not just lose a few battles but may very well be destined to lose the war. (Wilmarth, 1983, p. 3)

Bertram (1983) perhaps epitomized this discussion in stating:

Let us be clear, this is not an issue of competence, ethics, or morality. What we are dealing with here is turf. (p. 7)

Given this general caveat, we now move to considering the status of licensure regulation specifically for marriage and family therapists. Sporakowski (1982) put forth three major questions relevant to the licensing of marriage and family therapists:

1. Are specific guidelines available for preparing an individual to practice marriage and family therapy?
2. Are there ethical standards on which the professional will base practice?
3. Is there a need for control of the professional's practice?

A number of states have responded to these questions affirmatively in enacting legislation licensing marriage and family therapists.

Licensing Requirements for Marriage and Family Therapists

By 1985, state legislation creating licensing requirements specifically for marriage and family therapy was enacted in ten states: California, Connecticut, Florida, Georgia, Michigan, Nevada, New Jersey, North and South Carolina, and Utah. However, legislation is being introduced or pending in over twice as many states. Although the AAMFT has prepared a model regulatory code for marriage and family therapy licensure (AAMFT, 1979), significant diversity exists among enacted legislation.

Seven states, for example, regulate broad areas of counseling: Alabama, Arkansas, Idaho, Missouri, Ohio, Texas, and Virginia. These states do not, however, identify marriage and family therapy as a separate and distinct profession. These states' laws license "professional counselors," treating marriage and family therapy perhaps as a subspecialty within the more general counseling field. For instance, Virginia requires licensure as a professional counselor first and then allows for a specialty designation in marriage and family therapy (Clark, 1985). This section will address those states recognizing marriage and family therapy as having a distinct professional identity.

Sporakowski (1982) referred to existing licensure regulations as a "hodgepodge" given the variety of assumptions and definitions upon which they appear to have been based. Corey et al. (1984) provided the following partial definitions:

> Marriage and family counseling is that service performed with individuals, couples, or groups wherein interpersonal relationships between spouses or members of a family are examined for the purpose of achieving more adequate, satisfying, and productive marriage and family adjustments. (California)

> Marriage and family counseling also includes premarital counseling, predivorce and postdivorce counseling, and family counseling. It consists of the application of principles, methods and techniques of counseling and psychotherapeutic techniques for the purpose of resolving psychological conflict, modifying perception and behavior, altering old attitudes and establishing new ones in the area of marriage and family life. (Georgia)

> Marriage and family counseling consists of the application of established principles of learning, motivation, perception, thinking, emotional, marital and sexual relationships and adjustments by persons trained in psychology, social work, psychiatry, or marital counseling. (Nevada) (pp. 165–166)

Not only definitions but also essential terminology differ by jurisdiction. Not all of the ten states with licensure regulating marriage and family therapy refer to therapy-therapist. California, for example, refers to marriage, family, and child counselors. Michigan's 1974 act, by contrast, was specific to marriage counseling. Sporakowski (1982) suggested that this appeared to be as much a result of a states rights' attitude in legislatures as an attempt by states to meet the individual needs of their citizens. He further asserted other states' lack of legislation was directly related to the issue of the emergence of marriage and family therapy as a distinct profession. Although support from the various other major mental health professions has fluctuated, those representing medicine, psychology, social work, and the diverse group included in the American Association for Counseling and Development have generally been resistant to the anticipated intrusion of legislation into what they perceive as their professional domains.

Sporakowski (1982) outlined three issues as significant for marriage and family therapists: what and who are covered, required qualifications, and the licensure process.

Licensure Coverage

Most licensure legislation negatively defines the boundaries of practice by identifying exclusions or exemptions. For example, the state of Florida legislated the following exemptions in its licensure law:

(1) No person shall be required to be licensed under this chapter who:

(a) Is a salaried employee of a government agency; developmental services program, mental health, alcohol, or drug abuse facility . . . accredited academic institution; or research institution, if such employee is performing duties for which he was hired solely within the confines of such agency, facility, or institution.

(b) Is a student who is pursuing a course of study which leads to a degree in medicine or a profession regulated by this chapter who is providing services in a training setting, provided such activities or services constitute part of a supervised course of study, or is a graduate accumulating the experience required for any licensure under this chapter, provided such graduate or student is designated by a title such as "intern" or "trainee" which clearly indicates the in-training status of the student. . . .

(c) Is not a resident of the state but offers services in this state, provided:
   1. Such services are performed for no more than 5 days in any month and no more than 15 days in any calendar year; and
   2. Such nonresident is licensed or certified by a state or territory of the United States, or by a foreign country or province, the standards of which were, at the date of his licensure or certification, equivalent to or higher than the requirements of this chapter in the opinion of the department. . . .

(d) Is a rabbi, priest, minister, or clergyman of any religious denomination or sect when engaging in activities which are within the scope of the performance of his regular or specialized ministerial duties and for which no separate charge is made, or when such activities are performed, with or without charge, for or under the auspices or sponsorship, individually or in conjunction with others, of an established and legally cognizable church, denomination, or sect, and when the person rendering service remains accountable to the established authority thereof. (Psychological Services Act, 1983, sec. 490.014)

Similar exemptions exist in other states' licensure laws. One particular point of contention in regard to licensure coverage relates to other licensed mental health professionals claiming to practice marriage and family therapy. In California, for example, a psychologist was told by the state regulatory board that he would need the appropriate license (Marriage, Family, and Child Counselor) if he intended to advertise marriage and family therapy as a service. California has been specific in this regard; however, individuals practicing within the guidelines of another professional license are typically exempted so long as they do not claim to practice as a marriage and family therapist. This has generally been interpreted to mean that a licensed psychologist, psychiatrist, or social worker could treat marital or family problems but not advertise as a marriage and family therapist (Sporakowski, 1982).

Qualifications

Those states regulating marriage and family therapy all require that the prospective licensee possess a minimum of a master's degree in marriage and family therapy, social work, pastoral counseling, or relevant qualifications in behavioral sciences such as psychology or sociology. Some states go significantly beyond that minimum. New Jersey will accept only one master's degree, social work, or a doctorate in an appropriate field; Michigan requires a doctorate in a relevant field unless the master's degree is specifically in social work, marriage, or pastoral counseling.

In addition to these academic qualifications, states differ in their accompanying experience requirements. Qualifications vary from Nevada's 1 year of postgraduate experience in marriage and family counseling to New Jersey's 5 years of full-time counseling experience, at least 2 of which must have been in marriage counseling. Most states require that the majority of clinical experience be gained under supervision. Florida's licensure law, for example, requires marriage and family therapist applicants to have 3 years of experience in the practice of the profession in which licensure is sought. Two of the 3 years must be supervised; the applicant:

> . . . during his period of supervision, was subjected to oversight, guidance and evaluation by someone who meets the education and experience requirements for licensure in the profession for which licensure is sought by the applicant. . . . Supervision shall involve:
> (a) Face to face conversation with the supervisor.
> (b) A focus on the raw data from the student's clinical work, which is made directly available to the supervisor through such means as written clinical materials, direct observation and video and audio recordings.
> (c) A process which is clearly distinguishable from personal psychotherapy or didatic instruction. (Psychological Services Act, 1983, subsec. 120.53)

Florida's law also requires that of the 3 years required experience for licensure as a marriage and family therapist, the applicant must demonstrate 500 hours of direct involvement with individuals, groups, or families including work in at least two of the following four categories of cases: unmarried dyads, married couples, separating and divorcing couples, and family groups including children.

The Licensure Process

All state laws require prospective licensees to file a formal application, supplying letters of recommendation, giving proof of their academic credentials, and documenting hours of supervised experience. Most also request a written or oral examination or both.

After successful completion of all requirements, the license is awarded. Maintenance of the license is normally dependent upon paying renewal fees and obtaining a requisite number of Continuing Education Units prior to the time of renewal. For example, Florida requires that 30 hours of continuing education credit be earned during each biennial renewal period. Continuing Education Units must be relevant to the profession for which license renewal is sought and approved by the state regulatory body governing professional license renewal.

A license may be suspended or revoked for a variety of reasons that are typically defined within the legislation creating the license. Frequent violations cited include fraud or deceit practiced on the regulatory board, conviction of a crime, abuse of chemical substances, and unethical behavior. Identifying and reporting these violations is viewed as the responsibility of licensed individuals as well as the general public. Usually a "friendly remonstrance" is seen as sufficient unless violations are repeated or blatant and involved with criminal acts (Sporakowski, 1982). In such cases, legal action is taken, violation of the licensing law itself normally resulting in a misdemeanor action with possible fines and incarceration. Of course, associated criminal violations could garner more serious legal action and consequences.

In summary, the presence of and specific requirements for licensure as a marriage and family therapist vary from state to state. In seeking a license, prospective professionals should get in touch with the appropriate state agency for information about licensure laws and application requirements.

INTERDISCIPLINARY DIFFICULTIES FACED BY MARRIAGE AND FAMILY THERAPISTS

Over a decade ago, the professional literature testified to the roadblocks that systemically oriented marriage and family therapists faced working within a mental health delivery system entrenched in a traditional individualistic, linear epistemology (Framo, 1976; Haley, 1975). The medical model of pathology, which explains behavior in terms of intrapsychic dynamics, is still predominant within the mental health establishment. Consequently, marriage and family therapists are often subtly sabotaged by governmental agencies, community mental health administrators, and professional staffs (Piercy, McKeon, & Laird, 1983).

The difficulties derived from these circumstances are most evident in the community mental health movement in the United States originating in the mid-1960's, in part from a recognition that a prosperous post-World War II society was obligated to improve its delivery of human services. Extensions of Social Security, welfare, and unemployment benefits represent examples. The community mental health movement also arose out of a conviction that orthodox individual and group psychotherapy did not give enough attention to prevention and health. The major goal of the movement was to apply behavioral science knowledge to improve the functioning of persons in their environments and prevent serious emotional dysfunction (Iscoe, 1982).

Framo (1976) posited the parallel goals of family therapy and the community mental health movement's preventive/health orientation in stating:

> The symptoms of one or more family members may involve many community agencies and professional helpers, each dealing with a limited sector of the family process, leaving the system untouched. A marital difficulty, for example, may spill over into the children's presenting problems in school or in the community; it may involve the police, juvenile court, domestic relations court, social service agencies, psychiatrists, visiting nurses, Alcoholics Anonymous, religious organizations, and medical hospitals. In essence, the helping professions deal only peripherally with the effects of pathological family processes. Because they lack this awareness of the total family situation, there is inefficient duplication of services, and sometimes the various agencies and helpers work at cross purposes: one family I know had various family members simultaneously involved with eighteen agencies. By treating whole families, furthermore, contact can be made with asymptomatic people who bring others into treatment; these people may never seek treatment for themselves, and yet have great pathological impact on their intimates. The family approach, then, could move the helping professions into a heretofore unreachable part of the population. Moreover, since problems in families tend to repeat themselves from one generation to the next, treating the whole family gives us a chance to abort the problems in this generation—a truly preventative method. (p. 26)

Given this commonality of major goals, it seems ironic that marriage and family therapists should face obstacles in implementing their practice within community mental health settings. Haley (1975), however, asserted it is a fundamental error to assume that a marriage and family therapy modality can be added to a mental health setting in the same way one can add group therapy or a behavior therapy approach. He detailed a number of settings attempting to introduce marriage and family therapy, recoiling as they discovered the unexpected consequences, and "returning with relief to the tranquility of traditional individual therapy" (p. 3). Haley proposed that confrontations regarding theories of client motivation, diagnosis, and therapeutic technique are inevitable with the introduction of marriage and family therapy into a traditional mental health setting. The amount of energy spent in ameliorating marriage and family therapy as a representative force, either overtly or covertly, frequently becomes alarming. Marriage and family therapists must recognize these probable pitfalls in asserting their professional identity and practice.

Confrontations Over Theories of Causation

All mental health efforts are based upon a theory of causation. When the unit of diagnosis and treatment efforts is the individual, then the cause of behavior must rest within that individual. When the unit of diagnosis and treatment shifts to two or more persons, the cause of behavior no longer resides within the individual, but rather in the interaction between or among persons. Haley (1975) identified three confrontations occasioned when this shift in focus is introduced into a traditional mental health setting:

1. The most obvious confrontation is created by the marriage and family therapist's abandonment of traditional psychodynamic explanations of behavioral causation. Since the psychodynamic perspective is confined to one person, it becomes irrelevant by definition. In discarding psychodynamic theory, the dominant ideology for over half a century in mental health settings is cast aside.
2. A second confrontation occurs when the therapist abandons a theory of suppressed emotions as a cause of behavior. With two or more persons, "emotions" become a communicative behavior between persons, not a cause of one individual's actions.
3. By discarding the individual as the unit of diagnosis and treatment, the marriage and family therapist asks colleagues to believe that a client's history is not vitally relevant as a way of explaining the client's behavior. When cause is in the interpersonal context, it cannot be a program built inside an individual by his or her past.

Haley proposed that these confrontations result in a process of disorientation within a mental health setting. The two different views cannot reach agreement. The individually oriented therapist seeks to explore past causes; the systemically oriented therapist addresses the current situation. If either therapist attempts to adopt a partially systemic and individualistic perspective, he or she will be in a continual state of confusion.

Confrontations Over Diagnostic Systems

Another major confrontation facing marriage and family therapists involves the common requirement of an individually oriented assessment. Third party payment sources and traditional mental health practice itself mandate that records be geared toward individual diagnosis. Individually oriented diagnostic interviews require a psychosocial history, diagnosis, and treatment plan with a great deal of demographic data collected on the identified patient. This information, although potentially useful, is seen as incomplete by marriage and family therapists (Piercy et al., 1983). The individual focus of traditional assessment procedures ignores and sometimes even contradicts basic theoretical assumptions and intervention strategies implicit in an interactional marriage and family therapy model. Further, by identifying one individual as the focus of diagnosis and treatment, assessment procedures may actually support pathological homeostatic mechanisms within that person's family or environment.

The most glaring illustration of this is the *Diagnostic and Statistical Manual of Mental Disorders* (DSM III) (American Psychiatric Association, 1980), one of two widely accepted diagnostic systems in the United States. DSM III diagnosis is the vehicle used by mental health settings to classify clientele, demonstrate accountability, and thereby justify their place in the community. Furthermore, insurance companies will not pay for services unless a diagnosis is provided with a reimbursement claim (Seligman, 1983).

The DSM III's dominant focus is diagnosis of individual client dysfunction. Only 1 of its 17 diagnostic categories, the "V Codes" (Conditions Not Attributable to a Mental Disorder That Are a Focus of Attention or Treatment), reflect relationship diagnoses (e.g., Marital problem, Parent-child problem). V Code diagnoses, by definition however, are not the result of "mental illness." Consequently, most health insurance companies would refuse third party payment if a diagnosis of "V61.20 Parent-child problem" were submitted since it is not viewed as a mental disorder. While representing a useful and more accurate diagnosis from the marriage and family therapist's perspective, an individual diagnosis for the child or parent will ordinarily be necessary when insurance reimbursement is requested.

Formal diagnostic procedures and discussions are a dominant practice and part of the regular routine in traditional mental health settings. Haley (1975) asserted that significant disorientation can occur within a mental health setting when contrasting traditional diagnostic categories and marriage and family therapy actions are addressed. For example, traditionally, when a parent calls and reports that a child has a problem, one or both parents are interviewed together or individually and then perhaps with their child. After that, the child is seen individually and may be given a battery of psychological tests. These interviews and test results are written up, and a diagnostic case conference is held at which time the involved professionals discuss the case. A formal diagnosis is made and treatment begins. Treatment is almost always individual although group therapy or concurrent sessions with the parents (without the child present) can be an adjunct to the child's individual treatment.

The marriage and family therapist pursues a markedly different intake procedure. When a parent calls about a child's problem, the whole family is requested to come in for the initial interview. The therapist recognizes the clinical necessity of seeing the primary context within which the child functions and the relation of the child's problem to that context—his or her family. The marriage and family therapist combines an examination of the problem with immediate therapeutic interventions; from the perspective of the marriage and family therapist, part of any "diagnosis" is a family's response to suggestions for change. The therapist also seeks to take advantage of the crisis that brought the family to therapy as families tend to be most open to change during times of crisis. The case conference that might follow is not so concerned with diagnosis as it is with evaluating the effectiveness of the therapist's initial interventions.

Haley (1975) suggested that traditional case conferences become more pragmatic and thus valuable when a marriage and family perspective is pursued. He also asserted that compromise solutions in such situations are unlikely endeavors:

> If a clinic attempts to compromise and do both individual and family therapy, the diagnostic conference can become an unpleasant debate instead of a cooperative endeavor. The family therapist is asked to categorize an individual, which he considers pointless, and the individual therapist is asked to diagnose the interpersonal action in a family, which he considers secondary. Individual therapists object to the "disappearing" of the individual, insist that family therapists are ignoring deeper levels of character structure, and mourn the contamination of the transference. Family therapists object to fragmenting the family unit by focusing on the individual, argue that treating an individual is one way of intervening into a family and not the best way, and object to the hostile form the diagnosis always takes. The clinic patients become the field where battles between staff members take place. (p. 7)

Confrontations Over Change Strategies

Traditional clinical practice follows the belief that therapeutic change occurs when something inside the client changes. *Change* is defined as the client's insight into unconscious processes, the increased understanding of past causes for present behavior, the clearer perception of how he or she deals with others, the release of repressed emotion, and so on. With a shift to the interactions between two or more persons as the treatment focus, these various ideas of change are no longer logical. Instead, change must be defined in different terms, for example, as an altered sequence of behavior among intimates (Haley, 1975). Rather than having the therapist assist clients to better "understand," intervention is aimed at changing the ways a client interacts with others and vice versa. Marriage and family therapists are change facilitators of relationships and social structures and subsequent behavior sequences.

This latter stance calls for therapists to put aside the traditional techniques of passive interpretation where change is dependent almost solely upon what the clients say and do, not what the therapist does. Professional status in traditional settings is a strong social influence. A marriage and family therapy perspective requires the therapist to think strategically and become an active participant in bringing about client change. This requires that therapists expose themselves to greater vulnerability. Professional status becomes much less of a social influence; what one does, not who one is, facilitates change. Perceived loss of status and social influence is frequently followed by increased rigidity in any system, and the mental health setting is no different. As Framo (1976) related from personal experience:

> When some of the full implications of the systems' viewpoint become apparent—in terms of their effects on diagnosis and treatment procedures, admission policies, status, and so forth—establishment mental health finds it too threatening. . . . People get caught up in organizational structures with their rules and guidelines, and these systems develop a life of their own, with their own regulatory powers. (pp. 36–37)

Assuming Power Within the System

The recognition of the obstacles they may face represents the first step of marriage and family therapists in acquiring a sense of personal power for actively facilitating systemic change. Most established organizations resist major change. Smaller and more subtle changes, however, can be significant over time. Radical, system-wide change efforts will be met with strong resistance. Changes within the scope of one's position are more likely available and allow for opportunities to extend one's sphere of influence. For example, the therapist whose goal is to create an independent marriage and family therapy unit within a traditional mental health setting will soon encounter awe-inspiring obstacles. By directing his or her attention to ways of implementing a systemic perspective in working with his or her own clients, the therapist can attain a less grandiose, but still significant sense of power and accomplishment. Creating interest in one's work through successful client outcome also represents an initial step toward the greater future goal of an independent family therapy unit.

Another way of assuming power is learning the reasons for the policies of the system. A sound understanding of the objectives of the organization can strengthen any assessment of existing practices and make suggestions more acceptable to the executive structure. Alternatives should be informally addressed with colleagues prior to any formal proposals. Consulting with colleagues represents systemic practice and puts one in a much more powerful position; operating in isolation represents a weaker individualistic orientation.

Often professionals remain relatively powerless within a system because they have not made a concerted effort to order and pursue their priorities. Marriage and family therapists recognize that they cannot function autonomously in working with couples and families. The clients themselves represent equally critical components in the change process. Thus, negotiation and compromise among subsystems must occur regularly. By ordering priorities, the therapist can pursue compromise without sacrificing significant issues. In conjunction with this, clear communications with the executive structure is essential. Many times reasonable changes are resisted, not because they are unsound, but because the therapist did not attempt to join efforts with clinical supervisors and executive directors.

The most essential element in assuming power within a system is the recognition that one is a vital part of that system; marriage and family therapists cannot divorce themselves from the "system." Just as in actual therapy with client couples and families, being active in all parts of the process and using oneself as an essential tool within that process is critical to successful change outcomes (Corey et al., 1984).

Piercy et al. (1983) reported their growing dissatisfaction with individually oriented assessment procedures while working in a Community Mental Health Center (CMHC). They described their successful change efforts in creating and gaining acceptance for an assessment procedure congruent with their systemically oriented marriage and family therapy perspective. In their discussion of the process they offered the following recommendations:

> Institutional change, however, often faces resistance. A new approach may be perceived as a criticism of the status quo and thus create defensiveness. Resistance also springs from the need of CMHCs to respond to insurance companies who demand identification of a patient and the use of a diagnostic label.
>
> To reduce such resistance, efforts should be made to accommodate to the present system. While a family approach avoids labeling an identified patient, there is no reason why the counselor cannot open a case file under the name of one family member (e.g., the identified patient, principal wage earner, or initiator of therapy). Moreover, the problem of making individual diagnoses has become less of a concern with the advent of *DSM III*. The new "V" codes offer opportunities for broader and more generic diagnoses.
>
> Resistance also can be minimized by offering family assessment not as a replacement, but as an alternative means of gathering client information. Care should be taken not to portray it as being in competition with existing assessment procedures. On the contrary, it is important to be supportive of approaches already in use.
>
> If there is an existing structure to initiate a family assessment procedure, it is important to use it. In our case, family assessment was presented and accepted through a CMHC peer review system. Before a formal presentation on the family assessment process, however, the informal power structure within the CMHC was assessed and sensitively informed of the need for such a procedure. (p. 102)

PRAGMATIC ISSUES AND PROFESSIONAL IDENTITY

Marriage and family therapists' training prepared them to acquire an adequate repertoire of intervention strategies. They can select and tailor treatment plans for their clients. While at times these treatment tasks require attending to significant roadblocks, the competently trained clinician is ready to do so. Many marriage and family therapists' training, however, tends to provide them with a limited awareness of the array of choices they have when they make nonclinical professional decisions. Some of the more pragmatic professional identity issues facing marriage and family therapists include public relations (particularly advertising), professional growth through continuing education, and the importance of maintaining intraprofessional communications.

Professional Advertising

Almost all companies and individuals who provide a product or service to the public advertise. Traditionally, however, most professions have severely restricted their members with regard to advertising. The prevalent conception was that professionals are devoted to public service rather than making money. Advertising, it was felt, would change that image and undermine public confidence. Yet because advertising is the standard means by which people find out about available services and products, such restrictions tended to prevent average citizens from having equal access to professional help (Bayles, 1981).

In 1977 the Supreme Court declared that professional organizations' "ban on advertising" was restraint of trade. A compromise position has since evolved; now restrictions are generally placed on the style or content of information professionals may provide to the public (Van Hoose & Kottler, 1985). In an effort to come to terms with these new realities toward professional advertising, the American Association for Marriage and Family Therapy developed its *Standards on Public Information and Advertising* (AAMFT, 1982b). The 1985 revision of the *AAMFT Code of Ethical Principles for Marriage and Family Therapists* incorporated a seventh principle addressing "Advertising." Regulation of professional advertising was previously addressed only by the separate *Standards on Public Advertising*. Both of these guidelines are presently in effect and basically mirror each other (see Figure 8–1)

The AAMFT guidelines emphasize what members *cannot* do and detail what they should avoid. The following simplified checklist was derived from the AAMFT standards for therapists considering advertising (Ridgewood Financial Institute, Inc., 1984):

— *Self-praising should be avoided.* This relates not only to actual statements but is also reflected in the volume, scope or frequency of ads, or by use of unrepresentative biographical information. Use of inappropriate media can be self-praising.
— *Fee information demands special care.* It is very difficult to adequately provide complete and accurate enough information through advertising sources to avoid deceiving an uninformed layperson. If a set fee is advertised for a specific service, it obviously should be adhered to.

Figure 8–1   AAMFT Standards on Public Information and Advertising

The practice of marital and family therapy as a mental health profession is in the public interest. Therefore, it is appropriate for the well-trained and qualified practitioner to inform the public of the availability of his/her services. However, much needs to be done to educate the public to the services available from qualified marital and family therapists. Clinical Members of the American Association for Marriage and Family Therapy have a responsibility to the public to engage in appropriate information activities; Clinical Members shall not engage in misrepresentation, that is, the use of false, fraudulent, misleading or deceptive statements in keeping with the following general principles.

I. Information for the Consumer

Selection of a marital and family therapist by a layperson should be made on an informed basis. Advice and recommendations of third parties— other professionals, relatives, friends, business acquaintances, and other associates—may be helpful. Advertisements and publications, whether in directories, announcement cards, newspapers, or on radio or television, should be formulated to convey information that is necessary to make an appropriate selection. Information that may be helpful would indicate:

1. Office information, such as name, including a group name and names of professional associates, address, telephone number, credit card acceptability, languages spoken and written, and office hours;

2. Earned degrees, state licensure and/or certification, and AAMFT Clinical Member status;

3. Description of practice, including a statement that practice is limited to one or more fields of family therapy;

4. Appropriate fee information.

II. Name and Affiliation

As the name under which a marital and family therapist conducts his/her practice may be a factor in the selection process, use of a name which could mislead the public concerning the identity, responsibility, source, and status of those practicing under that name would be improper. Likewise, one should not hold oneself out as being a partner or associate of a firm, if he/she is not one in fact. One should not use or participate in the use of a professional card, office sign, letterhead, telephone directory listing, association directory listing, or a similar professional notice or device if it includes a statement or claim that is false, fraudulent, misleading, or deceptive. Practicing under a name that is misleading as to the identity, responsibil-

ity, or status of those practicing thereunder is improper.

III. Areas of Specialization

A marital and family therapist should be accurate in the representation of his/her professional background, training, status, and areas of specialization in order to avoid the possibility of misleading the consumer. A member should not hold himself/herself out as a specialist without being able to provide evidence of training, education, and supervised experience in settings which meet recognized professional standards. Public announcements which accurately describe that one practices in limited areas of specialization in marital and family therapy for which he/she has been so trained are helpful to laypersons.

IV. Fee Information

Marital and family therapists should exercise care to insure that fee information is complete and accurate. Because of the individuality of each problem, public statements regarding average, minimum, or estimated fees may be deceiving. Only factual assertions, and not opinions, should be made in public communications. Not only should commercial publicity be truthful, but its accurate meaning should be apparent to the average layperson.

V. Definition of False, Fraudulent, Misleading or Deceptive Statements

A statement is false, fraudulent, misleading, or deceptive when it includes a statement or claim which:

1. Contains a material misrepresentation of fact;

2. Fails to state any material fact necessary to make the statement, in light of all circumstances, not misleading;

3. Is intended to or is likely to create an unjustified expectation; or

4. Contains a representation or implication that is likely to cause an ordinary prudent person to misunderstand or be deceived or fails to contain reasonable warnings or disclaimers necessary to make a representation or implication not deceptive.

AAMFT Regulations

The American Association for Marriage and Family Therapy is the sole owner of its name, its logo and the abbreviated initials AAMFT. Use of the name, logo and initials is restricted to the following conditions:

1. Only individual Clinical Members may identify their membership in AAMFT in public information or advertising materials, not Associates or Students or organizations.

2. The initial AAMFT may not be used following one's name in the manner of an academic degree because this is misleading.

3. Use of the logo is limited to the Association, its committees and regional divisions when they are engaged in bonafide activities as units or divisions of AAMFT.

4. A regional division or chapter of AAMFT may use the AAMFT insignia to list its individual members as a group (e.g., in the Yellow Pages). When all Clinical Members practicing within a directory district have been invited to list, any one or more members may do so.

Note: From *AAMFT Standards on Public Information and Advertising* (unpaged), 1982, Washington, DC: AAMFT. Copyright 1982 by AAMFT. Reprinted by permission.

— *Past performance results are tricky.* It is almost impossible through advertising media to adequately explain all the relevant and important variables.

— *Only facts, not opinions, should be stated.* Facts represented should obviously be truthful, but also their accurate meanings should be easily understood by the average layperson.

— *There are no guarantees about the outcomes of therapy.* Even the best of therapeutic services are ultimately uncertain and thus explicit or implicit guarantees cannot be assured.

— *Watch out for appeals based on fear.* The use of brash or extravagant statements in seeking business could mislead and potentially harm laypersons, particularly those who are emotionally vulnerable.

— *Do not use misleading names.* Any information that could give an erroneous impression about identity, responsibilities, status, or improperly imply a link to any group should be scrupulously avoided.

Advertising by professionals is a relatively new venture. Conservative advertising in the Yellow Pages has tended to be the most accepted means of advertising professional services. The AAMFT encourages the use of its name and insignia by its state/regional divisions and their chapters as a means of advertising as a group. The following guidelines outline how this process can be pursued (Rotan, 1985):

1. The AAMFT logo listing is limited to clinical members. Clinical members in the local chapter or directory area who have been invited may advertise.

2. The bill for the AAMFT logo is sent monthly to one business number account. This is usually the member making the initial arrangements or another volunteer member with secretarial support. The listed members should then pay that individual for their portion of the entire year's cost of the logo listing.

3. A clean print of the AAMFT logo for the Yellow Pages representative may be cut from the top of the AAMFT stationary or an AAMFT office can be contacted for a copy.

4. A brief descriptive phrase may be added adjacent to the logo, according to any word limit imposed by the Yellow Pages. For instance, "Subscribing to a Professional Code of Ethics," or "Since 1942, The Professional Association for Marriage and Family Therapists," is appropriate. The chapter should be noted above the list of clinical members (see Figure 8–2).
5. If possible, the heading of the Yellow Pages listing should read "AAMFT—American Association for Marriage and Family Therapy." This will ensure that the alphabetical placement of the listing will be "AA" rather than "AM."
6. Any questions regarding this type of professional listing should be directed to the AAMFT Central Office in Washington, D.C. (212–429-1825). This phone number should be provided to the Yellow Pages representative for validation of the clinical members wishing to list under the logo.

Two other means of acceptably advertising mental health services include the announcement advertisement and the public service message (Kissel, 1983). Figure 8–3 illustrates an announcement advertisement suitable for newspaper or similar media use.

A less conservative approach to advertising is the public service message. Dentist, family practice physicians, and other professionals have been experimenting with paid for public service columns. An example of this type of advertising is presented in Figure 8–4.

Continuing Education

The continuing education of professionals in all fields has, in recent years, become a matter of great and pragmatic concern. There was a time when the basic information employed in practicing a profession, whether it be medicine, law, theology, or the like was relatively stable and could be mastered by a student in the course of a reasonable training

Figure 8–2   Sample Yellow Pages Logo

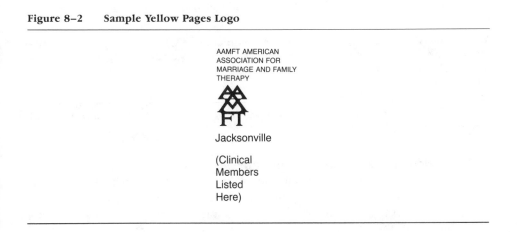

AAMFT AMERICAN
ASSOCIATION FOR
MARRIAGE AND FAMILY
THERAPY

Jacksonville

(Clinical
Members
Listed
Here)

Figure 8–3   An Announcement Advertisement

JANE KRANDELL, Ph.D.

Announces the opening of her office for the practice of marriage and family therapy. I am particularly interested in providing consultation and treatment services to couples and families where substance abuse is a concern.
Saturday and evening hours. 1st Avenue, Ocala, Florida 32217, 369-4390.

Note. From *Private Practice for the Mental Health Clinician* (unpaged), by S. Kissel, 1983, Rockville, MD: Aspen Systems. Copyright 1983 by Aspen Systems. Adapted by permission.

Figure 8–4   A Public Service Message

VIEWS ON FAMILY HEALTH

by Jane Krandell, Ph.D.

FACTS ABOUT CHILDREN'S EMOTIONAL PROBLEMS

Emotional problems, unlike certain physical ailments, may take years to develop to the point where symptoms cause concern and worry to the individual. The symptoms are indicators of too-heavy burdens, stresses, and conflicts. What are some of these signs for children? Mental health experts agree that the following are *possible* danger signals:

- Prolonged periods of unhappiness without apparent cause.
- Refusal to accept school or parental authority.
- Persistent avoidance of school.
- Excessive fears which are upsetting and interfere with normal functioning.
- Poor achievement in school subjects.
- Returning to activities associated with infancy, such as frequent (and not occasional) bedwetting, soiling, head-banging, thumb sucking, and little ability to tolerate frustration.

If too many of these signals are present, a consultation with your family physician, clergy person, school counselor, or a mental health expert such as a marriage and family therapist may be helpful.

A public service message with the aim of promoting more satisfying family home environments from the office of Jane Krandell, Ph.D., Marriage and Family Therapist, 1st Avenue, Ocala, Florida 32217.
Phone: 369-4390

Note. From *Private Practice for the Mental Health Clinician* (unpaged), by S. Kissel, 1983, Rockville, MD: Aspen Systems. Copyright 1983 by Aspen Systems. Adapted by permission.

---

period. The application of this knowledge was then largely a matter of professional skill. Changes in the professions were gradual and relatively easily incorporated by practicing professionals during their careers.

One of the most impressive and, to some extent, distressing developments in the professions during the last century has been the increase in change and development. Scientific and technological developments make it virtually impossible for a professional to rely on initial training in a field for any significant part of a career (Walker, 1981). As Vitulano and Copeland (1980) observed with regard to the health care professions in particular:

> First, the knowledge base for these professions is increasing at an astonishing rate. . . . One must continue to learn or suffer from professional obsolescence. Second, the enormous ethical responsibilities of our practice demand the highest standards. Licensure or certification solely at the beginning of one's career merely identifies a minimum standard for professional practice, not the ideal toward which one should strive. Third, lifetime education should constitute an important goal of the training and practice of the health professions. Fourth, a proactive commitment to the maintenance of competency over time would help maintain public confidence in the profession. (p. 891)

Students graduating from most professional programs today must immediately begin a program of continuing education and development to have any chance of survival in their chosen field. Should they fail to do this, by the end of 3 years (in most professions) their functioning would be substandard; by the end of 5 years that functioning would be seriously compromised; by the end of 10 years they would, no doubt, be totally incompetent (Walker, 1981). Professional organizations have increasingly responded to this dilemma by sponsoring and supporting continuing education efforts. Most have posited this pragmatic problem as an ethical responsibility as well, quite definitively stating their ethical codes. The *AAMFT Code of Ethical Principles for Marriage and Family Therapists* (AAMFT, 1985), for example, states, "Marriage and family therapists seek to remain abreast of new developments in family therapy knowledge and practice through both educational activities and clinical experiences."

To assist its members in pursuing and fulfilling their ethical professional development responsibilities, the AAMFT encourages all its clinical members to complete at least 150 hours of continuing education efforts every 3 years, at least 30 hours of which are "formal" activities. The Association has created a program known as Continuing Education in Family Therapy (CEFT) to structure these efforts. The AAMFT regards CEFT as part of a necessary and ongoing process of professional development to ensure competent, high quality professional practice. CEFT is not aimed at providing basic professional preparation for marriage and family therapists; it has been designed instead to build on basic knowledge and skills the professional acquired during initial academic and clinical training experiences. Specifically, CEFT is viewed as a process of learning aimed at keeping marriage and family therapists abreast of new developments, modifications, or extensions of basic skills evolving within the field (AAMFT, 1982a).

The CEFT program is currently voluntary based on marriage and family therapists' ethical obligation toward continuing professional development. It recognizes the value of both formal and informal continuing education endeavors and seeks to structure the most appropriate pursuit of both. The following outline represents the major aspects of the CEFT program (AAMFT, 1982a):

Category I: Formal CEFT

Completion of thirty hours minimum of formal CEFT is recommended every three years. Formal CEFT activities are those provided by sponsors approved by the AAMFT at either the national or divisional level according to AAMFT-established criteria. The approved sponsors at the national level include:

American Association for Marriage and Family Therapy
American Family Therapy Association
American Orthopsychiatric Association
American Psychiatric Association
American Psychological Association
Association for Advancement of Behavior Therapy
American Association of Pastoral Counselors
Canadian Psychological Association
National Association of Social Workers
National Council on Family Relations

All marriage and family workshops, meeting sessions, conferences, and the like offered by these organizations may be counted as formal CEFT activities provided they meet the following *general criteria*:

1. All offerings must be designed specifically for the purpose of providing continuing education rather than basic clinical training.
2. All offerings must deal specifically with theory, research, or practice related to family functioning and family therapy.
3. One hour of credit is claimed for each hour of contact.
4. Programs do not use multi-media films or other films which depict explicit sex acts.

Similarly, all post-graduate courses and programs in family therapy offered by educational institutions or clinical training centers accredited by the Commission on Accreditation for Marriage and Family Therapy Education are approved formal CEFT activities, provided the offerings meet the *general criteria* noted above.

Formally approved CEFT activities are also those family therapy conferences, workshops, institutes, and the like sponsored by state, regional, or provincial units of the nationally approved sponsors (i.e., Divisionally Approved Sponsors), provided these offerings meet the *general criteria*. Formally approved CEFT activities are also family therapy conferences, workshops, institutes, and post-graduate courses or programs given by regionally accredited educational institutions, provided the offerings meet the *general criteria*. Finally, programs offered by other sponsors located within a Divisionally Approved Sponsor that has been approved by the division's continuing education committee can be considered formal CEFT activities if both the *general criteria* and *specific AAMFT criteria* for such sponsors are met.

Category II: Informal CEFT

The CEFT program recognizes the value of informal as well as formal professional development activities and offers recommendations in this regard to assist in their pursuit. Sponsor approval is not required for Category II CEFT activities. These activities include:

1. *Non-AAMFT Sponsored or Approved Conferences.* Informal CEFT credit may be claimed for conferences dealing specifically with theory, research, or practice related to family functioning and therapy.
2. *Teaching/Consultation.* Informal CEFT credit may be claimed for contact hours of teaching marital and family therapy students in any regionally accredited institution. One hour of credit for each hour of consultation received from, or provided as, a qualified specialist in theory, research, or practice related to family functioning or therapy may be claimed.
3. *Publication.* Ten hours of informal CEFT credit may be claimed for each paper published in a recognized professional journal or for each book chapter authored and published on a family therapy topic.
4. *Individualized Self-Instruction.* Informal CEFT may be claimed on an hour for hour basis for activities that are not formally supervised, such as individual use of audio-visual materials, individual reading of professional journals, and participation in professional study and discussion groups.
5. *Other Marriage and Family Therapy Experiences.* Informal CEFT credit may be claimed for activities that do not fit into other categories provided that said activities are designed with appropriate consultation and assistance and answer specific CEFT needs in educationally defensible ways.

Activities That Are Not Acceptable as CEFT

Credit should not be claimed for education that is incidental to the regular professional activities of a marriage and family therapist, such as learning that may occur from clinical experiences or the conducting of research. Likewise, credit should not be claimed for organizational activities such as serving on committees or councils or as an officer of the AAMFT or one of its divisions.

While the CEFT program established by the AAMFT to help its members meet ethical obligations is voluntary, the accumulation of formal continuing education credits is normally a requirement for relicensure where marriage and family licensing legislation is in effect. State requirements differ, but there is a growing appreciation that lifetime competency in a profession is not guaranteed with the receipt of a license. Mandated continuing education experiences have increasingly become recognized as one method of protecting consumers of mental health services (Vitulano & Copeland, 1980).

Intraprofessional Communications

Professionals are part of the upper strata of the social structure of North American society. Their status is partly due to their being among the best-educated persons in society; however, it is also due to their assumption of responsibility for the public welfare inherent to the profession. The American Association for Marriage and Family Therapy, for example, states this position clearly in its promotional materials:

In a broader sense, the American Association for Marriage and Family Therapy is concerned not simply with the profession of marriage and family therapy but also with people—the needs and problems they face in relationships whether they are now married, have been married or may somehow be affected by marriage in our society. AAMFT is also concerned with the institution of marriage itself—its strengths and weaknesses, its changing patterns, its role in the lives of all people. AAMFT firmly believes that this most important and intimate of human relations demands increased understanding, research and education at all levels, and that the professional marriage and family therapist must take the lead to insure that these needs are met. (AAMFT, 1982c)

A major facet of this responsibility for the public good includes the preservation and enhancement of one's professional position as well as the profession itself (Bayles, 1981). This also, however, entails an understanding of the even more immediate and pragmatic need to maintain one's "personal good." Professional burnout is a phenomenon that has been the topic of numerous publications and has received tremendous attention at professional conferences and continuing education endeavors. *Burnout* is a state of physical, emotional, and mental exhaustion frequently associated with intense involvement with people over long periods. Burnout is particularly critical for professionals working in the mental health field. With so much emphasis on giving to others, there is often not enough focus on giving to oneself (Corey et al., 1984). Regular intraprofessional communications are one major means of preventing or remediating burnout as well as fulfilling other professional duties.

Professional organizations provide support, facilitate development, bring together colleagues with similar interests, offer opportunities for active participation in leadership roles, disseminate information, and generally provide a regular forum for intraprofessional communications. Both at the local, state/regional, and national levels, opportunities for intraprofessional communications are available for marriage and family therapists through active participation in relevant professional association affairs and through contact via professional journals, newsletters, and meetings. The two major professional affiliations identified for marriage and family therapists earlier in this chapter were the AAMFT and the AFTA.

The AAMFT publishes the quarterly *Journal of Marital and Family Therapy* "to advance the professional understanding of marital and family behavior and to improve the psychotherapeutic treatment of marital and family disharmony" (Instructions for authors, 1985). The *Journal* publishes articles on research, theory, clinical practice, and training in marital and family therapy. The Association also publishes a bimonthly newspaper, *Family Therapy News,* that disseminates information of current interest to the membership. AAMFT members receive the *Journal* and *Family Therapy News* as membership benefits. Paid subscriptions are available to nonmembers and institutions. A national conference is held annually to provide members and visiting participants with new ideas, techniques, and developments in the profession. Meetings and conferences are also conducted by state and regional divisions and chapters of the Association. Membership and other information relative to the AAMFT is available through its headquarters (1717 K Street, N.W., Suite

407, Washington, D.C. 20006). Although an academy of advanced professionals, the AFTA offers similar intraprofessional communications opportunities for more experienced marriage and family therapists. Its headquarters are located at 2550 M Street, N.W., Suite 275, Washington, D.C. 20037.

SUMMARY AND CONCLUSIONS

During the past 40 years, marriage and family therapy has developed from an interdisciplinary and nondistinct foundation of ideas to the recognized status of a profession. The theory, research, practice, and organization of marriage and family therapy have undergone a dramatic evolution that has increasingly delineated it as a separate entity—a peer to psychiatry, psychology, and social work. Many therapists who originally studied in these traditional professions have pursued further training and now identify themselves as marriage and family therapists.

With this evolution there has been an equally astonishing increase in those who have taken membership in the recognized controlling body for the profession, the American Association for Marriage and Family Therapy. Established in 1942, the then American Association of Marriage Counselors had 250 members in 1962; recent figures establish the number of members at over 12,000 (Riordan, 1985). With this rise in membership has come a slower, but equally important rise in the legislative recognition of marriage and family therapy as a distinct profession through the enactment of licensing laws. Therapists can no longer practice whatever they wish under the guise of an unregulated profession. Accountability is now firmly an active part of marriage and family therapy practice. As Sporakowski (1982) stated:

> At this point the question of the regulation of family therapists cannot be posed in the "To be or not to be" format. The profession and the public already have been working on the issues and, at least in nine states, come to grips with the task. . . . The family therapist will need to keep constantly abreast of these changes to maintain the credentials necessary for practice. Involvement in the process, not a let-somebody-else-do-it attitude, will be essential if professional credibility is to be continued. (p. 133)

Maintenance of professional credibility is a multidimensional process involving interdisciplinary difficulties that, at least at present, continue to confront marriage and family therapists. It also calls for active participation in one's professional development as well as actions to enhance the status and support base of the profession through appropriate public relations, continuing education, and intraprofessional communications. These are not separate processes; rather, they are an interrelated series of activities that foster marriage and family therapists' identity as members of a unique helping profession.

Chapter 9 provides further opportunities to consider specific situations and questions arising from identifying oneself professionally as a marriage and family therapist.

9

Professional Questions

Chapters 7 and 8 presented two predominant professional issues for the practice of marriage and family therapy. The first issue concerned the implications of valuing for professional therapeutic practice. The conviction that every therapist's professional position is formalized by his or her values was asserted. Moral, cultural, political, and therapeutic values represent the standards that direct actions and define, interpret, and judge all social phenomena. Marriage and family therapists actively draw upon the values they have derived from professional training and personal life experiences in understanding and intervening with couples and families. Therapists and clients define and interpret their respective positions by the values they maintain and all transactions between them ultimately involve negotiations about each's values.

This negotiation, a process of "valuing," frames the entire therapeutic endeavor. For marriage and family therapists, it represents assertions of the professional standards by which they establish criteria for the therapeutic process, define problems, select therapeutic goals, and fix parameters for interventions aimed at goal attainment. Valuing as a process was described as emanating from a systemic epistemology. This valuing process was construed as evolutionary and unfolding, occurring within the context of older beliefs, and is a direct contrast to linear notions of values as static entities.

As the profession of marriage and family therapy has grown, many new questions have naturally arisen. As with any young profession, marriage and family therapy is vulnerable to demands that it prove itself. In seeking to do so, these demands have frequently tended to result in defensive claims purporting systemic practices to be a panacea for all ills. It is important to reaffirm that a systemic epistemology represents a viewpoint and regardless of the treatment unit, this viewpoint can permeate and have a positive impact upon different types and forms of therapy efforts.

Another issue addressed was professional identity for marriage and family therapists. Marriage and family therapy is currently in an exciting, yet tempestuous, stage of development. Although the roots of marriage and family therapy can be traced to Freud, the profession did not receive formal recognition until the 1970s when the American Association of Marriage Counselors changed its name first to the American Association of Marriage and Family Counselors, and later to the American Association for Marriage and Family Therapy. The 1970s also saw the advent of state licensing laws regulating the profession's practice. When compared with some longer-standing professions such as medicine and law, marriage and family therapy is in its adolescence.

Adolescence is a time of many questions that evoke comparisons between what was, what is, and what may be. This chapter raises questions designed to provide answers to pragmatic inquiries about the application of valuing in the practice of marriage and family therapy, as well as to contribute to a more concise and "comfortable" professional identity.

QUESTION 1

A dhering to a systemic epistemology, I recognize the importance of conceptualizing problems as residing in systems as opposed to individuals, and consequently, emphasize change efforts directed to the system as a whole. However, within my overall commitment to a systemic epistemology, is there still a place for working with individuals in sessions?

Response

Experienced marriage and family therapists' employment of a systemic epistemology is not reflected by who is in the room, but rather by how many persons are involved in the therapist's thinking about the problem. Historically, the work of marriage and family therapists has encompassed a wide variation of ideas about who should actually be seen in sessions. While it is generally accepted that family therapy is the treatment of choice for marital or family dysfunction, many therapists use individual sessions as a part of ongoing family efforts. Murphy (1976) identified this practice of holding alternate individual and conjoint sessions by the same professional as *tandem counseling*.

Research has offered little firm support for either position. Although conjoint sessions have been shown to be superior to concurrent or collaborative sessions within marital therapy (Olson, 1975, 1976), there is almost no research data on the occasional use of individual sessions within conjoint therapy (Gurman & Kniskern, 1978). Therapists, therefore, must base their decisions on clinical judgment.

Berman (1982) proposed that individual sessions can be useful for a therapist operating within a systemic framework—first, as a part of the diagnostic/planning process, and then as a part of ongoing treatment.

Diagnostic/Planning Uses

Alliance Issues

Conjoint sessions allow a clear focus on the system, but may make it difficult for the therapist to gain the confidence of individual members. Having more than two persons in the room permits a reduction in intensity. Individual sessions can therefore frequently serve to intensify client-therapist relatedness that many believe deepens clients' commitment to the therapy.

History Taking

Marital partners and family members can profit from learning or reviewing each other's history, often adding considerably to it. However, histories taken one-to-one may be quite different from histories taken when a marital partner or family member is present. A client may omit crucial information because of guilt or embarrassment. In individual sessions, the recall process is often facilitated when a client does not have to worry about whether a spouse, parent, or child is recording potentially shameful incidents for future reference.

Assessing a Client's Manner of Acting Apart from the System

Systems are very much able to control and channel their members' behaviors. Rigid systems can produce highly polarized interactions among members when assembled together. An often startling therapeutic event is the change that can occur in persons apart from their family. Direct knowledge of clients' alternative behavioral repertoires is an invaluable therapeutic awareness.

Ventilation/Rehearsal

Many clients enter therapy so furiously angry that they are unable to express anything else. To help these clients rehearse more effective and positive ways of relating, it is frequently beneficial to allow some time for ventilating feelings without spouses or other family members present. The client can then be offered alternative ways of acting to "try on." Likewise, if a client is massively afraid of confronting a spouse or family member alone at home, it may help to first practice adaptive responses without feeling the pressure of the other present.

Secrets

Many clients have significant difficulty directly sharing certain past or present feelings and beliefs with marital partners and family members. Such "secrets" can seriously hinder therapy efforts. Individual sessions can provide a context wherein disclosure of relevant secrets is facilitated. Therapists who are aware of relevant, though unshared, marital or family information may find themselves in the difficult position of how to use it. No easy solutions are available in such situations; potential directions depend on the particular information and context. However, a therapist who is not privy to this kind of information may spend months doing unprofitable therapy while a marital partner is carrying on an affair, for example, or planning to pursue a divorce.

Individual Sessions During Ongoing Therapy

Individual Issues

One or more members of the marital or family system may be so involved in their own internal conflicts, transition issues, or irrational belief systems that efforts directed at altering their behavior consumes an inordinate amount of time during sessions. While the system in some way generates or supports individual concerns, it may be more efficient and ultimately effective to spend one or more individual sessions in a concerted effort to diminish that individual's internal conflicts so work on couple or family goals can proceed with less conflict.

Missing Puzzle Pieces

Occasionally information may be deliberately withheld or simply not shared early in therapy. Individual sessions may bring enhanced awareness. For example:

> A family had been participating in weekly therapy sessions for almost 4 months with no apparent progress toward agreed-upon goals. The therapist requested a second set of individual interviews. During her individual session the eldest daughter revealed that she had become pregnant shortly after therapy began and has been unable to tell her parents and brother.

Sexual Dysfunction

Many systemically oriented therapists identify certain issues as lending themselves particularly well to individual sessions. Sexual difficulties, for example, can generally be best addressed in a brief series of individual sessions with a same-sexed therapist, well-trained in human sexuality. Although most sexual education with marital partners should be undertaken with both present, it is often more productive to pursue some educational efforts in private.

Strategic and Structural Maneuvers

Individual sessions are a valuable means of unbalancing, giving private tasks, and the like to reduce overinvolvement or to reorder alliances. But Berman (1982) cautioned that before seeing marital partners or family members alone, therapists should discuss the proposed sessions with all members of the system together. Members of the system should be made aware that they may experience some concern or mistrust regarding what was shared outside their presence. The rationale for individual sessions should be explained as well as any confidentiality (or lack of confidentiality) to be in effect. While using individual sessions in the diagnostic/planning process is a matter of clinical preference, movement to individual sessions during ongoing therapy can be a choice facilitated by several common indicators: (a) therapy is not progressing for a significant period of time; (b) the therapist senses that a hidden agenda is blocking therapy efforts; and (c) a client requests private time (this last indicator calls for careful clinical judgment to balance the possibility of manipulation; that is, creating an unbalanced alliance versus trust in a client's sense of what is necessary) (Berman).

QUESTION 2

M y understanding of systemic understandings has so far emphasized the roles, relationships, rules, and balance of forces operating within marital and family systems. As a marriage and family therapist, I am recognized for my work with couples and families. How might my marital and family understandings and interventions be applied in working with other systems?

Response

Marriage and family therapy from a systemic perspective is not a method, but rather a viewpoint. It is a clinical orientation applicable to the problems of all systems, not just marital and family systems. For example, a systemic perspective has been extended quite naturally to the school context by a number of practitioners (Aponte, 1976; Fine & Holt, 1983; Pfeiffer & Tittler, 1983). An individual school is a part of a larger school system, with a hierarchy of faculty, staff, and administrative roles and relationships. Within an individual school, each classroom is likewise a subsystem characterized by the same roles, relationships, rules, and balances of forces operating within couple and family systems.

The following points and case illustration adapted from Fine (1985) provide an overview of what the application of a systemic perspective within a school setting can mean for marriage and family therapists serving as consultants.

1. There is no standard operating procedure for a systemic perspective. The perspective is just that—a perspective—a mental frame of reference for viewing function and dysfunction.
2. A systemic perspective views behavior contextually and in interaction terms. "What happens when a student does . . . .?" is more relevant than "Why does a student do . . . .?" What precedes undesirable behaviors? How are these behaviors generated and escalated by the host system? Understanding characteristic sequences of un-

desirable events presents the means for disrupting them and enacting desirable options.

3. A systemic perspective is concerned with the "fit" of students within the system, for example, the classroom. Do the present instructional components of the classroom match or clash with a student's learning style and developmental readiness to engage in certain learning and socialization experiences? These understandings offer the opportunity for modifying classroom variables such as seating, pace, and content of instruction; number and complexity of assignments; nature of teacher-student interactions; specific teacher control techniques; and more.

4. The systemic perspective recognizes that standard operating procedures in a situation may be exacerbating a problem and, in fact, may have defined the problem. Relevant examples include the use of certain labels that represent static views of students and teachers that, in turn, establish an expectation that influences interactions.

5. A systemic perspective is cognizant that systems overlap and thus influence each other and that systems seek stability and may resist change as a result of homeostatic forces exerting control. Because students live in multiple systems, one system might seek to influence the other to assume a particular stance. For example, parents who regularly complain to a teacher that their child refuses to listen can project this expectation into the school situation where that behavior may not be a predominant concern. Should the teacher come to accept this view of the student, the two systems become aligned.

Another illustration further clarifies the applicability of a systemic perspective within a school setting:

> John was a physically large, mildly retarded 14-year-old who had just completed a year of training in a residential rehabilitation facility because of a history of emotional acting out. Shortly after he enrolled in a primarily self-contained classroom in public school, John's teacher became very concerned. In refusing to do a number of tasks he found frustrating, John had pounded his desk and glared menacingly at the teacher. Given John's institutional background and sheer bulk, his teacher feared being attacked.

The consultant, a marriage and family therapist who worked regularly with school officials, was called upon for assistance. A review of John's background revealed no instances of physical acting out. It was decided to interpret John's actions to his teacher and school officials in a manner that would reduce their anxiety and offer a functional way of working with John's disruptive outbursts. His aggressive stance, therefore, was defined as "the way he's learned to act to keep away persons who might make frustrating demands of him." In essence, John's emotional outbursts were reframed as poor coping strategies.

Meeting with the teacher and other involved school personnel for several sessions (some of which included John), the consultant assured all that John had never displayed any instances of physical aggression except some minor "normal" scuffles with peers that had occurred more than 4 years previously. The consultant sought enactments among all present to reinforce the reframing of John's behavior as "faulty social learnings." Within this reframing, efforts and successes at teaching more adaptive interaction skills to John were punctuated. Simple diagramming was employed to show how behaviors and reactions were related and to illustrate what was occurring between John, the teacher, and other classmates and school personnel. John, in interaction with his teacher, received training as to how to more adaptively verbalize his frustration to the teacher (and the teacher to facilitate and reinforce the new behavior).

In summary, the consultant framed the situation in a way that changed the perception of the problem's severity and identified more adaptive roles for John, the teacher, and other school personnel. In effect, the consultant identified society as the "persecutor," John as the "victim," and the school as the "rescuer." This facilitated movement toward a positive "let's help each other" relationship between John and the school, with the society where John had previously learned his poor coping strategies as the "villain." This way of systemically triangulating relationships represented a constructive shift from the school's initial view as being victimized by both society and John.

QUESTION 3

I recognize that as a marriage and family therapist, I need to acknowledge the therapeutic influence of my values on a couple or family and attend to the transactions over values between us. However, I find it difficult at times to ascertain when I should actively seek significant change in a couple's or family's values. Are there guidelines to consider in identifying such situations?

Response

Negotiations over values are held at different levels of abstraction. They range, for example, from "marital partners should love each other" (general principle) to "this marital partner should love her mate" (particular implication) to "in these circumstances, this marital partner should demonstrate love for her mate in this particular manner" (operational application). The more abstract the value level, the more likely there is agreement between therapist and couple or family. Agreement is also more likely to occur if the therapist and couple or family share similar personal, socioeconomic, racial, cultural, and religious backgrounds. The closer interactions move to operational applications of a value or the greater the background differences between therapist and couple or family, the greater the probability of different values.

The model of therapy, the characteristics of clients, and the professional and personal styles of therapists all influence the degree and level of involvement a therapist has in addressing a couple's or family's values. As a general rule, Aponte (1985) recommended that "the therapist should attempt to exercise no more influence over the family's values than is required adequately to address the family's problems" (p. 335). In expounding this basic premise, Aponte differentiated between structure, function, and values. He identified three formative constructs in a social system, a social system being an aggregate of people who join in patterned *structures* to carry out a *function* or complex of functions in accord with a framework of standards of *values*. Aponte further described four situations (with case examples) wherein a change in a family's values will be essential to therapeutic change.

Value Conflicts as the Source of Dysfunction

When a conflict between members of a family or between a family and its community is a significant force in the dysfunction being addressed in therapy, a change in values will be essential to therapeutic change. Examples include marital dysfunction when partners are in conflict because they come from different racial, religious, ethnic, or socioeconomic backgrounds, or when a family has problems living in a community where it represents part of a racial majority experiencing conflicts due to its discrimination against the minority.

Conflicting values may simply serve as superficial issues obscuring deeper emotional issues. Family members may present a values conflict as their principal concern to avoid confronting emotional forces embedded in a structural conflict. For example, an adolescent and parent may present a conflict over values about dress style, but the more significant struggle may really derive from tension over the growing emotional distance, a developmental outgrowth of an adolescent's increasing separation from the family. But although emotional issues may represent the primary source of the family problem, the values conflict, although secondary, may sufficiently influence the predominant problem to demand the therapist's attention.

Incompatible Values, Functions, and Structures

A change in values is an issue when the family's values are incompatible with the function the family intends to carry out or the structures through which it is to operate. This lack of fit between the values of the family and its functions or structures most commonly emerges from evolutionary changes in the family or its social circumstances. For example, in a family where the parents cannot interact intimately within their marital dyad, an overriding value may be placed on centering family interactions around the children. As the children mature and move away from home, however, this priority no longer serves as an adequate standard by which to organize the parents' relationship to each other. When a family's social context changes, parents may continue to guide their children by standards appropriate to the old culture but not appropriate for the new situation. For instance, in moving from a culture where higher education is encouraged to where it is discouraged, not only will there be incompatibility between the family and surrounding society but also between the parents and children should the children have previously developed aspirations for advanced educational opportunities.

Underdeveloped Values

A change in family values is relevant to therapy efforts if a family or its members have not developed the values needed to guide the evolution of structures necessary to deal with functional issues. An underorganized family not only lacks structure but also lacks a well-elaborated, cohesive, and flexible framework of values. The development of a value framework influences how well-organized the structure of a family's relationships will be. A family that has primitive, inconsistent, conflicting, or rigid values will find it difficult to effectively establish functional relationships among its members.

Disagreement Over the Therapeutic Process

Value change represents a further issue in the therapeutic process. A family and therapist struggle to seek agreement on the values framework for addressing the family's dysfunction. For example, a therapist sought supervision in a case where a couple with two children were working to face the husband's ongoing affair with another woman. The therapy had consisted primarily of technical assistance being offered with regard to the couple's decision-making process and was stalled. The therapist was unable to incorporate the family's underlying emotional issues into this framework. The therapist lacked a framework of values to define and direct his approach for working with the couple's emotional struggle.

An exploration of the therapist's own family revealed a father who had carried on a long-term affair with his wife's knowledge while the therapist was a child. The therapist had been made part of the family's conspiracy of silence by sharing a number of recreational outings with the father and his woman friend and being cautioned to keep them quiet. Further, in the therapist's current life, problems over relationships were occasioned by the infidelities of a lover and consequent inability to establish a relationship with anyone based upon an enduring, exclusive commitment. The therapist was unable to decide what fidelity could be expected in a love relationship or marriage. The therapist (as well as the couple) had no personal reference point from which to organize the confusion of the couple being treated about their respective expectations of marital fidelity. Moreover, the therapist, who had not adequately dealt with personally relevant childhood conflicts, did not even think to consider the effect of the client-father's infidelity on the couple's young children. Without a values framework forged out of a resolution of personal life experiences, the therapist was approaching the family's dilemma without a means to guide interventions. The therapist obviously needed a clear set of values before he could guide the couple in efforts to resolve their conflict.

QUESTION 4

A s a marriage and family therapist seeking to act responsibly in clarifying my own values and assisting clients to do similarly, I am frequently confronted by ambivalence in myself and my clients. I recognize that at best, such ambivalence is nonproductive and at worst, promotes the disintegration and destruction of relationships. How might I address this ambivalence?

Response

Marital and family therapists often hear the following types of statements from clients: "I know I don't want a divorce, but I still can't get motivated enough to do what is needed to make the marriage better;" or, "We know our sex life is not great and want to make it better, but we can't seem to get together no matter how hard we try." Therapists might be making similar statements to themselves as well: "I know that this couple needs to discontinue their extramarital affairs if they are going to significantly improve their marital relationship, but I'm not sure it's my place to put my personal value on them." These statements reflect an ambivalence that keeps the speaker stuck midway between two points, simultaneously attracted toward and pushing away from each point.

Therapists need to be able to provide both themselves and their clients with a framework that can be used for probing the bases for their actions. Without such a framework, continued ambivalence will tend to sap available energy and prevent any commitment or concerted movement toward more adaptive options. Further, in interactions among therapists and clients, or within marital or family systems, decision-making tends to shift to nonambivalent members, forcing ambivalent members to take reactive and defensive positions. In effect, ambivalent members abdicate decision-making powers and become bystanders or victims instead of active participants.

Accepting the basic concept that actions reflect values—that at any given time, people are doing what is aligned with their most cherished beliefs—calls for a framework based on values analysis. Hof and Dwyer (1982) offered such a framework, suggesting that persons can perceive (or can be brought to perceive) between what is most important to them and what they actually do. This analysis of "behavior as being a consequence of values" was presented by Hof and Dwyer as having five conditions that must be fulfilled if persons are to engage in certain actions:

1. Persons must have some minimal perception of self-confidence. While the level or intensity of confidence can significantly vary, there still must be some minimal confidence or fear of failure will lead to avoidance of action or predestined attempts to fail. For example, the therapist who desires to confront a couple regarding the effects of extramarital affairs must believe that such a confrontation will ultimately result in the couple's greater commitment to their relationship and consequently lead to greater satisfaction. Further, the therapist must have the self-discipline to follow through and further assist the couple to fully examine the confronted issue.

2. Persons must perceive some values fulfillment, at least as potentially available. Rarely is attention directed at any action unless there is the belief it could potentially deliver values fulfillment. The therapist must have some sense of the importance of personal values that would find fulfillment through the couple's enhanced marital interaction.

3. Persons must perceive a reasonable probability that values fulfillment will be delivered. The perception of some relevant, substantial values is not enough by itself. Again, following the example, the therapist must perceive that confronting the couple's extramarital affairs will, very likely, deliver values fulfillment to the therapist.

4. Persons' perception of the costs to be paid by engaging in the behavior—values fulfillment to be given up—must be acceptable relative to the perception and probability of alternative values fulfillment. A behavior with a high cost in terms of value fulfillment means that a person would lose a great deal of fulfillment by engaging in the proposed behavior. On the other end of the cost continuum are behaviors that have a low cost in that a person would lose very little, if any, fulfillment when engaging in this behavior.

5. Persons' perceptions of the risks to other values involved in the behavior must be acceptable relative to their perceptions and probability of alternative values fulfillment. Not only are there perceptions of costs in all behavior changes, there are also perceptions of risks. A risk is believed to have a probability of less than 1 of occurring. It is therefore less definite, and only a possible consequence of engaging in the proposed behavior. The therapist may have only

a vague sense that something unknown may go astray or may worry about the possibility of the couple's rejection, premature termination from therapy, and the like.

To the extent that it can be seen as a function of values fulfillment, behavior constitutes the following equation:

$$\text{Behavior} = \text{confidence} + \text{value fulfillment} \times$$
$$\text{probability of value fulfillment} - \text{cost} + \text{risk}.$$

People can therefore be thought of as in a process of continuous calculation, often of a subconscious nature. With regard to a proposed behavior change, if the equation results in a negative or neutral conclusion, no change will take place; if it is positive, the behavior change will occur. Current behavior is always the product of a positive result. Any change in behavior requires a change in the amount or intensity of one or more of the five conditions until the end result of the calculation is pushed onto the positive side. In the end, if there is no change in behavior, current behavior is perceived to better serve values fulfillment.

Hof and Dwyer (1982) further offered a listing of areas for exploration and intervention for each of the five conditions. This listing and then an example illustrating the framework's use with a couple in therapy follow:

1. Confidence
   a. Gathering more facts and information
   b. "Testing the water," successive approximation to build confidence
   c. Asking others to assess competence
   d. Sharing with others for self-reinforcement and obtaining reinforcement from others
   e. Practice and rehearsal
2. Conception of Values Fulfillment
   a. Inventorying values to determine which might be positively affected by a behavior change
   b. Interviewing others about their values fulfillment
3. Probability of Values Fulfillment
   a. Trying out aspects of the new behavior likely to offer the most immediate values fulfillment
   b. Trying out the new behavior in contexts most likely to be supportive to values fulfillment
   c. Providing self-reward at preset milestones
   d. Seeking information on the success rate of others who have engaged in the new behavior
4. Perception of Cost
   a. Careful planning to assess and reduce costs
   b. Experimenting to assess and reduce costs
   c. Placing an upper limit on costs that would be incurred before quitting
   d. Realizing the option of backing out is always available

5. Perception of Risks
   a. Planning and taking appropriate precautions to reduce risks
   b. Sharing risks whenever possible
   c. Learning from experience; experimenting to reduce risks
   d. Assessing the worst that could happen and what that might mean to overall values fulfillment

Illustration

A couple with two children entered therapy with the intention of ending their marital relationship. It was soon evident that although the physical relationship change could be made rather easily, some factors were causing ambivalence, thereby inhibiting the decision-making process and blocking action. The values analysis construction was presented to the couple emphasizing the relevance of the five conditions, each of which was then considered separately.

1. Does the couple have the self-confidence regarding the task confronting them? Answer: Yes. Both partners were intelligent, self-responsible individuals. Both had achieved individual career success and were professionally well-established. Clearly both had had to make significant decisions and act upon them in their professional lives. They recognized as well that they would survive physically and emotionally if divorced and agreed that joint custody of the children would actually allow them to be even more effective parents. The question remained then: If they have the self-confidence needed to change, what is preventing them from changing?
2. Does the couple perceive values fulfillment in the proposed change? Again, the answer is yes. Exploration of their original marital "contract" indicated an early need by the wife to be taken care of by her husband as her family of origin had done. This dependency stance had since become aversive to her. She perceived divorce as enabling her to pursue and more fully achieve the personal fulfillment the independence in her career had provided her. The husband had brought forth needs to be "the head of the household" from his family of origin and sought to maintain a situation wherein these needs could continue to find satisfaction. His wife's desire for greater personal independence blocked his need. Divorce with potential remarriage to a woman more able to satisfy this need represented a clear values fulfillment. The question remained then: If they see values fulfillment, why do they not actively pursue change?
3. Does the couple believe they will find values fulfillment, that positive benefits would accrue to them if they made a decision and acted upon it? When pressed regarding the quality of their lives apart from each other, both maintained the belief that they would

develop the quality of life and find values fulfillment more easily if they ended their marriage. Both were finding such fulfillment only in professional endeavors at present because of their contrasting personal needs. Freedom to pursue more accommodating personal relationships would allow increased personal values fulfillment. The question again, then: If they believe that they will achieve values fulfillment by changing their situation, why do they not act to change it?

4. Does the couple perceive the cost of enacting the behavior change, and do the perceived benefits sufficiently outweigh the costs to move them toward the stated values fulfillment? Again, yes. Perceived costs (what would actually be given up in terms of values fulfillment if the behavior change is undertaken) included selling their current residence and having to move, some reduced income, loss of extended in-law family contacts, and guilt for creating a broken home for their children. These costs were perceived as being inevitable and were therefore direct costs of pursuing a divorce. Each of these costs was examined in-depth; for example, their guilt resulted from a clear breach of values that "children need both parents present." They did, however, present an understanding that these values were changing and needed to be balanced by the negative effects of remaining unhappy and frequently frustrated with their marriage on the children. The guilt was framed as appropriate, but not as necessarily crippling or debilitating. The question still remained: If they perceive the costs of the behavior change, and the cost/benefit ratio is in favor of the perceived benefits, what is preventing change from occurring?

5. Does the couple perceive the risks of engaging in the desired behavior change, and do the benefits sufficiently outweigh the risks to enable them to move toward actively pursuing the behavior change? Once more, a clear yes. Risks (values fulfillment that might be blocked, but with a perceived probability of less than 1) were noted as possible loss of children if either decided to seek single custody and loss of what little satisfaction they had in their marriage if other relationships were unable to produce greater satisfaction. The loss of the children was unlikely since both agreed on joint custody. Since their present satisfaction in their marriage was so low, it was not a very powerful deterrent to action. The question remained, however: If they perceive the risks of engaging in the behavior change and the risk/benefit ratio is in favor of the perceived benefits, why is no change actively being pursued?

The values analysis as undertaken and completed indicated that barriers to movement were not sufficient to deter the couple from taking the desired action. Yet ambivalence still prevailed. The therapist considered the possibility or probability that, although the five conditions were satisfied on an intellectual level in the here and now, perhaps one or more of them were not satisfied at a subconscious level. A review of the process with the couple again proved that this was the case. Condition 4 represented a long-time and strongly held value about family life. Both partners had long ago learned and continually been other- and self-reinforced in the belief that "children need two parents." At the subconscious level, only two options were being considered with regard to parenting: immediate presence as equaling love and caring, and nonimmediate presence through divorce as equaling rejection.

Identifying these beliefs and the early learning experiences that led to their formation did not result in instantaneous resolution of the couple's ambivalence. It did, however, lead to an agreement to seek resolution in this area through therapy efforts that ultimately led to satisfaction of this fourth condition and the originally desired behavior change—divorce.

QUESTION 5

A lthough my primary professional affiliation is as a marriage and family therapist, my initial training was as a psychologist. I have maintained my membership in the American Psychological Association which has taken a strong stance concerning sexism and sex-role stereotyping. The "Guidelines for Therapy with Women" were presented by the APA Task Force on Sex Bias and Sex Role Stereotyping in Psychotherapeutic Practice (APA, 1978) and the "Principles Concerning the Counseling and Therapy of Women" were developed by the Ad Hoc Committee on Women of the APA Division of Counseling Psychology (1979). Have similar guidelines for promoting gender equality been advocated by marriage and family therapists?

Response

At this time, the American Association for Marriage and Family Therapy has not adopted specific guidelines for promoting gender equality in marriage and family therapy. However, formal efforts within the profession to focus attention on and examine gender issues in marriage and family therapy theory, practice, research, and membership in associations have been active (e.g., Communication to the Family Therapy Community, 1985). Relevant recommendations have also been evident in the professional literature. One particularly pertinent set of recommendations was offered by Weiner and Boss (1985). These authors paralleled the APA "Guidelines for Therapy with Women" (APA, 1978) in offering recommendations focusing on gender role issues in marriage and family therapy necessary for the maintenance of therapists' responsibility to clients, own competence, integrity, and professional development.

Responsibility to Clients

— The conduct of therapy should be free of constrictions based on gender-defined roles, and the options explored between client and practitioner should be free of sex role stereotypes. (APA, 1978)

— Exploration of roles in marriage and family therapy should include evaluations of the marriage and family context by husband and wife as equals. Options for role flexibility (career, childrearing, sexuality, home care) should be examined for biased assumptions that males are only instrumental and achieving and females are only dependent and expressive. (Weiner & Boss, 1985)

— Psychologists should recognize the reality, variety, and implications of sex-discriminatory practices in society and should facilitate client examination of options in dealing with such practices. (APA, 1978)

— It may not be possible to separate politics from therapeutic issues at times. Discrimination against women is a current reality in many spheres. Responsible marriage and family therapists see couples in the context of their daily lives and maintain an awareness of contextual impediments faced by women (e.g., discrimination in employment). (Weiner & Boss, 1985)

— The psychologist should demonstrate acceptance of women as equal to men by using language free of derogatory labels. (APA, 1978)

— Outdated clinical labels (e.g., schizophrenic mother, castrating female, nagging wife, seductive woman, penis envy) are scientifically unfounded and derogatory. They should be abandoned as they reflect misogyny and do not promote the therapeutic process with women, couples, and families. (Weiner & Boss, 1985)

— The psychologist should avoid establishing the source of personal problems within the client when they are more properly attributable to situational or cultural factors. (APA, 1978)

— Marriage and family therapists should recognize the benefits of consciousness raising about situational or cultural demands on women's time and energy. Depression, for example, may be viewed as much as a response to unreasonable demands on women (e.g., the "super mom" who is expected to run the home, rear the children, and provide support for her husband while simultaneously maintaining a career) as to a disorder of a psychogenic nature. (Weiner & Boss, 1985)

— The psychologist should recognize and encourage exploration of a woman client's sexuality and should recognize her right to define her own sexual preferences. (APA, 1978)

— Sexual issues should be viewed in terms of both partners' sexual needs. Marriage and family therapists should challenge cultural double standards for sexual behavior and the dichotomous view of women as mothers (asexual) or seductresses (sexual) if either husband or wife has them. Marriage and family therapists should take a proactive attitude so that sexual issues can be explored in a non-biased setting. Bisexual and homosexual issues should be respected. Homophobia—fear of single sexual orientation—of marital partners or therapists should be identified, challenged, and reduced if possible. (Weiner & Boss, 1985)

Competence

— If authoritarian processes are employed as a technique, the therapy should not have the effect of maintaining or reinforcing stereotypic dependency of women. (APA, 1978)

— Marriage and family therapists choosing to use power techniques (e.g., strategic interventions) should be particularly cautious in employing any intervention that disenfranchises a woman's status or power because of likely prior socialization for dependency, inferiority, and subordination. (Weiner & Boss, 1985)

— The client's assertive behaviors should be respected. (APA, 1978)

— Marriage and family therapists should view the assertiveness of women who have been victimized as healthy growth and nurture it. Assertiveness in wanting to question the course of therapy, for example, should be viewed as progress. It may represent an adaptive first time assertion in setting protective boundaries. (Weiner & Boss, 1985)

Integrity

— The psychologist and a fully informed client should mutually agree upon aspects of the therapy relationship such as treatment modality, time factors, and fee arrangements. (APA, 1978)

— Wives and husbands should have equal input into discussions about therapeutic goals, fees, appointment times, and who is to be involved. (Weiner & Boss, 1985)

— The psychologist should not have sexual relations with a woman client or treat her as a sex object. (APA, 1978)

— Because of the traditional double power differential (between therapist and client and between man and woman) marriage and family therapists' responsibility in maintaining the integrity of the therapeutic process is magnified with regard to sexual relationships with clients. (Weiner & Boss, 1985)

Professional Development

— The therapist should be knowledgeable about current empirical findings on sex roles, sexism, and individual differences resulting from the client's gender-defined identity. (APA, 1978)

— Marriage and family therapists should be familiar with current reviews of gender research (e.g., Deaux, 1984; Gilligan, 1982) A therapist's proceeding without this knowledge is analogous to a surgeon's operating with outdated procedures. Professional development should also include familiarity with current research and clinical reports that address incest and other forms of sexual abuse. Marriage and family therapists should routinely ask clients about incest, family sexual abuse, and rape experiences. Claims that such inquiries are "too threatening to the client or the therapy process" may reflect therapists' resistance more than clients'. Marriage and family therapists should face any abhorrence of family sexual pathology through increased knowledge and active exploration of their own fears and attitudes. (Weiner & Boss, 1985)

— The theoretical concepts employed by the therapist should be free of sex bias and sex role stereotypes. (APA, 1978)

— Marriage and family therapists should regularly air their theories and clinical procedures in peer settings so that assumptions underlying practice can be regularly and rigorously challenged. Marriage and family therapists should recognize that even the best of therapists can at times be biased. (Weiner & Boss, 1985)

QUESTION 6

I am moving from my position in a publicly funded agency to pursue independent private practice as a marriage and family therapist. I know that in the past, advertising by the professions was frowned upon but today is acceptable with conditions. I recognize the importance of advertising in building and maintaining my practice and am concerned about proceeding appropriately. Are there issues relative to advertising my practice that I should be particularly aware of?

Response

As was mentioned in chapter 8, the American Association for Marriage and Family Therapy maintains its *Standards on Public Information and Advertising* (AAMFT, 1982c). In the 1985 revision of the *AAMFT Code of Ethical Principles for Marriage and Family Therapists* (AAMFT, 1985), Principle 7 incorporated the majority of the *Standards* within the *AAMFT Code.* Principle 7 states:

Marriage and family therapists engage in appropriate informational activities, including those that enable laypersons to choose marriage and family services on an informed basis.

7.1 Marriage and family therapists accurately represent their competence, education, training, and experience relevant to their practice.

7.2 Marriage and family therapists claim as evidence of educational qualifications only those degrees from regionally accredited institutions or from institutions accredited by states that license or certify marriage and family therapists, but only if such regulation is recognized by AAMFT.

7.3 Marriage and family therapists assure that advertisements and publications, whether in directories, announcement cards, newspapers, or on radio or television, are formulated to convey information necessary for the public to make an appropriate selection. Information could include:

1. Office information, such as name, address, telephone number, credit card acceptability, fee structure, languages spoken, and office hours
2. Appropriate degrees, state licensure and/or certification, and AAMFT clinical member status
3. Description of practice

7.4 Marriage and family therapists do not use a name that could mislead the public concerning the identity, responsibility, source, and status of those practicing under that name and do not hold themselves out as being partners or associates of a firm if they are not.

7.5 Marriage and family therapists do not use any professional identification (such as a professional card, office sign, letterhead, or telephone or association directory listing), if it includes a statement or claim that is false, fraudulent, misleading, or deceptive. This includes a statement that: (a) contains a material misrepresentation of fact; (b) fails to state any material fact necessary to make the statement, in light of all circumstances, truthful; or (c) is intended to or is likely to create an unjustified expectation.

7.6 Marriage and family therapists correct, wherever possible, false, misleading, or inaccurate information and representations made by others concerning their qualifications, services, or products.

7.7 Marriage and family therapists make certain that the qualifications of persons in their employ are represented in a manner that is not false, misleading, or deceptive.

7.8 Marriage and family therapists may represent themselves as specializing within a limited area, but may not hold themselves out as specialists without being able to provide evidence of training, education, and supervised experience in settings that meet recognized professional standards.

7.9 Marriage and family therapists who are AAMFT clinical members—not associates, students or organizations—may identify their membership in AAMFT in public information or advertising materials.

7.10 Marriage and family therapists may not use the initials AAMFT following their name in the manner of an academic degree.

7.11 Marriage and family therapists may not use the AAMFT logo. The Association (which is the sole owner of its name, logo, and the abbreviated initials AAMFT) and its committees and regional divisions, operating as such, may use the AAMFT insignia to list its individual members as a group (e.g., in the Yellow Pages), when all clinical members practicing within a directory district have been invited to list themselves in the directory.

7.12 Marriage and family therapists may use their membership in AAMFT only in connection with their clinical and professional activities.

The AAMFT Committee on Ethics and Professional Practices deals with violations to the *Standards on Public Information and Advertising* as well as the *Code of Ethical Principles.* Engelberg (1985) reported that the greatest number of complaints to this committee involved violations with respect to advertising and public information. Singled out were numerous members' violation of Principle 7.10, putting the initials "AAMFT" beside their name, connoting a degree.

To offer further response to the question herein, the following two relevant cases incorporate an analysis using Principle 7 from the *Code of Ethical Principles.*

> A marriage and family therapist joining a private partnership relocated from another state. The local licensing regulations required an endorsement of the therapist's out-of-state license by the state's Department of Professional Regulation. The therapist allowed the partner to place an advertisement in the telephone book and send out announcements indicating licensure as a marriage and family therapist prior to completion of the endorsement process.

Both the therapist and partner violated ethical principles in this case. The therapist's approval of the premature telephone book advertisement and announcements represented a direct violation of Principles 7.1 and 7.6. Not only did the therapist sanction an inaccurate representation of present licensure status but also made no attempt to correct the inaccurate information being disseminated by the partner when the partner presented intentions to do so. The partner's actions represented a particularly flagrant violation of Principle 7.7 in knowingly misrepresenting the qualifications of the therapist. Impatience preempted professionally ethical practice in this instance.

An announcement was mailed out by two partners in private practice. The brochure described the types of services available including marriage and family therapy and educational diagnostic services. No information indicating any distinction between the partners was included, although only one had training and licensure as a marriage and family therapist. The other, a school psychologist, had training and relevant licensure in educational diagnosis.

The brochure in this case violated Principles 7.4 and 7.5 since it misled the public in implying the school psychologist was competent to offer marriage and family therapy services and the marriage and family therapist was qualified to offer educational diagnostic services. Principle 7.6 was similarly violated; when informed of the misleading implication, the marriage and family therapist continued to use the brochure, justifying this action by a promise to correct the implications when the present stockpile of brochures had been disseminated and new ones could be printed.

QUESTION 7

S ince entering independent practice as a marriage and family therapist, I have become attuned to the ongoing attention needed to business-oriented details. A major example and area of concern in this regard has been clients who have fallen behind in their payments of fees and/or who have terminated therapy and failed to pay for those services already rendered. The typical business often resolves such situations by either absorbing the losses, by taking action against the debtor through a collection agency, or using other legal alternatives such as obtaining an attorney to attempt collection or bring suit. But should I as a marriage and family therapist, a professional person with whom clients have entered a complex confidential relationship, consider myself a "typical creditor" who possesses these options for action?

Response

Obviously the professional practice of marriage and family therapy requires that attention be given to business-oriented details if the therapist is to survive financially. However, because of the professional nature of the "business," extraordinary ethical and legal considerations must be considered, particularly with regard to employing external services to collect delinquent accounts.

Ethically, the question is whether the referral of a delinquent account to a collection service constitutes a breach of confidentiality. The *AAMFT Code of Ethical Principles for Marriage and Family Therapists* (AAMFT, 1985) states the following regarding confidentiality:

> Marriage and family therapists have unique confidentiality problems because the "client" in a therapeutic relationship may be more than one person. The overriding principle is that marriage and family therapists respect the confidences of their client(s).

Specifically, the problem is whether the referral of a client's name to a collection service may be interpreted as a confidence. One could readily dispute the contention that disclosing a client's name (and other relevant information such as address and phone number) constitutes a betrayal of confidences conveyed in the clinical relationship. There is, however, a consensus that clients have control over who knows that they have sought therapy (Pressman, 1979). Thus, clients' names could just as readily be viewed as a protected confidence of the therapeutic relationship. There is presently no clear general principle addressing referrals to collection agencies.

Still within the *Code of Ethical Principles,* using a collection agency may be clearly ethical if the therapist, prior to the initiation of therapy, provides the client with full knowledge of the financial conditions of the therapeutic relationship. The client can then decide from the outset whether to enter therapy under these conditions. The *AAMFT Code of Ethical Principles for Marriage and Family Therapists* (AAMFT, 1985) states, "Marriage and family therapists disclose their fee structure to clients at the onset of treatment."

Informed consent of clients at the beginning of therapy would therefore seem to settle any possible ethical concerns. If a client had not been properly informed of pertinent financial conditions, a warning that an account may be released (e.g., after the therapy had begun and a debt was incurred) would be a "paper tiger" and if acted upon, an ethical violation. In other words, warning clients that they had better pay their bills or else a collection service will be brought in would be unethical if the therapist lacked consent to release the relevant information from the outset of therapy.

Although some of the possible ethical ramifications of employing an external collection service may be arguable, much clearer consequences for marriage and family therapists are evident in considering potential legal vulnerability. Cohen (1979) reported that the most frequent legal complaint against psychologists involved fee disputes. In defining the nature of these disputes, Cohen wrote, "Included in this category were allegations of harassment by collection agencies retained by psychologists" (p. 10).

Clients terminate therapy and leave unpaid bills for numerous reasons. Some clients may be financially overextended and place greater priority on the payment of other accounts. Others may view the therapy efforts as not having been helpful, thus negating their financial obligation. Such clients may view the use of a collection service as harassment even when they gave their informed consent at the onset of therapy, and attempts to obtain payment from such clients may result in their bringing suit against the therapist. The therapist may be falsely accused of a variety of charges, some of which, such as sexual impropriety or abuse, may result in a difficult legal defense. Legal expert Cohen (1979) explicitly suggested, "One thing doctors should never do, however, is routinely turn accounts over to collection agencies. Collection agencies can be coarse in their treatment of patients, and they might push patients thinking about litigation into actually contacting an attorney" (p. 273).

The release of information by marriage and family therapists to a collection service is quite different than the release of material to facilitate a third party payment. In the case of third party payments, clients are normally aware of the information to be released since most will bring claim forms to the therapist or have to sign forms so reimbursement can be directed to the therapist. In most cases, clients encourage such a release of information to defray personal financial costs.

The ultimate pragmatic argument may be that a marriage and family therapist has as much right as any other businessperson to take action against debtors. Such an argument notes that clients enter an implied contract at the outset of therapy; services have a price and clients are obligated to pay for services rendered. Taken alone, this argument is undeniably true. Yet it may only hold true when considered in the absence of certain complexities evident in the therapeutic setting.

Faustman (1982) recommended that the best means of avoiding the potential ethical and legal problems created by resorting to collection services is to use billing strategies that prevent delinquent payments. He proposed requiring payment at the time of the visit, a practice becoming more common among other professionals (e.g., physicians, dentists). The acceptance of credit cards also provides immediate payment. Credit card receipts can be filled out so the confidential nature of clients' therapeutic status is insured (e.g., listing therapy as "services rendered" and avoiding information relating to the practice of marriage and family therapy). Using extended payment plans in cases of financial hardship offers another avenue.

In summary, while external collection services constitute one source of debt collection, potential legal risks should be considered and extreme caution taken in pursuing financial action against clients, particularly those who might have conveyed dissatisfaction regarding the quality or nature of therapy. When action is taken, clients should have been properly informed of these matters at the start of therapy and subsequently given their informed consent.

QUESTION 8

I am presently employed in an urban community mental health center and am considering moving to a small community that has no marriage and family therapist in residence. My training and experiences have been in more urban settings. What can I expect to confront in developing an independent practice in a small town?

Response

Information about independent mental health providers in small communities is scarce. The majority of potentially relevant professional literature has focused on practitioners employed by community mental health centers in rural areas. Many issues regarding the independent practice of marriage and family therapy in small communities do, however, bear a strong resemblance to those raised by rural community mental health workers, and a review of the professional literature in this area may prove fruitful.

Sobel (1984) raised a number of professional issues to consider relevant to "small town" practice from the viewpoint of a psychologist. These same issues are applicable to a marriage and family therapist seeking a similar situation and are summarized in the following paragraphs.

Generalist vs. Specialist

Urban-based practices allow marriage and family therapists to specialize, since other marriage and family therapists are available to deliver a full complement of services to the population. Small town practice does not permit specialization. For example, a therapist may specialize in marital therapy. The community may see drug abuse in adolescents as its major mental health problem. Although the marriage and family therapist may perceive adolescent drug abuse to be primarily precipitated by dysfunctional marital relationships of parents, centering a practice on marital therapy would probably fail since the community's defined need is not being met. However, were the therapist to initially establish a practice to work with adolescent drug abuse and demonstrate success to the community, credibility would be obtained to bring greater attention to marital dyads and develop a more direct demand for such services.

Community Agencies and Organizations

Involvement with community agencies and organizations is important for any independent practitioner, particularly from the standpoint of generating and maintaining referral sources. But in a small town setting, a marriage and family therapist will need to pursue an extraordinary involvement. Although one does not usually perceive independent practitioners as taking a major role in community education, the therapist in a smaller community must. Residents need to be educated about the identification of relevant problems and the availability of treatment resources. Thus, involvements with religious, professional, and social organizations become a regular part of the therapist's practice, though it is usually on a pro bono basis. Work within the schools is a particularly valuable service and source of referrals.

Professional Impact on Personal Privacy

The marriage and family therapist in a small town will likely live in the community. Thus, unlike a larger urban setting, some personal privacy is lost. The expectations of neighbors as well as other community people may call for the therapist to maintain a "professional image" at all times, lest credibility and practice suffer. Sensitivity to the community's standards is critical.

Funding Dilemmas

Small towns are likely to have fewer funding resources than urban communities. The financial resources of residents themselves and the general community revenues that often serve as a source of fees for marriage and family therapists in independent practice will be more limited. Innovative therapeutic practice (e.g., multiple family therapy) as well as innovative business practice (e.g., bartering) may be called for.

Professional Isolation

Independent practice can lead to professional isolation. The isolation of the marriage and family therapist is likely to be much greater in a small community than in urban areas. Peer consultation is not readily available. The therapist must rely on personal resources to keep abreast of new developments as well as creatively consider innovative interventions. Potentially the most frustrating isolation issue may be the lack of a full complement of mental health services within the community. The therapist may often be confronted with the decision of whether to refuse treatment or to deliver a service that is not the treatment of choice.

Continuing Professional Development

Closely tied to the issue of professional isolation is the increased need for continuing education. Needing to assume more of a generalist role calls for working with a wide diversity of presenting problems. To be successful, the therapist needs an eclectic orientation to provide the widest breadth of services possible. Thus, continuing education is critical.

Given the paucity of library resources and limited access to conferences, lectures, and seminars, a multifaceted program is recommended. Subscriptions to relevant professional journals and the regular purchase of appropriate books constitute necessary business expenses. Attendance at workshops, seminars, and professional meetings must be worked into a schedule even if significant travel is required. Therapists within a reasonable distance of each other, such as a 2–3 hour drive, might arrange monthly or bimonthly meetings to discuss professional issues and topics to maintain and enhance clinical skills.

Epilogue

Although less than 100 years old, professional psychotherapy has become a major influence in society. Therapists contribute to and considerably affect many aspects of modern life. During this time, psychotherapy has broadened its perspective. No longer is it practiced exclusively on a "one therapist-to-one client" basis. Group therapy efforts have become commonplace in almost every mental health setting. Likewise, the last several decades have seen the advent of another expansion within the psychotherapeutic field, that of marriage and family therapy.

Many therapists are increasingly replacing or supplementing their traditional individual and group models of practice with one emphasizing couples and families as the dominant treatment focus. This is not to suggest that contact with marital partners and other family members had been completely ignored. Rather, marital partners and family members had always been considered in light of the individual client's concerns and from an individually oriented therapeutic perspective.

A *new epistemology* (Hoffman, 1981)—a new framework for thinking about and conceptualizing the bases for clients' psychological problems and the most effective means of treating those problems—is being increasingly adopted. Therapists have recognized the limitations in working for individual change when the marital or family system in which a client lives remains unchanged. Consequently, marriage and family therapy has gained acceptance: the idea that other members of a relationship system will need to change in some way if changes are to be achieved and maintained for a particular member.

This book has sought to encourage a greater familiarization and expansion of knowledge relevant to ethical, legal, and professional issues necessary to supplement training and clinical practice in marriage and family therapy. We hope it has provided you with an introduction to some of the issues you may encounter; that it has stimulated you to think about your own position as a marriage and family therapist.

As marriage and family therapy assumes added importance in the psychotherapeutic community, these issues will take on even greater proportions. The new epistemology will be expanding, needing nurturance in the form of continuing contributions.

References

Abelson, R., & Nielson, K. (1967). History of ethics. In P. Edwards (Ed.), *The encyclopedia of philosophy* (Vol. 3). New York: Macmillan.

Abroms, G.M. (1978). The place of values in psychotherapy. *Journal of Marriage and Family Counseling, 4,* 3–17.

Alsager v. District Court of Polk County, Iowa, 406 F. Supp 10 (1975).

American Association for Counseling and Development. (1981). *Ethical standards* (rev. ed.). Falls Church, VA: Author.

American Association for Marriage and Family Therapy. (1979). *Marital and family therapy: State licensing and certification model legislation.* Upland, CA: Author.

American Association for Marriage and Family Therapy. (1982a). *Continuing education in family therapy (CEFT).* Washington, DC: Author.

American Association for Marriage and Family Therapy. (1982b). *AAMFT standards on public information and advertising.* Washington, DC: Author.

American Association for Marriage and Family Therapy (1982c). *AAMFT: What it is . . . what it does.* Washington, DC: Author.

American Association for Marriage and Family Therapy. (1983). *AAMFT membership requirements.* Washington, DC: Author.

American Association for Marriage and Family Therapy. (1984). *AAMFT: The approved supervisor.* Washington, DC: Author.

American Association for Marriage and Family Therapy. (1985). *AAMFT code of ethical principles for marriage and family therapists.* Washington, DC: Author.

American Jurisprudence 2d. (1976). Witnesses, Sec. 190.

57 American Jurisprudence 2d Negligence *1.

61 American Jurisprudence 2d 99.

American Psychiatric Association. (1980). *Diagnostic and statistical manual of mental disorders* (3rd ed.). Washington, DC: Author.

American Psychiatric Association. (1981). *The principles of medical ethics, with annotations especially applicable to psychiatry.* Washington, DC: Author.

American Psychological Association. (1973). Guidelines for psychologists conducting growth groups. *American Psychologist, 28,* 933.

American Psychological Association. (1974). *Casebook on ethical standards of psychologists.* Washington, DC: Author.

American Psychological Association. (1978). Guidelines for therapy with women. *American Psychologist, 30,* 1122–1123.

American Psychological Association. (1981a). *Ethical standards of psychologists* (rev. ed.). Washington, DC: Author.

American Psychological Association. (1981b). *Specialty guidelines for the delivery of services by clinical psychologists.* Washington, DC: Author.

American Psychological Association Division of Counseling Psychology. (1979). Principles concerning the counseling and therapy of women. *The Counseling Psychologist, 8*(1), 21.

Andolfi, M., Angelo, C., Menghi, P., & Nicolo-Corigliano, M. (1983). *Beyond the family mask: Therapeutic change in rigid family systems.* New York: Brunner/Mazel.

Aponte, H.J. (1976). Underorganization in the poor family. In P.J. Guerin, Jr. (Ed.), *Family therapy: Theory and practice.* New York: Gardner.

Aponte, H.J. (1985). The negotiation of values in therapy. *Family Process, 24,* 323–338.

Ard, B.N., & Ard, C. (Eds.). (1976). *Handbook of marriage counseling* (2nd ed.). Palo Alto, CA: Science and Behavior Books.

Atwood v. Atwood, 550 S.W. 2d 465 (Ky. 1976).

Baier, K. (1958). *The moral point of view.* Ithaca, NY: Cornell University.

Ball, P.G., & Wyman, E. (1977–78). Battered wives and powerlessness: What can counselors do? *Victimology: An International Journal, 2,* 545–552.

Barry, V. (1982). *Moral aspects of health care.* Monterey, CA: Brooks/Cole.

Bateson, G. (1977). The birth of a matrix or double bind and epistemology. In M. Berger (Ed.), *Beyond the double bind.* New York: Brunner/Mazel.

Bateson, G. (1979). *Mind and nature: A necessary unity.* New York: Bantam.

Bayles, M.D. (1981). *Professional ethics.* Belmont, CA: Wadsworth.

Beauchamp, T., & Childress, J. (1979). *Principles of biomedical ethics.* New York: Oxford University.

Becvar, R.J., Becvar, D.S., & Bender, A.E. (1982). Let us first do no harm. *Journal of Marital and Family Therapy, 8,* 385–391.

Bellotti v. Baird (II), 443 U.S. 622 (1979).

Bergantino, L.A. (1978). A theory of imperfection. *Counselor Education and Supervision, 17,* 286–292.

Berman, E.M. (1982). The individual interview as a treatment technique in conjoint therapy. *American Journal of Family Therapy, 10,* 27–37.

Bernstein, B.E. (1982). Ignorance of the law is no excuse. In J.C. Hansen & L. L'Abate (Eds.), *Values, ethics, legalities and the family therapist.* Rockville, MD: Aspen.

Bernstein, B.L., & Lecomte, C. (1981). Licensure in psychology: Alternative direction. *Professional Psychology, 12,* 200–208.

Berry v. Moensch, 8 Utah 2d 191, 331 P.2d 814 (1958).

Bersoff, D., & Jain, M. (1980). A practical guide to privileged communication for psychologists. In G. Cooke (Ed.), *The role of the forensic psychologist.* Springfield, IL: Charles C. Thomas.

Bertram, B. (1983). A threat to licensure. *American Mental Health Counselors Association News, 6*(6), 1, 7.

Besharov, D.J. (1982). Representing abused and neglected children: When protecting children means seeking the dismissal of court proceedings. *Journal of Family Law, 20,* 217–239.

Bieluch v. Bieluch, 462 A2d 1060 (Conn. 1983).

Black, M., & Joffe, W.A. (1978). A lawyer/therapist team approach to divorce. *Conciliation Courts Review, 16,* 1–5.

Black's Law Dictionary (4th ed.). (1968). St. Paul, MN: West.

Boszormenyi-Nagy, I. (1974). Ethical and practical implications of intergenerational family therapy. *Psychotherapy and Psychosomatics, 24,* 261–268.

Boszormenyi-Nagy, I., & Ulrich, D.N. (1981). Contextual family therapy. In A.S. Gurman & D.P. Kniskern (Eds.), *Handbook of Family Therapy.* New York: Brunner/Mazel.

Bourne, P.G. (1982). Ethical problems of therapists in government and industry. In M. Rosenbaum (Ed.), *Ethics and values in psychotherapy: A guidebook.* New York: Free Press.

Bowen, M. (1978). *Family therapy in clinical practice.* New York: Jason Aronson.

Brandt, R. (1959). *Ethical theory.* Englewood Cliffs, NJ: Prentice-Hall.

Bray, J.H., Shepherd, J.N., & Hays, J.R. (1985). Legal and ethical issues in informed consent to psychotherapy. *The American Journal of Family Therapy, 13,* 50–60.

Broadhurst, D.D. (1979). *The educator's role in the prevention and treatment of child abuse and neglect.* Washington, DC: National Center on Child Abuse and Neglect, U.S. Department of Health, Education and Welfare.

Brodsky, S.L., & Robey, A. (1972). On becoming an expert witness: Issues of orientation and effectiveness. *Professional Psychology, 3,* 173–176.

Bromberg, W. (1979). *The uses of psychiatry and the law.* Westport, CT: Quorum.

Brown, H.I. (1977). *Perception, theory and commitment.* Chicago: University of Chicago.

Bureau of National Affairs, Inc. (1976). *Uniform Parentage Act.* Washington, DC: Author.

Bureau of National Affairs, Inc. (1977). *HEW regulations—Child abuse and neglect.* Washington, DC: Author.

Bureau of National Affairs, Inc. (1982). *Uniform marriage and divorce act.* Washington, DC: Author.

Bureau of National Affairs, Inc. (1984). *Uniform premarital agreement act.* Washington, DC: Author.

Burgum, T., & Anderson, S. (1975). *The counselor and the law.* Washington, DC: American Personnel and Guidance Association.

Caban v. Mohammed, 441 U.S. 380 (1979).

Callis, R., Pope, S.K., & DePauw, M.E. (1982). *APGA ethical standards casebook* (3rd ed.). Falls Church, VA: American Personnel and Guidance Association.

Carl, D., & Jurkovic, G.J. (1983). Agency triangles: Problems in agency-family relationships. *Family Process, 22,* 441–451.

Chemerinsky, E. (1979). Defining the "best interests": Constitutional protections in involuntary adoptions. *Journal of Family Law, 18,* 79–113.

Clark, H.H., Jr. (1968). *The law of domestic relations.* St. Paul, MN: West.

Clark, H.H., Jr. (1974). *Cases and problems on domestic relations.* St. Paul, MN: West.

Clark, T.E. (1985). Licensed MFTs on par with AAMFT requirements. *Family Therapy News, 16*(4), 6.

Cleary, E.W. (Ed.). (1972). *McCormick's handbook of law evidence* (2nd ed.). St. Paul, MN: West.

Cobbs v. Grant. 8 Cal., 3d 229, 502 P.2d 1 (1972).

Coogler, O.J. (1978). *Structured mediation in divorce settlement.* Lexington, MA: Heath.

Cohen, R.J. (1979). *Malpractice: A guide for mental health professionals.* New York: Free Press.

Commission on Accreditation for Marriage & Family Therapy Education. (1981). *Manual on Accreditation* (3rd ed.). Upland, CA: Author.

Commission releases '85 MFT program roster. (1985). *Family Therapy News, 16*(4), 11.

Communication to the family therapy community. (1985). *The Family Therapy Networker, 9*(6), 17.

Connell, M.J. (1981). Property division and alimony awards: A survey of statutory limitations on judicial discretion. *Fordam Law Review, 50,* 415–449.

120 CONG. REC. 27, 36533 (1974).

120 CONG. REC. 31, 41381 (1974).

Corey, G., Corey, M.S., & Callanan, P. (1984). *Issues and ethics in the helping professions* (2nd ed.). Monterey, CA: Brooks/Cole.

Cormier, L.S., & Bernard, J.M. (1982). Ethical and legal responsibilities of clinical supervisors. *Personnel and Guidance Journal, 60,* 486–490.

Cruchfield, C.F. (1981). Nonmarital relationships and their impact on the institution of marriage and the traditional family structure. *Journal of Family Law, 19,* 247–261.

Danish, S.J., & Smyer, M.A. (1981). Unintended consequences of requiring a license to help. *American Psychologist, 36,* 13–21.

Daubner, E.V., & Daubner, E.S. (1970). Ethics and counseling decisions. *The Personnel and Guidance Journal, 48,* 433–442.

Davis, J.W. (1981). Counselor licensure: Overkill? *Personnel and Guidance Journal, 60,* 83–85.

Dawidoff, D.J. (1973). *The malpractice of psychiatrists.* Springfield, IL: Charles C. Thomas.

Day, D. (1977). Termination of parental rights statutes and void for vagueness doctrine: A successful attack on the *parens patriae* rationale. *Journal of Family Law, 16,* 213.

Deaux, K. (1984). From individual differences to social categories: Analysis of a decade's research on gender. *American Psychologist, 39,* 105–116.

Delaware Rules of Evidence, 503 (1981).

Dell, P. (1982). Beyond homeostasis: Toward a concept of coherence. *Family Process, 21,* 21–41.

Deli, P. (1983). From pathology to ethics. *The Family Therapy Networker, 7*(6), 29–31, 64.

DeKraai, M.B., & Sales, B.D. (1982). Privileged communications of psychologists. *Professional Psychology, 13,* 372–388.

Denkowski, K.M., & Denkowski, G.C. (1982). Client-counselor confidentiality: An update of rationale, legal status, and implications. *Personnel and Guidance Journal, 60,* 371–375.

DePauw, M.E. (1986). Avoiding ethical violations: A timeline perspective for individual counseling. *Journal of Counseling and Development, 64,* 303–305.

DeShazer, S. (1982). *Brief family therapy: An ecosystem approach.* New York: Guilford.

Deutsch, M. (1973). *The resolution of conflict.* New Haven, CT: Yale University.

Dincin, J., Selleck, V., & Streicker, S. (1978). Restructuring parental attitudes: Working with parents of the adult mentally ill. *Schizophrenia Bulletin, 4,* 597–608.

Doe v. Bolton. Rehearing denied, 410 U.S. 959 (1973).

Dooley, J.A. (1977). Malpractice: Professional liability and the law. *Professional Psychology, 9,* 467–477.

Douthwaite, G. (1979). *Unmarried couples and the law.* Indianapolis: Smith.

Eady v. Alter, 380 N.Y.S. 2d 737 (New York, 1976).

Efran, J., & Lukens, M. (1985). The world according to Humberto Maturana. *The Family Therapy Networker, 9*(3), 22–28, 72–75.

Engelberg, S.L. (1985). General counsel's report: Ethics committee's procedures outlined. *Family Therapy News, 16*(2), 16.

Erickson, M.H. (1967). Use of symptoms as an integral part of therapy. In J. Haley (Ed.), *Advanced techniques of hypnosis and therapy.* New York: Grune & Stratton.

Evans, J. (1983). The treatment specialist: An emerging role for counselors within the criminal court system. *Personnel and Guidance Journal, 61,* 349–351.

Everstine, L., Everstine, D.S., Heymann, G.M., True, R.H., Frey, D.H., Johnson, H.G., & Seiden, R.H. (1980). Privacy and confidentiality in psychotherapy. *American Psychologist, 9,* 828–840.

Family Educational Rights and Privacy Act of 1974. 20 U.S.C. 1232g.

Faustman, W.O. (1982). Legal and ethical issues in debt collection strategies of professional psychologists. *Professional Psychology, 13,* 208–214.

Felstiner, W.L., & Williams, L.A. (1978). Mediation as an alternative to criminal prosecution. *Law and Human Behavior, 2,* 223–244.

Fieldsteel, N.D. (1982). Ethical issues in family therapy. In M. Rosenbaum (Ed.), *Ethics and values in psychotherapy: A guidebook.* New York: Free Press.

Final regulations: Family Educational Rights and Privacy Act. (1976). *Federal Register, 41,* 24670–24675.

Fine, M.J. (1985). Intervention from a systems-ecological perspective. *Professional Psychology: Research and Practice, 16,* 262–270.

Fine, M.J., & Holt, P. (1983). Intervening with school problems: A family systems perspective. *Psychology in the Schools, 20,* 59–66.

Fisher, L., Anderson, A., & Jones, J.E. (1981). Types of paradoxical interventions and indications/contraindications for use in clinical practice. *Family Process, 20,* 25–35.

Fischer, L., & Sorenson, G.P. (1985). *School law for counselors, psychologists, and social workers.* New York: Longman.

Flax, M. (1977). *Couples therapy in battering relationships.* Paper presented at Colorado Women's College Conference on Battered Women, Denver.

Folberg, J. (1984). Custody overview. In J. Folberg (Ed.), *Joint custody and shared parenting.* Washington, DC: Bureau of National Affairs, Inc.

Folberg, J., & Graham, M. (1979). Joint custody of children following divorce. *University of California, Davis Law Review, 12,* 523–581.

Foster, H.H. (1976). An overview of confidentiality and privilege. *Journal of Psychiatry and the Law, 4,* 393–401.

Foster, H.H. (1978). Informed consent of mental patients. In W.E. Barton & C.J. Sanborn (Eds.), *Law and the mental health professions: Friction at the interface.* New York: International Universities.

Framo, J.L. (1976). Chronicle of a struggle to establish a family unit within a community mental health center. In P.J. Guerin, Jr. (Ed.), *Family therapy: Theory and practice.* New York: Gardner.

Framo, J.L. (1981). The integration of marital therapy with sessions with family of origin. In A. Gurman & D. Kniskern (Eds.), *Handbook of family therapy.* New York: Brunner/Mazel.

Fraser, J.S. (1984). Paradox and orthodox: Folie á deux. *Journal of Marital and Family Therapy, 10,* 361–372.

Freed, D.J., & Foster, H.H. (1981). Divorce in the fifty states: An overview. *Family Law Quarterly, 14,* 229–284.

Fretz, B.R., & Mills, D.H. (1980). *Licensing and certification of psychologists and counselors.* San Francisco: Jossey-Bass.

Fricke v. Fricke, 42 N.W. 2d 500 (Wis. 1950).

Gill, S.J. (1982). Professional disclosure and consumer protection in counseling. *Personnel and Guidance Journal, 60,* 443–446.

Gillespie v. Gillespie, 631 S.W. 2d 592 (Tex. App. 1982).

Gilligan, C. (1982). *In a different voice.* Cambridge, MA: Harvard University.

Glaser, B., & Kirschenbaum, H. (1980). Using values clarification in counseling settings. *Personnel and Guidance Journal, 58,* 569–574.

Glendon, M.A. (1976). Marriage and the state: The washing away of marriage. *Virginia Law Review, 62,* 663–720.

Glendon, M.A. (1980). Modern marriage law and its underlying assumptions: The new marriage and the new property. *Family Law Quarterly, 13,* 441–460.

Gomez v. Perez, 409 U.S. 535 (1973).

Gross, S.J. (1977). Professional disclosure: An alternative to licensure. *Personnel and Guidance Journal, 55,* 586–588.

Gross, S.J. (1978). The myth of professional licensing. *American Psychologist, 33,* 1009–1016.

Grosslight v. Superior Court of Los Angeles County, 72 Cal. App. 3d 502, 140 Cal. Rptr. 278 (1977).

Grunebaum, H. (1984). Comments on Terkelsen's "Schizophrenia and the family: II. Adverse effects of family therapy." *Family Process, 23,* 421–428.

Guernsey, T.F. (1981). The psychotherapist-patient privilege in child placement: A relevancy analysis. *Villanova Law Review, 26,* 955–966.

Guggenheim, P.D. (1979, March). The juvenile offender. *Bulletin, Area 11, American Psychiatric Association.*

Gulliver, P.H. (1979). *Disputes and negotiations: A cross-cultural perspective.* New York: Academic.

Gumper, L.L., & Sprenkle, D.H. (1981). Privileged communication in therapy: Special problems for the family and couples therapist. *Family Process, 20,* 11–23.

Gurman, A.S. (1978). Contemporary marital therapies: A critique and comparative analysis of psychoanalytic, behavioral and systems theory approaches. In T.J. Paolino & B.S. McCrady (Eds.), *Marriage and marital therapy: Psychoanalytic, behavioral, and systems theory perspectives.* New York: Brunner/Mazel.

Gurman, A.S., & Kniskern, D.P. (1978). Deterioration in marital and family therapy: Empirical, clinical and conceptual issues. *Family Process, 17,* 3–20.

Gurman, A.S., & Kniskern, D.P. (1981). Family therapy outcome research: Knowns and unknowns. In A.S. Gurman & D.P. Kniskern (Eds.), *Handbook of family therapy.* New York: Brunner/Mazel.

H.L. v. Matheson, 450 U.S. 398 (1981).

Hahman v. Hahman, 628 P.2d 984 (Ariz. App. 1981).

Haley, J. (1975). Why a mental health clinic should avoid family therapy. *Journal of Marriage and Family Counseling, 1,* 3–13.

Haley, J. (1976). *Problem-solving therapy: New strategies for effective family therapy.* San Francisco: Jossey-Bass.

Haley, J. (1984). Marriage or family therapy. *The American Journal of Family Therapy, 12*(2), 3–14.

Halleck, S.L. (1976). Another response to "Homosexuality: The ethical challenge. *Journal of Consulting and Clinical Psychology, 44,* 167–170.

Hammond, J.M. (1981). Children, divorce, and you. *Learning, 9,* 83–84, 88–89.

Handel, W.W., & Sherwyn, B.A. (1982). Surrogate parenting. *Trial, 18,* 57–60, 77.

Hare-Mustin, R.T. (1978). A feminist approach to family therapy. *Family Process, 17,* 181–194.

Hare-Mustin, R.T. (1980). Family therapy may be dangerous for your health. *Professional Psychology, 11,* 935–938.

Hare-Mustin, R.T., Marecek, J., Kaplan, A.G., & Liss-Levinson, N. (1979). Rights of clients, responsibilities of therapists. *American Psychologist, 34,* 3–16.

Harp, B.S., Jr. (1982). Post judgement proceedings. In *Program materials for seminars on family law practice.* Athens, GA: Institute of Continuing Legal Education in Georgia.

Haynes, J. (1978). Divorce mediation: A new role. *Journal of Social Work, 23,* 5–9.

Haynes, J. (1981). *Divorce mediation: A practical guide for therapists and counselors.* New York: Springer.

Hendrickson, R.M. (1982). Counselor liability: Does the risk require insurance coverage? *Personnel and Guidance Journal, 61,* 205–207.

Hendrickson, R.M., & Mangum, R.S. (1978). *Governing board and administrator liability.* (ERIC Higher Education Research Report No. 9).

Hennessey, E.F. (1980). Explosion in family law litigation: Challenges and opportunities for the bar. *Family Law Quarterly, 14,* 187–201.

Heppner, M. (1978). Counseling the battered wife: Myths, facts and decisions. *Personnel and Guidance Journal, 56,* 522–525.

Herrman, M.S., McHenry, P.C., & Weber, R.E. (1979). Mediation and arbitration to family conflict resolution. *Arbitration Journal, 34,* 17–21.

Herrington, B.S. (1979). Privilege denied in joint therapy. *Psychiatric News, 14*(1), 1, 9.

Hilberman, E., & Munson, K. (1977–78). Sixty battered women. *Victimology: An International Journal, 2,* 545–552.

Hines, P.M., & Hare-Mustin, R.T. (1978). Ethical concerns in family therapy. *Professional Psychology, 9,* 165–171.

Hof, L., & Dwyer, C.E. (1982). Overcoming ambivalence through the use of values analysis. *The American Journal of Family Therapy, 10*(1), 17–26.

Hoffman, L. (1981). *Foundations of family therapy.* New York: Basic.

Hoffman, L., & Long, L. (1969). A systems dilemma. *Family Process, 8,* 211–234.

Hogan, D.B. (1979). *The regulation of psychotherapists: A handbook of state licensure laws.* Cambridge, MA: Ballinger.

Hulnick, H.R. (1977). Counselor: Know thyself. *Counselor Education and Supervision, 17,* 69–72.

Huston, K. (1984). Ethical decisions in treating battered women. *Professional Psychology: Research and Practice, 15,* 822–832.

In re Carrafa, 77 Cal. App. 3d 788, 143 Cal. Rptr. 848 (1978).

In re Fred J., 89 Cal. App. 3d 168, 152 Cal. Rptr. 327 (1979).

In re Marriage of Gove, 572 P. 2d 458 (Ariz. App. 1977).

In re Marriage of Winegard, 278 N.W. 2d 505 (Iowa, 1979).

Instructions for authors. (1985). *Journal of Marital and Family Therapy, 11,* 113.

Iscoe, I. (1982). Toward a viable community health psychology: Caveats from the experiences of the community mental health movement. *American Psychologist, 37,* 961–965.

Jacobson, N.S., & Margolin, G. (1979). *Marital therapy: Strategies based on social learning and behavior exchange principles.* New York: Brunner/Mazel.

Jantsch. E. (1980). *The self-organizing universe: Scientific and human implications of the emerging paradigm of evolution.* New York: Pergamon.

Johnson, T.R. (1965). Medical malpractice-Doctrines of *res ipsa loquitur* and informed consent. *University of Colorado Law Review, 37,* 182–195.

Jones, W.T., Sontag, F., Beckner, M.O., & Fogelin, R.J. (Eds.). (1977). *Approaches to ethics* (3rd ed.). New York: McGraw-Hill.

Karpel, M.A. (1980). Family secrets: I. Conceptual and ethical issues in the relational context: II. Ethical and practical considerations in therapeutic management. *Family Process, 19,* 295–306.

Karpel, M.A., & Strauss, E.S. (1983). *Family evaluation*. New York: Gardner.

Katz, S.N. (1981). *Child snatching: The legal response to the abduction of children*. Chicago: American Bar Association.

Kazen, B.A. (1977). *When father wants custody: A lawyer's view*. Austin: State Bar of Texas.

Keary, A.O. (1985). Criminal law and procedure. In N.T. Sidney (Ed.), *Law and ethics: A guide for the health professional*. New York: Human Sciences.

Kelly, G. (1955). *The psychology of personal constructs*. New York: Norton.

Kempin, F. (1982). *Historical introduction to Anglo-American law* (2nd ed.). St. Paul, MN: West.

Kennedy, C. (1973). The psychotherapists' privilege. *Washburn Law Review, 12,* 297–315.

Kessler, S. (1978). *Creative conflict resolution: Mediation*. Atlanta: National Institute for Professional Training.

Kissel, S. (1983). *Private practice for the mental health clinician*. Rockville, MD: Aspen.

Kitchener, K.S. (1984). Ethics in counseling psychology: Distinctions and directions. *Counseling Psychologist, 12,* 15–18.

Kitchener, K.S. (1985). Ethical principles and ethical decisions in student affairs. In H.J. Canon & R.D. Brown (Eds.), *Applied ethics: Tools for practitioners*. San Francisco: Jossey-Bass.

Kitchener, K.S. (1986). Teaching applied ethics in counselor education: An integration of psychological processes and philosophical analysis. *Journal of Counseling and Development, 64,* 306–310.

Kluckhohn, F., & Strodtbeck, F.L. (1961). *Variations in value orientation*. Evanston, IL: Row, Peterson.

Kosinski, F.A. (1982). Standards, accreditation, and licensure in marriage and family therapy. *Personnel and Guidance Journal, 60,* 350–352.

Knapp, S., & VandeCreek, L. (1982). Tarasoff: Five years later. *Professional Psychology, 13,* 511–516.

Knapp, S., & VandeCreek, L. (1985). Psychotherapy and privileged communications in child custody cases. *Professional Psychology: Research and Practice, 16,* 398–407.

Knapp, S., VandeCreek, L., & Zirkel, P.A. (1985). Legal research techniques: What the psychologist needs to know. *Professional Psychology: Research and Practice, 16,* 363–372.

Krause, H.D. (1977). *Family law in a nutshell*. St. Paul, MN: West.

Krause, H.D. (1982). Child support enforcement: Legislative tasks for the early 1980's. *Family Law Quarterly, 15,* 349–370.

Kristensen v. Kristensen, 406 So. 2d 1210 (Fla. 5th DCA 1981).

L'Abate, L. (1982). Introduction. In J.C. Hansen & L. L'Abate (Eds.), *Values, ethics, legalities and the family therapist*. Rockville, MD: Aspen.

Lane, P.J., & Spruill, J. (1980). To tell or not to tell: The psychotherapist's dilemma. *Psychotherapy: Theory, Research, and Practice, 17,* 202–209.

Langsley, D.G., & Kaplan, D.M. (1968). *The treatment of families in crisis*. New York: Grune & Stratton.

Larson v. Larson, 24 Ill. App.2d 467, 192 N.E.2d 594 (1963).

Lavori, N. (1976). *Living together, married or single: Your legal rights.* New York: Harper & Row.

Lewis, J., Beavers, W.R., Gossett, J.T., & Phillips, V.A. (1976). *No single thread: Psychological health in family systems.* New York: Brunner/Mazel.

Loving v. Virginia, 388 U.S. 1 (1967).

MacDonald, J.M. (1969). *Psychiatry and the criminal* (2nd ed.). Springfield, IL: Charles C. Thomas.

Mace, D.R. (1976). Marital intimacy and the deadly love-anger cycle. *Journal of Marriage and Family Counseling, 2,* 131–137.

Madanes, C. (1980). Protection, paradox, and pretending. *Family Process, 19,* 73–85.

Madanes, C. (1983). Strategic therapy of schizophrenia. In W.R. McFarlane (Ed.), *Family therapy in schizophrenia.* New York: Guilford.

Margolin, G. (1982). Ethical and legal considerations in marriage and family therapy. *American Psychologist, 7,* 788–801.

Marlow, L. (1985). Divorce mediation: Therapists in the legal world. *The American Journal of Family Therapy, 13,* 3–10.

Marvin v. Marvin, 18 Cal. 3d 660, 134 Cal. Rptr. 815, 557 P. 2d 106 (1976).

Maslow, A.H. (1959). *New knowledge in human values.* New York: Harper & Row.

Massachusetts General Laws, ch. 119, *63.

Massachusetts General Laws Annotated, ch 233 *20B (e) (West Supp. 1980).

Matter of Atkins, 316 N.W. 2d 477 (Mich. App. 1982).

Maturana, H.R. (1978). Biology of language: Epistemology of reality. In G.A. Miller & E. Lenneberg (Eds.), *Psychology and biology of language and thought.* New York: Academic.

McCarty v. McCarty, 101 S. Ct. 2728 (1981).

McGoldrick, M., Pearce, J., & Giordano, J. (1982). *Ethnicity and family therapy.* New York: Guilford.

McG Mullin, R., & Carroll, M. (1983). The battered-woman syndrome: Contributing factors and remedial interventions. *American Mental Health Counselors Association Journal, 5,* 31–38.

McGuire, J.M., & Borowy, T.D. (1978). Confidentiality and the Buckley-Pell amendment: Ethical and legal considerations for counselors. *Personnel and Guidance Journal, 56,* 554–557.

McIntosh v. Milano, 403 A.2d 500 (N.J. 1979).

McKenzie, D.J. (1978). The setting up of a family court counseling system in Australia. *Conciliation Courts Review, 16,* 23–30.

Meyer, R., & Smith, S. (1977). A crisis in group therapy. *American Psychologist, 32,* 638–643.

Meyerstein, I., & Todd, J.C. (1980). On the witness stand: The family therapist and expert testimony. *The American Journal of Family Therapy, 8*(4), 43–51.

Milne, A. (1978). Custody of children in a divorce process: A family self-determination model. *Conciliation Courts Review, 16,* 1–10.

Minuchin, S. (1974). *Families and family therapy.* Cambridge, MA: Harvard University.

Minuchin, S., & Fishman, H.C. (1981). *Family therapy techniques.* Cambridge, MA: Harvard University.

Mnookin, R. (1973). Foster care in whose best interest? *Harvard Educational Review, 43,* 599–638.

Morrison, J.K., Layton, B., & Newman, J. (1982). Ethical conflict in clinical decision making: A challenge for family therapists. In J.C. Hansen & L. L'Abate (Eds.). *Values, ethics, legalities and the family therapist.* Rockville, MD: Aspen.

Mowrer, O.H. (Ed.). (1967). *Morality and mental health.* Chicago: Rand McNally.

Mulvey, E.P., Reppucci, N.D., & Weithorn, L.A. (1984). Mental health, law, and children. In N.D. Reppucci, L.A. Weithorn, E.P. Mulvey, & J. Monahan (Eds.), *Children, mental health, and the law.* Beverly Hills: Sage.

Murphy, J.M. (1976). A tandem approach: Marriage counseling as process in tandem with individual psychotherapy. *Journal of Marriage and Family Counseling, 3,* 13–22.

Napier, A.Y., & Whitaker, C. (1978). *The family crucible.* New York: Harper & Row.

Nathanson v. Kline. 186 Kan. 393, 350 P.2d 1093 (1960) affirmed on rehearing, 187 Kan. 186, 354 P.2d 1093 (1960).

National Association of Social Workers. (1979). *Code of ethics.* Washington, DC: Author.

National Center on Child Abuse and Neglect. (1983). *Report by the national center on child abuse and neglect.* Washington, DC: Author.

Newman v. Newman, 653 P.2d 728 (Colo. Sup. Ct. 1982).

New Mexico *ex rel.* Human Services Department v. Levario, 649 P. 2d 510 (N.M. Ct. App. 1982).

Nichols, M.P. (1984). *Family therapy: Concepts and methods.* New York: Gardner.

Nozick, R. (1968). Moral complications and moral structure. *Natural Law Forum, 13,* 1–50.

Olson, D.H. (1975). Marriage and family therapy: A clinical overview. In A. Gurman (Ed.), *Couples in conflict.* New York: Jason Aronson.

Olson, D.H. (1976). *Treating relationships.* Lake Mills, IA: Graphic.

Olson, D.H., Russell, C.S., & Sprenkle, D.H. (1980). Marital and family therapy: A decade review. *Journal of Marriage and the Family, 42,* 973–993.

Oppenheim, C.D. (1968). Valid consent to medical treatment: Need the patient know? *Duquesne Law Review, 4,* 450–577.

Orlando, F.A. (1978). Conciliation programs: Their effect on marriage and family life. *Florida Bar Journal, 52,* 218–221.

Osborne v. Osborne, 428 N.E. 2d 810 (Mass. 1981).

O'Shea, M., & Jessee, E. (1982). Ethical, value, and professional conflicts in systems therapy. In J.C. Hansen & L. L'Abate (Eds.), *Values, ethics, legalities and the family therapist.* Rockville, MD: Aspen.

Papp, P. (1984). The creative leap. *The Family Therapy Networker, 8*(5), 20–29.

Parniawski v. Parniawski, 359 A.2d 719 (Conn. 1976).

Pearson, J., & Thoennes, H. (1982). Mediation and divorce: The benefits outweigh the costs. *Family Advocate, 4*(3), 25–32.

Pell, E.R. (1979). A theory of imperfection: An imperfect theory? *Counselor Education and Supervision, 19,* 54–59.

Perry v. Fiumano, 403 N.Y.S. 2d 382 (1978).

Pfeiffer, S., & Tittler, B. (1983). Utilizing the multidisciplinary team to facilitate a school-family systems orientation. *School Psychology Review, 12,* 168–173.

Phillips, B.N. (1982). Regulation and control in psychology: Implications for certification and licensure. *American Psychologist, 37,* 919–936.

Piercy, F.P., McKeon, D., & Laird, R.A. (1983). A family assessment process for community mental health clinics. *American Mental Health Counselors Association Journal, 5,* 94–104.

Piercy, F.P., & Sprenkle, D.H. (1983). Ethical, legal and professional issues in family therapy: A graduate level course. *Journal of Marital and Family Therapy, 9,* 393–401.

Pittman, F. (1985). Gender myths. *The Family Therapy Networker, 9*(6), 24–33.

Planned Parenthood of Central Missouri v. Danforth, 428 U.S. 52 (1976).

Posner v. Posner, 233 So.2d 381 (Fla. 1979).

Pressman, R.M. (1979). *Private practice: A guide for the independent mental health practitioner.* New York: Gardner.

Professional Liability Predicament. (1985). *The Samaritan Institute Newsletter, 6*(4), 2, 4.

Prosser, W. (1971). *Handbook of the law of torts.* St. Paul, MN: West.

Psychological Services Act, Florida Statutes, Chapter 490 (1983).

Quilloin v. Walcott, 434 U.S. 246 (1978).

Reed, J.M. (1985). The origin and functions of American law. In N.T. Sidney (Ed.), *Law and ethics: A guide for the health professional.* New York: Human Sciences.

Reen v. Reen, 8 Fam. L. Rep. 2193 (Mass. 1981).

Rest, J.R. (1982, February). A psychologist looks at the teaching of ethics. *Hastings Center Report,* pp. 29–36.

Rest, J.R. (1983). Morality. In J. Flavell & E. Markman (Eds.), *Cognitive development* (Vol. 4). New York: Wiley.

Richman, J. (1979). Family therapy of attempted suicide. *Family Process, 18,* 131–142.

Ridgewood Financial Institute, Inc. (1984). *Psychotherapy finances: Guide to private practice.* Ho-Ho-Kus, NJ: Author.

Riordan, A.T. (1985). State divisions develop local chapters. *Family Therapy News, 16*(4), 5.

Roe v. Wade, 410 U.S. 113 (1973).

Rogers, C. (1980). *A way of being.* Boston: Houghton-Mifflin.

Rohrbaugh, M., Tennen, H., Press, S., & White, L. (1981). Compliance, defiance, and therapeutic paradox: Guidelines for strategic use of paradoxical interventions. *American Journal of Orthopsychiatry, 5,* 454–467.

Rokeach, M. (1968). A theory of organization and change within value-attitude systems. *Journal of Social Issues, 24,* 13–33.

Rokeach, M. (1973). *The nature of human values.* New York: Macmillan.

Rosen, C.E. (1977). Why client relinquish their right to privacy under sign-away pressures. *Professional Psychology, 8,* 17–24.

Rosenberg, M.S., & Hunt, R.D. (1984). Child maltreatment: Legal and mental health issues. In N.D. Reppucci, L.A. Weithorn, E.P. Mulvey, & J. Monahan (Eds.), *Children, mental health, and the law.* Beverly Hills: Sage.

Rotan, G. (1985). FAMFT members can use yellow pages to publicize. *Florida Family Therapy News, 1*(2), 7.

Roy, M. (1977). *Battered women.* New York: Van Nostrand Reinhold.

Ruback, R.B. (1982). Issues in family law: Implications for therapists. In J.C. Hansen & L. L'Abate (Eds.), *Values, ethics, legalities and the family therapist.* Rockville, MD: Aspen.

Ruback, R.B. (1984). Family law. In R.H. Woody & Associates (Eds.), *The law and the practice of human services.* San Francisco: Jossey-Bass.

Russell, C.S., Olson, D.H., Sprenkle, D.H., & Atilano, R.B. (1983). From family symptom to family system: Review of family therapy research. *The American Journal of Family Therapy, 11,* 3–14.

Salgo v. Leland Stanford, Jr., University Board of Trustees. 154 Cal. App. 2d 560, 317 P.2d 170 (1957).

Sauber, S.R., L'Abate, L., & Weeks, G.R. (1985). *Family therapy: Basic concepts and terms.* Rockville, MD: Aspen.

Sauerkof v. City of New York, 438 N.Y.S. 2d 982 (Sup. Ct. 1981).

Schoyer, N.L. (1980). Divorce and the pre-school child. *Childhood Education, 57,* 2–7.

Schultz, B. (1982). *Legal liability in psychotherapy.* San Francisco: Jossey-Bass.

Schwartz, S.H. (1977). Normative influences on altruism. In L. Berkowitz (Ed.), *Advances in experimental social psychology* (Vol. 10). New York: Academic.

Schwitzgebel, R.K. (1975). A contractual model for the protection of the rights of institutionalized mental patients. *American Psychologist, 30,* 815–820.

Schwitzgebel, R.K. (1976). Treatment contracts and ethical self-determination. *Clinical Psychologist, 29*(3), 5–7.

Schwitzgebel, R.L., & Schwitzgebel, R.K. (1980). *Law and psychological practice.* New York: Wiley.

Scott, E. (1984). Adolescents' reproductive rights: Abortion, contraception, and sterilization. In N.D. Reppucci, L.A. Weithorn, E.P. Mulvey, & J. Monahan (Eds.), *Children, mental health, and the law.* Beverly Hills: Sage.

Searight, H.R., & Openlander, P. (1984). Systemic therapy: A new brief intervention model. *Personnel and Guidance Journal, 62,* 387–391.

Seligman, L. (1983). An introduction to the new DSN III. *Personnel and Guidance Journal, 61,* 601–619.

Selvini-Palazzoli, N., Boscolo, L., Cecchin, G., & Prata, G. (1978). *Paradox and counterparadox.* New York: Jason Aronson.

Selvini-Palazzoli, N., Boscolo, L., Cecchin, G., & Prata, G. (1980). The problem of the referring person. *Journal of Marriage and Family Therapy, 6,* 3–10.

Seymour, W.R. (1982). Counselor/therapist values and therapeutic style. In J.C. Hansen & L. L'Abate (Eds.), *Values, ethics, legalities and the family therapist.* Rockville, MD: Aspen.

Shah, S. (1969). Privileged communications, confidentiality, and privacy. *Professional Psychology, 1,* 56–69.

Shah, S. (1970). Privileged communications, confidentiality, and privacy: Privileged communications. *Professional Psychology, 1,* 159–164.

Shalett, J.S., & Everett, C.A. (1981). Accreditation in family therapy education: Its history and role. *The American Journal of Family Therapy, 9*(4), 82–84.

Shea, T.E. (1985). Finding the law: Legal research and citation. In N.T. Sidney (Ed.), *Law and ethics: A guide for the health professional.* New York: Human Sciences.

Shipman v. Division of Social Services, 442 A. 2d 101 (Del. Fam. Ct. 1981).

Shrybman, J., & Halpern, W.I. (1979, March). *The mental health clinician's day in court.* Workshop presented at the Rochester Mental Health Center, Rochester, NY.

Sidney N.T., & Petrila, J.P. (1985). On being involved personally in a lawsuit, as a plaintiff, expert witness, or defendant. In N.T. Sidney (Ed.), *Law and ethics: A guide for the health professional.* New York: Human Sciences.

Siegel, M. (1979). Privacy, ethics, and confidentiality. *Professional Psychology, 10,* 249–258.

Silber, D.E. (1976). Ethical relativity and professional psychology. *Clinical Psychologist, 29,* 3–5.

Sims v. Sims, 243 Ga. 276, 253 S.E. 2d 763 (1979).

Slovenko, R. (1973). *Psychiatry and law.* Boston: Little, Brown.

Slovenko, R. (1978). Psychotherapy and informed consent: A search in judicial regulation. In W.E. Barton & C.J. Sanborn (Eds.), *Law and the mental health professions: Friction at the interface.* New York: International Universities.

Slovenko, R. (1980). Legal issues in psychotherapy supervision. In A.K. Hess (Ed.), *Psychotherapy supervision.* New York: Wiley.

Sluzki, C.E. (1978). Marital therapy from a systems theory perspective. In T.J. Paolino, Jr. & B.S. McCrady (Eds.), *Marriage and marital therapy: Psychoanalytic, behavioral and systems theory perspectives.* New York: Brunner/Mazel.

Sobel, S.B. (1984). Independent practice in child and adolescent psychotherapy in small communities: Personal, professional, and ethical issues. *Psychotherapy, 21,* 110–117.

Sosna v. Iowa, 419 U.S. 393 (1975).

Spencer, J.M., & Zammit, J.P. (1976). Mediation-arbitration: A proposal of private resolution of disputes between divorced or separated parents. *Duke Law Journal, V,* 911–939.

Sporakowski, M.J. (1982). The regulation of marital and family therapy. In J.C. Hansen & L. L'Abate (Eds.), *Values, ethics, legalities and the family therapist.* Rockville, MD: Aspen.

Stanley v. Illinois, 406 U.S. 645 (1972).

Stanton, M.D. (1981). Strategic approaches to family therapy. In A.S. Gurman & D.P. Kniskern (Eds.), *Handbook of family therapy.* New York: Brunner/Mazel.

State *ex rel.* Hickox v. Hickox, 410 N.Y.S. 2d 81 (1978).

State v. Driscoll, 193 N.W. ed 851 (Wisconsin, 1972) 50 ALR 3d 544 (1973).

State v. Vickers, 633 P. 2d 315 (Ariz. 1981).

Stensrud, R., & Stensrud, K. (1981). Counseling may be hazardous to your health: How we teach people to feel powerless. *Personnel and Guidance Journal, 59,* 300–304.

Straus, M.A. (1977–78). Wife beating: How common and why? *Victimology: An International Journal, 2,* 443–458.

Strickman, L.P. (1982). Marriage, Divorce and the Constitution. *Family Law Quarterly, 15,* 259–348.

Strupp, H.H., Hadley, S.W., & Gomes-Schwartz, B. (1977). *Psychotherapy for better or worse: The problem of negative effects.* New York: Jason Aronson.

Stuart, R.B. (1980). *Helping couples change: A social learning approach to marital therapy.* New York: Guilford.

Stude, E.W., & McKelvey, J. (1979). Ethics and the law: Friend or foe? *Personnel and Guidance Journal, 57,* 453–456.

Swanson, J.L. (1979). Counseling directory and consumer's guide: Implementing professional disclosure and consumer protection. *Personnel and Guidance Journal, 58,* 190–193.

Symonds, A. (1979). Violence against woman: The myth of masochism. *American Journal of Psychotherapy, 33,* 161–173.

Taggart, M. (1982). Linear versus systemic values: Implications for family therapy. In J.C. Hansen & L. L'Abate (Eds.), *Values, ethics, legalities and the family therapist.* Rockville, MD: Aspen.

Tarasoff v. Regents of the University of California, 13 Cal. 3d 177, 529 P.2d 553 (1974), vacated, 17 Cal. 3d 425, 551 P.2d 334 (1976).

Teismann, M.W. (1980). Convening strategies in family therapy. *Family Process, 19,* 393–400.

Terkleson, K.G. (1983). Schizophrenia and the family: II. Adverse effects of family therapy. *Family Process, 22,* 191–200.

Terkelsen, K.G. (1984). Response by Kenneth G. Terkelsen, M.D. *Family Process, 23,* 425–428.

Thompson v. County of Alameda, 167 Cal. Rptr. 70 (1980).

Tolbert, E.L. (1982). *An introduction to guidance: The professional counselor.* Boston: Little, Brown.

Torres, A., Forest, J., & Eisman, S. (1980). Telling parents: Clinic policies and adolescents' use of family planning and abortion services. *Family Planning Perspectives, 12,* 284–292.

Toulmin, S. (1950). *An examination of the place of reason in ethics.* Cambridge, England: Cambridge University.

Tymchuk, A.J., Drapkin, R., Major-Kingsley, S., Ackerman, A.B., Coffman, E.W., & Baum, M.S. (1982). Ethical decision making and psychologists' attitudes toward training in ethics. *Professional Psychology, 13,* 412–421.

U.S. Bureau of the Census. (1981). *Statistical abstract of the United States.* Washington, DC: Government Printing Office.

Van Hoose, W.H. (1980). Ethics and counseling. *Counseling and Human Development, 13*(1), 1–12.

Van Hoose, W.H., & Kottler, J.A. (1977). *Ethical and legal issues in counseling and psychotherapy.* San Francisco: Jossey-Bass.

Van Hoose, W.H., & Kottler, J.A. (1985). *Ethical and legal issues in counseling and psychotherapy* (2nd ed.). San Francisco: Jossey-Bass.

Vitulano, L.A., & Copeland, B.A. (1980). Trends in continuing education and competency demonstration. *Professional Psychology, 11,* 891–897.

von Weizsacker, E., & von Weizsacker, C. (1974). *Offene systeme I: Beitrage zur zeitstruktur von information, entropie and evolution.* Stuttgart, West Germany: Klett.

Vroom, P. (1983). The anomalous profession: Bumpy going in the divorce mediation movement. *The Family Therapy Networker,* 7(3), 38–42.

Wachtel, E.F. (1979). Learning family therapy: The dilemmas of an individual therapist. *Journal of Contemporary Psychotherapy, 10,* 122–135.

Wald, M.S. (1975). State intervention on behalf of "neglected" children: A search for realistic standards. *Stanford Law Review, 27,* 985–1040.

Wald, M.S. (1976). State intervention on behalf of "neglected" children: Standards for removal of children from their homes, monitoring the status of children in foster care, and termination of parental rights. *Stanford Law Review, 28,* 625–706.

Wald, M.S. (1982). State intervention on behalf of endangered children: A proposed legal response. *Child Abuse and Neglect, 6,* 3–45.

Walker, C.E. (1981). Continuing professional development. In C.E. Walker (Ed.), *Clinical practice of psychology.* New York: Pergamon.

Walker, L. (1977–78). Battered women and learned helplessness. *Victimology: An International Journal, 2,* 525–534.

Walker, L. (1979). *The battered woman.* New York: Harper Colophon.

Walker, L. (1981). Battered women: Sex roles and clinical issues. *Professional Psychology, 12,* 81–90.

Waltz, J.R., & Scheuneman, T.W. (1969). Informed consent to therapy. *Northwestern University Law Review, 64,* 628–650.

Watts, A. (1961). *Psychotherapy East and West,* New York: Random House.

Watzlawick, P., Beavin, J.H., & Jackson, D.D. (1967). *Pragmatics of human communications: A study of interactional patterns, pathologies and paradoxes.* New York: Norton.

Watzlawick, P., Weakland, J.H., & Fish, R. (1974). *Change: Principles of problem formation and problem resolution.* New York: Norton.

Weber v. Aetna Casualty & Surety Co., 406 U.S. 164 (1972).

Weiner, J.P., & Boss, P. (1985). Exploring gender bias against women: Ethics for marriage and family therapy. *Counseling and Values, 30,* 9–23.

Weiss, R.S. (1979). Issues in the adjudication of custody when parents separate. In G. Levinger & O.C. Moles (Eds.), *Divorce and separation.* New York: Basic.

Welfel, E.R., & Lipsitz, N.E. (1984). The ethical behavior of professional psychologists. *Counseling Psychologist, 12*(3), 31–43.

Wentzel, L., & Ross, M.A. (1983). Psychological and social ramifications of battering: Observations leading to a counseling methodology for victims of domestic violence. *Personnel and Guidance Journal, 61,* 423–428.

Weyrauch, W.O., & Katz, S.N. (1983). *American family law in transition.* Washington, DC: Bureau of National Affairs, Inc.

White, G. (1982, April 9). New laws help in collecting that check. *Atlanta Constitution,* p. 1B.

Widiger, T.A., & Rorer, L.G. (1984). The responsible psychotherapist. *American Psychologist, 39,* 503–515.

Wilcoxon, A., & Fenell, D. (1983). Engaging the non-attending spouse in marital therapy through the use of therapist-initiated written communication. *Journal of Marital and Family Therapy, 9,* 199–203.

Williams, R.M. (1968). Values, In E. Sills (Ed.), *International encyclopedia of the social sciences.* New York: Macmillan.

Wilmarth, R. (1983). A call for unity. *American Mental Health Counselors Association News, 7*(2), 3.

Winborn, B.B. (1977). Honest labeling and other procedures for the protection of consumers of counseling. *Personnel and Guidance Journal, 56,* 206–209.

Winkle, C.W., Piercy, F.P., & Hovestadt, A.J. (1981). A curriculum for graduate-level marriage and family therapy education. *Journal of Marital and Family Therapy, 7,* 201–210.

Wisconsin Statutes Annotated, 905.04 (1981–1982 Supp.).

Witmer, J.M. (1978). Professional disclosure in licensure. *Counselor Education and Supervision, 18,* 71–73.

Woody, R.H., & Mitchell, R.E. (1984). Understanding the legal system and legal research. In R.H. Woody and Associates (Eds.), *The law and the practice of human services.* San Francisco: Jossey-Bass.

Yaron v. Yaron, 372 N.Y.S. 2d 518 (1975).

Zablocki v. Redhail, 434 U.S. 374 (1978).

Zajonc, R.B. (1980). Feeling and thinking: Preferences need no inferences. *American Psychologist, 35,* 151–175.

Name Index

Abelson, R., 7
Abroms, G. M., 60
Ackerman, A. B., 10
Alsager v. District Court of Polk County, Iowa, 139
American Association for Counseling and Development, 5, 6, 9, 11, 17, 27
American Association for Marriage and Family Therapy, 5, 6, 9–11, 17, 27, 63, 82, 207, 208, 215, 226, 228, 231, 232, 234, 255, 256, 258
American Jurisprudence 2d Witnesses, 176
  57 American Jurisprudence 2d Negligence, 160
  61 American Jurisprudence 2d, 4, 5
American Psychiatric Association, 9, 11, 17, 27, 222
American Psychological Association, 5, 6, 9–11, 17, 27, 63, 251–254
Anderson, A., 52
Anderson, S., 4, 166
Andolfi, M., 193
Angelo, C., 193
Aponte, H. J., 185, 191, 241, 244
Ard, B. N., 206
Ard, C., 206
Atilano, R. B., 205
Atwood v. Atwood, 174, 177

Baier, K., 7
Ball, P. G., 14
Barry, V., 3

Bateson, G., 188, 189
Baum, M. S., 10
Bayles, M. D., 226, 234
Beauchamp, T., 11–13
Beavers, W. R., 194
Beavin, J. H., 46
Beckner, M. O., 3
Becvar, D. S., 188
Becvar, R. J., 188
Bellotti v. Baird (II), 138
Bender, A. E., 188
Bergantino, L. A., 186
Bergman, E. M., 238, 240, 241
Bernard, J. M., 178–180
Bernstein, B. E., 85, 127, 130, 131
Bernstein, B. L., 213
Berry v. Moensch, 122
Bersoff, D., 19
Bertram, B., 215
Besharov, D. J., 141
Bieluch v. Bieluch, 175
Black, M., 107
Black's Law Dictionary, 117, 122
Borowy, T. D., 168
Boscolo, L., 53
Boss, P., 252–254
Boszormenyi-Nagy, I., 51, 198, 200
Bourne, P. G., 58
Bowen, M., 55
Brandt, R., 3
Bray, J. H., 18, 162
Broadhurst, D. D., 100
Broadsky, S. L., 108, 115

Bromberg, W., 108
Brown, H. I., 190
Bureau of National Affairs, Inc., 97, 128, 134, 136, 143, 145–147, 149, 151
Burgum, T., 4, 166

Caban v. Mohammed, 136
Callanan, P., 4, 10, 213
Callis, R., 63
Carl, D., 55–58
Carroll, M., 12, 13
Cecchin, G., 53
Chemerinsky, E., 141
Childress, J., 11–13
Clark, H. H., Jr., 128, 135, 153
Clark, T. E., 215
Cleary, E. W., 109, 110
Cobbs v. Grant, 163
Coffman, E. W., 10
Cohen, R. J., 162, 178, 179, 258, 259
Commission on Accreditation for Marriage and Family Therapy Education, 209
Commission releases '85 MFT program roster, 210, 211
Communication to the family therapy community, 251
Connell, M. J., 146
120 CONG. REC., 169
Coogler, O. J., 107, 125, 142
Copeland, B. A., 231, 233
Corey, G., 4, 10, 18, 21–23, 47, 118, 213, 216, 225, 234
Corey, M. S., 4, 10, 213
Cormier, L. S., 178–180
Cruchfield, C. F., 132

Danish, S. J., 215
Daubner, E. S., 3
Daubner, E. V., 3
Davis, J. W., 212, 213
Dawidoff, D. J., 179
Day, D., 139
Deaux, K., 254
DeKraai, M. B., 18, 175, 176
Delaware Rules of Evidence, 175
Dell, P., 189, 192, 194–196
Denkowski, G. C., 16, 18, 22
Denkowski, K. M., 16, 18, 22
DePauw, M. E., 18, 63

DeShazer, S., 192, 193
Deutsch, M., 106
Dincin, J., 38
Doe v. Volton, 137
Dooley, J. A., 162
Douthwaite, G., 133
Drapkin, R., 10
Dwyer, C. E., 247, 248

Eady v. Alter, 180
Efran, J., 202
Eisman, S., 138
Engelberg, S. L., 63, 256
Erickson, M. H., 192
Evans, J., 101, 103
Everett, C. A., 210
Everstine, D. S., 18, 29
Everstine, L., 18, 21–23, 28, 29

Family Educational Rights and Privacy Act, 17, 168, 169
Faustman, W. O., 259
Felstiner, W. L., 106, 107
Fenell, D., 44, 45
Fieldsteel, N. D., 1, 38, 41, 47, 48
Fine, M. J., 241
Fischer, L., 98, 101, 160, 164–166, 168
Fish, R., 44, 115, 193
Fisher, L., 52, 54
Fishman, H. C., 49
Flax, M., 12
Folberg, J., 149, 150
Forest, J., 138
Foster, H. H., 144, 148, 161, 173, 174
Framo, J. L., 16, 219, 220, 224
Fraser, J. S., 53
Freed, D. J., 144, 148
Fretz, B. R., 213, 214
Frey, D. H., 18, 29
Fricke v. Fricke, 172

Gill, S. J., 31, 33, 214
Gillespie v. Gillespie, 177
Gilligan, C., 254
Giordano, J., 202
Glaser, B., 186
Glendon, M. A., 129, 132
Gomes-Schwartz, B., 120
Gomez v. Perez, 134
Gossett, J. T., 194

Graham, M., 150
Gross, S. J., 31, 33, 213, 214
Grosslight v. Superior Court of Los
    Angeles County, 176
Grunebaum, H., 39, 40
Guerney, T. F., 151
Guggenheim, P. D., 102
Gulliver, P. H., 107
Gumper, L. L., 17–20
Gurman, A. S., 42, 44, 46, 50, 51, 53,
    238

H. L. v. Matheson, 138
Hadley, S. W., 120
Hahman v. Hahman, 176
Haley, J., 34, 46, 52, 206, 219–223
Halleck, S. L., 30
Halpern, W. I., 104
Hammond, J. M., 143
Handel, W. W., 137
Hare-Mustin, R. T., 27, 28, 30, 34, 41,
    44, 47, 51, 191, 197
Harp, B. S., 152
Haynes, J., 108, 125, 143
Hays, J. R., 18, 162
Hendrickson, R. M., 118, 123
Hennessey, E. F., 133, 153
Heppner, M., 13
Herrington, B. S., 19, 176
Herrman, M. S., 106
Heymann, G. M., 18, 29
Hilberman, E., 13
Hines, P. M., 41, 51, 191
Hof, L., 247, 248
Hoffman, L., 49, 52, 53, 56, 57,
    187–189, 194, 263
Hogan, D. B., 214
Hovestadt, A. J., 206
Hulnick, H. R., 186
Hunt, R. D., 139, 141
Huston, K., 9, 11–14

In re Carrafa, 129
In re Fred J., 175
In re Marriage of Gove, 174
In re Marriage of Winegard, 172
Instructions for authors (AAMFT), 234
Iscoe, I., 220

Jackson, D. D., 46
Jacobson, N. S., 34

Jain, M., 19
Jantsch, E., 190, 191
Jesse, E., 37, 42, 44, 46, 48–50, 52, 53,
    60
Joffe, W. A., 107
Johnson, H. G., 18, 29
Johnson, T. R., 162
Jones, J. E., 52
Jones, W. T., 3
Jurkovic, G. J., 55–58

Kaplan, A. G., 27
Kaplan, D. M., 49
Karpel, M. A., 24–26, 190, 198–201
Katz, S. N., 129–131, 133, 142, 151
Kazen, B. A., 149
Keary, A. O., 91
Kelly, G., 202
Kempin, F., 89
Kennedy, C., 173
Kessler, S., 107
Kirschenbaum, H., 186
Kissel, S., 102, 229, 230
Kitchener, K. S., 5, 7, 11
Kluckhohn, F., 185
Knapp, S., 22, 89, 91, 174, 176
Kniskern, D. P., 42, 44, 46, 50, 51, 238
Kosinski, F. A., 207
Kottler, J. A., 3, 4, 117, 125, 179, 214,
    226
Krause, H. D., 130, 133, 135, 136, 144,
    146–148, 152, 153
Kristensen v. Kristensen, 177

L'Abate, L., 55, 187, 205, 212
Laird, R. A., 219
Lane, P. J., 96
Langsley, D. G., 49
Larson v. Larson, 142
Lavori, N., 132
Layton, B., 60
Lecomte, C., 213
Lewis, J., 194
Lipsitz, N. E., 6
Liss-Levinson, N., 27
Long, L., 56, 57
Loving v. Virginia, 128
Lukens, M., 202

MacDonald, J. M., 108
Mace, D. R., 51

Madanes, C., 39, 54
Major-Kingsley, S., 10
Mangum, R. S., 118
Marecek, J., 27
Margolin, G., 10, 14–16, 19, 23, 25, 33–35, 41, 46, 197
Marlow, L., 156
Marvin v. Marvin, 132, 133
Maslow, A. H., 185
Massachusetts General Laws, 164
Massachusetts General Laws Annotated, 176
Matter of Atkins, 177
Maturana, H. R., 195
McCarty v. McCarty, 147
McGoldrick, M., 202
McG Mullin, R., 12, 13
McGuire, J. M., 168
McHenry, P. C., 106
McIntosh v. Milano, 96
McKelvey, J., 9
McKenzie, D. J., 106
McKeon, D., 219
Menghi, P., 193
Meyer, R., 175
Meyerstein, I., 114–116
Mills, D. H., 213, 214
Milne, A., 106, 107
Minuchin, S., 47, 49
Mitchell, R. E., 85, 89, 92, 94, 109, 125
Mnookin, R., 139
Morrison, J. K., 60
Mowrer, O. H., 3
Mulvey, E. P., 87
Munson, K., 13
Murphy, J. M., 238

Napier, A. Y., 42
Nathanson v. Kline, 161
National Association of Social Workers, 5, 6, 9, 11, 17, 27
National Center on Child Abuse and Neglect, 97
Newman, J., 60
Newman v. Newman, 172
New Mexico ex rel. Human Services Department v. Levario, 174
Nichols, M. P., 52, 53, 197, 205, 212
Nicolo-Corigliano, M., 193
Nielson, K., 7
Nozick, R., 7

Olson, D. H., 205, 238
Openlander, P., 192
Oppenheim, C. D., 162
Orlando, F. A., 144
Osborne v. Osborne, 172
O'Shea, M., 37, 42, 44, 46, 48–50, 52, 53, 60

Papp, P., 193, 194
Parniawski v. Parniawski, 172
Pearce, J., 202
Pearson, J., 106
Pell, E. R., 186
Perry v. Fiumano, 176
Petrila, J. P., 101, 110, 125
Pfeiffer, S., 241
Phillips, B. N., 213
Phillips, V. A., 194
Piercy, F. P., 200, 219, 222, 225
Pittman, F., 202
Planned Parenthood of Central Missouri v. Danforth, 137
Pope, S. K., 63
Posner v. Posner, 131
Prata, G., 53
Press, S., 54
Pressman, R. M., 258
Professional Liability Predicament, 124
Prosser, W., 119, 162, 163
Psychological Services Act, Florida Statutes, 217, 218

Quilloin v. Walcott, 136

Reed, J. M., 88, 89
Reen v. Reen, 148
Repucci, N. D., 87
Rest, J. R., 5, 8
Richman, J., 49
Ridgewood Financial Institute, Inc., 226
Riordan, A. T., 235
Robey, A., 108, 115
Roe v. Wade, 137
Rogers, C., 214
Rohrbaugh, M., 54
Rokeach, M., 185
Rorer, L. G., 116
Rosen, C. E., 30
Rosenberg, M. S., 139, 141
Ross, M. A., 12
Rotan, G., 228

Roy, M., 12
Ruback, R. B., 88, 129, 131–133, 136, 137, 140, 143–148, 150, 152, 153
Russell, C. S., 205

Sales, B. D., 18, 175, 176
Salgo v. Leland Stanford, Jr., University Board of Trustees, 161
Sauber, S. R., 55, 187, 212
Sauerkof vs. City of New York, 168
Scheuneman, T. W., 162
Schoyer, N. L., 143
Schultz, B., 18, 117–123, 125
Schwartz, S. H., 6
Schwitzgebel, R. K., 30, 109, 121, 123
Schwitzgebel, R. L., 109, 121, 123
Scott, E., 138
Searight, H. R., 192
Seiden, R. H., 18, 29
Seligman, L., 222
Selleck, V., 38
Selvini-Palazzoli, N., 53, 57
Seymour, W. R., 187, 197
Shah, S., 16, 18, 21
Shalett, J. S., 210
Shea, T. E., 88, 90, 92
Shepherd, J. N., 18, 162
Shipman v. Division of Social Services, 177
Shrybman, J., 104
Sidney, J. T., 101, 110, 125
Siegel, M., 21
Silber, D. E., 44
Sims v. Sims, 151
Slovenko, R., 16, 108, 151, 163, 179, 180
Sluzki, C. E., 37
Smith, S., 175
Smyer, M. A., 215
Sobel, S. B., 260
Sontag, F., 3
Sorenson, G. P., 98, 101, 160, 164–166, 168
Sosna v. Iowa, 144
Spencer, J. M., 106
Sporakowski, M. J., 215, 216, 218, 219, 235
Sprenkle, D. H., 17–20, 205
Spruill, J., 96
Stanley v. Illinois, 136
Stanton, M. D., 34

State ex rel. Hickox v. Hickox, 176
State v. Driscoll, 174
State v. Vickers, 174
Stensrud, K., 47, 48
Stensrud, R., 47, 48
Straus, M. A., 12
Strauss, E. S., 190, 198–201
Streicker, S., 38
Strickman, L. P., 144
Strodtbeck, F. L., 185
Strupp, H. H., 120
Stuart, R. B., 185
Stude, E. W., 9
Swanson, J. L., 31, 33
Symonds, A., 13

Taggart, M., 190–192
Tarasoff v. Regents of the University of California, 92, 94, 96
Teismann, M. W., 41–44
Tennen, H., 54
Terkelsen, K. G., 39–40
Thoennes, H., 106
Thompson v. County of Alameda, 96
Tittler, B., 241
Todd, J. C., 114–116
Tolbert, E. L., 182
Torres, A., 138
Toulmin, S., 7
True, R. H., 18, 29
Tymchuk, A. J., 10

Ulrich, D. N., 198–200
U.S. Bureau of Census, 145, 151

VandeCreek, L., 22, 89, 91, 174, 176
VanHoose, W. H., 3–5, 8, 117, 125, 179, 214, 226
Vitulano, L. A., 231, 233
von Weizsacker, C., 192
von Weizsacker, E., 192
Vroom, P., 106

Wachtel, E. F., 46, 48
Wald, M. S., 139, 140
Walker, C. E., 231
Walker, L., 12, 13
Waltz, J. R., 162
Watts, A., 192
Watzlawick, P., 44, 46, 52, 115, 193

Weakland, J. H., 44, 115, 193
Weber, R. E., 106
Weber v. Aetna Casualty & Surety Co.,
    133
Weeks, G. R., 55, 187, 212
Weiner, J. P., 252–254
Weiss, R. S., 149
Weithorn, L. A., 87
Welfel, E. R., 6
Wentzel, L., 12
Weyrauch, W. O., 129–131, 133, 142
Whitaker, C., 42
White, G., 153
White, L., 54
Widiger, T. A., 116
Wilcoxon, A., 44, 45

Williams, L. A., 106, 107
Williams, R. M., 185
Wilmarth, R., 215
Winborn, B. B., 31, 32
Winkle, C. W., 206
Wisconsin Statutes Annotated, 174
Witmer, J. M., 33
Woody, R. H., 85, 89, 92, 94, 109, 125
Wyman, E., 14

Yaron v. Yaron, 176

Zablocki v. Redhail, 129
Zajonc, R. B., 6
Zammit, J. P., 106
Zirkel, P. A., 89, 91

Subject Index

Abortion, 137
Accessory to a crime, 165, 166
Accountability, 24, 62–82, 201, 202
  ethical, 62–82
  realistic, 201, 202
Accreditation, 209–212
Adjudicatory hearing, 104
Administrative law, 89
Adoption, 135
Advertising, 82, 226–230, 254-257
Alliance, 238
Alsager v. District Court of Polk County,
  Iowa, 139, 140
Alternating custody, 150
American Association of Marriage and
  Family Therapy (AAMFT), 63,
  206–212, 234, 235
  accreditation, 209–212
  approved supervisor, 208, 209
  clinical membership, 207, 208
  headquarters, 234, 235
American Family Therapy Association
  (AFTA), 212
  57 American Jurisprudence 2d
  Negligence, 160
American Law Reports, 94
Annulment, 141, 142
Approved supervisor, 208, 209
Arkansas Statutes Annotated, 93
Assessment of behavior, 239
Atwood v. Atwood, 174, 177
Autonomy, 11, 13, 14

Battery, 121, 122, 163
"Battle for structure," 42
Blackman, Justice, 138
Black's Law Dictionary, 94
Battered woman's syndrome, 11–13
Bellotti v. Baird (II), 138
Beneficence, 11, 12
Berry v. Moensch, 122
Bieluch v. Bieluch, 175
Bifurcated proceedings, 105
Boszormenyi-Nagy, Ivan, 197, 198
Bowen, Murray, 196
Breach of contract, 163
Buckley Amendment, 167–170
Burnout, 234

Caban v. Mohammed, 136
California Reports, 93
*Casebook on Ethical Standards of
  Psychologists*, 63
Case law, 89
Cases, 65–82, 155–180
  Buckley Amendment, 167–170
  child custody and privileged
    communications, 173–179
  confidentiality, 68–71
  criminal liability, 163–167
  divorce mediation, 155–158
  fees, 80–82
  informed consent, 160–163
  legal responsibility of clinical
    supervisors, 177–180

liability in crisis counseling, 158–160
professional competence, and integrity, 71–75
responsibility to clients, 65–68
responsibility to students, employees, and supervisees, 75–77
responsibility to the profession, 77–80
Causation, 189
Change agent, 46–51
Change strategies, 223
Changing Families, 47
Child abuse and neglect, 97–101, 103–105
  defined, 97–98
  physical and behavioral indicators, 99, 100
Child custody, 148–150
  divided, 150
  joint, 150
  sole, 149, 150
  split, 150
Child support, 151–153
Circularity, 189
Civil law, 91
Client, 6, 9, 14–16, 27, 64–68, 174, 175
  information clients should have, 27
  multiple, 14–16
  referrals, 6
  responsibility to, 64–68
  sexual relationships with, 9
  waiver, 174, 175
Clinical membership (AAMFT), 207, 208
Cobbs v. Grant, 163
Code of ethics, 3–6, 8–11, 17, 26, 27, 35, 63
Code of Federal Regulations, 93
Cohabitation, 128–133
Common law, 88
Communication, privileged, 16–21
Community agencies and organizations, 260, 261
Components of valuing, 197–202
  acknowledgment and claim, 199, 200
  balance of fairness, 200
  obligation and entitlement, 198, 199
Concurrent custody, 150
Confidentiality, 16–18, 23–26, 68–71
  accountability, 24
  exceptions to, 18

privacy, 16, 21–23
privileged communication, 16–21
reparative strategies, 25
Consent to act, 161
Contempt proceedings, 152
Continuing education, 229–233, 261, 262
Contract law, 117, 118
  fiduciary relationship, 117
  tort liability, 118
Contributing to the delinquency of a minor, 164, 165
Corpus Juris Secundum, 94
Court decisions, 90–92
  civil law, 91
  criminal law, 91
  parts of, 90–92
  typical court names, 91
Court decisions, parts of, 90–92
  dicta, 91
  facts, 90
  holding, 91
  issue, 90
  rule, 90
Courtroom testimony, 110
Criminal law, 91
Criminal Law Reporter, 93
Cross examination, 112–114

Damages, 121
Danger of violence to others, 22
Debt, 199
Decision making, 5–10
  formulating, 7
  implementing, 7, 8
  integrating, 7, 8
  interpreting, 6, 7
Defamation, 122
Delaware Rules of Evidence, 175
Delinquency of a minor, contributing to, 164, 165
Deterioration effect, 50, 51
  deterioration, 50
  relapse, 50
Diagnostic and Statistical Manual of Mental Disorders (DSM III), 222
Diagnostic/planning, 238–239
  alliance issues, 238
  assessing behavior, 239

Diagnostic/planning, *continued*
history taking, 239
secrets, 239
ventilation/rehearsal, 239
Diagnostician, 101, 102
Diagnostic systems, 223
Dicta, 91
Direct examination, 111, 112
Discipline, 4
informal, 4
formal, 4
Disclosure statement, 31, 32
Divorce, 142–148
division of property, 146–148
spousal maintenance, 145, 146
Divorce Mediation Research Project, 108
Doctrine of recrimination, 143
Doe v. Bolton, 137
Dualism, 187, 188
Due care, 5
"Duty to warn," 22, 23, 92–97
Tarasoff v. Board of Regents of the
University of California, 93–97
McIntosh v. Milano, 96
Thompson v. County of Alameda, 96,
97
Driver v. Hinnant, 94

Eady v. Alter, 180
Education records, 169
Employees, responsibility to, 75–77
Epistemology, 187–190, 263, 264
causation, 189
circularity, 189
definition, 187
dualism, 187, 188
evolution, 190
linear thinking, 188
new, 263, 264
Ethical accountability, 62–82
advertising, 82
confidentiality, 68–71
fees, 80–82
professional competence, 71–75
responsibility to clients, 64–68
responsibility to students, employees,
and supervisees, 75–77
responsibility to the profession, 77–80
Ethical considerations, 36–60
agency triangulation, 54–59
agent for change, 46–51

convening therapy, 38–41
defining the problem, 38–41
paradoxical procedures, 52–54
Ethical Standards Case Book, 63
Ethics, 1–35
client welfare, 10–13
codes of, 3–6, 8–11, 17, 26, 27, 35
confidentiality, 16–18, 23
decision making, 5–10
defined, 3
due care, 5
formal discipline, 4
informal discipline, 4
informed consent, 26–31
malpractice, 4
multiple clients, 14–16
referrals, good faith, 6
sexual relationships with clients, 9
therapist competence, 5
Ethics Committee (AAMFT), 63, 64
Evolution, 190
Examination, 111–114
cross, 112–114
direct, 111, 112
redirect, 114
Expert witness, 108–116
courtroom testimony, 110
preparation, 110
rules of, 108–110
systemic understanding, 114–116
Expressed waiver, 175

Fairness, balance of, 200–202
realistic accountability, 201, 202
rejunction, 200, 201
Family Educational and Privacy Rights
Act, 17, 168, 169
Family Law, 126–153
annulment and divorce, 141–148
child custody and support, 148–151
marriage and cohabitation, 128–133
parental rights and responsibility,
139–141
parent–child relationships, 133–138
Family Law Reporter, 93
Family Therapy News, 234
Fatal flaw, 186
Federal Register, 93
Federal Reporter, 93
Federal Rules, 93
Federal Supplement, 93

Fees, 80–82, 257–259
  collection of, 257–259
Fidelity, 11–13
Fiduciary relationship, 117
Formulating ethical justification, 7
  critical-evaluative level, 7
  intuitive level, 7
Fourth Amendment, 21
Freud, 237
Freudians, 205
Funding, 261

"Gender brokers," 202
Gender equality, 251–254
  competence, 253
  integrity, 253
  professional development, 254
  responsibility to clients, 252, 253
Generalist vs. specialist, 260
Gestalt Prayer, 198
Gillespie v. Gillespie, 177
Gomez v. Perez, 134
Greenberg v. Barbour, 94
Grosslight v. Superior Court, 176

H. L. v. Matheson, 138
Hahman v. Hahman, 176
Haley, Jay, 47
History taking, 239
Homosexuality, 129

Implementing, 8
Implied waiver, 175
Imprisonment, false, 123
Individual sessions, 240, 241
Informed consent, 26–31
  information clients should have, 27
  in marriage and family therapy, 33
  professional disclosure statement, 31,
    32
  therapeutic contracts, 27–29
Injury, 120
In re Carrafa, 129
In re Fred J., 175
In re Marriage of Gove, 174
In re Marriage of Winegard, 172
Integrating, 7, 8
Interdisciplinary difficulties, 219–225
  assuming power, 224, 225
  change strategies, 223

diagnostic systems, 223
  pragmatic issues, 225–235
  theories of causation, 221
Interpreting, 6, 7
Isolation, professional, 261

Journal of Marital and Family Therapy,
  234
Justice, 11, 12
Juvenile delinquency, 102

Kristensen v. Kristensen, 177

Labor Law Reports, 93
Larson v. Larson, 142
Lawyer's Edition of United States
  Supreme Court Reports, 93
Legal capacity, 162
Legal Consultation Plan (AAMFT), 92
Legal education, 88–92
  administrative law, 89
  case law, 89
  common law, 88
  court decisions, 89–91
  research sources, 93, 94
  regulatory law, 89
  statutory law, 89
Legal issues, 85–125
  expert witness, 108–116
  professional liability, 116–124
  referral resource, 101–108
  roles and responsibilities, 86–91
  source of information, 101–108
Legally adequate consent, 162
Legal rights, 157
Legislative regulation, 212–219
  licensing requirements, 215–219
  licensure, defined, 213
Legitimacy, 133
Liability, 116–124
  contract law, 117, 118
  insurance, 123, 124
  intentional torts, 121–123
  malpractice, 118
Licensing requirements, 215–219
  licensure coverage, 216, 217
  licensure process, 219
  marriage and family counseling,
    defined, 216
  qualifications, 218

Licensure, 213, 216, 217, 219
  coverage, 216, 217
  defined, 213
  process, 219
Linear thinking, 188
Locality rule, 119
Loving v. Virginia, 128, 129

Malpractice, 4, 118–121
  damages, 121
  injury, 120
  professional relationship, 118
  proximate cause, 119, 120
  standard of care, 118, 119
Marriage and family counseling, defined,
  216
Marriage, 128–133
  ceremonial, 128
  common law, 128
  prenuptial agreement, 130
  types, 128
Marvin v. Marvin, 132, 133
Maternalism, 14
Matter of Atkins, 177
McCarty v. McCarty, 147
McIntosh v. Milano, 96
Mediation, 105–108
  Divorce Mediation Research Project,
    108
  stages of, 106, 107
Mental distress, infliction of, 123
Mental health as a condition of waiver,
  176, 177
Merit, 199
Michigan Reports, 93
Minor, 164
Morality, 3
Moral predicates, 3
Muller v. Oregon, 94

Nathanson v. Kline, 161
Negligence, 163
Negotiation, 190–193
  reframing, 193
  resistance, 193
  script, 193
Newman v. Newman, 172
New Mexico ex rel. Human Services
    Department v. Levario, 174
Nonattending spouse, letter to, 42, 43

Nonmaleficence, 11, 12
Northwestern Reporter, 93

Osborne v. Osborne, 172

Paradoxical procedures, 52–54
Parens patriae, 139
Parental rights and responsibilities,
  139–141
Parent-child relationships, 133–138
  abortion, 137
  adoption, 135
  legitimacy, 133
  paternity, 134
  surrogate, 136, 137
Parniawski v. Parniawski, 172
Paternalism, 14
Paternity, 134
Peoplemaking, 47
Perls, Frederick, 198
Perry v. Fiumano, 176
Planned Parenthood of Central Missouri
    v. Danforth, 137, 138
Police power, 139
Posner v. Posner, 131
Power, 224, 225
Practice implications, 193–197
  accepting what is, 196–197
  doing therapy without pathology, 196
  living without objective knowledge,
    195
  taking personal responsibility, 195
  taking responsibility for pathologizing,
    195, 196
Practice, "small town," 260–262
  community agencies and organizations,
    260, 261
  continuing professional development,
    261, 262
  funding, 261
  generalist vs. specialist, 260
  isolation, 261
  privacy, 261
Pragmatic issues, 225–235
  advertising, 226–230
  continuing education, 229–233
  intraprofessional communications, 233
Prenuptial agreement, 130
Privacy, 16, 21–23, 122, 123, 261
  invasion of, 122, 123

personal, 261
Prizing, 186, 187
Professional affiliation, 206–212
  American Association of Marriage and
    Family Therapy (AAMFT), 206–212
  American Family Therapy Association
    (AFTA), 212
Professional disclosure statement, 162
Professional identity, 204–235
  interdisciplinary difficulties, 219–225
  legislative regulation, 212–219
  pragmatic issues, 225–235
  professional affiliation, 206–212
  profession or professional
    specialization, 205, 206
Professional issues, 183–262
  identity, 204–235
  valuing, 184–203
Property, division of, 146–148
Prosecution, malicious, 123
Proximate cause, 119, 120
Puzzle pieces, missing, 240

Quilloin v. Walcott, 136

Redirect examination, 114
Referrals, good faith, 6
Reframing, 52, 53, 115, 193
Regulatory law, 89
Rejunction, 200, 201
Relationship, professional, 118
Research sources, 93, 94
Resistance, 192
Resource expert, 103, 104
Roe v. Wade, 137
Rogerians, 205
Roles and responsibilities of therapist,
  86–91

Salgo v. Leland Stanford, Jr., University
  Board of Trustees, 161
Satir, Virginia, 47
Sauerkof v. City of New York, 168
Script, 193
Secrets, 239
Self-fulfilling prophecy, 156
Sexual dysfunction, 240
Sexual relationships with clients, 9
Shared parenting, 150
Shepard's Case Citations, 94

Shepard's Law Review Citation, 94
Shepard's Ordinance Law Citations, 94
Shepard's United States Citations, 94
Shipman v. Division of Social Services,
  177
Sims v. Sims, 151
Sosna v. Iowa, 144
Spousal maintenance, 145, 146
Standard of care, 118, 119
Standards on Public Information and
  Advertising (AAMFT), 226, 227
Stanley v. Illinois, 136
State ex rel. Hickox v. Hickox, 176
State v. Driscoll, 174
State v. Vickers, 174
Statutory law, 89
Statutory waiver, 176
Strategic maneuvers, 240, 241
Strategies, reparative, 25
Structural maneuvers, 240, 241
Students, responsibility to, 75–77
Suicide potential, 49
Supervisees, responsibility to, 75–77
Supervision, AAMFT approved, 208–209
Supreme Court Reporter, 93
Surrogate, 136, 137
Systemic perspective, 241–243

Tandem counseling, 238
Tarasoff, 93–97
"Tender years" doctrine, 148
Theories of causation, 221
Therapeutic contracts, 27–29, 163
Therapist
  advertising, 82, 226–230, 254–257
  "battle for structure," 42
  change agent, 46–51
  communications, 233
  competence, 5, 253
  continuing education/development,
    229–233, 261–262
  convening therapy, 41–46
  "duty to warn," 92–97
  expert witness, 108–116
  fees, 80–82, 257–259
  isolation, 261
  letter to nonattending spouse, 44, 45
  liability, 116–124
  licensure, 212–219
  malpractice, 118–121

Therapist, *continued*
 privacy, 261
 professional affiliation, 206–212
 professional competence and integrity,
  71–75, 253
 professional disclosure statement, 31,
  32
 professional identity, 204–235
 referral resource, 101–108
 responsibility to client, 64–68, 252,
  253
 responsibility to students, employees,
  and supervisees, 75–77
 responsibility to the profession, 77–80
 roles and responsibilities, 86–91
 source of information, 92–101
 therapeutic contracts, 27–29
 withholding treatment, 42, 43
Therapist as referral resource, 101–108
 mediation, 105–108
 resource expert, 103–104
 treatment provider, 104–105
 treatment specialist, 101–103
Therapist as source of information,
 92–101
 child abuse and neglect, 97–101
 "duty to warn," 92–97
Therapy, convening, 41–46
 "battle for structure," 42
 enabling, 43
 letter to nonattending spouse, 44, 45
 withholding treatment, 42, 43
Therapy, withholding, 42, 43
Third-party rule waiver, 175, 176
Thompson v. County of Alameda, 96, 97
Tort, intentional, 118, 121–123
 battery, 121, 122
 defamation, 122
 false imprisonment, 123
 infliction of mental distress, 123
 invasion of privacy, 122, 123
 liability, 118
 malicious prosecution, 123
Treatment provider, 104, 105
Treatment specialist, 101–103
 child abuse and neglect, 103–105
 diagnostician, 101, 102
 juvenile delinquency, 102
 person in need of supervision, 102,
  103
Triangulation, agency, 54–59

defined, 54, 55
 prevention, 58, 59
 systems dilemma, 57, 58

Unfit parent, 148
Uniform Child Custody Jurisdiction Act,
 151
Uniform Premarital Agreement Act,
 170-172
Uniform Reciprocal Enforcement of
 Support Act, 152
Uniform States Code, 93
Uniform System of Citation, 94
United States Law Week, 93
United States Supreme Court Reports, 93

Values analysis, 247–251
Values clarification, 186–187
 acting, 187
 choosing, 186
 epistemology, 187
 prizing, 186, 187
Values conflicts, 244–246
 disagreement over the therapeutic
  process, 245, 246
 underdeveloped values, 244
Values, underdeveloped, 244
Valuing, 184–203, 237
 components, 197–202
 definition, 185
 epistemology, 187–190
 negotiation, 190–193
 practice implications, 193–197
 values clarification, 186–187
Ventilation, 239

Weber v. Aetna Casualty & Surety Co.,
 133
Welfare, client, 10–13
 autonomy, 11, 13, 14
 beneficence, 11, 12
 fidelity, 11–13
 justice, 11, 12
 nonmaleficence, 11, 12
Words and Phrases, 94

Yaron v. Yaron, 176

Zablocki v. Redhail, 129